Human Res

st P   iversity Centra

Human Resource Development

Foundations, Process, Contexts

3rd Edition

Stephen Gibb

Senior Lecturer, Department of Human Resource Management,
University of Strathclyde, UK

First edition published 2002
Second edition published 2008
Third edition published 2011 by
PALGRAVE MACMILLAN

Palgrave Macmillan in the UK is an imprint of Macmillan Publishers Limited, registered in England, company number 785998, of Houndmills, Basingstoke, Hampshire RG21 6XS.

Palgrave Macmillan in the US is a division of St Martin's Press LLC, 175 Fifth Avenue, New York, NY 10010.

Palgrave Macmillan is the global academic imprint of the above companies and has companies and representatives throughout the world.

Palgrave® and Macmillan® are registered trademarks in the United States, the United Kingdom, Europe and other countries.

ISBN 978-0-230-24710-9

This book is printed on paper suitable for recycling and made from fully managed and sustained forest sources. Logging, pulping and manufacturing processes are expected to conform to the environmental regulations of the country of origin.

A catalogue record for this book is available from the British Library.

A catalog record for this book is available from the Library of Congress.

10   9   8   7   6   5   4   3   2   1
20   19   18   17   16   15   14   13   12   11

Printed in China

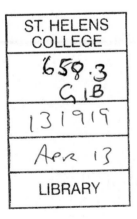

In memory of my Dad

Contents

List of Figures and Tables

Figures

Tables

Preface

This third edition has been updated in structure and content to reflect the changing agenda in HRD. Reviewers of the draft of this third edition, to whom I owe a debt of gratitude, were helpful in finding a balance between two demands. One is the demand for a text to support those studying HRD with pragmatic concerns, as part of their undergraduate development or professional development. The other is the demand from those seeking a text that is more challenging, exploring ideas as well as practical and operational realities. This balance is sought in the three main parts: in foundations, exploring theory, knowledge and values; in process, exploring concepts and methods in practice; and in contexts, exploring the organisational, national and intellectual issues of HRD.

What's new in the third edition at a glance:

- Re-structured to lead with theory and consideration of knowledge bases;
- New chapters on ethics/values, talent management, comparative HRD and critical HRD;
- New cases with questions and model answers;
- Addressing social science, reflective practice and ethical/values issues throughout;
- Identification of key texts, articles and Web sources for each topic.

HRD matters because it is integral to creating wealth and opportunity, sustaining and transforming good working lives and advancing on the higher goals that individuals, organisations and countries have for themselves. HRD has long been recognised as a catalyst for economic growth and opportunity significant and a force for greater and broader social good. Organisations that are successful in managing HRD are better placed to meet their goals and fulfil their purposes, becoming assets to the societies they work within, fostering productivity and an improving quality of life. The continuance and sustainability of such wealth creation and opportunity depends upon the management of HRD, now more than ever as the scale and extent of skill and expertise needed to confront the challenges ahead grows. This is why understanding better why and how HRD can be managed matters to more people, from the affluent developed countries to the still impoverished parts of the developing countries. I continue to be mindful of five education value propositions for undergraduate and postgraduate learners alike who seek knowledge and understanding about HRD:

- HRD education contributes directly to society by facilitating economic development and service; graduates and postgraduates learning about HRD will have responsibilities for those ends.
- Through HRD education it is possible to inspire and involve people to engage with human development.
- HRD education provides graduates with a portfolio of competences that enable meaningful contributions to organisations engaged in a variety of enterprises and pursuits, and provides significant life-long economic benefit to graduates.
- HRD education produces well-rounded graduates who can help to strengthen the connection between business and society.
- HRD education helps to produce and disseminate cutting edge ideas and theories that facilitate the advance of organisational efficiency and effectiveness. HRD education provides a fertile environment for the development and incubation of research, reflective enquiry and new ideas.

There are modifications and enhancements to the structure and content in this second edition. These seek to better combine the values of the human sciences within the disciplines of business and management. One stronger message, that I am ever more convinced needs to be promoted, is that students of HRD need to appreciate and be much more values and ethics conscious. We need to be more aware of how values and ethics shape and frame what is done and how it is done in HRD, not just social science or economic argument. This, in my experience, is as important for a students' professional development as the grasp of theory and the appreciation that comes from understanding theory coherently.

I also continue to believe that hands-on HRD at work activity, and observation of the actual organisational world of work, provide the wellsprings of experience that can support learning. Models, concepts and cases are resources to explore in the safety of the classroom without the turbulent and complex flow of action and consequence that accompanies process and practice in organisations. Even so, the best models, concepts and cases are the results of others' observations and speculations about workplace and organisational experiences, not authoritative and definitive accounts of organisational reality. They are simplifications. As such these 'constructions' and simplifications of others, including mine, should be approached as open to question, challenge and change. 'Critical' study of organisations, models, concepts and cases is a way of doing that, where that means getting beyond only knowing and having a reliance on others' constructions. Critical and independent thinking alone is though not sufficient. Time and experience in action is also necessary to secure effective professional development.

To support that there are five features used in each chapter

(1) Practice examples: which describe aspects of HRD practice, and illustrate what HRD involves in practice;

(2) Perspectives: reference to studies, evidence and resources underpinning knowledge in HRD;

(3) Exercises: activities for learners to try;

(4) Cases: individual, organisational and national cases to illustrate topics and themes;

(5) Debates: questions to explore.

HRD has a growing literature associated with it. Suggestions for key reading and associated resources for each topic are provided as starting points for exploring this at the end of each chapter. Keeping abreast of current writing and debate is getting tougher with much more being written; it is worth the effort.

Acknowledgements

I am greatly indebted to the reviewers of this third edition, for their feedback. I have worked with many colleagues, and students, on programmes and projects too numerous to mention individually, and I thank them all. I especially mention Nicole for her contributions on corporate universities, and Khan for his insights to Pakistan. Of course the responsibility for any errors or omissions is mine.

Every effort has been made to trace all the copyright holders, but if any have been inadvertently overlooked the publishers will be pleased to make the necessary arrangements at the first opportunity.

PART I

Foundations

Part I introduces Human Resource Development (HRD). HRD is concerned with the process of learning and change in work and employment to enable skilled people to perform competently in their roles, the key to sustainable organisational success. It describes and reviews the areas of theory which are relevant to understanding learning, change and the management of these in work and employment. The core process, policies and strategies for developing people in work and employment are described. Value-based and ethical concerns as well as economic issues are highlighted as significant in motivating and shaping human development in work and employment.

Human Resource Development

Learning Objectives

By the end of this chapter you will be able to:

- Define Human Resource Development (HRD);
- Describe a model of organisational value bases influencing learning and change in work and employment;
- Connect HRD and organisational learning and change challenges;
- Identify and critically reflect on contemporary challenges in HRD.

Question 1.1

> Adult Learning and Change; How Long Does It Take?
> How long on average does it take an adult to learn a new habit, to change?

Introduction

Human Resource Development refers to the process of learning and change in work and employment. This process has the purpose of enabling skilled people to perform competently in their roles. Knowledge of this, from theories to methods and practices, has wellsprings in the study of human development and work organisation, and the professional development and practical management in work. The major goals of HRD in the work and employment context can be to enable and improve competitiveness, control, creativity and collaboration. The challenge of HRD is to shape and advance personal, group, organisational and national learning and change to achieve these goals. The nature of the challenge does vary with industry sectors and organisations, reflecting the particular performance, employment and strategic concerns that prevail in different industry sectors and organisations. These aspects of HRD are introduced to be considered in more depth in later chapters.

Human Resource Development

Human Resource Development is concerned with the process of learning and change in work and employment to enable skilled people to perform competently in their roles (Nadler and Nadler 1970, Swanson and Holton 2001, Reid et al. 2009, Stewart and Rigg 2011). That's a formal way of operationalising and defining the subject. Well-trained and developed people are able to work safely, effectively and efficiently. For those who are passionate about it, and study it as they aim to work professionally in HRD, the meaning of HRD is often more than that; it is about realising the potential of people, teams, organisations and countries. HRD is a necessary and critical foundation of success at all these levels. And how success is to be achieved is integral to how people understand their lives, work and societies (Kuchinke 2010) not only producing effective and skilled employees. A recent OECD report on 'Human Capital' (see Perspective 1.1) concluded that HRD is central to achieving economic growth and skilled employment and much more. It is this broader valuing, meaning and purpose of HRD that inspires people to ask questions and seek answers about adult learning. As a field of study, a discipline, HRD is emerging as the home of the study of adult learning and change, and the theory and practice of success (see Practice 1.1).

HRD in the 'big picture' is to be understood as being concerned with training people for and in work and employment, with the theory and practice of adult

---

Perspective 1.1: United Nations 'Human Capital' Report

The OECD is a forum where the governments of 30 democracies work together to address the economic, social and environmental challenges of globalisation. The Human Capital report pulls together a lot of ideas and data about that, focussing on human development. Economic success crucially relies on human capital – the knowledge, skills, competencies and attributes that allow people to contribute to their personal and social well-being, as well as that of their countries.

Education is the key factor in forming human capital. People with better education tend to enjoy higher incomes, health levels, community involvement and employment prospects. Yet even in developed countries, as many as one-fifth of young people fail to finish secondary school, which severely limits their subsequent employment prospects. Learning beyond the years of formal education, continued training and education, will become ever more important as economies evolve and people work longer. To study HRD is to engage in debates on some of the key issues that affect our societies and economies today.

Source: Keely, B., (2007).

Practice 1.1: Recognition of HRD

The recognition and status of HRD in the workplace as a significant process, worth attention and investment, has been established over time. The original term 'HRD' has been used since 1970 (Nadler and Nadler 1970), though since then several important bodies and networks have evolved and shaped how we understand HRD. They include:

- Academy of Human Resource Development (AHRD)
- University Forum for HRD (UFHRD)
- Chartered Institute of Personnel and Development (CIPD)
- American Society for Training and Development (ASTD)
- International Federation of Training and Development Organisations (IFTDO).

HRD Academic Journals

- *HRD International*
- *Advances in Developing Human Resources*
- *HRD Quarterly*
- *HRD Review.*

---

learning at the core of HRD connecting areas of theory, concepts and contexts which inform and direct thinking on adult learning and change that go well beyond training for employment (see Figure 1.1).

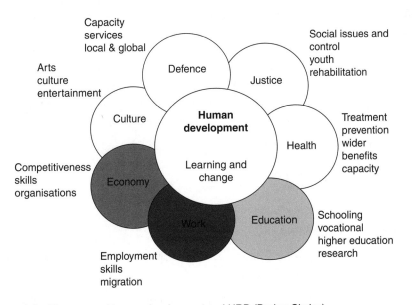

Figure 1.1   The scope of human development and HRD (Darker Circles)

The antecedents of producing capable and successful people, teams, organisations and countries are not confined to training for and in employment. These are part of the bigger picture where the organisation of learning and change to support human development is, in contemporary societies and cultures, associated with many contexts and outcomes (Seligman 2002, James 2007, 2008, Butler-Bowden 2008, Gladwell 2008, Ehrenreich 2009, Foley 2010). There is an interrelationship where human development for work both depends upon and contributes to human development in other contexts (see Perspective 1.2). In knowledge about HRD the foundations are understanding successful human development while the specific focus is the process of managing learning in work.

Perspective 1.2: Do firms that make large investments in Human Capital perform the best?

There are, in the simplest terms, two systemic views of Human Capital. There is the systemic view that a cycle of high skills, high wages, and long term success is initiated and sustained by investing in people, in human capital. There is the alternative view that a cycle of low skills, low costs underpins short term success. In this case employees are disposable costs, not assets to be invested in.

Subjectively the former view is appealing, but is it objectively true? Do, for example, firms that make large investments in employee development outperform the stock market . One study claims this is indeed the case (Bassi & McMurrer 2008). The evidence base is not robust, but the analysis of why this might be true is interesting; it is not just about the level of individuals' skills, but about the positive reciprocal relationship between leadership and human capital investment. Investing in people challenges leaders and managers to be better; developing better leaders and managers results in an interest in upskilling other people too. The opposite is also seen; where the workforce is low skill there is little demand for improving leadership and management; and where leadership and management is limited there is not much motivation to upskill people, so this is a constraint on development. A cluster of practices produce a virtuous cycle underpinning success;

- Learning Capacity (training)
- Leadership
- Employee Engagement
- Knowledge Accessibility (learning)
- Workforce Optimisation

Human Capital means more than upskilling individuals, it raises challenges for managerial and leadership capacity too.

Source: Bassi, L. and McMurrer, D. (2008) Towards A Human Capital measurement methodology, Advances in Developing Human Resources, 10(6), 863–881

Success: Individual and Organisational

The heart of HRD is about achieving successful human development for and in work. Capable, successful people, teams, organisations and countries are an outcome of many people working together with shared and contested definitions of success. The past and present results of working for success suggest there are both peaks and troughs that are encountered by individuals, organisations and societies in the extent to which human development as an ideal is actually attained. The peaks of the past and the present are represented by people, organisations and societies that flourish and achieve rewarding and fulfilling work and employment which contributes to potential being realised. The troughs in the past and the present are represented by people, organisations and societies that languish and decline, where potential is unrealised. If we better understood success, the probability of achieving and sustaining peaks and removing troughs would be increased. How we understand individual success has inspired many writers (Butler-Bowden 2008) and contemporary analyses (Gladwell 2008). In these, individual success is understood as emerging from a set of characteristics shared by successful people. These characteristics can be listed and commonly include the following:

- Optimism
- Having a definite aim and purpose
- Being willing to work
- Being disciplined
- Curiosity
- Risk taking
- Expecting the best
- Seeking mastery
- Well-rounded/balanced.

The iteration of such characteristics is hardly recent (Marlow 1984, De Bono 1985, Covey 1989), but their reiteration in evolving systems of personal development (Cottrell 2003, Sieger 2004) and reinforcement with the rise of positive psychology (Barrell and Ryback 2008, Dweck 2008) makes them a central and significant feature of the HRD landscape. Evidence for the validity of these factors as 'the' recipe for individual success, as the cause of individual success, is mixed. This perspective which has been implicit for some time has been made more explicit by the growth of Positive Psychology (Seligman 2002), which proposes that research and action should be about identifying and working with core strengths. Understanding these characteristics, and applying that knowledge to developing individuals, groups, organisations and societies, is a significant field of research and practice. While there are no large-scale meta-studies of individual success exploring these factors (Ng et al. 2005), they have a degree of face validity.

These individual factors do not operate in isolation. Gladwell (2008) identified a mix of culture, community and family factors that are shared by exceptionally successful people.

The same issue, understanding success and the lack of a clear profile of success, occurs as the picture is broadened, beyond individual success, looking at success for teams and organisations. Successful teams, and often sporting examples are first to come to mind here, are also perceived to share characteristics that researchers seek to turn into models and factors explaining group success (Belbin 1996). Combing these levels, from creating capable and successful individuals and teams to creating capable and successful organisations and countries, makes HRD an interdisciplinary field of study. This means that it draws on evidence, knowledge and research from a range of disciplines. These conventionally include economics, education, management, sociology and psychology (Swanson and Holton 2001). The advantage of HRD being an interdisciplinary field of study is that it leads to learners exploring diverse and potentially fascinating areas of knowledge and research. The disadvantage of HRD being an interdisciplinary field of study is that the breadth of diverse bodies of evidence, knowledge and research can mean learners skim the surface of disciplines and do not develop a robust and deep understanding of any of them.

Other writers critique aspects of the lists of common characteristics of individual, team and organisational success which are found in the popular literature. Both Foley and James critique such lists of characteristics of success as being part of the problem, not the solution. They argue that these are not neutral profiles of success, but they are expressions of values perpetuating perspectives on human development which may bias and distort our understanding of successful development. HRD influenced by these, and that can mean educational systems, workplace training priorities and cultures perpetuate, in the name of success, negative qualities; including greed and attention-seeking, and also a sense of entitlement, with overall an ideology of the 'strenuous life' as the way to succeed. This does not create success; it produces resentment and dissatisfaction for individuals, organisations and cultures. James argues that people, societies and cultures influenced by the search for success are driven to channel potential into performance in work and employment and attain affluence beyond the aspirations of previous generations; yet levels of mental distress, depression and dissatisfaction in those societies also have never been greater. Debate 1.1 invites you to consider if some value-based definitions of success may be part of the problem as they bias and distort how we perceive HRD. Developing skills for work and employment is the focus, yet an awareness of and reflective thinking about value bases is integral to that. HRD is a process that begins with the development of children in families, moves on to include learning in educational institutions and eventually entails training and development inemployment.

Capable, successful people, teams, organisations and countries are an outcome of many people working together with shared and contested definitions of success. Theories of HRD provide explanations of what works to support learning and change that makes capable and successful people for work and employment.

Success is also an issue at a regional and national level; with different cities, regions and countries facing different challenges in producing the people and organisations that can create wealth and provide the services, work and employment, to their people. The contexts in which this can be studied, and the realities of human development most broadly as well as the work and employment concerns of different countries vary dramatically (see Perspective 1.3).

Perspective 1.3: United Nations Human Development Index (HDI)

One model for measuring levels of Human Development is the UN HDI. This uses data about three areas to produce an overall, single figure which places a country in one of four bands: Low, Medium, High and Very High. The data is about education in the form of net enrolments in primary, secondary and tertiary education; standard of living based on GDP per capita; and health based on longevity. The bands are

Very High and High HDI	0.8 to 1.000
Medium HDI	0.500 to 0.800
Low HDI	< 0.500

High HDI countries tend to have high levels of enrolment in primary, secondary and tertiary education; high levels of GDP per capita; and populations with the greatest longevity.

High HDI nations are affluent, developed nations. The top 10 in the 2010 review were Norway, Australia, Ireland, Canada, Ireland, the Netherlands, Sweden, France, Switzerland and Japan. Medium HDI status nation are developing nations with critical challenges. The top 10 in 2010 in this category are Armenia, Ukraine, Azerbaijan, Thailand, Iran, Georgia, Dominican Republic, China, Belize, and Samoa.

Low HDI status nations are those facing multiple problems (the changing village). These in 2010 include Afghanistan, Sierra Leone, Central African Republic, Mali, Burkina Faso, Congo, Chad, Burundi, Guinea-Bissau, Mozambique and Ethiopia.

Source: http://www.facebook.com/pages/Human-Development-Index/108073452
547813; http://hdr.undp.org/en/

Debate 1.1: Outliers or Peelers as the Challenge?

Outliers is a book that explores stories of individual and remarkable success (Gladwell 2008). The stories Gladwell recounts range from Canadian elite ice hockey players through to computer industry leaders and mathematicians, and pilots who successfully manage potentially fatal incidents, and musicians. One conclusion is that 10,000 hours are the amount of practice needed for remarkable success. But such hard work and natural talent also combine with 'arbitrary' factors (luck) and cultural legacies which for some nurture success but not others. All these together provide a tide of advantage, which leads an individual to remarkable success.

Peelers: Foley takes a different perspective, seeing increasing levels of absurdity to be found in modern life rooted in attitudes that are about a sense of entitlement to success without much effort. 'It is a shocking and profoundly regrettable, but, apparently, sales of oranges are falling steadily because people can no longer be bothered to peel them. As soon as I read this I began buying oranges more frequently and eating them with greater pleasure. Now I peel an orange very slowly, deliberately, voluptuously, above all defiantly; as a riposte to an age that demands war without casualties, public services without taxes, rights without obligations, celebrity without achievement, sex without relationships, running shoes without running, coursework without work and sweet grapes without seeds' (Foley 2010, p. 112).

Which view of the contemporary challenge of channelling potential into performance are you more sympathetic towards? If lucky breaks, arbitrary advantage and cultural legacies underpin patterns of remarkable success, how do we manage learning and change to enable more opportunities for more people in work and employment? Or if our 'age' is one in which people are increasingly 'not bothered' but have a rising sense of entitlement, how does that shape the challenges to be found in channelling potential into performance in work and employment?

HRD, Organisational Values and Success

What makes for a capable and successful person is a contested and complex area of study in itself. This contest and complexity is found again when organisational success is the focus. There are four types of work and organisational value that underpin success (Cameron et al. 2000) that shape HRD and learning in work and employment. To succeed can mean to

(1) Compete: do things fast and change to do them faster

(2) Control: do things right and change to do them better

(3) Create: do things first and change to break new ground

(4) Collaborate: do things together and change to have greater consensus and cooperation.

In some areas of work and employment individuals, groups and organisations create value by being fast; they have performance, management and strategic concerns which are about competing robustly, moving swiftly and being very customer focused. In other areas of work and employment individuals, groups and organisations create value by robustly 'doing things right', and have performance, management and strategic concerns around controlling processes, managing quality and moving steadily. In other areas individuals, groups and organisations create value by being first, being creative, and they have performance, management and strategic concerns about breakthrough learning, innovation and generating and protecting ideas and intellectual capital. Finally, in some areas of work and employment individuals, groups and organisations have performance, management and strategic concerns about collaboration, and are most focussed on building relations with many partners working together, strong teams cohering over time, developed over the long term and with building/sustaining what has been called 'social capital'.

Exercise 1.1: Learning and Change, Priorities and Focus

Identify examples of people, groups and organisations which represent the four different performance priorities and focus:

Compete: do things fast, do them faster:

- person
- group
- organisation

Control: do things right, do them better:

- person
- group
- organisation

Create: do things first, break new ground:

- person
- group
- organisation

Collaborate: do things together, consensus and cooperation:

- person
- group
- organisation.

With these examples of different kinds of people, groups and organisations, you will have reference points. These are useful to keep in mind to understand that different kinds of learning and change challenges will be present for individuals, teams and organisations. What people need to know, be able to do, value and cope with, varies with these.

To an extent all these kinds of value and success are a concern in most industries and organisations. At some times or in some units in an organisation there will be a dominant concern in one value to a greater degree in some areas of work and employment. In the work and employment context what HRD means and involves and how it is managed will differ according to the value created and the kinds of learning and change which are dominant in that form of organisation. Learning and change in organisations where doing things fast is the core value will be quite a different strategic and management challenge to learning and change where consensus among partners and collaboration is the core value.

Dependence and reliance on some forms of value creation more than others is also a concern at the national level. This is evident between economically developed and developing countries and economies, and also within developed and developing countries and economies. As the global economy has seen supply chains re-configured the relative significance of, for example manufacturing and service activities, involving control and competition as drivers of learning and change can change dramatically to work and employment requiring learning and change driven by creativity and collaboration.

HRD in Practice

Value-based modelling shows the big picture within which HRD has evolved and features. The shared concerns in any work and employment are that success, potential being realised in performance, requires learning and change. Particular concerns with learning and change, with the development of people and organisations, are shaped by the extent to which competition, control, creation and collaboration, and working faster, working better, working differently and working together, require learning and change.

There is a breadth and depth to HRD that makes the practical aim of understanding and channelling potential into performance a topic of some complexity. In HRD more narrowly considered the focus is the theory, policy and practice of learning and change in work and employment. The scope of HRD is centred on work, and related to that context also extends to economics and education. That narrower scope itself can be drawn quite tightly by some, with HRD being exclusively about learning and change inside employing organisations – training at work, aspects of vocational education and as a feature of economic growth. The ends here, the outcomes, are people teams, organisations and nations with the knowledge, skills and emotional intelligence required to work and succeed in employment. The major topics in this text reflect this, with the process of identifying needs and designing training in employment at the fore, and the use of methods like coaching and mentoring situated in the organisational context, along with analyses of the HRD connection to significant management concerns. These include the items outlined in Practice 1.2.

The definition and scope of HRD here is the narrower one. This includes the HRD process at work, the identification of needs and analysis of individual, team and organisation needs. Design involves determining objectives for learning and change, and choosing methods to achieve those objectives. Action, in professionally delivering this learning and change involves skilled practice in supporting individual, group and organisational learning and change. Results are evaluated at a number of levels to measure individual, group and organisational learning and change. The HRD process forms a significant part of HRM and the strategy, structure and culture of a successful organisation.

Practice 1.2: Practical HRD Process Concerns

- **Direction and goals**: The direction of the HRD function in the organisation: the primary mode of operation of the HRD function; the goals of the HRD function; how new programs are initiated.

- **Responsibility**: major organisational change; define training plans: determining the timing of HRD and the target audiences; responsibility for training results; systematic, objective evaluation designed to ensure that people are performing appropriately on the job.

- **Perceptions**: Management involvement in the training process: ensure that training is transferred into performance on the job; HRD staff's interaction with line management: HRD's role in major change efforts; How managers view the HRD function.

- **Programmes**: HRD programmes; How investment in HRD is measured primarily; routine HRD efforts: New HRD programs.

Practice 1.2: (Continued)

- **Resourcing**: Budgeting for HRD; principal reason for HRD expenditures; HRD is focus; leadership of the organisation.
- **Manager and employee involvement**: Top management's involvement in the implementation of HRD programs; Line management involvement in conducting HRD programs is; employee engagement in HRD; self-directed learning.

Human Development, how learning and change are possible and to be enabled, happens not just in employment and work. Learning and change, wherever it happens, can provide HRD.

One snapshot (VA 2009) of what matters in typical organisation identified the following as the top learning and change needs:

- Leadership
- Managing people
- Communication
- Customer service
- Quality
- Performance management
- Attitude and motivation
- Teamwork
- Change management.

Definitions

These two sides of HRD, the values-based context and the goals for HRD in practice combine to present stakeholders in learning and change in employment with issues in individual, team, organisational and national development. As a distinct area of study, with research, journals and professional bodies, HRD is emerging as a subject that shapes practice in these, progressing and advancing our knowledge and management of learning and change in work. Other terms can be used, and textbooks may use the phrase 'HRD' (Reid et al. 2009) or 'Learning and Development' (Harrison 2009). An inclusive definition of the area is:

> HRD is any process or activity that, either initially or over the long term, has the potential to develop adults' work-based knowledge, expertise, productivity and satisfaction, whether for personal or group/team gain, or for the benefit of an organization, community, nation or, ultimately, the whole of humanity. (Mclean and Mclean 2001)

This is a definition emphasising some key words: 'processes', 'adults' as the focus and an interest in 'benefits'. Processes are significant, and need to be understood, though HRD is more than a sum of processes. Adult learning is the heart of HRD, though HRD may be seem to begin, to have roots, well before adulthood; from the early years of education, as part of the goal of general education. Finally, the idea that there need to be tangible benefits/gains is something which concerns all stakeholders; though the wider benefits and purposes of learning and change for stakeholders in employment and outside employment should not be overlooked.

A different approach to defining HRD, with an emphasis on other key words is:

> HRD is quite a complex subject. The curriculum is not easy to define as the subject continues to evolve and to adopt different concepts. HRD is clearly concerned with professional practice and so needs to be open to and reflective of that context. (Sambrook and Stewart 2007, p. 8)

The keywords here are 'complex', evolving and 'reflective'. Complexity is a key word in contemporary management, and complexity theory is worth thinking about a bit more. Complexity theory is a heterogeneous body of theories originating in evolutionary biology, and general systems theory (Fenwick 2010). The key theme is emergence, that complex systems interact according to simple rules that are recursively re-enacted. Such systems are self-organising. That is, they can maintain form without some externally imposed discipline or organising device. Complexity theory considers the relations that produce things, not the things themselves. New possibilities for action are constantly emerging among these interactions of complex systems, and HRD occurs therein. Learning is to be defined as expanded possibilities for action, or becoming 'capable of more sophisticated, more flexible, more creative action' (Davis and Sumara 2006). In HRD applications of complexity theory, attention would be drawn to the relationships among learners and their environment.

> For example, an organizational change initiative would focus on enabling connections instead of training individuals to 'acquire' understanding of the new policy – connections between this initiative and the many other initiatives likely to be lurking in the system, between parts of the system, between the initiative and the system's cultures, and between people, language and technologies involved in the change. It would encourage experimentation among people and objects involved in the change, and would focus on amplifying the advantageous possibilities that emerge among these connections as people tinker with objects and language involved. (Fenwick 2010, p. 109)

There are different aspects to complexity:

- Intricate, with many different and connected parts;
- Hard to predict;
- Embodying and entailing human subjectivity, meaning and belief.

For example, an aeroplane, a computer or the brain are complex in the first sense, but not the second nor self-evidently the third sense; they have many parts, but their behaviour is predictable. The weather, and climate, is complex in the second sense, but not the first or third sense; there are fewer factors involved, which can be measured, yet it is still hard to forecast what the weather or climate will actually be at any point in the future, or the definitive direction of climate change. Finally there are individuals, groups and organisation which are 'complex' in the third sense. 'Complex' in an individual psychological sense can refer specifically to a system of interrelated, emotion-charged ideas, feelings, memories and impulses. These may be repressed and can give rise to abnormal or pathological behaviour in individuals, groups or organisations. The sense in which complex is used here is less evaluative and more broad; that people are complex as they are cultural animals (Baumeister 2005), whose combinations of motivation, thinking and feeling as individuals and in groups is complex to map and engage with.

> Human behaviour responds to meaning, which is not a physical reality but depends upon the shared understanding of a cultural group. (Baumeister 2005, p. 61)

HRD is of course to be understood as engaging with complexity in this third sense. There are no well-defined and clear boundaries, and certainties, grounded in a single social science; as we will explore further in Chapter 2 on theory in HRD. Ethical perspectives and values as well as an active imagination can be integral to making sense of and being successful in HRD as well as the rational and logical isolation of constructs and concepts from social science.

Beyond that learning and change at work and in employment is a subject in which all these senses and forms of complexity are present. It has its intricacies, as we will explore in relation to aspects of the process and the practices involved in HRD. And learning and change, our knowledge of these, as we engage with systems, individual human beings, groups and organisations, may entail some fairly easy to measure aspects but remains nonetheless difficult to predict. Altogether, how we come to know and understand what capability and success for individuals, groups and organisations is complex.

The positive part of this complexity is that it justifies HRD as an academic area of study, with HRD being about more than 'training' for skills. That in itself is not to be overlooked or looked down upon. In the pragmatic, practical and cost-conscious contexts of work and employment effective training is, ideally, like a machine for developing the operational capability of the workforce. Yet as HRD evolves as a subject that is more academic, this brings in theoretical ambiguities, permeable boundaries to the subject, and produces what has been called 'an anxious vigilance' on maintaining connections to practice (Garavan and Morley 2006).

In reality, Sambrook and Stewart (2010) find that HRD as a subject is less well established in educational contexts; mainly situated within HRM programmes as a module, rather than being the subject of a dedicated programme in itself. At undergraduate level HRD modules are usually part of broader business and management education, and are given limited space and time within that broader business education. At postgraduate level HRD programmes are for professional practitioners. In that context the development of critical reflection is often a significant issue, and HRD as a subject, what is taught and how it is taught, can enable that. Yet in each case HRD is a junior partner in human resource management (HRM).

Finally, critics of the evolution of HRD as a subject question and challenge the perceived dominance of human capital theory, that what matters most in human development is the development of skills for work and employment, in the field (Fenwick 2004). They perceive this to reflect a particular set of values, with consequence either intended or unintended. These include a commodification and subjugation of human development to organisational interests, rather than a motivation to invest in people, skills and development. HRD forms part of a system as a form of 'soft control', that entails surveillance, classification, normalisation and cultural engineering of individuals and teams. In total HRD, and human development for work and employment, may be seen to distort rather than fulfil people's potential.

Human Resource Management

As HRD most often is located within HRM, and approaches to HRM can vary, it is worth saying a bit about the HRM context. HRM can be used to define a particular approach to the management of people at work, and is contrasted with other approaches, such as the more conventional terms 'personnel management' or 'industrial relations'. In this sense HRM is seen as being a more strategic and managerial set of activities, often emphasising development. In focusing on employees as individuals and development some see a trend to playing down the significance of employee relations systems, managing conflict and the legitimacy of trade unions.

In this text HRM is used in a general and neutral sense to mean the whole of people management, the combination of employee resourcing, employee relations, employee reward and HRD concerns in business and management. HRD is thus one key function of the broader HRM of an organisation; it is not an isolated and stand-alone activity. Organisations' strategies and policies for attracting and retaining staff, and the ways in which stakeholders define their different and common interests at work, can of course have a great impact on HRD policies and practices. In the context of work and organisations, 'development' was usually reserved to describe what was, in effect, learning for managers and professionals. There was a status issue involved. These groups, with career paths, had a course of development to follow; not just periods of vocational training. Employees were to be trained; managers and professionals were to be developed. Development tended to signify higher status and more sophisticated forms of learning and growth. Now personal development is becoming an integral part of working life for many employees, and the concept of development is being applied more broadly throughout work, employment and organisations. Development, and the growth it entails, is of interest as a domain of learning involving many more in the workforce.

Describing the core terms in use signposts several areas of study, each complex in its own right, each with a stake in making up a full and useful understanding of learning and development at work. Skills and economic factors, the psychology of development, the social and institutional features of education: these all contain the seeds of an interest in knowledge and professionalism, development and ethics, learning and science. Following are the issues that matter in the HRM context.

Planned and Informal Learning

Planned and formal practice learning and change, such as training courses, are tangible, manifest and explicitly managed as HRD. This is not the whole story of HRD though. Emergent and informal learning and change, learning from experience, also matters; though it is by its nature more implicit, embedded and self-managed. HRD service delivery in organisations, the common approach is dominated by the delivery of the tangible and the explicit; short courses, typically of 1–3 days duration. However, understanding what works, how it works, and the organisational role of learning and change professionals in managing learning and change, includes also understanding the more implicit and embedded aspects of learning.

Performance Management

HRD exists in an environment where performance management in the organisation as a whole provides the context for managing learning and change. HRD is a means to an end, not an end in itself. That end is acknowledged to be getting better results in work, from teams and individuals, by reviewing and managing performance within an agreed framework of organisational goals, objectives and standards. HRD in this context is only one, albeit important, means of achieving organisational goals, objectives and standards.

Talent Management

Much activity and discussion in HRD is couched in terms of talent management and development (Tulgan 2001, Rothwell and Kazanas 2003). The emergence of this perspective represents an evolution of thinking on succession planning among the senior echelons of organisations, extending to values about identifying potential and developing the workforce as a whole. In some cases talent management will mean what is done with the development of people towards or in the senior echelons of the organisation; in others it will mean what we refer to here as HRD, the development of all in the workforce.

Change Management

The literature about change management is large and multi-faceted (Iles and Sutherland 2001).

- It contains contributions from several different academic disciplines including psychology, sociology, business policy, social policy and others.

- Its boundaries can be set differently, according to the definition of change management employed.

- Valuable contributions to the literature have been made in all of the last five decades, with the later not necessarily superseding the earlier.

- It contains evidence, examples and illustrations generated in a wide variety of organisations and from a diverse range of methodologies with varying degrees of rigour.

- Some material is not readily accessible to non-specialists and does not readily lend itself to cumulative review.

- The concepts included within it range in scale from whole academic schools, through methodologies to single tools.

Perhaps because of these difficulties, the literature is dominated by descriptions of the various models and approaches, prescriptive advice and anecdotal accounts of organisational change (see Practice 1.3). A major problem in this field has been the dominance of gurus who prescribe courses of action without any basis in evidence. The recourse to such prescriptions should be seen as part of the problem, not the solution. Articles based on empirical research are relatively rare and are predominantly single-site case reports, often conducted by a member of the target organisation.

Practice 1.3: Change, Kotter

Few businesses are renowned for successful change process, and many get bad reputations. Kotter identifies eight steps that should guide through a change to avoid failures in managing change.

'Skipping steps creates only the illusion speed and never produces a satisfying result' (Kotter 1995, p. 3). The steps in Kotters (1998) model are as follows:

(1) Establishing a sense of urgency

(2) Forming a powerful guiding coalition

(3) Creating a vision

(4) Communicating the vision

(5) Empowering others to act on the vision

(6) Planning for and creating short-term wins

(7) Consolidating improvements and producing still more change

(8) Institutionalising new approaches.

Describing the core terms in use signposts several areas of study, each complex in its own right, each with a stake in making up a full and useful understanding of learning and development at work. Skills and economic factors, the psychology of development, the social and institutional features of education: these all contain the seeds of an interest in knowledge and professionalism, development and ethics, learning and science.

Contexts

As well as having levels and a scope which includes a core process with key concepts and methods HRD can be studied in context. HRD contexts are the economic, social, technological and political environments which will bring shared and different interest into play. Employers, employees, institutions of learning, government, professional bodies, trade unions and others all have a common interest and concerns. The different concerns and interests of these stakeholders converge on HRD policy and practices.

HRD contexts have been increasingly prominent as individual, team, organisation and broader national development have become more prominent. Learning societies are communities dependent on the lifelong learning and change of all their members, in contrast with industrial societies, which required more limited and narrow learning and change for many. Knowledge economies are those in which value and wealth creation comes from the application of know-how alongside the manufacture of goods and provision of services. In this context HRD becomes more than a minor function of HRM, or an interesting perspective on work and employment. It is the essential and critical task confronting individuals, teams, organisations and nations.

The belief that HRD is a 'good thing' is replaced with the conviction that HRD is the wellspring of success. Individuals succeed by engaging in learning and change; employers succeed where they invest in their people. Government succeeds with workforce development. At times an industrial relations perspective has dominated management, social and economic thinking, and consequently people management problems and solutions. At times people management was dominated by employee-resourcing perspective arising from changes in organisational and employment structures, such as the rise of flexible firms, and the establishment of 'new deal' employment practices and policies. These industrial relations and employee-resourcing perspectives are not irrelevant in an era where HRD is more prominent. Yet the provision and quality of HRD at work are acknowledged as key factors in adapting to change; economic change, social change, organisational change and technological change. As the traditional industries with their old forms of knowledge and skill base declined, new knowledge and skill bases had to be established to enable job creation and growth. In a context of dealing with unemployment and aspirations to eliminate historical discrimination and inequalities, the foundations for the social inclusion agenda were established. And as work organisations changed from standard bureaucracies with classic divisions of labour to flatter structures for lean, world-class manufacturing or service delivery, so a new agenda for HRD at work was needed, both as a means of effecting such change and as a consequence of it. And finally, as new technologies, particularly information technologies, were invented and adopted, so a whole range of other changes to organisations and jobs required new HRD at work.

There are signs that the valuing of HRD at work and in employment is still increasing. This prominence may be unstable: it might be threatened if the industrial relations or work and employment situation were to worsen. However, at present the proponents of the learning society, of knowledge economies, of flexible organisations and careers, and the developers of new technologies all agree that the future will see greater demands upon employers, governments and individuals to participate in and improve HRD. It is in this context that HRD can claim to be a significant and challenging part of the future of HRM; much more than a passing concern for everyone except those aspiring to be specialist trainers who had to learn 'how to train' people.

HRD at work seems to offer the ultimate win–win outcomes for everyone. In an era characterised by the volatility of the change to a learning society and a knowledge economy, HRD at work promises to provide the levers that can be manipulated in order to control the future of work and organisation to ensure individual career success and competitiveness for those currently prosperous, and a route to prosperity for those currently 'struggling to get by' or 'going nowhere'.

For those with a more sceptical approach to such consensus in areas of management, this may all sound too good to be true. The sceptics have a point, and, to avoid the pitfalls of succumbing to the rhetoric of some with a lot to gain from over-promoting HRD, we need advocates who can give a balanced and professional view; those with the ability to reflect critically on HRD, using what the human sciences have to offer; on the problems of HRD strategies in organisations; on how National HRD (NHRD) policy is made; on the potential of e-learning; and on how to connect HRD with the theory and practice of knowledge management.

Conclusion

Human Resource Development (HRD) refers to the process of learning and change in work and employment. The process of learning and change in work and employment has the purpose of enabling skilled people to perform competently in their roles. What successful performance means, for individuals and organisations, can vary though all require learning and change. A narrow or a broader view of HRD can be taken. A broader, inclusive, views the subject in theory and practice as influenced by knowledge of human development, definitions of success and organisational values. HRD is simultaneously a distinctive subject of study, an area of theory and practice, and at the same time an integral part of larger and longer established areas of theory and practice; human development and organisational and social analysis. HRD is commonly perceived to be part of the solution to securing the best possible future and equally challenged to demonstrate its distinctive and knowledge-based relevance in various contexts; organisational, economic, social and political.

The narrow view, up close and in practice, perceives HRD as training in employment. The topics that come to the fore then are formal learning, performance management, talent management, change and HRM. Among the key decisions to be made about the workforce, central to the problem-solving and decision-making which at the heart of this is the question 'what are the kinds and levels of learning and change that we need to manage?'. If these needs are recognised and dealt with, the conviction is that success and sustainability in wealth creation, service delivery and employment can be founded on investing on the right kinds and levels of learning and change for the good of people, organisations, and national success.

Understanding both human development and practical management of learning in work and employment are then equally significant to examine and deal with issues and challenges encountered in achieving success for people and organisations. The roots and branches are part of the same system, and contribute together to the overall functioning and well-being of the system as a whole. Ideas, motivation and action relevant to learning and change in work, organisation and management have not evolved separately and are not independent from the values, study and thinking of human development most broadly (see Debate 1.2 and 1.3).

Assuming the list of success characteristics given have a degree of face validity, explore where you stand on these. Complete the grid below.

Exercise 1.2

Do you attribute your relative success, however you define that, to the factors you are high and low in? What might you do to change any of these if you conclude that your current assessment of it is lower than you would like?

Successful people/teams/ organisations/ nations	Where are you, and where would you like to be?	Failing people/ teams/ organisations/ nations
Optimism	10 9 8 7 6 5 4 3 2 1	Pessimistic
Definite aim and purpose	10 9 8 7 6 5 4 3 2 1	No clear aim and purpose

Willingness to work	10 9 8 7 6 5 4 3 2 1	Unwilling to work
Discipline	10 9 8 7 6 5 4 3 2 1	Unfocused
Curiosity, Prolific reading	10 9 8 7 6 5 4 3 2 1	Lack curiosity
Risk taking	10 9 8 7 6 5 4 3 2 1	Risk averse
Expecting the best	10 9 8 7 6 5 4 3 2 1	Expecting the worst
Mastery	10 9 8 7 6 5 4 3 2 1	No Mastery
Well rounded as a person	10 9 8 7 6 5 4 3 2 1	Imbalanced as a person

Debate 1.2: Connections to Human Development

Some scholars see HRD as including community and national development, not just individual and organisational learning and change. For them HRD as a way to achieve not just organizational competitiveness but broader goals, such as the eight UN Millennium development goals.

- Eradicate extreme poverty and hunger
- Achieve universal primary education
- Promote gender equality and women's empowerment
- Reduce child mortality
- Improve maternal health
- Combat HIV/AIDS, malaria and other diseases
- Ensure environmental sustainability
- Develop a global partnership for development

Source: McLean, G. (2006) 'National Human Resource Development: A Focussed Study in Transitioning Societies in the Developing World', *Advances in Developing Human Resources,* 8(1), 3–11.

Do you think that HRD is an area of study in which these kinds of goals should be part of the picture or are they not within the scope of a subject whose heart is developing skills for work and employment?

Debate 1.2: (Continued)

What are the implications of either including or excluding these from the meaning and purpose of HRD ?

Further reading: Kuchinke, P. (2010) 'Human Development as a central goal for human resource development', *Human Resource Development International*, 13–5, 575–585.

Debate 1.3: What Do You Think?

Could HRD and greater HRD be contributing to the problems that writers like Foley and James perceive? Those problems are mental distress and dissatisfaction. Is the perspective that all people, organisations and countries must realise their potential primarily in work and employment an ideology that fits the interests of some but distorts the lives and well-being of many?

Some individuals have successful careers; many don't. Some organisations succeed; many fail. Some countries continue to get wealthier; others remain poor.

HRD encourages people to channel their efforts and energies into the value producing activities of work organisations to obtain career, material and economic outcomes, but at the price of happiness and well-being?

Case: HRD and BROADCAST ORG

The following case study illustrates how one organisation, BroadcastOrg, is concerned with learning and change. As you read it think about what HRD is in this organisation in terms of the value creation of the organisation, the challenges it faces in channelling potential into performance; and the goals, scope and levels of HRD that arise.

The value creation drivers for the BROADCASTORG:

- Compete: do things fast, and change to do them faster;
- Control: do things right, and change to do them better;
- Create: do things first, and change to break new ground;
- Collaborate: do things together, and change to have greater consensus and cooperation.

Goals of learning and change; what are the HRD priorities that arise in meeting the challenges of change and working towards a people management agenda for the future?

The scope of learning and change; which kinds of HRD initiatives and methods are being used to provide development around the values and behaviours the organisation want?

Levels of learning and change; what is the focus and combination of individual, team and organisational levels of learning and change?

Section 1: Background

BROADCASTORG is a media broadcaster with activities in Television, Radio and online broadcasting for a local population of around 5 million people. It is part of a larger organisation BROADCASTORG, which serves a national population of around 58 million and which has a worldwide audience too. BROADCASTORG is a public service broadcaster, funded by a licence fee that is paid for by households.

The overall BROADCASTORG mission is 'To enrich people's lives with programmes and services that inform, educate and entertain'. Their vision is 'To be the most creative organisation in the world.' Trust is a key value, the foundation of BROADCASTORG as an independent, impartial and honest. Pride in delivering quality and value for money is also a key value.

BROADCASTORG work to achieve this with around 1250 staff, producing 7000 hours of radio annually and 300 hours of TV across 4 channels programmes, from news and current affairs to drama, music and entertainment.

They have a clear concern with people management at the heart of this;

> BROADCASTORG is a diverse and flexible place where people never stop learning and can stretch their creativity, imagination and expertise to create content and services that our audiences love and value.

BROADCASTORG is constantly evolving and changing. Currently BROADCASTORG face change in the form of:

- Revenue streams are less than anticipated
- They have twenty-first century ambitions but are housed in a nineteenth century buildings
- The need to connect with audiences in new and different ways
- Technology enables and demands flexible responses, interactivity, content 'on demand'
- Competition for audiences has never been more acute
- The parent organization expect them to become a 'centre of excellence' in specific areas contributing to the national scene not just delivering for their North area regional audience; in children's programming, comedy, entertainment, factual and drama.

BROADCASTORG regional development strategy commits them to increase network production from BROADCASTORG as part of a plan to increase total spending in the Regions by a third.

The following graphic captures the broad people management agenda BROADCASTORG has for the near-term future:

At the heart of this agenda BROADCASTORG see HRD initiatives that will be needed. These centre on key values and behaviours:

- Collaborate at all levels
- Trust each other to deliver
- Be open to change and developing new skills
- Have a strong bond with audiences.

It was decided that investment and a major change, in a move to a new purpose built building, would be necessary to provide the foundation for this. This provided BROADCASTORG HRD staff with plenty of challenge and opportunity to show they could deliver. This would make BROADCASTORG a pioneer, being able to leap to new ways of working and technologies as they occupied their new building and facilities.

Section 2: Other Aspects of Change

As well as the positive HRD agenda outlined above BROADCASTORG also needed to take into account:

Reduce staff: they need to increase productivity and make significant savings, reducing costs and staffing in some areas and enable smarter redeployment. Specifically reduce by 230 posts over 5 years – a big redundancy/redeployment programme

Enable change through engaging staff and unions: work with our unions and staff to deliver the change agenda ahead

New ways of working: encourage new ways of working through greater movement and sharing of resources, with more collaboration across genres, and more flexibility in roles, and streamlined systems.

Reflections on the Case

The value creation core here is complex. BROADCASTORG has people, groups and is an organisation with all the forms of value creation present:

- Compete: do things fast, and change to do them faster; in news production, for example
- Control: do things right, and change to do them better; the technical control of broadcasting
- Create: do things first, and change to break new ground; using the internet, for example, and the capacities that has for broadcasting
- Collaborate: do things together, and change to have greater consensus and cooperation; most projects entail staff inside the organisation and contractors working on projects.

If I were to put these in a hierarchy of value creation for the organisation as a whole, I would suggest it is an organisation that values:

- Collaboration: ever-changing projects involving groups of highly skilled professionals is the core of the organisation
- Creativity: by definition programing and production are about being creative, doing new and different things
- Control: the production and broadcasting process requires a lot of quality control
- Competing; being funded by a licence fee means that competing is less critical for the BROADCASTORG than it is for other media organisations.

Goals of HRD; the HRD priorities to be dealt with here are as follows:

- Attract, recruit, retain and share the best talent with the right skills and attitude to deliver their ambitious plans.

- Re-skill: maintain strength in specialist skills and re-skill our existing workforce for a digital, multi-platform environment, through the continued delivery of the T&D priorities for core and future skills.
- And be transformational, engaging people.

Designing and delivering HRD in such a complex situation with so many needs and limited resources, and a need to keep on broadcasting through major changes like a shift of building, is critical. 'Three-day training programmes' are less likely to succeed than innovations which integrate learning with work, and which fits with a culture in which so many people are creatives or associated with creativity. The 'Where and when' options could include reference to:

- Small numbers/hands-on training and whole organisation wide events and information
- On-site: classroom environments for training along with links to the new production and working facilities
- Innovative: this is a creative organisation, so expect some creative initiatives!
- Delivered just in time with migration/continuous output with change of building

The evaluation of returns on investments in seeking to focus resources on key areas in the short term to make the move of the building need to be balanced with expectations about changing the values (more collaboration) which can only be discerned in the longer term.

The opportunity of the major change to a new building with new technology is balanced by the threat which the scale and scope of this change brings. It is not just the logistical challenge of the move. There are engagement priorities to evaluate.

Engage staff in the overall vision of BROADCASTORG Change programme

Engaging them with the new workspace and the new technology

Encouraging collaboration and innovation

Equip leaders with the tools and skills to engage their staff in the challenges ahead

Scope of HRD

To recap, they want;

Collaborate at all levels

Trust each other to deliver

Be open to change and developing new skills

Have a strong bond with audiences

Consider how initiatives might include the use of training, team building, mentoring, e-learning, communities of practice and strategic HRD. HRD initiatives need to relate to providing;

Deliver a full training and development programme to support business priorities – including specialist skills to support network growth strategy. So specialist technical training from experts is part of the picture;

Gives clear and consistent direction and a compelling reason for change. Some joined up, open/honest pan communication over the period of the change would be expected – special newsletters, special events, access to senior decision-makers for questions and answers, and so on.

Collective leadership: demonstrating a different and collective leadership, engaging people in the challenges ahead can be signalled through who is promoted, hired, exited at the top. Part of this might entail the use of coaching and mentoring methods as part of a talent management strategy.

An annual employee engagement survey to help managers understand issues and drive employee engagement

Leadership and management development is essential, the platform for change: equipping leaders and managers first with key skills and tools to engage our staff to address the challenges ahead. Again succession planning/talent development framework for key leaders

As a user of advanced digital technologies the role of e-learning could be critical; but it is appropriate to be balanced, and blend it in rather than letting it take over, a risk in such an environment.

Levels of HRD

Learning and change needs identification is assisted by the level of change involved, where demands on HRD to support individuals, groups and the whole organization is self-evident. The logistics of providing the right HRD for so many people in so many ways (technical, organizational, cultural) is a huge task. Training Priorities and targets in:

- Core technologies
- Underpinning skillsets
- All staff and freelancers across the country.

Working at the basics across people management and HR remain the platform on which effective HRD depends. This situation combines the classic combination of a change of technology and change of social relations. So it is about cultural change; that can be a long haul with few quick wins in the early days as the technology is introduced and existing relations are disrupted. When the demands of handling downsizing are included this makes it tougher. These people are very aware of and dealing with that.

Approaching this as Strategic HRD. Sponsorship and Leadership engagement are critical – who's on the journey with the HRD staff as they plan and deliver? This matters from the top levels down through all the key groups to the sometimes neglected but critical staff in easy to over-look but perhaps critical roles – the staff in security, in canteens and in support services need to given attention and not just the big name talents and established technical professions at the heart of the of the broadcasting organisation. Be clear what you need to deliver and what your partners, including in this case trade unions, need to deliver; working in partnership with various stakeholders to define needs, engage with HRD and appreciate its significance for individuals, groups and the whole organisation.

Deficiencies in Knowledge Management. There is also a partnership between the BROADCASTORG HRD and BROADCASTORG to consider. BROADCASTORG were pioneers as they had the chance to move to the new building and technologies built in, but this did mean they could get it wrong. They needed to feel that this was OK. When there is no model to import because this is a leading organisation there needs to be an appreciation of learning from mistakes, and sharing that knowledge.

Winning hearts and minds is essential to the momentum needed to see these changes through, so to keep communicating even as things get very complex and difficult is essential. All kinds of initiatives to communicate about the changes in general, and the move to the new building especially, were worked on as a priority in real-life.

The Scope of HRD

Human Resource Development (HRD) is concerned with the process of learning and change in work and employment to enable skilled people to perform competently in their roles.

The theory, policy and practice of HRD has roots in the study of Human Development and thinking about organisations and management. The field of Human Development (see Figure 1.1) provides ideas and movements that have inspired and impassioned people from the philosophers of education to businesses and politicians engaging with the demands of contemporary and future social and economic challenges. From Socrates and Confucius, through Marx and Freud to the myriad and diverse writers and researchers on Human Development in the kaledeoscope of areas in which questions and answers about human development matter now.

Keeping a broad sense of the area of HRD can be helpful. With a looser and broader view HRD show is then potentially implicated and involved in more areas of public theory, policy and practice. And questions and answers from these other areas of human development can be potentially relevant to understanding and exploring HRD. The challenges of adult learning and change are not confined to work and employment, and education; they are a feature of every aspect of public life, from defence to criminal justice systems. The ends of HRD, the outcomes of HRD, can then be seen learning and change which provide advances in these areas of public life; including, for example, defence, welfare, justice, culture and health.

Selected Further Reading

Butler-Bowden, T. (2008) '50 Success Classics' (London, Nicholas Brealey Publishing).

Ehrenreich, B. (2009) 'Bright-Sided' (New York, Metropolitan Books).

James, O. (2007) 'Affluenza; How to Be Successful and Stay Sane' (London, Vermillion).

Reid, M.A., Barrington, H., and Brown, M. (2009) 'Human Resource Development; Beyond Training Interventions', 7th Edition (London, CIPD).

Stewart, J. and Rigg, C. (2011) 'Learning and Talent Development' (London, CIPD).

Seligman, M. (2002) 'Authentic Happiness' (New York, Free Press).

Swanson, R.A. and Holton, E. F. (2001) 'Foundations of Human Resource Development' (San Francisco, Berret-Koehler).

3 Key Texts

(1) Baumeister, R. (2005) 'The Cultural Animal: Human Nature, Meaning, and Social Life' (USA, Oxford University Press).

(2) Cameron, K.S., Quinn, R.E., Degraff, J. and Thakor, A. (2006) 'Competing Values Leadership: Creating Value in Organizations' (Cheltenham, UK, Edward Elgar).

(3) Gladwell, M. (2008) 'Outliers: The Story of Success' (London, Allen Lane).

3 Key Articles/Reports

(1) Keely, B., (2007) 'Human Capital: How What You Know Shapes Your Life', OECD.

(2) Kuchinke, P. (2010) Human Development as a Central Goal for Human Resource Development', *Human Resource Development International*, 13–5, 575–585.

(3) Sambrook, S. and Stewart, J. (2007) Teaching, Learning and Assessing HRD; FINAL REPORT, Higher Education Academy: Business, Management, Accounting & Finance.

3 Key Web Links

(1) UN facebook site: http://www.facebook.com/pages/Human-Development-Index/108073452547813.

(2) Butler-Bowden texts on success: http://www.butler-bowdon.com/home.

(3) Dictionary of HRD; Key terms defined: http://www.eric.ed.gov/ERICWebPortal/search/detailmini.jsp?_nfpb=true&_&ERICExtSearch_SearchValue_0=ED367907&ERICExtSearch_SearchType_0=no&accno=ED367907.

2

Knowledge Bases and Theory

Learning Objectives

By the end of this chapter you will be able to:

- Describe three sources of knowledge in HRD: evidence-based social science, reflective professional practice and ethical/ideological beliefs;
- Analyse social science theories as macro-formal and micro-substantive forms of knowledge;
- Compare and contrast realist and constructivist views of knowledge;
- Reflect critically on the presence and contribution of values and ethical/ideological perspectives in HRD.

Question 2.1

Either
   What is your own current knowledge base about 'what works' to help adults learn and change? Take a few minutes to write down the sources of ideas you currently have about how adults learn and change
   Or
   Describe a knowledge base you are aware of that relates to 'what works' in adult learning and change. To what extent do you consider this knowledge base to be valid and evidence based?

Introduction

In Human Resource Development (HRD), knowledge bases can emerge from and be attributed to three broad areas, with varying kinds of validity and evidence bases. First are the social science disciplines and theories, especially psychology, sociology and economics. In social science as it applies to HRD there are concerns with the validity and evidence bases of macro-formal or micro-substantive theory and research. Second is the 'reflective practice' literature of HRD. The validity and evidence base of this is grounded in experience, presenting concerns with respect to the norms of social science. Third is the knowledge embodied in values and ethical/ideological beliefs. The mapping of these, and understanding how they connect with understanding 'what works' and influence what is done in practice, can be critical for appreciating the rhetoric and reality of HRD. It can be helpful to combine all these in comparing and contrasting realist and constructivist paradigms for useful knowledge in HRD and professional practice.

What is Knowledge?

The pragmatic question at the fore of most peoples' exploration of HRD is 'what works'? To understand 'what works' and engage with adult learning in employment, it is not essential to be aware of social science theory, but it is desirable to be able to think critically. Many of the professionals, managers and others directly engaged in HRD may have some reference points in formal and codified knowledge about human development and adult learning, but not any substantial education in the contributing social science disciplines. The absence of social science grounding in itself does not preclude being an effective developer of people, but the absence of critical thinking may. Part of critical thinking is to understand, engage with and evaluate knowledge bases, in their own terms.

Such critical thinking is constantly emerging in HRD, especially as specialist journals publish research in HRD. Jun Jo et al. (2009) completed a review of four specialist HRD journals that have been publishing research on HRD, some since 1990 and up to 2007. They reviewed over 1,300 articles and identified two key topics which attracted critical thinking. One key topic was empirical and conceptual research into learning and performance, with debates about the 'learning' or 'performance' rationales of HRD. The other key topic was theory and theory building, reflecting the significance of this as a concern in the area of HRD as a subject aiming to become more professional and mature. The previous chapter introduced and outlined how the former concerns, with successful performance for individuals, organisations and nations exist in HRD, and ideas about process, methods and contexts which exist in the study of adult learning and change in work and employment.

This chapter now looks at the latter concern in HRD, the nature of the knowledge in the subject. There are three sources of knowledge in HRD: (1) theory-driven social science, (2) reflective professional practice, (3) and values or ethical/ideological beliefs. Understanding and evaluating the relevance, validity, evidence bases and impact of all these is an integral part of understanding HRD.

Theory-based social science is the dominant force in academic and study contexts, as it provides a structure and language for knowledge to be generated, communicated and critiqued. However other sources of knowledge are possible too, and help to identify important questions, as well as suggest answers to them. Perspective 2.1 provides some examples of knowledge present in HRD. These have emerged from research, professional experience and ethical/ideological beliefs. They are all considered to be to some extent relevant, valid evidence based and have an impact on practice in HRD. They will each be considered in more depth in later chapters. The concern here is to consider the general issues that arise in generating and using knowledge in HRD.

Perspective 2.1: Examples of Knowledge in HRD

Learning styles: adult learners have patterns of preferences in how they go about learning depending on the way they process information.

Action learning: adults learn best in learning systems designed around principles of 'action learning' and problem-solving not those more commonly used in the education of young people.

Learning organisations: if employees can be helped and encouraged to share what they know, organisations are more efficient and effective.

Organisational cultures shape learning: nurturing an organisational culture is an integral part of creating an environment at work which supports learning, productivity and well-being.

Scientific management: systematic observation and analysis of jobs can provide the foundations for training people in skills and roles at work.

Lifelong learning: societies need to encourage adult participation in learning throughout life, not only in fixed periods of formal education and training.

The Structure and Sources of Knowledge and Theory

What counts as useful knowledge about a subject evolves in an organised way over time, with different threads offered, described and communicated, shared and analysed by a community of stakeholders. Those stakeholders include academics, professionals, policy-makers and groups involved in the area; in the case of HRD that includes employers, employees and institutions of adult learning. When a subject is first encountered, it is these 'threads' of knowledge that a student encounters and accumulates. The chapters which follow hereafter develop those threads, and together they form a whole picture of adult learning in work and employment. But to make sense of any thread, it is always helpful to have some understanding of how it fits into the 'whole' from the outset. To guide learning as the threads are assembled together. Following from this analogy, some questions arise. Are all the threads available, or are there gaps in knowledge of learning and change? How are new threads to fill in any gaps there may be to be made, and advance to a fuller, and more complete whole picture of learning and change?

Social Science Theory

A common and general definition of theory is that the 'theory' of an area is that which is written down, to explain and guide learners in advance of their actually doing something in practice. Anything which is written down with the intention of explaining HRD, including this whole book, is a form of theory in this general sense. More specifically theory in social sciences provides a structure and language with which knowledge can be generated, communicated and critiqued.

Theorising is establishing and developing systems of ideas intended to explain. Theory helps us to explain by 'using a statement of relations among concepts within a set of boundary assumptions and constraints' (Bacharach 1989). Where we want to advance knowledge in a discipline, guide research towards important question and develop evidence-based professional practice, then theory matters.

The topics in HRD we seek to explain, as the examples of theory above show, include learning, change, performance, organisation, success and talent. To generate knowledge, it is desirable to make explicit underlying assumptions we have about these and then to gather evidence, to do research. This is part of the function of theory, to direct and set boundaries for gathering evidence to test and refine explanations of these topics. Ultimately, the aim is indeed to explain what works for whom, in what circumstances, in what respects and how. This is another part of the function of theory, to enable and encourage stakeholders in HRD, including learners new to the subject as well as experienced professionals, to adopt an exploratory rather than judgemental perspective. The focus is not on certainty, which is unobtainable, but on understanding how things work in contexts and settings (Pawson et al. 2004). Pawson emphasises the value of theory for:

- Making explicit underlying assumptions: encountering theory is not just about reading other peoples' ideas, but about making explicit any assumptions; these may be your assumptions, another writer's assumptions, an organisation's assumptions.

- Gathering evidence to test and refine these: you will read articles where others have gathered evidence to test and refine their theories, but you also need to be able to gather your own evidence while learning about HRD.

- Influence sense-making and shifts in thinking: ultimately the success of knowledge and a theory is its impact or otherwise in shaping and shifting peoples thinking.

This is relevant and significant in HRD because the 'same' thing, the same 'treatment', cannot be repeated in an identical manner or in an identical setting with adult learners. No training programme or course is ever delivered as an exact duplicate; even the most standardised programme is never repeated in the say way in different organisations; and so on. 'What works' in one situation once is no guide to what will work in a different situation at another time. So even the most apparently authoritative theory is open to modification in implementation as actual people make use of it.

Theories are systems of ideas intended to explain something, based on general principles. Such systems of ideas and principles may also be the basis for practice, but not necessarily. Systems of ideas may be the subject of speculation and interest in themselves, outside of any practical application. Exploring theory may then be both a means of managing practice or a means of engaging in debates about the nature and merits of systems of ideas themselves, critically reflecting on these. The value of each of these is strongly defended by its advocates, those concerned with action or those concerned with critical reflection. For the learner new to HRD and experienced professional a synthesis of concerns, expecting theory to help understand and meet the demands of practice is important, and so is questioning and critique of the knowledge which forms the knowledge base of HRD.

This is because, at any level, developing and using theory involves making explicit underlying assumptions and gathering evidence to test and refine these, explaining what works for whom, in what circumstances, in what respects and how (Pawson et al. 2004). The ultimate purpose is to influence sense-making and shifts in thinking. As such the desire for theory can be said to begin in the head, of researchers, policy-makers and others; to pass into the hands of practitioners and managers; and, sometimes, into the hearts and minds of users and participants (see Debate 2.1).

Debate 2.1: Status of Theory

The status of theory in HRD is ambiguous. On the one hand are those who desire a foundation of professional practice in HRD that is formed by an appreciation of valid and robust theory. Alternatively there are those who adopt a pragmatic approach, believing that managing HRD at work requires familiarity with an accumulated body of knowledge around best practice, not commitment to a theory.

This reflects the more general debate between these positions in management as a whole. The proponents of theory-based learning about HRD are concerned to contest 'normative' and prescriptive biases of a pragmatist approach to learning;

concerned just with what is current 'best practice'. This can be seen to select from and distort knowledge and understanding about learning and change, leading to poorly realised processes, hit or miss practices, and a detachment from ongoing research and evidence. Theory is a disciplined way of acquiring truth about causes and effects.

The response of the pragmatists is that devoting time to getting to grips with systems of theory, and theory development, which are diverse and contested is a distraction rather than a useful contribution to organising adult learning in practice. They may see the proponents of research and theorising as detached from the real-world concerns of practitioners. And they may be sceptical that research and evidence can ever construct certain scientific knowledge that is worth basing their practice on.

If we think of theory as providing a language with which to define, examine and discuss knowledge about HRD, there is no universal, single language. Chalofsky (2007) identified several different disciplines, or language, incorporating scholarly dialogue and perspectives from many sources. The major ones are psychology, sociology and economics, and each of these and their connections with HRD are introduced next.

Psychology

The first discipline and knowledge base that most associate with the theoretical exploration of learning and change in work and employment is psychology. HRD at work can appear to have much of its professional and theoretical underpinnings as a form of applied psychology. The fields and associated theories of the psychological literature provide for understanding the principles and problems of HRD at work (Arnold et al. 2010). In this human science there are, however, competing theories emerging from the various schools of psychology. These provide different and diverging explanations of the principles and problems of learning and change.

Hardingham (2000) provides a good example of bridge between theory-based psychology and HRD. Psychology for her is to be defined as a 'frame of mind' rather than a specific school of theory. It can help people understand how to establish a learning partnership, but it is not a source of a complete recipe for success in managing learning and change. Hardingham touches on many significant and useful points about the HRD process, and concerns with processes working and not working, emphasising delivery, with aspects of design and evaluation also considered. Design is about getting information across, and ensuring the transfer of learning. Delivery involves understanding things that stress trainees and trainers, how to build rapport and establish credibility, work in groups and handle conflicts. That is frame of mind which is sensitive to a set of assumptions and debates (see Perspective 2.2).

Perspective 2.2: The Psychological Frame of Mind; Assumptions and Debates	
Popular assumptions about people and learning	Debates in adult learning
There is an exercise of personal freedom involved in learning; motives and control matter and can be influenced to promote learning	The extent to which determinism exists and factors beyond the control of the person have a big impact on learning
Situational contexts matter: environment can have a big impact for good in advancing learning	The extent to which 'innateness' is the heart of capability, with inborn characteristics setting the boundaries on what is possible
People are unique and therefore each has a different development pathways which needs to be facilitated and respected	The extent to which 'universality' applies, with most people following the same or similar development pathways over a lifespan
Being proactive, taking the initiative, shapes learning positively	To what extent being reactive, driven by external stimuli, shapes learning for most people most of the time
Optimism is warranted about learning; significant change is possible for all	To what extent is pessimism about learning warranted is warranted; as most people tend to be stable and unchanging, not open to learning

Learning is about involving people in processes rather than transmitting data to them. Hardingham argues that in many cases the information required to underpin performance and learning can be condensed to a single A4 sheet, and most time in learning is spent on activity and discussion. This is not a waste of time; it all aids perception, attention and short-term memory and helps because people learn best when they are active, free to engage in activities, with lots of variety and stretch on development.

The two dominant families of theory in psychology are those formed, broadly, around the behaviourist and cognitive perspectives. For behaviourists the principles and problems of HRD at work are the principles and problems of conditioning and reinforcing desired behaviours. Learning fails if the conditioning is not secured and transferred from the learning experience to subsequent behaviour in work. For those adopting a cognitive perspective the principles and problems of HRD at work are those of enabling and influencing sense-making and information processing (Pinker 1997). Learning fails if it is not constructed to best fit with people's natural learning styles and harness people's natural abilities to learn.

Cognitive science attracts the most current attention, with research and knowledge about the brain seeming the most productive and constructive basis for exploring the what and how of learning and change (see Practice 2.1). The evolution of technologies in MRI scanning, which can show areas of the brain 'lit up' when involved in tasks and activities, is believed to hold potential not just for medical diagnosis but also for enlightening us about learning and change. If we can observe the brain, and changes in it, we can measure and evaluate all kinds of things; including the effectiveness of learning and change interventions. This is the culmination of a long developing mix in cognitive science, practice and knowledge deriving from primary contributing disciplines which are computer science and linguistics as well as neuroscience and cognitive neuropsychology (Thagrad 1996). Whatever the technologies used to measure brain activity, cognitive scientists aim to construct causal accounts by linking three levels: (1) the behavioural, (2) the cognitive and (3) the biological.

To understand theory in HRD is then to encounter, if only superficially, an analysis of the biology of the brain and mind and brain-friendly learning. The rationale of cognitive science is that the human brain, the site of learning, can best be understood in terms of the use of representational structures in the brain and the computational procedures that operate on those structures. The brain is a machine for creating and using representational structures in the form of logical propositions, rules, concepts, images and analogies. It uses procedures on these such as deduction, search, matching, rotating and retrieval. The cells of the brain, the neurons, embody these representations and enable such computation.

Practice 2.1: Brain-friendly Learning

- The brain is 'plastic' across its lifespan; people are naturally able to learn and re-learn.
- Learning is achieved best with all five senses engaged.
- Learning takes time, as it involves a balance of input and accommodation/assimilation (reflecting on feedback) and output (practice).
- Emotional well-being is essential for learning; high challenge stimulates learning, but high anxiety impedes it.

The costs of this information-processing capacity for the organism are the resources needed to develop and maintain the sense system it requires and the need to learn symbol systems – the resources required for the brain and consciousness. These costs are varied and considerable. They include females having to cope with long pregnancies, and the risks of giving birth to babies who have large skulls. They also include the young being exposed to a prolonged period of dependence in development through to maturity and competence. The mechanics of data representation in people's heads takes the form of visual, phonological and grammatical data transformed into modes of inscription in the neural networks of the brain. Neural networks act to enable cognition based on set symbols being manipulated by basic rules and procedures.

The empiricist model of the brain asserts that nurturing determines what is imprinted on the blank slate of the brain: thus culture is the most powerful force in forming the mind. This kind of computational theory asserts rather that there is hard wiring in the brain, selected, through evolution, for obtaining and handling information. The brain is not an empty slate. This hard-wiring was formed from people's evolution of stereoscopic vision, bipedal walking (which freed the hands for using tools), group living and hunting (which required coalitions and reciprocity among the group). A view that the brain is pre-wired, not a blank slate, is the classic rationalist view. In the contemporary human environment, with the lifestyle challenges and risks it involves, these original hard-wired elements of the human brain, determining its functions and structures, remain the same, but the context and the goals of intelligent behaviour are now different. Evolutionary theory implies that the brain and mind, and the use of learning in their operations, are ultimately to be judged in terms of how they help in the survival and replication of the species.

For analysts, these analogies of hard-wiring lead to the conclusion that the emotions are mechanisms that set the brain's highest level goals. Exploring emotions, scientifically, as drives to deploy the intellect in pursuit of certain goals means bracketing any judgements about whether those emotions are 'good' or 'bad'. They have the function of keeping people in tune with their environment, and the risks and opportunities that presents, at all times. Most evidently, this is seen to be true at critical points in survival and evolution; points of fight, flight and reproduction. In a scientific sense their function is to help people connect with and secure the cooperation of others in these contexts while pursuing their individual interests and goals.

Social Theory

The dominance of psychological theory and knowledge bases, in either the behaviourist or cognitive form, can often seem to the beginning and end of theory in HRD. But other streams of knowledge and therefore theory do exist which are at least equally as important for appreciating and analysing adult learning challenges and issues at work (Lave and Wenger 1991, Boud and Garrick 1999, Hager 1999). There is a considerable amount of social science theory related to and relevant for understanding learning and change as social processes, involving relationships and group dynamics. This is not surprising, given that the natural way in which HRD at work has been organised for most of human history has not been in the form of professional mediated systems grounded in psychological validated methods and models of the brain. It has been in the context of human relationships and groups. Relationships matter, and are central; from the parent–child relationship, through learning in the community then formal education and onto learning the complex organisations of work and employment. What existed and has evolved socially has implications the success or otherwise of these relations and their institutional features. No advances in the technology of brain-scanning enabling greater understanding of the neuropsychology of learning and change have, or will, displace the social facts and circumstances that shape the opportunities and challenges of learning and change for people as members of communities and societies.

For example, in the past in work and employment much learning occurred in apprenticeships, in an age of more organic social relations, with stable close tries in small communities. These involved a learner totally immersed in learning with a master and mentor. The context for the HRD process which this entailed, for a master to structure and supervise learning constantly, and then require the person to make their own way as their own master, was the archetypal learning and change journey and story. Much modern HRD has displaced or rendered this journey and story apparently obsolete. In the age of large employers and industrial organisation and institutional systems, the apprenticeship altered and changed to fit within large-scale organisation. With the decline of that manufacturing-based context in many areas the apprenticeship system became obsolete. The journey and story changed; it changed to feature longer periods in formal education, including higher education; and to prepare people for employability rather than employment in one kind of job and career.

Yet even with such dramatic change in work, organisation and career journeys and stories, learning is still often 'situated' (Lave and Wenger, 1991) in social contexts; in the complex working environments of financial, creative and service contexts as well as modern manufacturing. These provide a context and role for social theory and theorising to investigate what HRD at work entails and how it happens in practice and may be improved.

That entails one form of social context in itself; the motivation and capacity to engage in education. Alongside this occupational development in education much HRD still occurred in the workplace. The learning that occurred outside the educational environment, the classroom and formal learning, involved learning in these situations and contexts. Understanding the principles and problems of, making sense of and managing, HRD is therefore bound up with theory about social relationships and the institutional contexts of learning, both formal and informal. Constructs from social science are relveant to illuminate and explore this.

The social science perspective highlights how people and their behaviour are the products of social situations and contexts. For learning people will be embedded in social relations, which they may find amenable or in which they may find uncomfortable and challenging. Consequently they may be involved in or excluded from communities of practice. The principles and problems of HRD are of having effective relationships in formal learning settings or within those communities of practice, whether they be found in work or within special education and training institutions. The quality of access to and relationships within a community of practice can determine how effective learning will be. To be excluded from these communities of practice is to be excluded from effective HRD. To be part of a thriving community of practice is to be accessing the best HRD possible. This is significant not only locally, for individuals in communities; it is significant globally, among nations.

Economic Theory

As well as the psychology and the social relations concerns there are also sources of knowledge in economic theory (Chapman 1993, Machin and Vignoles 2001) which can be drawn upon to understand and make sense of HRD. Here the problems and decisions associated with HRD at work are investigated within a context of economic models and theories; assuming that individuals are rational actors seeking to maximise their self-interest in an environment where financial rewards are the most significant. Problems and solutions with situations such as skill shortfalls which affect performance and growth can only be managed by training provisions that make economic and business sense. One recent case, widely reported, was a situation in train operating companies. The situation had arisen where many people wanted to be managers, and few wanted to be train drivers. Consequently any managerial job in a train operating company received many applicants, but there were not enough staff to actually run the trains. This represents a problem in labour market relations, and can be theorised about as such. In general such skill shortages or oversupply represent a form of market failure. How these market failures can be dealt with by economically informed thinking on the part of governments, firms and individuals will depend on the theoretical position adopted, the answer as to 'why' is this failure occurring?

There is often a primary concern in economic sense-making about HRD with macro-level policy concerns, and with arguments over which interventions should be supported by governments, to help make HRD pay. The possible economic benefits of HRD may be perceived to be threefold:

1. To the individual in terms of higher wages and better job prospects;
2. To the firm in terms of increased productivity and profitability;
3. To the economy as a whole in terms of higher economic growth and other benefits to society.

However, there is a lack of data and evidence to back up claims that 'HRD pays', from an economist's perspective, in any of these respects. Notwithstanding the considerable discussion of Human Capital, one reason for this and an important gap in the literature currently is that little is known about the cost side of the HRD equation. Information on identifying the benefits of training, which is not simple to do either, is merely the first step in calculating the overall private (and social) return from training investment. The HRD and policy research communities are interested in researching and obtaining better measures of training effectiveness and impact. For instance, data may differentiate more effectively between the different types of employer-provided training, rather than lumping it altogether under the heading 'training'. Such primary research could be able to provide evidence more sophisticated and credible than just 'training pays'. It could also be possible to tell individuals, firms and policy-makers which types of training yield what level of private and social returns. This area of HRD will be discussed in more detail in the chapter on National HRD policy.

For organisations, profit-oriented, public service or other, these conceptual and theoretical concerns increasingly involve a discussion of human and intellectual capital. New models of enterprises and how they create value have led to the development of the idea of intellectual capital. Instead of defining value in terms of short-term profits, and seeking to identify gaps between balance sheet values and market valuation, there is a concern with the intangible assets. Traditional accounting systems are challenged to find ways of describing and valuing intellectual capital as an asset of the organisation. Increasing intellectual capital, through learning, rather than through cost cutting or the introduction of new technologies, becomes a strategic imperative. The growth of intellectual capital, in theory, depends on HRD in practice.

Some argue that, to date, HRD has been relatively un-informed by economic thinking as what attention there has been has been subsumed in general discussions of broader industrial policy or industrial relations systems, including wage bargaining at the heart of that. With more prominence to HRD that may change. Others worry, conversely, that the focus on HRD is a worrying narrowing of policy concern, with the focus on skills displacing a broader concern with industrial relations systems; one effect is to cut off economic thinking from HRD policy.

There are different economic approaches to analysing HRD at work that could be better explored as the bases for policy. The first is the market failure approach, explaining shortfalls in training provision and highlighting several areas of fact, for example the levels of young people participating in education. There has been an increase in some forms of training (job related in the 1980s), but there is a bias to academic achievement not vocational training, as seen in the expansion of higher education. Large numbers of people receive no training, or only enough for low-level qualifications.

This happens because, at existing costs, individuals cannot afford training they would otherwise undertake. There is also the 'free rider' problem: firms fail to train, because they fear poaching. There are contract restrictions: employers and employees ideally need continual re-contracting to reflect changes in value, but this works against the advantages of fixed wages. Market failure as a consequence of these explains the dominant fact – the under-provision of HRD. It implies that interventions in markets will be the remedy, and cooperation among various stakeholders is required for such a remedy.

Another economic theory influenced theory framework is human capital theory, developed in the 1960s. Earnings follow a lifecycle pattern, first rising to a maximum and then declining. This is because wages are determined by human capital, which depends on education, training and job experience, as attainment in these leads to higher productivity. Individuals with higher skill levels may be rewarded with higher wages in recognition of their superior productivity. Human capital acquisition through training and education reflects the rational investment decisions of actors in the system. In the 1960s this line of thinking was suggested to explain why the nations defeated in the Second World War recovered so spectacularly. The significant factor was investment in human capital, not physical capital. It also highlights how for developing countries there is a trap: they need human capital aid, not physical aid, but as they develop their people those people often leave for other countries. It could also explain the life-cycle of earnings: low for the young with little human capital, increasing as human capital is gained, and then declining as outmoded human capital loses its relevance.

The concept of human capital emerges and centres around the core argument; that individuals and firms can be seen as wealth maximisers who calculate the value of different training options, and given transparency on who benefits from training determine and accept who should pay for it. In this context skills and training for them can be defined as either 'general and portable' or 'specific and non-transferable'. In general and portable skills and training there is an increase in the trained person's marginal productivity by the same amount for any firm. This benefits workers, through higher earnings for them as a more skilled and productive person. As they benefit so they should pay for the training. With specific and non-transferable training there is a productivity increase of use only to the host firm. The firm acquires the gains from the skills and training, no other organisation can benefit, so it should meet the costs.

An implication of this general analysis of human capital and rational actors making decisions was that anything which impeded the operation of a rational system in HRD was an 'externality'. If, for example, individuals could not get the resources to increase their human capital as capital markets did not give credit for training that was an externality. Further, inter-firm factors also applied to complicate the picture. The prisoners' dilemma model and game theory suggest that how people behave in situations where there are possible win–win outcomes available do not always to maximise those win–win outcomes. Each party seeks to avoid losing, the net effect being a lose–lose situation emerges. This dynamic could be seen where firms could invest in training to increase human capital, but fear doing so, as they think they will lose that investment as people move out of the organisation. They as firms therefore pursue sub-optimal strategies, collectively losing out as neither provides training.

Finally, the institutional school of economic theory sees issues in HRD, including differences between organisations, as being explained by their emphasis on external or internal labour market forces. HRD will be carried out within organisations where recruitment is limited to certain ports of entry. For occupational labour markets wages are set by market supply and demand, so wages will be equalised across firms because of mobility. But, once hired, the internal labour market becomes paramount. Progress to different skill levels and inter-firm differences in this respect mean that wages vary, reducing mobility. Firms seek to buy in cheap at certain levels, develop specific skills through learning by doing and then protect their internal market against poaching.

Levels of Theory

Social science knowledge and theories can be classified according to the level they are providing knowledge at (see Figure 2.1). In HRD, perceived as a field of applied knowledge, there are two levels of theory which are particularly important. These are macro-formal theories and micro-substantive theories. Theories that seek to map and classify HRD as a whole are macro-formal theories. Theories that seek to focus on 'what works' in practice are micro-substantive theories; theories that focus on 'what works' in policy terms tend to be macro-formal theories. These are the main form in which useful knowledge from social sciences are adopted as useful knowledge in HRD.

Macro-formal and micro-substantive theories consider different levels, but both seek to explain the causes and effects of a series of observations in a way that focuses attention on possibilities, actions and choices. Developing these theories, about HRD as a whole or about a specific practice in learning and change, also bring out differences, and new questions. In finding answers we generate new questions, and so continue to educate ourselves, apply ourselves to reasoning and arguing about possibilities, actions and choices. Without theories, both macro-formal and micro-substantive, bad reasoning, flawed evidence and vested interests may shape thinking about and practising HRD.

HRD has the best and worst of both worlds in terms of levels of theory. There is scope for both micro and macro studies, alongside an interdisciplinary

SCOPE		
	Micro	**Macro**
Formal	Micro-formal General forms of social organisation of HRD, e.g., manager–employee relationships	Macro-formal Structure, function and development of workplace HRD in societies and cultures; comparative organisational and country studies
Substantive	Micro-substantive Specific organisations or situations, e.g., mentoring and coaching relationships, Trainer–learner interaction, single e-learning platforms	Macro-substantive Specific HRD strategies and policies in particular workplaces, practices like e-learning, coaching

Figure 2.1   Scope and generality theory
Source: Based on Hammersley and Atkinson (1992, pp. 204–206).

foundation for HRD, making it a potentially social science rich, credible, effective, professional domain. Psychology, social relations and economics all have well-developed theory which claim to offer some kind of scientific foundation for understanding and practising HRD. The big challenge is the diversity of the social science knowledge base itself, and identifying connections and applications to HRD as a domain of applied knowledge.

The validity and reliability of knowledge from social science is generally high, though its connection to and influence on practice is an issue. The exchange of knowledge from research communities to practitioners occurs institutionally, at conferences and through some publications, and individually as researchers work with organisations. Whether enough of that exchange happens, or if there is a tendency for researchers to communicate among themselves, and for practitioners to look to other sources of knowledge to inform practice, is a critical issue in HRD.

Reflective Practice Literature

The founts of social science theory are not the only wellspring of knowledge. There is much literature which is reflective practice literature; written by, and usually for, HRD professionals, people who have experience and who work in the field of HRD, drawing on their experience and wisdom. The usefulness of this as a source of knowledge is disputed. Its relevance and impact can be perceived to be high, as the concepts and practices discussed emerge from practical experience. Validity and reliability can often be low, as such knowledge is based on limited theorising and evidence. This kind of knowledge is not uncommon in management in general. It can be found in the wisdom literature that practitioners of HRD write and disseminate. HRD is replete with wisdom literature, work written by and for practitioners. This literature encompasses texts on 'how to do it' (refs) and popular writers on learning and change (for example, Covey 1989). This kind of knowledge is a popular resource, both among experienced practitioners and often with new learners too. It is often popular precisely because it does not address questions and issues of theory. That can be an advantage for professionals not schooled in social science, but means it has weaknesses as a credible resource for constructing useful knowledge about HRD.

Reflective practice research and knowledge generation can be done with regard to the norms of social science, but its nature and purpose is not to produce social science knowledge. The risks are that as knowledge is developed it is based on observations that are inaccurately made. Data are collected selectively rather than comprehensively. There is usually only evidence to generalise from a few cases. Researchers tend to retain impressions rather than have well-structured data available to analyse. The practitioner as researcher tends to be emotionally/personally involved in the process, not a detached researcher. Connections or conclusions may be made up to fill gaps and remove uncertainty. The researcher may form views and stick to them. There may be a view that some things are beyond analysis, and in some way remain mysterious.

Debate 2.2: Reflective Practice or 'Normal Science'

If the norms of social science are not adhered to in doing research and developing knowledge, what are the risks? The following are some of the issues that can arise.

Reflective practice	Normal science
Observe inaccurately	Decide what to observe carefully
Observe selectively	Observe systematically
Generalise from a few cases	Sample
Retain impressions	Collect data
Get emotionally/personally involved	Respect scientific norms
Make things up to fill gaps	Stick to the evidence
Form views and stick to them	Constantly revise views
Some things remain mysterious	All is knowable; research it

In some cases this feeds a predisposition to causal explanations (Wolpert 2008) which produces knowledge based on:

- Quick decisions;
- Bad with numbers;
- Seeing patterns in randomness;
- Influenced by authority;
- Liking for mysticism.

The underlying concern is that knowledge from reflective practice theory, or wisdom, is rarely based on systematic research, evidence collection and valid forms of argument, and tends to reflect the problems of 'common-sense' thinking rather than the rigour of normal science (see Debate 2.2). Reflective practice literature tends to express prescriptions about what works, based on one person's experience in the situations they have experienced. Such advice emerging from personal experience, and prescriptions for good practice, can be useful and stimulating. Reading the reflective practice literature can give checklists of 'what to do', providing 'know-how' knowledge. This is enduringly popular with hard-pressed action-oriented practitioners; and new learners looking for material to use in assignments and exams. Indeed the reflective practice literature tends to see problems with learning and change at work as a consequence of ill-prepared and unprofessional trainers and managers seeking to manage learning and change in an ill-informed way. Understanding the experience of successful trainers and others the reflective practice literature provides admonitions, recipes, tips and techniques for supporting effective learning and change.

The validity and reliability of such knowledge about HRD at work, and the sense-making it involves, is that those who have experience are often the best placed to explain and discuss what works and what does not work. The weakness of the reflective practice literature is that the research base is not rigorously collated or presented. The implication, sometimes expressed explicitly in this literature, is that theorising actually gets in the way of good and effective practice. Clearer and better prescriptive accounts of the best practice, not an engagement with the complexity of pure theory, is the solution. Yet every author and experienced practitioner has a theory. The critique is not just that the norms of social science are absent, but that there is no atheoretical position to adopt. It may not be their main concern to explain and evaluate a theory or different theories, but in prescribing the best way and 'getting results' they are agents of unexamined theory (see Practice 2.2).

Practice 2.2: Unexamined Theory

Reading the reflective practice literature can involve interpreting and evaluating the theories that are being used.

Mager (2000) provides a good illustration of a writer providing a practitioner's wisdom about the field of HRD. Mager has produced a text that is aimed at managers involved in HRD, rather than being for specialist trainers or student learners. He is critical of much training as 'a fraud' or 'an extravagance', which managers have rightly been sceptical about in the past. He claims to explain how and why HRD at work from a personal wisdom based on experience.

He believes that knowledge of learning theory will not in itself make a person good instructor so learning the theory is not essential. Yet he concludes that it is important to be able to describe the relevant characteristics of adult learners and know the key principles of supporting effective learning.

Mager argues that effective HRD can provide performance improvements through instructions in skill, and can help develop employee self-efficacy; but it is up to managers to provide the opportunity and support that translate instruction in skills into improved performance. There are often other, non-training, means to the same end. What Mager is articulating is a version of a theory of behaviourism. Both these aspects of theory – of how adults learn best, and general principles for supporting learning – are presented by Mager as simply being 'common-sense' guides. Yet contrary perspectives are possible on both these aspects of his theory. His arguments are not based on citing studies or evidence; this knowledge comes from knowing reality and being experienced.

Values and Ethical/Ideological Beliefs

The final source of knowledge present in HRD is values, and ethical or ideological beliefs. The meaning of the term 'value' here needs to be clear. First, organisations are used to identifying their own values, the general principles they adhere to in doing business. These will be relevant to HRD, but they are not a source of knowledge. Equally, the concept of value introduced in Chapter 1, to describe the ways organisations create value through competing, controlling, creating and collaborating, is also significant; but again, this does not produce knowledge about HRD, it rather sets the context as to what is required. The concept of value here is,

> 'an enduring belief that a specific mode of conduct or end-state of existence is personally or socially preferable to an opposite or converse mode of conduct or end-state of existence' (Rokeach 1973, p. 5).

According to Rokeach values have a 'transcendental quality' that guides 'an actor's actions, attitudes and judgments' beyond immediate goals to more ultimate ends (1973, p. 18). While values are, in some sense, natural and ideal, they are not necessarily mutually supportive. For example there are potential contradictions of being thrifty and charitable, both worth behaviors. As these value conflicts are resolved, either consciously or unconsciously, a hierarchical arrangement evolves into a value system. A value system is simply a rank ordering of values that serves to resolve social and personal conflict and direct the selection of alternatives.

As Rokeach explains value systems are organised around two main objects. Some values, called terminal, refer to desirable end states. Other values, called instrumental, refer to modes of conduct. Those values may be about self or other people or about ways of living (Morris 1965), or about any other aspect of being that bears on how people should live and what ends they should pursue. The analytical interest was in different value systems, value systems within specific cultures and across different cultures. It was also about how social conditioning and relationships underpin the creation, assimilation and evolution of value systems. This was partly evolving in the context of arguments about re-orienting human sciences on understanding human experiences and human problems in ways that were considered relevant to enhance the 'humanising' rather than the 'de-humanising' of human science theory and practice (Brewster Smith 1974).

Polanyi was critiquing the amorality of disciplines in science others were noting the evolution and importance of beliefs in everyday life. The view that value systems are central to human behaviour and understanding, and provide the basic wellspring for peoples beliefs, provided another mode of analysis of belief in the middle of the twentieth century. Here the interest was in 'axiologies'; the things people take as generally accepted or self-evidently true, that they believe, because of their core value systems.

Yang (2004) identifies six kinds of value system, and ethical/ideological thinking which can be used to frame an understanding of the aim and purpose of HRD, and along with that implies a focus for and content of the type of knowledge relevant to guide practice. One ethical/ideological position is behaviourism; which assumes that the purpose of learning and development are to produce behavioural change in the desired direction to increase performance. Another is humanism; which assumes the purpose of learning and development are to facilitate a self-actualised, autonomous person. There is also liberalism; which values learning and development centred on knowledge gained in and from official institutions and sources such as texts and universities. Yang also defines 'progressivism'; which favours learning and development grounded in experience and unofficial sources, as this is linked ultimately to social well-being. There is also a position described as human capitalism; which assumes that learning and development are required to increase returns on investments, improving organisational performance. Finally there is radicalism, which sees learning and development as potentially challenging the existing status quo, and critiques learning and development practices reinforcing the status quo and constraining the development of peoples potential. They might see that existing systems tend to privilege a few, and over-value performance concerns at the expense of social responsibility.

These values based ethical/ideological beliefs for making sense of HRD as a whole, of seeing adult learning in employment, exist and coalesce around these forms because they are a 'package' of answers to fundamental questions:

- Ontology: what is the basic nature of reality? In the case of HRD, for example, what exactly are the material bases of learning and change?

- Epistemology: how do I know what is true? In the case of HRD, for example, how do we determine which of many competing interpretations of what constitutes effective learning and change to invest in?

- Ethics: what should I do? In the case of HRD, for example, what is right and what is wrong, what is considerate and responsible, when it comes to investing in and managing HRD?

Values and ethical/ideological knowledge and theory matters as it can offer answers to these questions, and make more visible some of the issues under the surface of practically managing effective adult learning and change. They can inform how we think about the purpose and focus of the design of learning systems and interventions. They can provide insights and guidance on issues of motivation and environment: how to diagnose problems to get results, and how to analyse problems with learning transfer. These theories are all ways of exploring how people learn that can be related to managing learning better, either by informing the work of specialists supporting learning, or by providing insights for learners into what they can do to learn how to learn.

The validity and reliability of values, and associated ethical/ideological beliefs as a foundation of knowledge, depends on the social, cultural and political perspective that individuals and institutions. Knowledge that fits with a person's values, ethics or ideology will be perceived as valid and reliable. Knowledge that does not fit with, and even questions, a person's values, ethics or ideology will be perceived as invalid and unreliable. If dialogue follows from encountering these areas of disagreement, then constructing knowledge can be a useful focus for debate. If positions harden and become contests, then constructing knowledge can become a site of considerable antagonism.

Putting it Together

Links to Practice

Professionals and practitioners producing and organising knowledge, based on social science, reflective practice or values-based beliefs, are equally concerned to have an impact on practitioners. Social science advocates would argue that theorist–practitioner interactions can form in four areas: (1) formulating problems, (2) developing theories, (3) collecting evidence and (4) applying findings (see Practice 2.3). If theorists and practitioners can interact at these four theory-building stages, a theory has the highest potential to be successful, to fulfil the dual purpose of advancing knowledge and guiding practice.

Practice 2.3: The Role of Theory

Problem formulation: consists of developing a concrete description of the symptoms, conditions, or anomalies as they exist in the real world on a topic or issue. Recognition of these perceptions or facts is acquired through experience, observation, or judgments of a problem, opportunity, or issue existing in a realistic situation. It produces a research question and the body of knowledge that is relevant to the research problem.

Conceptualization: A conceptual model is the mental image or framework that an investigator brings to bear on the research problem. Selecting the conceptual model is perhaps the most strategic choice that an investigator makes, for it significantly influences the research questions to ask, and the kind of propositions and hypotheses that will be set forth to answer these questions.

Theory building: Theory building consists of developing clear statements of relationships or comparisons between two or more constructs that are expected to hold within a set of assumptions or boundary conditions. A theory consists of propositions at a middle range of abstraction, and it consists of hypotheses at an operational level of concreteness.

Research designs: This connects a theory with empirical evidence. It involves the selection and execution of operational procedures for bringing valid scientific evidence to bear to examine a theory that addresses the research question about the problem or issue as it exists in reality.

Source: Storberg-Walker, J. (2003).

The problem as generated from organisational reality must be relevant, the concepts of the theory must be valid, the research must provide evidence and the research must have an impact on the science and profession of HRD.

It is important to bear in mind that there are espoused methods for developing theory and 'in use' methods, how it is actually done (Van de Ven 1989). The main espoused method of theory development in social science can be called the realist one; empirical events are observed, particular circumstances are understood and laws of causality are identified. The critique of this is that it entails accumulating lots of individual research studies, co-relational studies, with empirical evidence but not providing scope for identifying any substantial kind of causality or truth. The questions that need to be asked and answered, beyond the empirical confirmation of cause–effect relationships, when evaluating theory are as follows:

- What's new?
- So what? This changes what?
- Why so? What is the logic and assumptions?
- Is it complete and thorough?
- Is it well written? Flow, accessible, standards
- Why now?
- Who cares? Both narrowly and broadly

In use, in reality, much knowledge is not produced this way. And even if it is, it may not impact on HRD practice. HRD theories which say something new, and change the view of practice, based on good logic, well communicated and which connect with the concerns of stakeholders will be successful; and these may emerge from any of the sources of knowledge discussed above. Each of these can provide insights into the 'how' and the 'why' of managing and improving learning at work. With macro-formal theories of HRD itself, and a concern with the underlying and competing philosophies in play, the picture is more complex. Macro-formal theories cross disciplines, combining ideas from a range of knowledge bases. Debates about macro-formal theories of HRD are a crossroads and meeting point of ideas, debates and argument (see Perspective 2.3).

Perspective 2.3: From a Key Thinker to Diagnosing Performance Problems

HRD theorising can be stimulated by reviewing key thinkers like Rogers' on positive regard (Rogers 1969) people have a drive to grow and achieve, and a secure sense of self-supported by others positive regard is central to that. Such growing involves both pleasure and pain, as people become aware of what they can and cannot do; sustained positive regard whatever happens is a highly desirable environment for growth.

As people grew up how others have defined them and treated them, their positive regard or it absence, had a big influence on development. Peoples' experiences in HRD are implicated in this, being both fulfilling and an arena in which disappointment may be experienced. Problems often arise in later life where people as adults may continue to feel they have to deny a part of themselves to secure and sustain positive regard; even to the extent that they may sacrifice expression of their true self to secure and sustain positive regard.

This interferes with engaging people in learning. It may alienate people even from participating in learning at all, or block learning dependent on a person gaining personal awareness; which features in a lot of the learning on softer skills associated with work and employment. Blocks can be removed if secure, and unconditional, positive regard is offered. Then change and growth will happen driven by the person themselves, as they work things out for themselves.

Successful learning and development in a learning environment requires, in essence, a 'space' for a person to feel good in rather than a web of rewards and punishments to direct learning and change. This in turn connects to wider concerns about 'systems thinking'; for any individual learning and change enabled in a learning environment may be hard to sustain if the broader system of work and employment does not also provide a space in which positive regard is forthcoming.

There are also influences on knowledge and theory emerging from different conceptions of the purpose of HRD at work and the focus of learning and change at a macro-formal level. One approach (see Figure 2.2) is to distinguish between a positivist form, a phenomenological form and a reflexive form (Gill and Johnson 1991, Easterby-Smith et al. 1992, Hammersley and Atkinson 1992).

In a positivist approach theory is prospective; it is established a priori, and determines the ultimate outcome; hypotheses and theory are either confirmed or disconfirmed. The status of any hypotheses of theory is linked to the confidence

	Positivist theory building	Phenomenononological theory building	Reflexive theory building
Origins in relation to research practice	A priori hypotheses	Final stage explanations	Developed throughout
Typical form	Causal statements based on quantified data	Case studies	Necessary core and reasons for variations Variety of data sources
Status	Procedures and testing determine validity and reliability	Fidelity to the subject in its natural setting determines validity and reliability	Fidelity and testing
Approaches	Positivism	Naturalism/phenomenology	Analytical induction Action research

Figure 2.2 Approaches to theory building

with which procedures have been followed, and the degree to which results stand up to further testing/retesting. A good prospective theory is one that enables testing and leads to a causal evaluation of a body of data.

In a naturalist approach theory is retrospective; it is established through the research process, and is only complete when the research process is complete. Theory gives an explanation of the qualitative data collected. The status of any theory here is linked to the plausibility with which it offers a plausible account of such data. A good retrospective theory is one that exhausts the data collected and leads to an accomplished account of actor's subjectivity.

There is a third option: reflexive theory. This is neither purely prospective nor retrospective. That means it is neither solely produced a priori nor after data collection; it develops as data are collected. Its status is neither linked solely to procedures nor the 'completeness' of its analysis of qualitative data; it can be evaluated in relation to the logic of the experiment, observations and tests, but deals with qualitative data. A good reflexive theory will not struggle to justify itself in terms of how detached the researcher has been from the data. Such an approach can be associated historically with 'analytical induction' explored by Hammersley and Atkinson (1992).

Reflexivity makes sense if it is accepted that researchers are part of the social world they study, and there is no ontologically privileged stance available in any research tradition. Researchers rely on working with common-sense knowledge and methods are simply a refinement of everyday human skills and capacities. Their research has an impact on their subjects.

Conclusions

There is not in HRD what one writer called 'superstrong knowledge'. Rather there is an eclectic body of knowledge from past and present, including knowledge from three domains: (1) theory, (2) reflective practice and (3) values. That eclectic body of knowledge includes evidence-based research, lessons from professional experience and tenets emerging from ethical/ideological belief and argument. Systems of ideas, theories, emerge and evolve to explain learning, and if they are successful can impact on policy and practice. The validity and reliability, truthfulness and trustworthiness, of these forms vary; from the evidence based and impactful, judged in terms of the tradition in which they belong. Each is present and of concern in the professional field. In social science there are different levels at which theory can be developed and applied. There are several social science disciplines which provide micro-substantive theories of HRD. There are several macro-formal theories which aim to define and explain HRD as a whole. Familiarity with these can be helpful to the learner engaging with HRD as an area of policy and practice, and for the experienced professional confronting challenges in policy and practice. It is also helpful, in the academic context, to be aware of and appreciate the difference between a realist and constructivist.

Exercise 2.1: Consider the Validity and Evidence Base of Knowledge

The examples of knowledge outlined at the start of this chapter (duplicated below) were given as relevant and impactful. But are they valid and reliable?

What kinds of things would you need to know before accepting these theories as valid and evidence based?

Knowledge	Need to know to be valid and reliable
Learning styles: different people have different preferences for how they go about learning	
Action learning: adults learn better with systems designed around principles other than those used in the education of young people	
Learning organisations: if people in organisations are helped and encouraged to share what they know, organisations are more efficient and effective	
Human relations: managing relationships is an integral part of creating an environment at work which supports productivity and well-being.	
Scientific management: systematic observation and analysis of jobs can provide a structure for training people in the skills of roles in mass production	
Lifelong learning: societies need to encourage participation in learning throughout life, not only in periods of formal education	

In developing professional effectiveness in HRD it is not essential to apply theory, but it is desirable to develop critical thinking (see Debate 2.3). And a part of critical thinking is to understand, engage with and evaluate theory; in its own terms, not solely in relation to 'what works'. Critical thinking, in the realist tradition is about questioning validity and evidence bases. Critical thinking in the constructivist tradition is about accepting that relevance and impact are earned not by strict use of the scientific method in theory development but by the bringing together of stakeholders around pragmatic solutions to real questions in practice.

Understanding theory in HRD is more about appreciating and applying insights and less about the search for absolute truth and superstrong knowledge, as the tests of evidence and usefulness have not yet produced knowledge about learning and change which is comparable to the strong knowledge found in natural sciences. The constructivist frame of mind for thinking about the HRD, exploring insights from wisdom, psychology, from social studies and economics is the main discourse. These can give insights to designing HRD interventions, diagnosing problems with implementing HRD systems in organisations and evaluating the application of innovative solutions in HRD demands, such as introducing e-learning or new government policies.

Response to Debate 2.3: "Think about what characteristics make an area of study a robust academic discipline?"

Whether HRD can be considered a real discipline itself, a branch of knowledge or teaching, depends on how a discipline is defined. One set of features that can constitute a discipline are as follows; do these seem to be present in HRD?

- members exist professionally and academically and share a sense of identity/ethics;
- there is a community/network, traditions/heritage;
- there is a mode of inquiry (syntactical structure for inquiry and critique);
- there is a technical language;
- all these are passed on in teaching.

Source: Chalofsky, N. (2007).

Exercise 2.2

Theory	Need to know to be valid and evidence based
Learning styles: different people have different preferences for how they go about learning	Few of the instruments developed to measure learning styles are valid and reliable. We do not yet know enough about the brain and learning to conclusively model learning styles
Action learning adults learn better with systems designed around principles other than those used in the education of young people	The principles of adult learning amount to those of 'facilitation', and the creation of systems such as 'action learning' are perhaps useful but not scientific
Learning organisations: if people in organisations are helped and encouraged to share what they know, organisations are more efficient and effective	There are dynamics in organisations which impede the sharing of knowledge, and so the theory is not complete; it is prescriptive, not descriptive

Theory	Need to know to be valid and evidence based
Human relations: managing relationships is an integral part of creating an environment at work which supports productivity and well-being	Not necessarily true for all kinds of organisations, and not necessarily a function of employing organisations
Scientific management: systematic observation and analysis of jobs can provide a structure for training people in the skills of roles in mass production	Putting roles into boxes and targeted training in chunks of skill does not produce the kind of employee that is desired in many organisations
Lifelong learning: societies need to encourage participation in learning throughout life, not only in periods of formal education	There are recurring questions about the extent to which periods of formal learning, in schools, colleges and universities, produce the goods; sorting that out and not lifelong learning is the priority.

Case: Retail Motivation Training

Read the following case, and the 14 focal areas that were the heart of the HRD provided. First considering those 14 tips identify which form of social science, reflective practice or value-based knowledge might have justified the inclusion of the focal areas in the accompany. What is the underlying 'philosophy' you can see, in Yang's terms, at work here? My analysis is given for comparison.

Case

A leading retailer RetailCo was continuing to experience difficulties competing to retain its once leading position. It decided to use some HRD, sending up to 56,000 staff on a £10 million pound initiative in retail motivation training. This is a day-long training session run by a motivational guru. Staff from stores will attend the event in groups of 5,000, attending at a major exhibition venue. Each store group would be led by team leaders, and the stores should vie with each other to show team spirit at the event; they are advised that they can dress unusually, or in football strips, and take mascots with them representing their store and part of the country.

Each day session will begin with a psychological self-assessment; starting with assessing peoples' good points (fun to be around, brave and determined) and then their bad points (don't care attitude, moody and negative). This is followed by tips on how to treat customers. Successful sales people operate in a 'can do' circle, and avoid the circle of apathy and indecision. They are given other advice like 'when a customer approaches disengage courteously if talking with a colleague'. The staff then leave with a list of reminders, including a fake dollar bill with 'Don't pass the buck-take ownership and responsibility', a gold starfish and an ace of spades card; along with a pocket-sized plastic card reminding them of key slogans. The top 14 tips they were given during their HRD were as follows:

1. Life can be thought about in three concentric circles: an inner circle is what you can control; the next is what you can influence but cannot control; the third is what is outside your control. Work on things in circles one and two on things you can do and control or influence.

2. Even in situations where you have no control over events you can still choose your reaction

3. Communicate what can be done in an upbeat, courteous, confident language – you and the customer will feel better.

4. It's natural to bitch and complain and feel sorry for yourself. The key is how quickly you snap out of it.

5. Be a 'can do', solution-oriented person.

6. Good attitudes are listening deeply, being gracious and empathetic, communicating clearly and assertion.

7. Bad attitudes are being problem-oriented, interrupting, rude, vague, passive or aggressive, defensive and withdrawn.

8. A compelling vision, mission or sense of purpose is a vital first step to ensuring motivation to achieve goals.

9. If a mission is overly complex and without spirit, it will just be ignored.

10. People do not leave organisations, they leave managers.

11. Customer service is about people helping people competently, genuinely and enthusiastically.

12. Be optimistic rather than resigned and pessimistic. Optimism fuels motivation, stamina and creativity.

13. Adopt an open and positive stance towards criticism. See it as a gateway to improved relationships.

14. Look after your self-esteem, it provides you with the confidence and desire to make the difference.

Focus for HRD	Knowledge source: social science, reflective practice, values/ethics	Issue
Know Concentric Circles		
Choose reactions		
Be upbeat		
'Snap out of it'		
Can do outlook		

Good attitudes to be supported *Bad attitudes to be eliminated*		
Vision		
Keep it simple		
People leave managers		
Helping is good		
Optimistic		
Take feedback		
Self-esteem		
Overall conclusion?		

Selected Further Reading

Arnold, J, Randall, et al. (2010) *Work Psychology*, 5th Edition (London, Pearson).

Boud, D. and Garrick, J. (1999) *Understanding Learning at Work* (London, Routledge).

Chapman, P. (1993) *The Economics of Training* (London, Harvester Wheatsheaf).

Lave, J. and Wenger, E. (1991) *Situated Learning: Legitimate Peripheral Participation* (Cambridge, Cambridge University Press).

Mager, R. (2000) *What Every Manager Should Know About Training* (Chalford, Management Books).

Machin, S. and Vignoles, A. (2001) *The Economic Benefits of Training to the Individual, the Firm and the Economy: The Key Issues* (Centre for the Economics of Education, London School of Economics).

Pawson, R., Greenhalgh, T., Harvey, G. and Walshe, K (2004) 'Realist Synthesis: An Introduction, ESRC Research Methods Programme', RMP Methods Paper.

Reynolds, A., Sambrook, S. and Stewart, J. (1997) *Dictionary of HRD* (London, Gower).

3 Key Texts

(1) Boud, D., Garrick, J. (1999) *Understanding Learning at Work* (London, Routledge).

(2) Hardingham, A. (2000) *Psychology for Trainers* (London, CIPD). Available in a 2009 version as an e-book.

(3) Schon, D. A. (1987) *Educating the Reflective Practitioner* (San Francisco, Jossey-Bass).

3 Key Articles/Reports

(1) Chalofsky, N. (2007) 'The Seminal Foundation of the Discipline of HRD: People, Learning and Organizations', *Human Resource Development Quarterly*, 18 (3), pp. 431–442.

(2) Storberg-Walker, J. (2003) 'Comparison of the Dubin, Lynham, and Van de Ven Theory-Building Research Methods and Implications for HRD', *Human Resource Development Review*, 2, pp. 211–222.

(3) Yang, B. (2004) 'Can Adult Learning Theory Provide a Foundation for Human Resource Development?', *Advances in Developing Human Resources*, 6 (2), pp. 129–145.

3 Key Web Links

(1) Resources for Trainers, illustrating the range of type of knowledge involved: http://www.completetrainer.co.uk/.

(2) Positive Psychology Resources: http://www.centreforconfidence.co.uk/pp/positive-psychology.php.

(3) Changing Minds Resources: http://changingminds.org/.

3

Organising Learning

Learning Objectives

By the end of this chapter you will be able to:

- Define the HRD process in the work and employment context;
- Describe the organisation of learning using systematic training, performance improvement and continuous development approaches;
- Analyse the challenges and opportunities involved in organising learning in work and employment.

Case: Corporate Universities

Corporate Universities are 'in-House' universities in work organisations. Since being established in some companies in the 1950s there has been an expansion.

They aim to coordinate learning and share knowledge, aligning with organisational business strategy, incorporating e-learning and promoting a culture of learning throughout the company. Thus, Corporate Universities (CUs) are education institutes of the organisation, which support the strategic management, learning and problem-solving in the form of an integrated and continuous process and are always inimitable constitutions (Andresen 2003, Rademakers 2005).

CUs are not only a setting for training, but also can offer postgraduate certificates by cooperation with established universities (Glotz and Seufert 2002, Wimmer et al. 2002). Wimmer et al. found 326 companies in Germany had a CU. The first CUs in Germany were from major international enterprises such as Lufthansa with their Lufthansa School of Business, followed by Bertelsmann, Siemens and DaimlerCrysler (Gebauer 2006, Zimmermann 2008). Most are amongst others the automobile industry, banks, media industry and IT industry (Hanft and Knust 2007).

Among the factors behind this were critics of traditional Universities. These were perceived to be not sufficiently application-oriented nor international enough (Schamari 2001, Simon 2002, Knoll et al. 2003). Organisations needed to build up their own company, own training and development facilities to ensure a better transferability of knowledge into the workplace, a supporter for business' strategy. The major aim was to combine teaching of theoretical knowledge with specific organisational expertise and economic information (Heuser 2001).

Various types of CUs have been evolved in the process of systematisation training and development activities. The range is enormous between CUs which are seen as only profit centres such as outsourced training centres, and strategic catalysts for change like, for example General Electrics' CU and Lufthansa's School of Business. The type of a CU is influenced by the corporate culture and factors such as the chosen effect or target group, regardless of which kind of CU an organisation aims to employ to support their business' strategy. Some CUs focus on the top management with an emphasis on the exchange of experiences and information, whereas others are rather directed on all employees and want to enhance the overall qualification and expertise by teaching and training knowledge transfer takes place by either imparting already existing knowledge or by generating new expertise out of the development process in form of a learning lab for project teams. Programmes can concentrate only on company's own employees or on structures, where external and internal applicants are coached and trained together to benefit from external experiences. Other forms of CUs are these, which are affiliated on a real Campus and do employ their own professional staff. Most CUs are working together with other traditional universities, or have only a virtual company's own university.

One example is AutoCoUni. AutoCo was founded in the early twentieth century and is today one of the international leading automobile manufacturer, with about 368,500 employees. Additionally, it consists of 359 group companies worldwide and various brands. AutoCos current main strategy is aiming to be the most successful and fascinating worldwide leader in the automobile research and industry and to be among the most respected employers in all brands and societies. This is to be achieved through a high-qualified and trained workforce, as well as a partnership-based and valued employer–employee relationship, sustainability and supporting of staff's development. As part of this AutoCo founded the AutoCoUni in the early twenty-first century, and is working together in close cooperation with over 40 national and international academic universities. Most important is the partnership with a local research centre for automotive engineering industry. The programmes of the AutoCoUni are directed to top managers and employees and are being developed around internal questions, problems and knowledge. In addition, the AutoCoUni is an institution which is based on university structures, research and postgraduate level and aims to link expertise with science (Hanft and Knust 2007). The main types of activities of the AutoCoUni are presentations, conferences, offers of studies and research projects, and supervising doctorates programmes. Aim of the CU is to ensure an enhanced transfer of academic knowledge into AutoCo and to gain competitive advantage due to knowledge advantages.

Introduction

If the theory of learning reflects pragmatic management, applied social science and ethical/ideological imperatives these all also influence the organisation of learning. What is done, how and by whom. A process can be described and mapped using various methods, some scientific and some artful. The former emphasise quantification, measurement and the 'hard' side of organising learning. The latter emphasise values, ethics and the 'soft' side of organising learning. In Human Resource Development (HRD) there is one form of process mapping that has been dominant which combines these hard and soft aspects. This is the process mapping of a 'training cycle', the inputs, activities and outcomes which professionals need to be familiar with and competent in managing. It is the core of the common sense which has been, and is still, in use; for example it has been used to organise and communicate occupational standards for those who work to provide learning and development at work.

Organising Learning at Work

HRD Factors

The following 30 factors are the key aspects of organising learning in most organisations. They relate to the direction and goals of HRD, responsibilities, perceptions, programmes, resourcing and manager involvement. How these are approached and managed will give concrete shape to the theory, values and practical concerns of organisations in HRD. There is an exercise at the end of this chapter which expands on these, which can be completed once the chapter is read and understood.

Direction and goals

1. The direction of the HRD function in the organisation...
2. The primary mode of operation of the HRD function...
3. The goals of the HRD function...
4. How new programmes are initiated...

Responsibility

5. When a major organisational change is made...
6. To define training plans...
7. When determining the timing of training and the target audiences...
8. The responsibility for training results...
9. Systematic, objective evaluation designed to ensure that trainees are performing appropriately on the job...
10. New programmes are developed...
11. Costs for training and OD are accumulated...

Perceptions

12. Management involvement in the training process...

13. To ensure that training is transferred into performance on the job...

14. The training staff's interaction with line management...

15. HRD's role in major change efforts...

16. How managers view the HRD function...

Programmes

17. HRD programmes...

18. How investment in HRD is measured primarily...

19. The HRD effort consists...

20. New HRD programmes are implemented

21. During a business decline at my organisation, the HRD function will...

Resourcing

22. Budgeting for HRD is based on...

23. The principal reason for HRD expenditures is...

24. HRD is most celebrated where we can

25. The Leadership of the organisation emphasise that

Manager's involvement

26. Top management's involvement in the implementation of HRD programmes...

27. Line management involvement in conducting HRD programmes is...

28. When an employee completes a training programme and returns to the job, his or her manager is likely to...

29. If an employee attends an outside seminar, upon return he or she is required to...

30. Managers are most likely to come to HRD when

The HRD Process

Process analysis in organisations involves identifying the inputs, activities and outcomes of an area of management. Processes in HRD in organisations are the inputs, activities and outcomes associated with learning and change. Processes can be mapped using various methods. In HRD one form of process mapping has been used for establishing occupational standards for those who work to provide learning and development at work (LLUK 2010). This process mapping identifies areas of a 'training cycle' (see Perspective 3.1) and inputs, activities and outcomes which professionals need to be familiar with and competent in managing. The ways in which organisations manage the training cycle is not a case of one form or size fits all (Allen 1994, Lynton and Pareek 2000, Dealtry

2009). How research, planning, facilitation and quality are managed can vary in different organisations. These differences reflect the different kinds and degrees to which formal and informal learning and change are being managed, and how they are managed.

Debate 3.1: Potential Learning Experiences

Where and when does learning begin? One view is that learning begins with discrepancies – between past experiences and current ones that cannot be encountered automatically –when people cannot perform 'unthinkingly'. There is then a potential to learn. That potential may lead to:

- **Non-learning**: same routines, too preoccupied to learn, rejects opportunity to learn
- **Non-reflective learning**: unconsciously internalise, practice new skill, memorise information
- **Reflective learning**: contemplate, think, reconsider and experiment

Professionals who learn reflectively have the time to

- Frame the context
- Respond to triggers
- Interpret experience
- Examine alternative solutions
- Choose learning strategies
- Produce alternative solutions
- Assess intended and unintended consequences
- Evaluate lessons learned.

Source: Jarvis (1987).

As with the organisation of any aspect of people in work HRD be viewed and mapped as a process. A process is a sequence of events, actions and behaviours which are connected together and come to be analysed in a standard way. Process analysis in organisations involves identifying all the events, actions and behaviours as the inputs, activities and outcomes of a process. The HRD process in work and employment organisations is made up of the inputs, activities and outcomes associated with individual, team and organisation learning. Processes can be mapped using various methods. In HRD one form of process mapping has been used for establishing occupational standards for those who work to provide learning and development at work (LLUK 2010). This process mapping identifies areas of a 'training cycle' (see Perspective 3.1) and inputs, activities and outcomes which professionals need to be familiar with and competent in managing (see Debate 3.1).

Perspective 3.1: Process Mapping in HRD and Occupational Standards

Key area A: Research learning and development needs

(1) Identify collective learning and development needs

(2) Identify individual learning and development needs

Key area B: Plan and develop learning and development opportunities

(3) Plan and prepare learning and development programmes

(4) Plan and prepare specific learning and development opportunities

(5) Develop and prepare resources for learning and development

Key area C: Facilitate learner achievement

(6) Manage learning and development in groups

(7) Facilitate individual learning and development

(8) Engage and support learners in the learning and development process

(9) Assess learner achievement

Key area D: Maintain and improve quality standards

(10) Reflect on, develop and maintain own skills and practice in learning and development

(11) Internally monitor and maintain the quality of assessment

(12) Externally monitor and maintain the quality of assessment

(13) Evaluate and improve learning and development

The ways in which organisations manage the training cycle is not a case of one form or size fits all (Allen 1994, Lynton and Pareek 2000, Dealtry 2009). How learning is organised, the research and planning behind it and the ways delivery and quality are managed will vary in different organisations.

These differences embody, among other things, how in different contexts there is a spectrum of formal and informal learning (Practice 3.1). In some organisations different parts of this spectrum may be more visible than others. In some the formal is most visible. In others the informal is most invisible. In some there is a mix.

Practice 3.1: Formal–Informal Learning Continuum

Informal Formal	Unanticipated experiences and encounters that result in learning or change as an incidental by product, which may or may not be consciously recognised

	New job assignments and participation in teams, or other job-related challenges that are used for learning, change and self-development
	Self-initiated and self-planned experiences – including the use of media (print, etc.), seeking out a tutor, coach or mentor, attending conferences, travel, consulting
	Total quality groups/action learning or other vehicles designed to promote continuous learning for continuous improvement
	Planning a framework for learning which is often associated with career plans, training and development plans or performance evaluations
	Combination of less organised experiences with structured opportunities, which may be facilitated, to examine and learn or change from those experiences
	Designed programmes of mentoring and/or coaching or on-the-job training
	Just-in-time courses, delivered as classes or through self-learning packages, with or without the use of technology
	Formal training courses
	Broad programmes leading to some official qualification

Source: Stern and Sommerlad (1999). *Workplace Learning, Culture and Performance*, London: Institute of Personnel and Development.

HRD Process Forms

The patterns seen in organising learning, the HRD process, reflect the presence of and preferences for ways of organising the inputs, activities and outcomes of HRD. These can be described and analysed as three distinctive kinds of vision and value-based frameworks for HRD, emerging from foundations in the distinctive kinds of information and analysis preferred, the main agents involved, and the measures of outcome which are most valued. These forms of organising learning are as follows:

- Systematic training;
- Performance improvement;
- Continuous development.

These forms of organising can be seen as evolutionary. That is they appear to emerge in a chronological sequence, with systematic training (ST) the first, then performance improvement (PI) following from that and continuous development (CD) most recently. The environmental change bringing forth changes of emphasis in the HRD process has varied, though a common sense of disenchantment with an established and prevailing 'prescription' for organising learning, and the problems this has given rise to with the quality and quantity of HRD. Disenchantment with the prevailing ways of organising learning is often accompanied by a sense of insufficient connection between HRD and key concerns in work and employment. There are also concerns with the quality of learning, as well as opportunities offered by new technologies, which prompt fresh process thinking. However, if the HRD process were subject to evolutionary change we might expect to see the earlier forms of HRD process fading away or falling into the shadow of more advanced and superior forms: from ST to PI to CD. This is not the case, as there is no clear or definitive replacement of one kind of organisation of learning by another. The comparative approach is to consider how they each embody aspects of the foundation on which HRD is to be based, the systemic things to which most attention is given, and the main agents implicated (Practice 3.2).

Practice 3.2: Comparative Features of the Organisation of Learning

HRD Process	Inputs; Foundation for HRD is . . .	Systemic things to get right are . . .	The main agents involved are . . .	Outcomes measured
Systematic training process	Job analysis	Formal courses	Training professionals	Training programmes delivered
Performance improvement process	Organisational objectives and performance	Critical incidents arising in performance	Managers	Performance Improvements
Continuous development process	Self-directed needs analysis	Coaching and mentoring	Learners themselves	Potential fulfilment

Systematic Training

An ST approach is often still the process which is most visible and striking in many contemporary organisations when HRD is being discussed and examined.

The emphasis is on being systematic rather than ad hoc and fragmented. In one sense, this is simply adopting a common-sense view. Yet it also a broader mindset; that of a scientific view of management and organisation, with the organisation thought of as a machine made up of parts which all need to fit and mesh if the machine is to work properly. Skilled people are parts too. This way of thinking assumes that there are right ways and wrong ways to perform, and these can be identified and directly controlled by expert authorities. This results in a control strategy in which the HRD process is to be managed systematically by dedicated professionals. Just as management itself emerged to keep control of work in the hands of specially trained expert managers, so HRD emerges as an area where control of learning and change is in the hands of specially trained trainers.

This organisation of learning will include being systematic, thorough and detailed in the formal assessment of needs by an HRD expert. It will be most visible in the planning and organisation of formal on-job training and off-job courses by HRD experts. Off-job courses may be run either inside the organisation or by outside providers, but in either case the emphasis is on professional trainers and developers taking the leading role in learning and change. Such courses are to be designed and delivered by training specialists. Training is to be formally evaluated by professionals or experts. The typical outcomes are validated by testing, and this is often recognised or accredited, leading to certification and the award of qualifications.

This approach to HRD process is commonplace and taken for granted. Its underlying assumptions and distinctiveness as a way of managing a process can be overlooked. Critiques of it make this more apparent. Critiques highlight how control through ST can encourage a bureaucratic approach to HRD that may produce a proliferation of substantial, formal training programmes, particularly off-job training programmes. Professionalism and expertise in HRD become professionalism and expertise in training course design and delivery. This emphasis on specialists designing and implementing training programmes and evaluating these programmes means that the whole HRD process is 'owned and controlled' by specialist trainers. This can become a concern, and a source of weakness, for dedicated and expert trainers are often not best placed to identify performance issues, and deliver and evaluate HRD in the context of understanding those issues.

Use and support for ST is greatest during periods of clearly identified skills shortages which need to be assessed and met by large-scale interventions. This is true both historically, and structurally; ST is prominent at times and in industry sectors where skill shortages require large-scale interventions. In the United Kingdom, for example, the most recent re-organisations of Sector Skills Councils (SSCs) and skills academies for manufacturing is a classic example of the re-discovery of ST. The viability of ST depends upon the commitment among employers to organising the analysis, programmes and HRD staff needed. It also depends upon a willingness among individuals in or seeking employment to participate in formal training programmes. To manage this, the HRD profession has to be seen as guardians of the systematic, as a specialist training function.

Performance Improvement

Developing and investing in generic courses and initiatives for HRD to reduce skill shortages or to close skill gaps can be, or can become, detached from the evolution of a business and a sector. A lot of HRD might be systematically delivered, but it might not necessarily be keeping in touch with the ultimate ends of improved organisational performance. In periods and industry sectors where dissatisfaction with ST arises, there usually emerges a call for a more PI organisation of learning to be adopted. Catalysts for this may come from concerns around the relevance of the corporate curriculum, the courses on offer and the effectiveness of learning in the 'classroom', either in the workplace or elsewhere. There may also be complaints about the costs and time taken to sort out high volumes of 'sheep-dip' training, which is training where every member of staff has to have their period of 'immersion' in the same course, along with the cost of the training system that it entails.

Alternatives that provide better ways of delivering HRD are sought in order to impact directly and quickly on the development and performance of the business. The PI is the option that emerges. The language used to define it can vary from national culture and organisational culture and from time to time. In essence it entails the location and embedding of HRD processes more firmly in the critical performance imperatives faced by organisations and at the heart of their objectives. This means a much greater emphasis on managerial involvement in HRD.

Such a strategy offers an alternative rational and common-sense position. The PI is, nonetheless, also a partial and limited way of perceiving and managing the practices of HRD at work. It is partial because the demands arising in 'performance' as the managers and employees of the time understand them are not the only force that can inform investments in HRD. Other demands on the workforce – longer term trends – may be neglected if the issue of performance today is the primary lens for seeing learning needs. If HRD is mainly focused on the organisation 'here and now', it may fail to evolve to keep up with changes in the longer term. For example, it may be of no interest to a particular individual organisation that their workforce is improving its IT skills 'here and now'. But that factor might become critical over the longer term for a society. It is also limited because it may be that, in emphasising business needs, other stakeholder needs which are equally legitimate and significant are neglected or ignored. It may not be of much interest to an employer in the 'here and now' to support their workforce's engagement in learning beyond their current job roles; but it may be very desirable socially, and ultimately economically, for that to be happening.

A PI way of thinking about HRD processes can become part of the problem and not part of the solution. Its existence and popularity reflects a particular balance of power among stakeholders in employment, not evidence about the best way to promote HRD at work. That is a balance in favour of the employers rather than a partnership between them and employee representatives. Were there true partnership between employers, employees and government, there might be less pure PI and perhaps more effective and efficient HRD. This is because PI can de-contextualise HRD issues; it considers them only with reference to the existing workplaces within which learning and development occurs, in isolation from the broader social, educational and economic context. One area of contention that often arises from this de-contextualisation is the idea that HRD for work ought to be dealt with more centrally in basic education rather than academic learning. The conclusion, especially from business interests, is that to change an education system to accommodate employers' needs for skills is sensible and desirable. Yet, as critics will argue, this is to overturn the rationale and direction of educational development for young people as requiring general academic development.

More importantly for other critics, the popularity of PI raises issues about integrating investment in learning and development, and skill formation, with concerns about how that learning and development then gets used. Beyond debates about education and workforce development, there are concerns around changing work organisation, job design, industrial relations and participation in decision-making, and other aspects of formal and informal people management systems. These should form a natural part of discussions about how HRD is managed, not a solely business-oriented view of how it is created and then used and renewed.

The point is that PI ignores or overlooks interests in and links between HRD, citizenship and life outside work. For example, mention may be made of education for adult life, for lifelong learning. In comparison with perceived leaders in this and HRD, such as the Scandinavian countries, and their development of the notion of the learning society, the reality for many seems to be that education and training to enhance citizenship, voluntary activities, parenthood, or political, social and cultural life, have limited appeal to those only concerned with workplace learning. For most, it is a business-oriented organisation of learning that prevails.

Continuous Development

The conclusion can be drawn, then, that a PI approach may be a limited and even distorting way to think about HRD processes. This is particularly relevant when observing and thinking about adults whose jobs demand limited skills or which are evolving and changing rapidly, and for whom other sources of motivation to engage or re-engage with opportunities for learning might be more fruitful than an agenda dominated by a PI. This is one reason why, alongside ST and PI processes, CD processes are developed. The concern with CD is on how to work with the informal and less structured ways in which learning occurs in everyday situations, rather than organising formal, structured HRD in special learning environments. The emphasis in the workplace changes from sending staff on courses to equipping employees with new skills through workplace-based problems and action learning as an ongoing process (see Perspective 3.2).

Perspective 3.2: Activities of Informal Learning

Lohman (2005) identified eight activities for informal learning;

- Talk with others
- Collaborate with others
- Observe others
- Share material and resources
- Search the Internet
- Scan professional magazines and journals
- Trial and error

There were two kinds of engagement with informal learning among groups in employment using these, which Loman calls 'interactive' and 'independent'.

Often there are issues with time, access and money for independent learning being limited; so people relied on interactive learning, talking and sharing. People, Lona concludes, need time to learn built into their work.

Much of the recent proliferation of research in and books about organisational and workplace learning represents a 'discovery' of CD and a renaissance of strong values propositions incorporating humanistic values and aspirations. This culminates in the new, received wisdom that HRD does not necessarily have to mean formal training, linked or otherwise to existing business needs. Instead, most of us are engaged in a naturally occurring process of continuous learning and development for which we can take greater personal responsibility, supported by coaches and mentors.

One implication of CD is that it places an emphasis on individuals and their managers organising ongoing development in the course of normal work, and making use of options such as on-job coaching rather than drawing upon the help of professional trainers in classrooms. If development is an ongoing process, then observations about HRD needs are an integral part of work, and planning for meeting those needs should be integrated with work. If this is so, then it is limiting to depend on sending staff on courses now and then to achieve development; delivery must be integrated with work as well. In practice, this meant the growth of new kinds of HRD processes.

While investment in structures for competence-based HRD was proceeding apace in many countries, a quite different basis for HRD processes was also evolving: self-development. Two principles inform the self-development processes. The first is that almost any form of HRD is good in and of itself because it involves embracing the new and changing skills and capabilities. The second principle is that the HRD that has the most potency to achieve change is that chosen and specified by the learners themselves. This has led to learners being given the central responsibility for managing the whole HRD process which, in practice, is often centred on establishing Personal Development Plans (PDPs). Problems that arise with this HRD strategy include the need for individuals to perceive that their ambitions can be satisfied by HRD, rather than by spending time 'politicking' their way up the career ladder; that people need 'space' to grow through HRD at work; and that it is critical to manage the way people learn from their own mistakes in the course of self-development.

The challenges for PDPs were identified in a study by Antonacopoulou (2000) which looked at self-development initiatives in three retail banks. It found that moves to PDP were accompanied by tensions and contradictions, based on encouraging choice and self-direction in learning among individuals. The essence of a PDP system is development of the whole person, willing and indeed determined to commit to actions on their own part for their own reasons. But is this of benefit to the organisation? Do banks actually require lots of people exercising individual initiative? PDP enhances individual confidence and abilities that can be directly integrated with better work performance. Development of self and development by self go together, and are unified in the workplace. Changing organisations need changing people, and self-development is the way to support and achieve this. Although mutual benefits can be seen, the process is nevertheless one that requires much negotiation; the organisation is dependent on individuals growing and changing, but individuals are also dependent on the organisation supporting their growth and change. Balance and synthesis between these interests and priorities are far from easy to manage, but the problems of this are the issues that HRM practitioners need to confront and deal with.

Organisational cultures and the attitudes of top managers affect the way initiatives take shape and have effect. If an organisation does not allow mistakes, does not welcome ambition and does not create space to grow, then self-development cannot take root. If people are blamed when things go wrong, if there is no scope for promotion and if there is no empathy with concepts of personal growth in the workplace, then self-development will fail, even though it might have seemed attractive as a way of managing HRD. There are problems for the individual as well as for the organisation. If individuals either are unwilling to follow, or actively resist, the self-development philosophy, then it will fail as a basis for HRD and HRD will fail. Learners often rely on the organisation to manage development for them; they may have neither the interest, the will nor the skills to handle self-development. They could be developed so that they had the ability and the inclination; but the suspicion is often that this is a way to put the burden for development onto the individual, and for the organisation to avoid responsibility. Employees may then resist self-development-based HRD.

Exercise 3.1:

Identify for an organisation you are familiar with the kinds of HRD inputs, activities and agents involved, and the things which are measured. Use the grid below to map these. What does this show about the main approach to organising learning in use in the organisation?

	STP	PIP	CDP	Other
HRD inputs				
HRD activities				
Agents				
Measures				

Process Maturity

The organisation of learning be also be analysed as a more or less mature process (see Figure 3.1). The maturity standards for the management of the training cycle can range from the least mature, informal planning and an ad hoc culture to HRD, to highly mature processes in the organisation which are significant and which have definite associations with strategy.

Organisations and their management of the training cycle and processes can be located and analysed along this maturity continuum. The least mature situation is one of apparent neglect of HRD processes. This is sometimes perceived to be the case in smaller and medium-sized organisations, where there is no formal HRD policy or presence. It may also sometimes be perceived to be the case for units or parts of the workforce in larger organisations. The opening case example of CUs represents a more mature approach, focussed and strategic in this sense.

The motivation to attain greater management maturity of processes, and have a clear policy and presence for HRD in the organisation and managing it both informally and formally, is the same as for any process; it can be done more effectively and efficiently if the process is mapped and managed well. As this

Focused, Strategic
Formalised, Connected
Piecemeal, Isolated
Neglected, Overlooked

Figure 3.1   Maturity standards for organising learning

engagement with process maturity is sought the inclusion and management of both formal and informal learning and change becomes more of an issue (Colley et al. 2003, Natrins and Smith 2004, Marsick 2009).

The motivation to have more mature management of the training cycle and HRD processes is to accommodate greater and better formal and informal learning and change. Process maturity is not, however, to become confused with increasing control of informal learning and change. There may be scope for managing some informal learning and change more systematically, but seeking to control all learning and change formally and is potentially fruitless and counter-productive. Mayo (2001) proposes a framework beyond a narrow view of HRD strategy which helps to put the value of mature processes in context. He identified three variables that influence how the training cycle is operated:

- Variable 1: Maintaining core competencies;
- Variable 2: Values and beliefs in people development;
- Variable 3: Organisation's mission, vision, values and goals.

In order to maintain core competence, follow through on beliefs, and connect to visions, organisations training cycles would be shaped by responding to two reactive drivers:

- Competence reactive drivers: operational issues, individual needs, team needs, external changes;
- Mission reactive drivers: business strategies, business goals, plans, change, Initiatives.

HRD strategies, management of the training cycle and HRD processes would be different forms of beliefs and policies, directions, processes, plans, resources and measures in different organisations. So as well appreciating and managing the formal–informal spectrum of learning and change, there is a need to be 'focused and strategic' about HRD. What this means is addressing three factors: (1) the organisations core competencies, (2) values and (3) mission. Addressing these can help clarify and focus the value and purpose of a mature HRD process, and help various audiences appreciate what learning and change provides. The audiences of interest may be strategic (senior managers), operational (line managers and users of HRD) or external (regulatory and other agencies).The value and purpose may be helping these stakeholders to plan, consult, communicate or prioritise options for HRD in the organisation.

Accordingly the HRD process can also be mapped as follows:

- Articulate a commitment to people development;
- Identify how organisational goals link to HRD;
- Have goals for HRD itself;
- Identify priority activities;

- Define roles and responsibilities;
- Define measurements of success and performance.

In many organisations these aspects of process are expressed in and managed as an explicit and integrated HRD policy. That is helpful, however, there is more to managing processes than adopting generic good policies and practice. For organisations which have mature processes can still have significant variation in what they do and how they do it in the name of HRD. This reflects the existence of distinctive value propositions and business models. Supermarkets, for example, compete with each other on the basis of different value propositions: from the cheapest offering discounts and limited lines to the higher end brands, with premium prices and prestige. The basics of what HRD processes are might be similar in all supermarkets, but how they do it may be very different. In part this difference will be a consequence of variations, as Mayo notes, in different core competence, values and mission in organisations. In part it may also reflect how stakeholders, including HRD professionals, understand and fulfil their roles.

A final factor is that HRD processes can be located within and be reciprocal with the broader business strategy. This merits detailed treatment later, in the chapter on Strategic Human Resource Development (SHRD). It is necessary here to note that there are debates, with those who question if HRD is, or can be, a strategic-level issue in the purest sense; that is, an area of policy that requires consideration and decision-making by the most senior executives of an organisation. For some HRD is to be considered more as an ad hoc, contingent and 'downstream' activity in business, one which is of very little concern to an organisation's senior management team. That is why it does not often feature as a constituent part of business-level strategies. The activity of compiling annual training plans can be a focus for some senior team discussion about performance issues and HRD initiatives, but such training plans do not in themselves amount to developing strategic HRD.

Others take a more positive view, arguing that HRD is as important an area of decision-making in the organisation as any other. Accordingly HRD plans should be developed reciprocally with business plans. This involves more than just planning for the purposes of managing mature processes and setting and managing budgets for HRD. It involves the heart of the business and its future success.

Exercise 3.2

Re-visit the organisation whose approach to learning you mapped in Exercise 3.1. Is it possible to gauge the maturity of the organisation of learning in this case, and also to identify where there might be weaknesses in managing either aspects of formal or informal learning and change?

Exercise 3.3

The following 30 items are relevant factors in how HRD is organised in an organisation. Select an organisation you are familiar with to review. Select the option which most reflects how HRD is managed in that organisation for each of the 30 items. At the end score and profile the organisation:

1. The direction of the HRD focus of the organisation:

   a. Shifts with requests, problems and changes as they occur.
   b. Is determined by Human Resources and adjusted as needed.
   c. Is focused on innovation and initiatives.
   d. Is based on a mission and strategic plan for the function.

2. The primary mode of operation of the HRD function is:

   a. To help management react to fast changing situations and reach solutions through training programmes and services.
   b. To respond to requests by managers and other employees to deliver training programmes and services.
   c. To support enterprise and innovation and transform people, groups and the whole organisation.
   d. To implement training programmes in collaboration with management to keep and develop our talent.

3. The goals of the HRD function are:

   a. Set by the training staff/managers based on perceived demand for programmes.
   b. Developed consistent with human resources plans and goals.
   c. Driven by transformation needs of individuals and the organisation.
   d. Developed to integrate with operating goals and strategic plans of the organisation.

4. Most new programmes are initiated

   a. To respond to what competitors have done.
   b. When a quality issue emerges as a significant problem.
   c. when major transformation initiatives are drawn up.
   d. By request of top management in consultation with other stakeholders.

5. When organisational change happens it is usually:

   a. To be better than our competitors.
   b. To improve quality.
   c. To do things differently.
   d. Necessary to reach a consensus and collaborative approach with the workforce.

6. To define training plans:

   a. Employees are asked about their training needs.
   b. Management is asked to choose training from a list of existing courses.
   c. We look ahead for innovation.
   d. Think about the needs of our key talent first and foremost.

7. When determining the timing of training and the target audiences:

   a. We tie specific training needs to specific customer facing individuals and groups.
   b. We have lengthy, nonspecific training courses for operational staff.
   c. Those involved in innovation and enterprise are considered first.
   d. The needs of the top talent pool are taken into account.

8. The responsibility for training results:

   a. Rests primarily with the training staff to ensure that the programmes are successful.
   b. Is a responsibility of the training staff and line managers, who jointly ensure that results are obtained.
   c. Is a shared responsibility of the training staff, participants and managers all working together to ensure success.

9. Systematic, objective evaluation designed to ensure that trainees are performing appropriately on the job:

   a. Performance metrics are expected to improve after training is completed.
   b. Quality standards are expected to improve if the training was effective.
   c. Innovation is expected to be started or completed if the training was effective.
   d. Trust, collaboration and top talent satisfaction are expected to greater if training was effective.

10. New programmes are developed:

    a. Internally, using a staff of instructional designers and specialists.
    b. By vendors. We usually purchase programmes modified to meet the organisation's needs.
    c. In the most economic and practical way to meet deadlines and cost objectives, using both internal staff and vendors.
    d. Following strategy development or review by senior leaders.

11. Costs for training and HRD are identified:

    a. With a core budget for a HRD team in house and flexibility to respond to emerging needs quickly.
    b. With a core budget for predicted year on year training programmes.
    c. On a programme-by-programme basis.
    d. Over the long term, with external partners and commitments.

12. Management involvement in the training process is centred on:

    a. The performance targets they and their staff have.
    b. The quality of the processes they are responsible for.
    c. Supporting innovation and enterprise in their areas of responsibility.
    d. Talent management of their key people.

13. To ensure that training is transferred into performance on the job, we:

    a. Track performance metrics and sales data.
    b. Track quality improvement data.
    c. Check on the success of innovations and initiatives.
    d. Check the retention and use of top talent.

14. The training staff's interaction with line management is:

    a. About performance metrics and issues.
    b. About quality metrics and issues.
    c. About innovation and enterprise.
    d. Focused on key talent pools.

15. HRD's role in major change efforts is:

    a. training to support quick change.
    b. training to support process improvements.
    c. training to support transformation.
    d. Training to develop leaders and managers.

16. Most managers view the HRD function as:

    a. A support for doing things better.
    b. The guardians of getting things right.
    c. A driver of innovation and change.
    d. supporters of talent, leadership and management development.

17. HRD programmes are:

    a. Individual results-based. ('The participant will reduce his or her error rate by at least 20 percent.')
    b. Subject-based. ('All supervisors attend the Performance Appraisal Workshop.')
    c. Associated with major initiatives in the organisation.
    d. A way of enabling networking among talent from across the organisation.

18. The investment in HRD is measured primarily by:

    a. Return through improved productivity, cost savings.
    b. Better quality.
    c. The success of initiatives and change.
    d. Workforce trust, collaboration and commitment.

19. The HRD effort consists of:

    a. A full array of courses to meet individual needs.
    b. Usually one-shot, seminar-type approaches.
    c. A variety of training and development programmes implemented to bring about change in the organisation.
    d. Substantial programmes for key talent and leaders.

20. The results of HRD programmes are evaluated and communicated about as a part of:

    a. Performance management.
    b. Quality reviews.
    c. Change initiatives.
    d. Strategic reviews.

21. During a business decline at my organisation, the HRD function will:

    a. Look for opportunities to enhance competitiveness.
    b. Look for opportunities to improve quality.
    c. Look for opportunities for major transformations.
    d. Look for opportunities to retain existing and find new talent.

22. Budgeting for HRD is based on:

    a. Whatever the training department can 'sell.'
    b. Last year's budget.
    c. The scale of change to be encountered in the year ahead.
    d. Sustaining the development of a pool of top talent.

23. The principal reason for HRD expenditures is:

    a. Competitiveness.
    b. Quality of operations.
    c. Major change initiatives.
    d. Developing peoples' potential and top talent.

24. HRD is most celebrated where:

    a. We can demonstrate results.
    b. We can quantify the value of our efforts (classroom, CBT, Web courses, self-study, etc.).
    c. We can support a new initiative or system companywide.
    d. We have provided excellent individual support for key talent.

25. The Leadership of the organisation emphasise that:

    a. The marketplace is continually increasing competitively.
    b. Continuous improvement and process improvement are highly valued.

c. Devising new methods and solutions for delivering services.

d. Talent management decisions are the critical thing to get right, identifying future potential.

26. Top management's involvement in the implementation of HRD programmes:

a. Includes monitoring progress, opening/closing speeches, and presenting information on the outlook of the organisation.

b. Includes limited to sending invitations, extending congratulations and signing certificates.

c. Includes programme participation to see what's covered, conducting major segments of the programme and requiring key executives to be involved.

d. working with partners to commission and design talent management systems like coaching and mentoring

27. Line management involvement in conducting HRD programmes is:

a. Very minor: usually HRD specialists conduct programmes.

b. Limited to a few specialists conducting programmes in their areas of expertise.

c. Extensive, closely concerned with developing staff.

d. Very significant: programmes are conducted by managers, and they coach and mentor.

28. When an employee completes a training programme and returns to the job, his or her manager is likely to:

a. Make no reference to the programme.

b. Ask questions about the programme and encourage the use of the material.

c. Require use of the programme material and give positive rewards when the material is used successfully.

d. Not need to know as they have been involved in coaching/mentoring conversations.

29. If an employee attends an outside seminar, upon return he or she is required to:

a. Explain the connection to competitiveness.

b. Explain the connection to quality improvement.

c. Identify any new and innovative thinking.

d. Share their experience with their close network.

30. Managers are most likely to come to us when:

a. Management has mandated performance changes.

b. New processes or methods have been introduced in their department.

c. They need to identify what motivates people to change actions or behaviours.

d. They want to offer our top talent professional development and qualification.

Conclusion

The organisation of learning to effectively provide for learning may be associated with encouraging or requiring people to attend training, but this cannot make them learn or change. To explore what is done, how it is done and who does it, means mapping the HRD process. Three major frameworks for organising learning and achieving the main goals of HRD at work are definable. Each has its strengths and weaknesses. For example, ST training is based on a system that involves professionals and experts conducting thorough analysis of needs, job analysis and performance appraisal processes. Other elements of the organisation's HRD strategy have to be consistent with this. In practice, this kind and degree of thorough and complete analysis is too time-consuming and complex, and may not be done entirely well.

One clear conclusion is the need to manage each approach well where it is in use, as befits its activities, main agents and outcomes. A maturity analysis helps to do this. There are no intrinsic reasons for preferring one kind of organisation of learning over another; each one has some potential to deal with aspects of the contemporary HRD agenda. Another challenge is that multiple and combined processes may exist and be adopted as the organisation aspires to evolve and improve its HRD. Then the challenge is how to manage these multiple and combined processes in a balanced way, how to address all these different aspects of managing and organising HRD. Finally organisations may use different processes to deal with different groups. For example, for many employees HRD may be managed through STP, whereas for managers it will be managed through a CDP route.

Ranking

Note the total number of response in the table below:

	A	B	C	D
Number of				

Organisations showing mainly A's will tend to be focused on performance improvement, and tend to be organisations whose value creation is centred on competing, it terms of the model introduced in Chapter 1.

Organisations showing mainly B's will tend to be focused on systematic training, and tend to be organisations whose value creation is centred on control, it terms of the model introduced in Chapter 1.

Organisations showing mainly C's will tend to be focused on continuous development, and tend to be organisations whose value creation is centred on creating, it terms of the model introduced in Chapter 1.

Organisations showing mainly D's will tend to be focused on collaboration, and tend to be organisations whose value creation is centred on collaboration, it terms of the model introduced in Chapter 1.

Corporate Universities Re-Visited

CUs are a very mature form of organising the HRD process, combining ST, PI and CD. CUs are not always successful and meaningful strategies to generate a good HRD in an organisation. There do exist several complications Human Resource manager and specialists have to deal with; from general difficulties of HRD to specific problems of CUs. These issues can emerge in the stage of construction and development and again in the process of operating a CU. Initial problems can arise when a CU is only implemented to rename an already existing HRD concept without any structural or content-related changes, in order to achieve a higher reputation, demand and to give the actions more weight. On the other hand, some think that many CUs are too close to traditional universities in their curriculum and direction.

Another factor many companies are struggling with is the necessity to assess organisations' and individuals' current potentials, strength, weaknesses and competences, and in return to identify future challenges and training needs (Zimmermann 2008). Therefore, it is important to integrate employees', divisions' and especially managers' interests into the process of generating programmes and finally into the development of careers (Gebauer 2006). And it might be risky to create a curriculum without taking external influences into account such as competitors, political regulations or demands from potential students internal and external, if the CU gives places to external customers. A meaningful and structured evaluation is necessary to be able to react to difficulties and to ensure a successful turn-around early enough. The challenge exists firstly in the problems to measure an enhancement in soft skills like, for example communication skills, teamwork skills or leading skills, and secondly in the need for a continuous evaluation; not just directly after a programme but also in the following time after the action. An appropriate and aim-directed evaluation to gain information about training and development outcomes seems to be one of the main factors of issues and failure of CUs.

Moreover, the monetary aspect of building up a CU is another main problem, which needs to be recognised in forehand to avoid problems in liquidity after foundation and while operating a CU. Questions must be answered, whether a company own university is economic efficient and the outcomes value enough to exclude the possibility to gain cheaper experience from the job market; in matters of money, time and effort. (CUs are only efficient for bigger companies with a high number of employees and enough participants to ensure economies of scale and a long-term financing. The support of a CU can become insufficient and unclear after a while, especially in times of financial crisis or inconsistencies, such as a change in the supporting party, from stakeholder or in the board. Situations like redundancies and cost saving can cause a neglect of HRD, with again results in conflicts with resistance and unmotivated staff. Not only external factors can cause tensions and disadvantages for an organisation, but also when employees have benefited from training and development and leave the company afterwards, taking the expertise and skills with them; this means that not only the employee but also all efforts and investments into training and development are lost.

By the use of company-specific training facilities, unique and organisation-specific skills and talents can be aimed and outcomes-oriented developed as they are needed. The organisational standing of training and continuous education is increasing organisational efficiency, reputation and quality, and is generating a strong commitment, loyalty and corporate culture towards the company and is strengthening the psychological contract. Especially when a CU strategy includes directing informal learning actions, employees are enabled to learn from mistakes and success in order to use their experiences to re-define problems and to find new strategies.

Wimmer et al. (2002) found that 74 per cent of companies built a CU because of the advantages of an improved distribution and implementation of organisations' strategy with the aims to achieve training (47 per cent) as well as strategic (41 per cent), structural and cultural change (12 per cent). CUs make sense when enterprises do value HRD as a strategic tool to gain greater performance, enhanced learning culture and improved competitive advantage. Thus, companies are aiming for renewals in which the qualifications and competencies needed fit with the strategic direction based on the overall business strategy. This takes place by using case studies and examples out of the organisation's own working environment. So, CUs are a supporting model for the dissemination of knowledge, expertise and inter-cultural understanding in the organisation.

Additionally, a CU is a place where colleagues can be collaborating together to share experiences and knowledge and therefore strengthen the team spirit and corporate culture. A CU means a place for exchange and development and thus creates an instrument for an improved internal and external communication. In particular the term 'University' creates a picture of a superior and privileged training facility, which in return leads to a higher reputation as well as to a crucial competitive factor. The invitation to participate in courses or even to gain a degree like a 'Bachelor' or 'MBA' in a CU provides additionally to salary or promotions a huge meaning of an incentive for employees. Organisations can achieve important advantages by acknowledging training investment as expenditures in human capital and competitive advantage and is a contribution to business success.

Selected Further Reading

Antonacopoulou, E. (2000) 'Employee Development through Self-Development in Three Retail Banks', *Personnel Review*, 29 (3), 491–508.

Baumard, P. and P Starbuck, W. (2006) Is Organisational Learning a Myth? Executive Briefing. London, Advanced Institute of Management (AIM)

LLUK (2010) National Occupational Standards for Learning and Development Final version approved March 2010, Lifelong Learning UK.

Lynton, R. and Pareek, U. (2000) 'Training for Organisational Transformation: Part I for Policy Makers and Change Managers (London, Sage).

Dealtry, R. (2009) 'The Design and Management of an Organisation's Lifelong Learning Curriculum', *Journal of Workplace Learning*, 21 (2), 156–165.

Miller, L., Rankin, N. and Neathey, F. (2001) *Competency Frameworks in Organisations* (London, Chartered Institute of Personnel and Development).

Stern, E. and Sommerlad, E. (1999) *Workplace Learning, Culture and Performance* (London, Institute of Personnel and Development).

Natrins. N. and Smith, V. (2004) *Rethinking the Process: Strategies for Integrating On- and Off-the-Job Training* (London, Learning and Skills Development Agency).

3 Key Texts

(1) Jarvis, P. (1987) *Adult Learning in the Social Context* (London, Croom Helm).

(2) Mayo, A. (2001) *Creating a Training and Development Strategy* (London, CIPD).

(3) Colley, H., Hodkinson, P. and Malcom, J. (2003) *Informality and Formality in Learning: A Report for the Learning and Skills Research Centre* (London, Learning and Skills Research Centre).

3 Key Articles/Reports

(1) Lohman, M. (2005) 'A Survey of Factors Influencing the Engagement of Two Professional Groups in Informal Workplace Learning', *Human Resource Development Quarterly*, 16(4), 501–528.

(2) Marsick, V. J. (2009) 'Toward a Unifying Framework to Support Informal Learning Theory, Research and Practice', *Journal of Workplace Learning*, 21(4), 265–275.

(3) Bates, R. and Chen, Hsin-Chih (2004) 'Human Resource Development Value Orientations: A Construct Validation Study', *Human Resource Development International*, 7(3), September, 351–370.

3 Key Web Links

(1) National Occupational Standards in Learning and Development: http://www.ukstandards.org.uk/Find_Occupational_Standards.aspx?NosFindID=4&FormMode=ViewModeSuite&SuiteID=2174.

(2) National Training Awards: http://www.nationaltrainingawards.com/.

(3) Lifelong Learning: http://www.lluk.org/.

4

Values and Ethics

Learning Objectives

By the end of this chapter you will be able to:

- Define and analyse the role of 'ethics' in determining HRD actions;
- Describe four different perspectives on ethics;
- Reflect on the problems of acting ethically in the HRD context.

Introductory Exercise 4.1

If a code of ethics was to be written for HRD practice in a workplace, what might it contain?

Use the following categories to flesh out what a code of ethics might look like to guide adult learning in a work organisation.

Section 1: Define HRD:

(1) HRD is . . .

(2) Our commitment is . . .

(3) HRD seeks to . . . .

Section 2: Basics:

(1) The Primary client of HRD is . . .

(2) Significant features of the Social context that matter to us are . . .

(3) Equity for us means . . .

(4) Empowerment involves . . . .

Section 3: Process Issues:

(5) Our duty of care is . . .

(6) Transparency

(7) Confidentiality

(8) Cooperation.

Section 4: Professional Regard:

(10) Professional Development of HRD practitioners should involve...

(11) The Boundaries we recognise to our work in supporting learning are...

(12) Self-care for people organising learning is advocated by....

Introduction

Knowledge and organisation of learning in work and employment are both affected and shaped by values and ethical concerns and perspectives. In the contemporary context the most prominent example of this is the achievement of social change and progress towards managing diversity. This means that Human Resource Development (HRD) policy and practice are expected to play a part in social change. HRD is a discipline and a profession that participates in the contest that accompanies social change, and the power dynamics in society, and more broadly the global economy, which accompany that (Cervero and Wilson 2001). Neutrality, HRD as a set of methods to assist individual and organisational development towards effective performance based on skills is possible. To ignore values and ethics and deal only with performance concerns is to neglect the reality of what matters to many stakeholders, what they think, feel and are motivated by. This is especially so as experiences in workplace learning and HRD activities may now have as great an impact on the lives and fortunes of individuals and social groups as access to education was previously perceived to have. If this is so, it has a special responsibility. Workplace HRD can be viewed through the lenses of political and ethical agendas.

HRD, Values and Ethics

There is evidence that HRD professionals appear to operate from a structured set of values (Bates and Chen 2005), and these values can be explored. The construct of values examined by Bates and Chen was a model (see Practice 4.1 and Table 4.1) with six sets of values classed as follows:

1. Building learning systems;

2. Enabling meaningful work;

3. Providing individual learning experiences;

4. Building socially responsible organisations;

5. Improving organisational performance;

6. Improving individual job performance.

Practice 4.1: Organisational Value Propositions and HRD Processes

- Building learning systems where HRD is focused on transforming or building organisations into learning systems in order to learn and apply that learning more quickly, thereby helping with change processes
- Establishing meaningful work where HRD is focused on helping individuals to create work that is meaningful to a sense of self and spiritually energising, fulfilling important 'inner needs'
- Providing individual learning is a focus on individual learning experiences that build work-related expertise, increasing work skills and behaviour
- Building socially responsible organisations is focused on building organisations which are socially responsible and contributing to the good of the community, contributing to a larger social and ecological good beyond organisational goals
- Improving organisational performance has its focus on meeting organisational goals and objectives
- Improving individual job performance focuses on work-related performance among individuals to meet or exceed demands at work.

Source: Bates, R. and Chen, Hsin-Chih (2004).

Table 4.1   Respondents selection of Key values Driving HRD

Sets of values	Percentage of respondents selecting this as the key value
Improving individual job performance	41.75
Improving organisational performance	30.42
Building learning systems	12.26
Providing individual learning experiences	5.90
Building socially responsible organisations	5.42
Enabling meaningful work	4.25

In the study respondents felt the most important guides to the practice of HRD should be those emphasising performance-related outcomes, firstly at the individual level then in the organisational context (see Table 4.1).

This suggests 'that there may be a good deal of agreement about the relative importance of the values that should guide HRD practice ... the largest percentage of respondents believed the practice of HRD should be guided largely by performance-focused values, and to a lesser degree by learning and meaning-in-work values' (Bates and Chen, p. 364). Yet as well as the consistency of this general value pattern favouring performance values, the results do show variation in top-priority values; around 30 per cent selected values other than individual and organisational performance as the core value. There were also significant differences in the comparative importance of values. Only about 40 per cent of individual ratings were in agreement that one specific value guided the HRD process, acknowledging that other values, and potential value conflicts, were significant. This evidence of the values based foundations of HRD opens up the question of how values, and ethics, operate and influence HRD.

Ethics

Ethics are about making judgements concerned with moral right and wrong, here related to employment and, more specifically, HRD at work (Hatcher 2002, Fisher 2005). Ethics provide the ground rules that determine how people think about what is right and wrong, and then how they act. They offer a constraint on selfishness and self-interest, and a potential basis for justifying actions. One simple, common-sense list of ethical qualities is the following:

- Honesty;
- Fairness;
- Respect for others;
- Promise keeping;
- Trustworthiness.

HRD professionals can be connected with ethics in a number of ways. Sometimes HRD professionals are faced with the responsibilities of implementing ethics initiatives (Foote and Ruona 2008). More broadly HRD professionals are expected, as part of their professionalism, to have and abide by a code of ethics, as advanced by for example the Academy of Human Resource Development. The interest here is mainly in considering the latter, and appreciating how what HRD is and how it is done raises and reflects values, ethical and political stances and dilemmas.

In significant areas, such as the management of diversity, the impact on HRD at work does not have to emerge from legislation; it can be embedded in the promotion of these ethical qualities at work. Whether a legislation-driven approach, such as affirmative action, or an organisational 'best practice' approach is valued, there is a deeper level of analysis that might help throw some light on the opportunities and threats of managing diversity. These are the opportunities and threats of shaping people management practices to combine a 'contribution to the business' and dealing with the 'humanness' of the human resource.

There are three possible responses to an ethics-embedded approach. The first is to deny it wholly, arguing that work organisations are places where 'anything goes' as long as performance is achieved. Ethics ought to be kept out, and firms left to pursue their interests. Work organisations are not institutions that can rescue groups in society from social problems. By pursuing their own interests organisations will recruit the best, promote the best and develop talent. Economic imperatives drive high standards, not a commitment to ethics. This stance extends to HRD. It is not the function of a company's training strategy to right the wrongs of prejudice and discrimination; the role of HRD is to improve performance.

The second position is that ethics are to be left to individuals' personal conscience, and work organisations should not be expected to go beyond ensuring compliance with basic standards. It is society that needs to socialise people with the norms and beliefs about matter such as diversity, not work organisations. If people take their norms and beliefs with them into organisations, then that has to be managed but cannot be changed or eradicated. No amount of organisational action in HRD can or should seek to change a person's conscience. The third position is to argue that work organisations ought to lead, and are crucial stakeholders in setting and upholding ethics, and acting to change. Such leadership emerges from their own core values, which are commonly expressed as being consistent with high standards in, for example, diversity management. The challenges arise if values and codes of best practice remain on paper only, or now if the organisation gets bogged down in 'equal opportunities' for some specific group rather than valuing diversity in the workforce as whole. The emergence of targets that are set and monitored for specific groups rather than culture change promoting diversity is an issue.

Defining Ethics

In the third sense, where organisations do accept the relevance of an ethical perspective on their activities and HRD, it can be helpful to analyse issues about organisational practice and debates around them by appreciating different foundations for ethics. Four perspectives on ethics have been described (Legge 1997):

1. Utilitarian: what is done is to be judged according to the consequences of actions; with the greatest good for the greatest number being the ideal. If HRD as a means to the end of effective performance provides the greatest good for the greatest number, then it is ethical. If minorities are unable to benefit from this that is acceptable.

2. Rawlsian: what is good is what is agreed by consensus. The key to this is dialogue and consultation with all stakeholders. Whatever HRD emerges from dialogue and consultation with all stakeholders is the best. Practices are justified as long as the stakeholders participate in decisions.

3. Aristotelian: individuals should be able to achieve self-actualisation within healthy communities. If HRD enables that, it is ethical. If it does not, it is not. This line of thinking can be directly connected to human relations

thinking, and in HRD ideas of the learning organisation which go beyond what is necessary for pragmatic performance.

4. Kantian: treat all people with respect, as rational beings with individual dignity. Justification of actions in terms of economic aims or ends is a distortion of ethics. This means promoting human development, not just resource development. Both what is done and how it is done should be consistent with and contribute to respecting people and their dignity.

In terms of HRD generally, and diversity specifically, the conclusions are quite different. The utilitarian would seek to calculate the overall costs and benefits and take up those options representing the greatest good of most; an approach often phrased in terms of the business case for HRD. The Rawlsian would also be calculating, but seeking groups' views and a consensus; an approach often associated with ensuring dialogue between employers, employees and other stakeholders. The Aristotelian would be most prescriptive and positive about HRD being framed in terms of fulfilling potential rather than performance. The Kantian would be more concerned with collective action on human development in all contexts, and high standards around doing the right thing with regard to respecting to people and their dignity.

An alternative way of framing the way ethics can impact in HRD is given by Fisher (2005), who maps the different stances that may be seen to be taken. These he defines these as modernist, neo-traditonalist, traditionalist and postmodern. Depending on a person's stance, certain identities in principle and policy roles tend to follow. As Fisher defines these ethical positions the

> traditionalist sees a unified world united by time-hallowed values. The other three positions see the ethical world as fragmented but have different responses to this perception. The modernist believes that unity can be constructed by the rational development of individuals. The neo-traditionalist believes unity can be restored only by a return to neglected traditional values. The postmodernist accepts the inevitability of fragmentation and enjoys it. (p. 242)

To say the ethical world is fragmented is to say that there are no common, secure, shared position on what is right in all circumstances and situations; there is uncertainty, ambiguity and contest. The postmodernist accepts this, and does not seek to remove uncertainty and ambiguity by asserting a general ethic. For others a general ethics may provide a shared base for understanding and guiding HRD practice, as traditionalists, modernists and neo-traditionalist would see it albeit in their own ways.

Social Contexts of Learning Relationships

HRD is expected to use effective learning relationships to redress discrimination and inequalities, but often there are problems with this actually being fulfilled, despite best intentions. After many years of policy development and practice there are still challenges in organisations with 'leaky pipelines'; that is to say that the expectations of attracting and developing people to progress in talent development pipelines is not happening to the extent desired. For example, with women into engineering or leadership roles, a major multinational organisation in computer manufacture and e-business development recognised that even following years of promoting policies the level of women entering engineering career paths and going through the pipeline in senior positions was decreasing not increasing.

There is a need to identify circumstantial and conditional contexts which bring into relief the social forces concerned. For example:

- The hardest to reach often go untrained; they do not get into the workplace or the HRD system and learning relationships;
- Trainers may have professional knowledge but not the resources to make change happen in contexts of inequality;
- Training cannot sweep away structural forces that lead to discrimination and continue to hold sway over people.

Even so learning relationships can make a difference, looking beneath discrimination forms to underlying status difference and shifts (Pawson 2004). Development and change is a matter of status change and shift, as well as knowledge increase and skill development. The respective social standing of the partners as well as historical inequalities exists. To learn and change is to overcome status barriers, and HRD is the environment in which this is evident. One classification of status terms and differences, outlining the journeys people face in learning is

- Status in a hierarchy: going from 'low' to 'high' up occupational ladders. HRD accompanies going from the low to the high;
- Status in an oppositional context: going from 'being without' something to possessing it. HRD provides knowledge and skill;
- Status in source: Inherited status versus Achieved status. HRD is a way that insiders maintain control of progress confined to fellow in-group members, or HRD enables achievement for those of 'outsider' groups.

These sources and dynamics of status may all matter, and combine to produce individual and collective learning journeys which are about outsiders who move to become marginals before becoming insiders.

- Development and change is about outsiders to marginals;
- Development and change is about marginals to insiders;
- Development and change is about outsiders to insiders.

Individual and collective learner orientation to change in this context is crucial. Understanding reference group positioning can illuminate a learners appetite or otherwise for change; the social self and the allies or opponents of the reference group. Three stances tend to result:

1. Aspiration: those who are ready and willing to change, looking to an 'out-group';
2. Acquiescent: those ambiguous about change, in a flux between existing reference groups and new reference groups;
3. Antagonism: those who resist change, committed to their current 'in-group', even if it is discriminated against/isolated/different culture and values.

HRD in this context can be a key to change a negative message:

- Positive: helping entry and change;
- Autonomous: laissez-faire on entry and change;
- Antipathy: obstructionist on entry and change.

If HRD is going to be positive, this usually means gaining a reputation for four things:

1. Advocacy: positional resource, network and promote;
2. Coaching: aptitudinal resource, encourage and coax in skills;
3. Direction setting: cognitive resource, choices and decisions;
4. Affective contacts: emotional resource, hand of friendship, feel different.

We can map all this onto an integrative model (Figure 4.1), with three pathways; one short 'up', one medium 'along' and one big leap.

	HRD Roles			
New reference group	**Advocate:** positional resource, network and promote	**Coaching:** aptitudinal resource, encourage and coax in skills	**Direction setting:** cognitive resource, choices and decisions	**Existing reference group**
Insider				**Aspirational**
Marginal	**Affective contacts**: emotional resource, hand of friendship, feel different			**Acquiescence**
Outsider				**Antagonism**

Figure 4.1 Status change journeys and HRD roles

Where motivated learners are aspirational and HRD practitioners can assume positive affective contact, then direction setting, coaching and advocacy are the levers to work with. But HRD professionals and managers may also have to deal with other situations; development pathways:

(a) Identity development needs to shift from antagonism to aspiration;

(b) Achievement development to shift from outside to insider;

(c) Engagement development to shift from antagonism to insider.

Development programmes, and their goals and challenges, contain all these pathways, and we identify what to do to manage:

- From outsider to insider; get qualifications and in-group associations

    o So coaching then advocating

- From hostile to aspirational change emotional loyalties and forward thinking

    o So trust and reflect anew, promote alternatives.

In successful development relationships between trainers and learners where there are equality/discrimination issues and challenges, there are moves across status and resource differences. These can be managed to match the intended shift in the learner's standing and thinking, combining advocacy, coaching, direction setting and the affective

The converse is that unsuccessful learning relations will entail a reinforcement of status and resource differences, the application of inappropriate mechanism, and a continuation of inequalities and discrimination. Values and ethics matter as:

- HRD status and reference groups will influence the resources they bring to situations where inequalities exist (possession of capacity in advocacy, coaching, direction setting, affective);
- Learner status and reference group will influence responses to learning opportunities (need to encounter and benefit from advocacy, coaching, direction setting, affective);
- Development interactions may be focused on one level (advocacy, coaching, direction setting, affective) depending on the situation.

Long moves across status and identity positions are the hardest to sustain. It is sensible to split this into shorter processes of change; from antagonism to aspiration, then to being insiders. To support longer moves HRD needs not just additional resources in advocacy, coaching, direction setting and the affective but the values and ethics to work on this.

Politics

Cervero and Wilson suggest that there are three possible meanings for this ethical and political context for HRD, its political significance. Firstly, it can mean that the 'political is personal' in HRD. This means that there is no specific conscious and deliberate politicisation of HRD policy and practice, to achieve general aims for groups. Rather it means that the cultural approach to HRD, how it is done, as a whole should reflect certain tenets, often associated with a learner-centred view of the adult learner in workplace HRD. Development is not something that should be done 'to' people, as this assumes a control and direction of the person by an authority which perpetuates a basic cause of a general problem; that people feel subject to the control of others. Some may indeed 'learn' knowledge and skills, but others may respond to that by withdrawing rather than engaging. Even those who learn knowledge and skills may become in the course of that passive and dependent on others. The way HRD is done may preclude and prevents people from growing as whole people. HRD is then an area where the 'personal is political' in the sense that developing and having systems of learning and development where adult learners are independent, questioning, engaged and committed, requires mutual control of development and learning. The concern is not to change governments, or policy, but to embed a system of practice that makes the means by which HRD is delivered a contributor to the end of producing mature and fulfilled adults.

Second, it can mean that in HRD the 'political is practical'. This means that stakeholders should be concerned with what is done with whom, and have an ability to get things done in the face of conflict and contention by managing political relationships. Those relationships exist in work and in society. They take shape around what learning and development is done and who benefits. This may imply that certain groups should be given special attention and support through HRD, to advance and progress in circumstances where there are still disadvantage, and legacies of disadvantage.

Thirdly, it may mean that in HRD the 'political is structural'. This means recognising that using HRD to support personal progress, or even more targeted progress for set groups, is an incremental process which encounters obstacles as long as the structural relationships remain the same. Inequalities are perpetuated despite HRD and other efforts as the structural forces behind inequality and discrimination persist. Workplace HRD in itself, overcoming past inequalities by development opportunities rather than obstructing progress by limiting them, cannot transcend these. Deeper and more profound change is required in systems, including government policies or even forms of government; to attain HRD ends entire cultures, values, systems and leaderships can come into question. This applies equally to developing, developing and under-developed economics and countries. In developed economies there are the challenges of the consequences of affluence for well-being, as well as continuing disparities in wealth and material well-being. In developing economies there are challenges of managing leaps in progress which bring progress to some but not all. In low-development countries there are the challenges of meeting basic human development needs in security, health and education.

In this book the political meaning in the first sense is relevant to and considered in discussions of learning design and the growth of development partnerships. In the second sense it is relevant to and considered in the context of HRD strategies, talent management and Strategic HRD. In the third sense the political is considered in the contexts of national and Comparative HRD. These are not novel or exceptional connections to make in the context of HRD. However the discussion of the politics of HRD is often neglected in introductory texts in favour of neutral social science treatments of process management. The current and future demands on HRD make this an omission that is significant. These issues provide as real a challenge to critical thinking and understanding, the prominence to the management of diversity particularly and ethics more generally, as do questions of organising learning and managing the HRD process to improve performance. They are two sides of the same coin, with breakthroughs in one being contingent on breakthroughs in the other.

Diversity

Managing diversity has emerged as a major concern in many areas of management, including HRD (Briley 1996, Kirkton and Greene 2000, Mavin and Girling 2000). It can be a real testing factor for the existence of good practice in human development (James 2007). The changing nature of the workforce is the underlying reason for this in the HRD context. These changes include:

- Higher levels of employment participation by women;
- A significant percentage of the workforce with dependent children or 'carer';
- Responsibilities;
- Increased number of dual income families;
- Changes in the family structures of employees, for example sole parents, fewer men and women in traditional family roles;
- An ageing workforce;
- High levels of cultural diversity with substantial labour migration.

There are also some organisational factors which create greater concerns with diversity. Some of these are as follows:

- Aspirations to alter the traditional perceptions of male and female work roles and careers;
- Changes to workforce profiles as a result of downsizing and outsourcing;
- Fewer levels of management and a reduction in 'command and control' styles of management;

- Impact of globalisation and technology on HRD practices;
- Trends towards knowledge work.

Diversity management concerns present a special challenge, manifestly significant for HRD. In organising learning this has included, alongside responding to equal opportunity legislation, concerns with issues of gender, race, culture, age, family/carer status, religion and disability. Organisations need to improve awareness, review their management practices and develop new and creative approaches to organising learning in this diversity context. This is not just about complying with the law; it is also about clarifying, reviewing and advancing in general the 'ethical' grounds of contemporary HRD as more than rhetoric. To stress the need for the HRD process and practices to be diversity-supportive means appreciating core ideas and concepts relating to the management of diversity and the role of ethics in HRD.

Why Manage Diversity in HRD?

Equality has been a strong theme and focus of policy in HRM as a whole. At some points in many organisations, it can become most significant. Overcoming inequalities and dealing with unjust discrimination can provide a major perspective with which to make sense of many issues and problems in the workplace. The ethical case for social justice and the business case for talent management combine and can come to the fore, if sometimes uneasily, as dual drivers of change in the workplace. The outcome has been to question and change decision-making processes in selection practices and in reward systems; as well as in career management and development.

It is often only once this has happened that deeper issues appear. Following such change in decision-making processes and practices, a further agenda for action emerges around promoting diversity. Two deeper concerns are often highlighted. First is a difference in strategy between liberal and radical proponents on how to pursue consolidation and momentum in advancing diversity. Liberal proponents advocate individual freedom to compete as the strategy that will secure diversity in the workplace. Critics of this strategy tend to highlight two concerns. First is that, in the short term, not much seems to change if we rely on the freedom to compete. A few people from groups experiencing discrimination compete and succeed, but not enough to deliver true diversity. The second concern is that this approach to diversity fails to challenge the biggest problem, the pre-existing templates of success. If the previous ideal, for example the 'ideal leader', is still assumed, that invariably favours those who in the past have fulfilled those ideals; previous 'ideal leaders' who were primarily male. Those who fit the ideal are still at an advantage, rather than the newer and more diverse competitors. They are then still most likely to succeed, as they are more 'suited' for the role. Until visions of, for example, leadership are reconstituted to be more diverse themselves then this will be a source of blockage to the progress of diversity. That is why some advocate more systemic change, such as forms of positive discrimination in favour of key groups among those discriminated against. This would overcome the weaknesses of the liberal strategy. The acceptability of these more radical approaches is constrained by a mix of legal and political issues, reflecting concerns among organisations and their stakeholders.

The second, deeper issue is the inertia of organisational culture. The impact of changing policy in major decision-making areas, such as selection, reward and career management, opens up a period of possible transition as new kinds of entrant or successors in senior roles, the pioneers, emerge. Given the gradual pace of this, the transition from small changes in the beginning to more fully realised change establishing a different equilibrium reflecting diversity can be a long one. If the transition is to be successful, rather than reverting to old patterns, there will need to be a culture change over the long term as much as personnel policy changes in the short term. In this context HRD has been seen as a tool of culture change, a means of supporting the evolution of equality in the organisation as a whole, supporting these pioneers.

Alongside the use of HRD as a means of achieving longer term equality goals there have also been voices directly considering and exploring what equality means inside HRD. The diversity concern has been a touchstone of those who advocate non-traditional and distinctive approaches to adult learning. Non-traditional approaches are those which are grounded in learning relations outside the classroom, in development partnerships such as coaching, mentoring and action learning. In this context, distinctive approaches are those emerging from exploring adult and workplace learning specifically rather than approaches derived from applying principles of psychology to adult and workplace learning needs. It has been evident to many working in this field that the standard 'expert–novice' relationship template is deeply misplaced, and is not a helpful perspective to adopt, or appropriate for supporting and sustaining diversity.

Alongside this long-standing concern there has emerged another concern, understanding organisational learning. Attention has been given to concepts of learning organisations, and on cultivating a culture of learning, putting greater responsibility for learning and shared approaches to learning with individuals, with facilitators and learners carrying out HRD activities together. Within this tradition the question of the relationship between these two groups has been mainly concerned with re-conceptualising the role of the 'trainer', and the learner has been neglected. But if in cultivating learning organisations the role of trainer changes, so too must the role of learner. One source for the concern with equality in HRD may be the humanist articulation of new structures for adult education. These were first proposed in the1960s and progressive movements promoted adult and experiential learning in 1970s. They have become incorporated in HRD as themes around the political aspects of advocating access to learning. Providing 'freedom to learn' meant not just leaving it to the individual but an openness to hearing learners' own ideas and engaging employees as active partners in learning. But the relationship between learners and those helping them, including coaches, mentors and HRD professionals, will always be unequal in the sense that the former have a development demand and the latter have a development offer. Under-examined prescriptions about how facilitators and learner can be 'partners' in learning, and how organisational learning is to be fostered through treating each other with respect, mutuality and trust, provide an interesting domain of research.

Prior to the greater impact of demographic forces increasing awareness about the potential 'business case' for valuing diversity, there had been a long history of political and ethical concerns about tackling prejudice and discrimination in HRM. The focus was initially one of pursuing 'equal opportunity', then more recently 'diversity'. Three kinds of reason are relevant for HRD:

1. Economic reasons: get and use the best talent, globalisation and international business;
2. Social reasons: changing composition of societies (e.g. migration and movements of ethnic groups) and workforces (e.g. greater participation of women) means that the 'traditional' profile of the workforce changes;
3. Political reasons: legislation on equal opportunities.

Governments and companies have created initiatives to improve standards so that all kinds of decisions in employment, from selection to promotion and reward, are based on merit alone. Discrimination is both explicitly, in law, and tacitly, in cultural terms, proscribed; yet significant problems seem to persist. We still then need to consider the basics: why does unfair discrimination occur, and how might that impact on HRD? Unfair discrimination occurs when decisions or behaviour are based on prejudice. Prejudice is a negative attitude towards a particular group of people who, for cultural or social psychological reasons, are considered to be 'different'. Prejudice may be focused on a range of groups:

- Women;
- Ethnic minorities;
- Disabled people;
- Age – young or old;
- Part-time workers;
- Personal (e.g. people with red hair).

Discrimination and diversity issues arise where people are treated unfairly because of their membership of a particular group. Discrimination in the world of employment was a major part of the agenda that inspired the growth of a concern with civil liberties/human rights throughout the twentieth century. As the promotion of civil liberties gained ground in general, in political and social contexts, it was natural to expect change and progress in the employer – employee relationship. The highest profile area for this in the past has concerned discrimination in employment against women as a group on the grounds of their sex, and discrimination against ethnic minority groups on the grounds of their race. Race is defined here with reference to a person's colour, race, nationality, ethnic or national origin. The concern here is not with the specifics of employment law in the field of discrimination, which are bound to national legislative systems. Rather the concern is with general principles of discrimination and diversity and their connections to HRD at work.

1. Specifying what misconduct leads to discrimination; considering direct and indirect discrimination.
2. Identifying the grounds of prohibition: which bases of discrimination will be prohibited. Four major groupings are sex, race, ideological, other.
3. Specifying what exceptions are permitted to these general rules: discrimination relevant to the inherent requirements of a job, state security and special measure of protection.
4. Considering the field of application: which elements of employment will be covered, for example pre-employment, general terms and conditions, specific issues such as pay, harassment.
5. Considering how these laws will be implemented, what agencies will be created and what competence they will have.

It is important to distinguish between direct and indirect discrimination. In employment we can describe direct discrimination as occurring when people are judged in terms that do not relate to their competence to do a particular job. Direct discrimination occurs when, on the grounds of someone's sex or on racial grounds, an employer treats a person less favourably than he treats or would treat a person of a different sex or racial background. If a job application is rejected or a promotion denied because the applicant is a women or a member of a specific racial group, that is direct discrimination. Direct discrimination is the exercise of prejudice, either openly or masked by reasons which cannot be justified in terms of the person's ability. Rooting out such direct discrimination is the first concern of any equal opportunity policy.

One of the major problems with identifying and challenging such direct discrimination is that it can be difficult to detect. Few employers are likely to be explicit about their prejudices. It is often only when an employer's HRM procedures are analysed, following a complaint from an individual, that such direct discrimination comes to light. For example, if an employer is systematically evaluating all applicants for a job but rejecting women even where they are objectively the best applicants, it would be evidence that direct discrimination is occurring. One of the positive side-effects of equal opportunity initiatives is that they often force organisations to adopt or improve basic HRM procedures so that people are only judged on their merits relative to the job.

However, even if all direct discrimination could be eliminated, it is still likely that discrimination would persist. This is because the legacy of the past is an institutional set of 'common-sense' ways of thinking and practices which can lead to indirect discrimination. Indirect discrimination means that a requirement is applied equally to all, but it is not relevant to the job and disadvantages a particular group. In employment indirect discrimination may create or perpetuate inequality. Dealing with indirect discrimination is an abiding issue in many national, occupational and organisational contexts. The use of affirmative action policies to try to deal with the problems of this legacy from the past has led to much debate in the USA and other cultures which have been influenced by the 'civil rights' approach.

In any legal system there will be scope to specify the bases on which discrimination will be prohibited. Anyone can suffer discrimination in the context of employment. It is possible to identify four main groupings of bases for discrimination which can be prohibited: sex, race, ideology and other reasons. The category of 'other reasons' has been taking greater form recently, with legislation around disability, sexuality and ageism being prominent. Sex and race issues remain major concerns.

There are some exceptional circumstances where discrimination is permitted on grounds that are normally prohibited. The main categories are jobs in which sex, race or some other criterion is inherent. Jobs may be specifically listed, or indications of the type of job concerned may be given. Other grounds for exception to normal anti-discrimination rules include jobs related to the security of the state.

Whenever a human resource decision is made there is a risk of unfair discrimination. It is useful to look at HRM in terms of three areas where employment law has an impact; pre-employment, terms and conditions and other specific issues.

In pre-employment, access to training can be crucial. Without access to training there will not be an option to apply for jobs and develop careers in the area concerned. Providing positive images of role models for women or racial groups in occupations can be an essential catalyst for individuals to pursue path-breaking careers. Employment services, both public and private, can be important in ensuring that equal opportunity precepts are maintained in recruitment matters. It is also relevant to monitor advertisements and scrutinise methods such as psychometric tests for discriminatory elements. Recruitment should be based on competence only. Thus the development of job descriptions, person specifications or equivalent systematic and objective tools for helping with selection needs to be emphasised. Training in selection methods such as interviewing is also critical. Untrained interviewers are prone to making mistakes which can be discriminatory, such as seeking to confirm their initial impressions of a candidate rather than probing for relevant information.

With terms and conditions of employment any and all terms and conditions can be considered relative to equal opportunity issues. The example of promotion is illustrative; for even where direct discrimination against women has been explicitly dealt with in pre-employment terms there can still be problems inside the organisation. Even where women are recruited, for example, to management posts they may find their path to the very top of the management system is hampered. There appears to be a 'glass ceiling' which women come up against; an invisible barrier beyond which they cannot go. As the management of careers is becoming a hotter issue in general, due to organisations downsizing and the career 'ladder' seeming to disappear, such issues raise fundamental questions.

There are a number of specific HRM issues that the promotion of equal opportunities has brought to the fore. Concerns about diversity and HRD have to be seen in this context. These include equal pay, probably the most crucial 'bottom-line' issue in the field of discrimination. For individuals it can mean increased earnings, for organisations it can mean increased wage bills. Not surprisingly it is a hotly contested area of debate and analysis. The principle of equal pay for work of equal value has been promulgated at length. The validity of the concept of equal value and the practicalities of altering occupational payment structures has its advocates and its detractors. Another equal opportunities issue is sexual harassment, which can be defined as any unwanted conduct of a sexual nature or other conduct based on sex affecting the dignity of women and men at work. It includes all unwelcome sexual advances, requests for sexual favours, verbal or physical conduct of a sexual nature.

Machinery for preventing discrimination and applying, supervising and enforcing the principle of equal opportunity is needed. This may be a direct government role, or agencies, either general or specialist, can be set up. Whatever machinery is implemented special features for dealing with complaints need to be considered. For example, complainants may be afraid of initiating proceedings as, unlike unfair dismissal proceedings, they will still be in the organisation and may feel exposed. It can also be difficult to substantiate allegations. The approach often adopted is that, if a complainant can establish a prima facie case, the burden of proof shifts to the employer. In organisations clear commitments to equal opportunity policies, and procedures to ensure fairness and monitoring of policies in practice are all required at the organisational level.

In practice, the management of equal opportunity in this context comes down to employers striving to ensure that there is meticulous attention to systematic HRM procedures. If there is any evidence of 'bad housekeeping' in HRM procedures inferences of discrimination may be brought from that alone. It is thus vital to introduce and monitor a good equal opportunity policy. Companies need to:

- Have formal statements;
- Stress equal opportunities in principle;
- Intend to have no discrimination;
- Stress employee responsibility.

Even with international conventions, constitutional backing or legislative support for equal opportunities there remain big challenges. Some think it is possible to go beyond such measures, and legislate for 'positive' or affirmative action. The experience of the USA, and its affirmative action principles which grew out of the civil rights era, can be reflected on. The USA is a distinctive context to analyse. On the one hand, it is one of the least 'regulated' labour markets in the world, with a culture that enshrines entrepreneurial zeal and organisational autonomy. On the other hand, it is a society with ethnic divisions at its heart, given its social composition and history. And, as a nation, Americans are perceived to be among the most prone to pursuing litigation, as part of the 'compensation culture', when any hurt or pain is suffered. The affirmative action argument is that the law above all else can help to reshape behaviour where there are significant costs for failing to comply. Legal solutions are important as a statement of value, even if they cannot cover all the unacceptable forms of discrimination which can occur.

The alternative to affirmative action is promoting a strategic and coordinated approach to organisational practice. The following 'Ten Point Plan' suggests an outline for this:

(1) Develop an equal opportunity policy;

(2) Set an action plan, including targets;

(3) Provide training for all;

(4) Monitor position and progress;

(5) Review HR procedures regularly;

(6) Draw up clear and justifiable job criteria;

(7) Offer pre-employment training and positive action training;

(8) Consider your organisation's image;

(9) Consider flexible working;

(10) Develop links with local community group, organisations and schools.

Conclusion

The prominent concern with managing diversity, which features strongly in HRD, is one example of the way that values and ethics are at the heart of what HRD is and how it is done. How HRD is influenced by ethics, by engaging in status shifts and by perceptions of the political all combine to make it an area of professional practice in organisations and societies where neutrality, HRD as a set of methods to assist individual and organisational development towards effective performance is limiting. To ignore values and ethics and deal only with performance concerns is to neglect the reality of what matters to many stakeholders, what they think, feel and are motivated by. Workplace HRD in general, and in specific situations, can usefully be viewed through the lenses of values, ethics and politics. These themes will be re-visited in future chapters, especially in critical HRD.

Exercise 4.1:

Follow Up

The following is a suggested outline code of ethics:

Section 1
Human Resource Development is a field of professional practice for training, trainers and managers as coaches and mentors. While practices and constituencies may differ, they have in common a commitment to their learners as their primary clients, and to the power of HRD to transform individuals, organisations and situations.

HRD is a prerequisite for performance and well-being. HRD seeks to actively engage all, especially those who are challenged by participation in learning. The following principles are informed by this core position.

Section 2: Basics

1. **Primary client**
    Our primary client is the organisation.

2. **Social context**
    Our work is not limited to facilitating organisational performance but also to have a positive impact on individuals.

3. **Equity**
    Our work promotes equality of opportunity and outcome. Our practice is equitable and inclusive.

4. **Empowerment**
    We seek to enhance learner's capacity for positive action by:

    enabling them to clarify and pursue their chosen priorities;

    building skills of decision-making, engagement and cooperation;

    making power relations open and clear;

    supporting constituents in holding those with power accountable.

    Our starting point is that learners are capable of assessing and acting on their interests.

Section 3: Process issues

5. **Duty of care**
    We will avoid exposing our learners to the likelihood of harm or injury.
    We will not seek to advance ourselves, our organisations or others, personally, politically or professionally, at the expense of our learners.

6. **Transparency**

   Engagement with the adult learner or community, and the resulting relationship, will be open and truthful. Potential conflicts of interest will be openly declared.

7. **Confidentiality**

   Information provided by learners will not be used against them, nor will it be shared with others who may use it against them. Learners should be made aware of the limits to confidentiality. Until this happens, the presumption of confidentiality should apply.

8. **Cooperation**

   We will actively seek to cooperate with others in order to secure the best possible outcomes for our learners.

Section 4: professional regard

9. **Professional development**

   We will work reflectively, identifying and using the information, resources, skills, knowledge and practices needed to improve our capacity to meet our obligations to learners.

10. **Self-awareness**

    We should be conscious of our own values and interests, and approach cultural and other difference respectfully. While the need to challenge may arise, we must try first to understand.

11. **Boundaries**

    The HRD relationship is a professional relationship, intentionally limited to protect the learner and the purpose of our work. These limits should be clarified, established and maintained. The relationship with an individual learner is based on trust and is not available for unprofessional engagement.

12. **Self-care**

    HRD practice should be consistent with preserving the health of HRD workers.

Case: AROCo, Developing Woman Leaders

Read the following case and answer the question; would you suggest that organising and providing a single-sex leadership training course for women would be the best way of helping more women to achieve advancement into senior management positions in this case?

Company Background

AROCo repairs and overhauls aero engines for the commercial and military markets. At one of their plants they have 1,100 employees. Most of these employees, predominantly male, are working on the engine repairs, with around 270 professional and technical support staff. Of these professional and technical staff 63 are female, some 23 per cent. All of these women work full-time at the factory. The majority of them are aged between 26 and 35. Many were recruited into AROCo directly from school, with a minority recruited from university or from another AROCo plant or outside companies. Most of them were recruited as trainees in professional areas, with around a third being initially recruited in secretarial or administration roles. A few had been employed as professional entrants or as managers but since been re-deployed. The lack of women in senior management roles in the company was perceived to be a weakness. The company decided to research the attitudes of their existing female workforce to explore potential points of action to change this. They had been proud that many of these women had been recruited as trainees and progressed into a professional role during their time at AROCo. Within the next ten years, the great majority of the women would like to move up in the organisation. They also found that, while these women did not perceive any barriers to career progress, only two of them saw themselves as having the potential to reach senior management positions.

None of the women believed that age or length of service would prevent someone moving on at AROCo, with only a few believing gender was a problem. Many women did feel that AROCo did not do enough to develop its employees. The main reasons they cited for lack of progression were line managers' negative opinions, a lack of opportunities at AROCo and a person's home life. Despite these factors nearly half the women said that they personally felt no barriers to progression. However a majority did feel that restriction on their geographical mobility and pressures in their home life did affect them, and stop them from aspiring to further their career development.

The majority of these women did not believe that women as a group required special attention regarding their development as potential senior managers. They saw themselves as being equal with men and feared that special attention would in fact mark them out as inferior in men's eyes. Those few who felt that women should receive more help thought that women needed to be brought on a par with men to get around the 'Old Boys Club' networks at AROCo. Some people made comments which suggested that there was a culture of 'favouritism' at AROCo; that is, that those who get on with current management best are the ones who progress, not those with the greatest talent. This it was felt often meant men in senior management favouring other men.

There were substantial existing HRD provisions in the company. Formal further education was available at AROCo, with many of women participating in this at one time or another to obtain qualifications. General internal training courses existed, and most of the women participated in these courses. Appraisal also existed, with the majority of women taking part in this process. Many of them regarded mentoring as an important and available source of development, but only a few had actually had a mentor at any point in their career. Prime responsibility for managing development was felt by some to lie with themselves, for others with the line manager; with some seeing it to a joint responsibilities with management.

3 Key Texts

(1) Cervero, R. and Wilson, M. (2001) *Power in Practice: Adult Education and the Struggle for Knowledge and Power in Society* (San Francisco, Jossey Bass).

(2) Hatcher, T. (2002) *Ethics and HRD: A New Approach to Leading Responsible Organizations* (New York, Basic Books) 1st edition.

(3) Kirkton, G. and Greene, A. M. (2000) *The Dynamics of Managing Diversity: A Critical Approach* (Oxford, Butterworth-Heinemann).

3 Key Articles

(1) Bates, R. and Chen, H. (2005) 'Value Priorities of Human Resource Development Professionals', *Human Resource Development Quarterly*, 16 (3), pp. 345–368.

(2) Fisher, C. (2005) 'HRD Attitudes: Or the Roles and Ethical Stances of Human Resource Developers', *Human Resource Development International*, 8 (2), pp. 239–255.

(3) Mavin, S. and Girling, G. (2000) 'What is Managing Diversity and Why Does It Matter?', *Human Resource Development International*, 3 (4), pp. 419–433.

3 Key Web Links

(1) AHRD (2012) Guidelines on Ethics: http://www.ahrd.org/displaycommon.cfm?an=1&subarticlenbr=17.

(2) Ethical issues and human resource development; Simon Longstaff: http://www.ethics.org.au/ethics-articles/ethical-issues-and-human-resource-development.

(3) Guide to issues in business ethics: http://managementhelp.org/ethics/ethxgde.htm.

PART II

Process, Concepts and Methods

This part of the text looks at organising learning at work how HRD fits with the social and technological contingencies that exist in particular organisations; and how they deal with issues of control, competition, creativity and collaboration in work and employment. There is a common process being managed. In this part there are chapters on the key concepts and methods that are used in HRD to understand and fulfil that common process. These include identifying learning needs, designing, delivering and quality managing learning HRD activities. Other key concepts in practice are talent management, development partnerships, ways to categorise individual differences and the challenges of learning relationships, and the use of technologies in HRD.

5

Identifying Needs

Learning Objectives

By the end of this chapter you will be able to:

- Describe the first part of the HRD process, observing, researching and assessing needs;
- Identify causes and effects of gaps in learning and development;
- Describe and analyse three levels of need: personal, work and organisational;
- Describe and observe three types of need: know what, know how and know why;
- Use skills and techniques to identify HRD needs.

Introduction

The first part of the Human Resource Development (HRD) process is to observe and research; to identify and assess HRD needs. What is to be observed and researched? Who is doing the observation and research? What methods are there to help correctly identify needs? Three levels of need analysis are common: (1) personal needs, (2) work needs and (3) organisational needs. Skills in obtaining evidence and relating this to the performance challenges in an organisation by identifying the know-what, know-how and know-why issues for individuals, jobs and organisations.

Exercise 5.1:

List five signs of poor performance you can think of which might indicate there was a need for HRD.

Identifying Needs

One ideal might be to have a 'needs scanner', a tool with which it was possible to scan people as they joined an organisation. Like a luggage scanner at airport security, or an MRI scanner for the body and brain, this would get beneath the surface and show us what lay inside. In the case of HRD, a person's knowledge, skills and capabilities to the standards they currently existed. Such a scanner might also show the extent to which the person had the capacity to develop more knowledge, skill and capability. It would, while the wish list is being drawn up, also help if it could reveal aspects of the person's personality and learning styles, and their working styles too.

In fact all we have is the technological equivalent of a barcode scanner at a supermarket checkout; where the 'barcode' of basic information we have is made up of information about the person's qualifications and history of work experience. A quick scan of this to check the facts is about all that can be done as people enter the organisation. That's what HR recruitment staff do – scan the barcode. And like other barcodes it tells the price, not the quality.

In the absence of a new technology to scan people for the information of interest the options are to use 'old technologies' to collect data and information and to help inform HRD; essentially using forms of social science and professional skills. The first question is usually: is a performance gap worth closing? (see Practice 5.1). HRD needs to emerge most typically from forms of performance review and the broad performance management context for the observation of HRD needs in the workplace. There are a range of possible causes of performance gaps, and interventions to deal with these. Some of these are not attributable to deficits in knowledge, skill and attitudes, or are not to be resolved solely through the HRD process. This requires consideration of context and an estimation, or calculation, of costs and benefits. For a performance problem that is mission critical, where the benefits of closing the gap are evident and greater than the costs, there is a clear case to proceed with more detailed research and needs analysis. Equally, where the performance problem is an apparently minor concern for which a 'quick fix' is available, and which might take a lot of resource and time to deal with through training, there is no case for further research into HRD needs. The difficult and challenging cases and situations are those which are less black and white, and where some research and investigation of HRD issues and options is worthwhile.

Practice 5.1: Are Performance Gaps Worth Closing?

Identifying performance gaps does not necessarily mean that actions, HRD related or otherwise, have to be taken. A way of structuring the observation of any gap that exists to consider whether, and what, action is needed involves the following stepwise analysis:

1. **Define** specifically whose performance is at issue: which person, or which group?

2. What is the actual performance **discrepancy**? Describe the actual and the desired performance.

3. **Estimate the cost** in some way so that a solution can be found that costs less than the consequences of living with the problem. Is the problem worth solving? Is it a big enough problem to bother about? How much does the problem cost? What happens if you ignore the problem?

4. Options to choose from other than full HRD include:

   a. Is it possible to apply a **fast fix**? If a light goes out we try changing the bulb first rather than calling out an electrician.

   b. Do the people involved **already know how** to perform effectively? Could they perform in the past? Are the tasks performed often? Perhaps better feedback is needed, or some refresher practice or job aids.

   c. Are expectations clear, and are resources adequate? Is performance quality visible, and is **feedback** on performance being given?

   d. Consider **task changes** as solutions: simplify the task, remove obstacles to performance.

   e. Are the '**consequences**' properly balanced? Or are people in some way rewarded for doing things wrong? List all the negative and positive 'consequences' of poor performance that are evident, from the point of view of the people involved.

5. Does the poor performers have the **potential** to change?

6. If it seems after all this that the performance gap is worth closing, and HRD is appropriate, then describe the **training solutions** and calculate the costs. Select the most practical and cost-effective HRD solution and implement it.

Source: Mager (2000).

If the answer is affirmative, then an HRD needs has been identified. This emergence of needs from performance gaps is one source of identifying needs. The other major source is the clear and coherent outline of expectations and roles which organisations develop. Expectations and roles may be simple or complex, and can be challenging to specify precisely and completely. There are methods of generating job descriptions and competence profiles for roles which provide a starting point and benchmark for HRD.

The forms in which organisations develop and use methods are themselves influenced by ways of seeing and thinking about organisational roles and work. The ways that organisational roles and work are perceived may take different forms; previously the extent to which control, competition, creative and collaborative expectations and roles have been described. There are other perspectives available too. Perspective 5.1 sets out some different ways of seeing and thinking about roles and work in an organisation. These perspectives reflect and embody various ways of perceiving of organisation which can influence how needs for HRD are understood and enacted.

Perspective 5.1: Different Lenses for Thinking about Performance Management

Identifying a core value proposition for the business. This involves determining the value streams in a business; the extent to which the business model is, for example, brand or cost driven. Determining this provides an underlying context for success, and what managers need to work on for success; making the brand perform or controlling and reducing costs are not mutually exclusive, but the concerns they highlight about managing performance can be distinctive. (See Finkelstein et al. 2006).

Identifying key performance indicators (KPI). This involves setting specific, measurable, attainable, time-bounded objectives for a range of activities in the organisation. This is the model of performance management that many people have, and which many organisations adopt. It is associated with conventional top-down strategic management in the private sector, and with value-for-money initiatives in the public sector.

Kaizen, TQM. This involves developing, planning and monitoring systems to achieve continuous improvement. It is most associated with the lessons of successful manufacturers, with origins in Japanese companies.

Becoming 'excellent' or 'world class'. Adopting, or establishing, the standards of the best in order to compete. This is associated with, for example the work of Peters and Waterman (1990) on 'excellence' and, in the contemporary context, with standards such as the European Quality Management Foundation (EQMF).

High-commitment organisations. This involves ensuring that the workforce is fully and enthusiastically engaged in achieving the tasks of the organisation. It is associated with trends in organisations to develop organisational cultures that embody this concern, often focused on customer service.

Business process re-engineering. This involves reviewing organisational structures to achieve tasks faster with fewer resources. It is associated with the 'flattening' of hierarchies, 'downsizing' of workforces, and 'outsourcing' of activities.

Developing balanced scorecards. This involves identifying measures across a broad range of areas to monitor and evaluate. It is associated with the work of Kaplan and Norton (1996). They identify four areas that need to be balanced: translating the vision, feedback and learning, business planning, and communicating and linking.

Learning organisation. This involves keeping abreast or ahead of the competition by ensuring there is an effective collective learning process that facilitates change and innovation. It is associated with the work of Senge (1990) in the USA and the ideas of Pedler et al. (1994) in the United Kingdom.

> **Organisation development.** This involves using behavioural sciences to diagnose and solve organisational problems. It is most associated with the 'academic' literature on management and organisations (e.g. Robbins, 1993) and the use of 'action research' projects, where researchers and managers work together.

These perspectives will influence the extent to which HRD needs are observed and assessed: that is, they define the type and shape of the issues that will be identified and encountered. By using these approaches, explicitly or implicitly, organisations will be able to observe and identify certain kinds of gap between their desired performance and their actual performance. This is about observing patterns in organisational roles and work offer different ways of defining and translating the basic goals of the organisation into different levels of responsibility, including unit, team and individual performance tasks and challenges. Different perspectives also offer different ways of thinking about the process of planning goals, setting objectives, and agreeing measurable standards or outcomes in organisations.

Exercise 5.2:

Why might the needs analysis phase be skipped?

If there are HRD issues underlying and causing performance problems, observation and assessment of need is then appropriate. This will involve exploring the interplay of organisational, work and individual factors. Each of these calls for a careful and considered observation of situations and circumstances and what a best practice process might be (see Perspectives 5.2 and 5.3).

Perspective 5.2: HRD Process Modelling

Gratton and Ghosal (2006, p. 6) have taken this further, and suggested an important distinction that can be of use here, the distinction between 'best practice' processes and 'signature' processes.

'The search for, and adoption of, best practice processes is a crucial component in the creation of a high performance company .... The more effective these processes are the more likely the company is to enjoy a competitive advantage .... What our research into high-performing companies shows, however, is that the adoption of best practice processes only gets you a seat at the table; it is not enough to assure you of winning the game ... for sustained competitive success, however, something extra is required. We have discovered that other types of

---

Perspective 5.2: (Continued)

---

processes, which we call signature processes are crucial. Signature processes are different from best practice processes. They are processes that evolve internally from executives' values and aspirations, while best practice refers to ideas developed outside the boundaries of the business unit or company'.

Perspective 5.3: Best Practice and Signature Process Modelling Compared

---

Best practice modelling	Signature processes modelling
Origin Starts with external and internal practice processes	Evolves from a company search for best specific history
Development 'Bringing the outside in'	'Bringing the inside out'
Needs careful adaptation and alignment to the business goal and industry context	Needs championing by executives
Core Shared knowledge from across the sector	Organisation values

Source: Gratton, L. and Goshal, S. (2006).

Objective and Subjective Factors

Objective observations of needs centre on defining levels of expected performance and performance gaps in tangible and quantifiable ways. They may be based on financial results, productivity or product/service quality levels. Productivity is the average output produced by inputs, a combination of human and capital resources. We can describe it in economic terms – for example, in manufacturing measuring the number of goods produced per hour – or in terms of customer satisfaction (see Figure 5.1).

Countries can also be compared in these terms. As with organisations, differences in productivity may reflect HRD issues in human capital productivity, a lack of investment in HRD or structural differences such as having more part-time and temporary staff. An absence and lack of HRD can be seen as a principal barrier to increased productivity.

When defining and measuring objective, empirically measurable, productivity criteria some generic challenges with obtaining accurate information at reasonable costs are encountered. There are also challenges specific to industry sectors, where productivity may be less dependent on internal organisational factors and more on external factors. Even where such contextual challenges are overcome the use of objective data on its own is often of limited use in HRD needs analysis. It is usually only meaningful when compared with some internal or external benchmark standard, and/or with trends over time. It is this

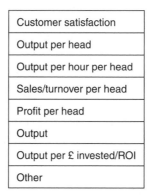

Figure 5.1 Productivity measures

comparative aspect, rather than stand-alone, isolated, observations, that generates effective assessments of HRD need. To take a basic example, the level of sales a sales person achieves will not indicate whether there are performance issues; it is only when we compare that person's sales with those of other people in the same organisation, or in similar companies, that we may see whether a difference exists which warrants being called a performance gap.

The objective challenge, then, is to establish norms for performance. Measures of central tendency, such as arithmetic means and deviations from these, provide the control limits and standards of acceptable performance. If an organisation's performance as a whole lies outside these standard thresholds, then its continuing viability will be in doubt. If a retailer is failing to make as much sales revenue per person employed or per area of retail space as its competitors, or perhaps as other similar stores in the same group, then this is usually a signal that something significant needs attention. Trend analysis in performance is more helpful: tracking trends over time can be one of the most useful sources of information about gaps in performance.

However, what is objectively measurable isn't necessarily all that is important or meaningful in assessing needs. The attempt to become more forensic in identifying needs can even interfere with effective observation of HRD needs. This is because only tracking tangible and easily measured aspects of performance may mean neglecting more intangible and qualitative aspects of performance. A manager, for example, may have a sales team that meets and exceeds all their sales targets; yet that manager may be creating an environment in which morale is low, staff are experiencing severe stress, and are likely to either leave the organisation or become ill.

Qualitative and subjective observations may also be appropriate, and may indeed be more useful. Qualitative and subjective observations about people, work and organisational performance are usually captured as attitudes and feelings. These may be collected from customers, managers or other team members to identify where performance issues arise. For example, managers may form perceptions in the course of their work, through conducting staff surveys or by getting feedback on individuals from a range of sources in the course of performance appraisal. Perceptions may also be derived from focus group discussions among managers, staff and customers on important performance themes and issues. These perceptions may be cross-checked through surveys of customers or other stakeholders.

Subjective perceptions of need usually remain private and confidential, inside the organisation, or inside the unit or team. This is in contrast to the often publicly available objective observations and measures on productivity. One of the issues with using and including subjective perceptions and measures of need is their reliability. Norms for subjective perceptions can be established, and many employee surveys now in common use seek to do that. Trends showing variation over time are more valuable than snapshots for revealing issues for which HRD might be useful.

A combination of objective and subjective approaches to assessing HRD need will reflect organisational cultures and priorities. Variation occurs in terms of sectors: for example, for-profit organisations often observe and measure clear financial measures whereas not-for-profit organisations may be more 'values-based', for example valuing being compassionate and caring, and concerned to see and track HRD needs relevant to achieving that. Variations in perception, observation and measurement will also exist according to the different business strategies followed by organisations; depending on the relative importance of, for example, innovation, quality or cost-leadership strategies. The underlying challenge is to identify, observe and measure the key strategic drivers of performance before investing in any HRD. Without specifying relevant and specific performance improvement outcomes – no matter how much is to be spent on HRD or how professional HRD delivery may be – the prospects for sustained impact from HRD activity will be poor.

Observing and assessing HRD needs is the first phase in providing the learning opportunities required to achieve the goals, standards and objectives of the organisation. These can be articulated through organisational, team and individual levels of analysis.

Organisational Needs

In discussing and analysing overall organisational effectiveness, senior directors, managers and others naturally consider the extent to which HRD needs may exist. In dealing with the identification of HRD needs at the organisational level, it is again to be stressed that this is a particular example of a general activity; research to inform problem-solving and decision-making. The methods and techniques of data collection and analysis are not unique to the identification of HRD need.

One kind of organisational need is that of the whole organisation, which we can define as needs that are common to all members of the organisation.

Everyone, from the top to the bottom and across all departments/units, may need learning and change of a particular kind. This might include induction or basic health and safety training. Other common examples are learning about new information systems or new product introductions. If organisational restructuring is proposed, in the course of which jobs and job specifications will change, the cognitive capacities and capabilities required will also have to change. Or, as often applies in restructuring exercises, culture changes are also sought, and these may necessitate major behavioural and attitudinal changes among all employees to align with the desired new culture.

Often, in this regard, organisations have completed their own internal mapping of values and competence. These are outlines of the key qualities and behaviours associated with effective performance in the workforce as a whole. They can be used for many purposes, from compiling selection profiles to development planning and reward. Second, organisational HRD needs may be defined in terms of a performance gap that is seen to affect the organisation as a whole, not just a part of it. With this kind of organisational need assessment, gaps between desired performance and actual performance can come in many shapes and sizes. In the pursuit of effective performance – which may be defined as either doing things well, doing them better or doing them differently – learning and change may become a central strategic issue, and of major concern to the organisation's senior management team. Much information may already be available within the organisation, in the form of plans and data sources about the goals and customer satisfaction, limiting the need for special and original observation and research in assessing HRD needs.

In undertaking a needs analysis it should be the business needs that provide the rationale for what is to be done, not what a training manager or anybody else with a professional view thinks might be useful. Many stress this point, because otherwise there is a risk that trainers and training managers may drift into providing 'more of what has been done already', maintaining a catalogue of courses as a ready-made solution to performance problems. Such familiar and easy-to-manage catalogues or menus of courses may even be popular with managers and staff, but they can be out of touch if they are not founded on proper needs analysis and a general analysis of the environmental factors that impinge on the organisation and its development. Existing sources of information and other HR systems that may be relevant to learning and change needs analysis are set out. These include

(1) Human resource plans: data on future demands for staff to ensure that there is a supply of the right kinds of people, whether that means maintaining a steady state, expanding or rationalising. From these, we can derive some perceptions of the extent and kind of HRD needs – for example the replacement rates of certain kinds of role.

(2) Succession planning data: identifying concerns with employee flows related to promotions, retirements and leavers.

(3) Reviews of critical incidents: organisations often experience and analyse unforeseen events that turn out to be of great importance. By reviewing such 'accidents', good or bad, and discrepancies, they develop a database for learning.

(4) Management information systems: data from various sources are collated and can be integrated to support analysis for decision-making. In manufacturing, for example, enterprise resource planning systems provide managers with data on real-time performance.

(5) Individual performance appraisal systems and records: performance reviews based on attainment of targets offer a potentially rich source of information about HRD needs. However, it is possible to have the trappings of a performance management system, particularly an individual appraisal system, without the data fromthat being collated and processed for the management of HRD.

If existing sources of information are not available, then identification of HRD needs may be the prompt to establish more complete sources of information, which others may use in their own contexts. If, for example, there are performance problems that catalyse HRD needs analysis, but there are no current measures of productivity with which to gauge the impact of any HRD, then such measures will need to be developed. Thus, analysing HRD needs may have important implications for motivating and driving performance management in general.

Work and Occupation Analysis

HRD needs can also be observed at the level of areas of work and occupation. In this respect there is an abundance of frameworks to choose from. Government, other agencies and companies often conduct exercises to map and specify the skills and knowledge needs of an area of work or an occupation. Professional associations and bodies do the same for almost every area of work, from general management to customer service. The resulting comprehensive maps, often defined as 'competence' frameworks, are needed to inform the design of vocational courses and qualifications for those who aspire to work in that area or occupation. They specify what is needed to be able to perform to the standards expected in employment. These general maps may not exactly match the behaviours that any specific organisation needs or expects from people in those roles. Nonetheless, someone who holds a qualification in a particular area may have demonstrated sufficient competence for an organisation to infer equivalent competence in its specific sphere of concern.

Where more general HRM plans and systems do exist in an organisation, it is usually because some kind of job analysis has been undertaken. These may range from simple job specifications to more highly structured job grading systems. Job specifications typically identify roles, key tasks, competences and performance standards. Job and task analysis will have been used to create these specifications, and HRD needs can be logically and directly derived from them. It makes economic sense to use such existing reference points, based on traditional forms of scientific job and task analysis of existing data about jobs and competences. However, there are concerns with these, and one major problem with depending on these kinds of job specification and analysis is that they produce an inflexible notion of needs related to discrete job families. This model often seems outmoded and inappropriate alongside contemporary views of changing organisational structures and cultures that emphasise flexibility, innovation, project and team-working.

At a national level, specifications for occupational categories can be highly detailed and very well defined, and integrated into many development systems and activities, such as career guidance and advice. These occupational categories can be used to characterise overall supply and demand in the labour market and associated systems such as further and higher education. Accordingly, various institutions have an interest in defining and managing the HRD needed to provide the year-by-year replacements in occupations, depending on expansion or contraction in the particular area of work in the short and long term. On the basis of such forecasts governments provide funding for HRD in educational institutions, and organisations provide their own HRD for those pursuing careers in occupations they depend on.

Job Analysis

Within organisations, job, task and occupational analyses are required to support HRM systems in many areas of practice, ranging from templates for recruitment processes to performance appraisal systems and rewards. Some suggest that, even where job specifications already exist, a distinct HRD needs analysis may raise issues about the validity and reliability of these specifications. This is because it can be dangerous to assume that existing models of work and occupation can be directly adopted for the purpose of HRD needs analysis. Examining existing job specifications for their robustness in the HRD context means understanding something of methods of job analysis. Job analysis is, in essence, any systematic procedure used for obtaining detailed information about a job. The methods may vary, but they should all produce the following outcomes:

- Specifications that have 'face validity' – that is, they are acceptable to current job-holders and their managers;
- Clear role definitions specifying the purposes and main functions of the job;
- Specification of key tasks – describing the main parts of the job;
- Specification of competences – what people need to know and be able to do to perform the tasks;
- Specification of performance standards – what will be measured and reviewed.

These outcomes can help to identify what HRD will be relevant, and where HRD efforts might need to be focused. They can also be used to help structure the planning of HRD, by suggesting areas where specific aims, goals and objectives for HRD activities will be needed. Sometimes, though, a performance gap seen to be associated with the way a task or occupation is managed is not relevant for HRD needs analysis at all.

A framework for analysis is needed where jobs or tasks must be reviewed in order to identify HRD needs. For instance, examples of job outputs could be 'to take orders over the phone', 'to assemble a piece of furniture' or 'to write marketing reports'. Duties related to these kinds of output can be described using job analysis. These descriptions may vary from the general to the highly specific. In the examples cited above, the resulting titles might be 'call centre operator', 'furniture maker' or 'marketing manager'.

Boundaries are the limits to the job, delineating where responsibilities end. These are the interfaces with other jobs and roles in the organisation at which job-holders must interact to achieve overall outputs. For example, call centre operators will not manage budgets, furniture makers will not sell chairs and marketing managers will not design the products. These tasks will all be part of other jobs.

Behaviours are defined in this context as the observable actions involved in performance, whereas competences are defined as the capabilities underlying effective performance. When describing jobs, we usually use a mixture of behavioural and competence statements, though some jobs emphasise one rather than the other. For example, furniture-making will focus on behaviours, whereas management and professional roles are more often described in terms of competence, because they involve the application of capacities that are not directly observable. A good example would be a medical doctor: he or she cannot guarantee to produce the outcome of a 'successful' operation or course of treatment – that is, a healthy or 'live' patient. What doctors can, and should, guarantee is that, in dealing with patients, they follow the procedures laid out for such operations or courses of treatment in a competent fashion.

Personal-level HRD Needs

HRD needs assessment would be a blunt and ineffective instrument if it were confined to a generic analysis of organisational or occupational needs. Not everyone whose work includes the same or similar tasks, whether new or existing staff, will have the same kinds or degrees of learning and change need. A 'one-size-fits-all' approach, which is a consequence of analysing only at the organisational or occupational level, is pejoratively known as sheep-dip training. Everyone is processed through the same things, regardless of their individual needs. Yet the workforce is not a flock of cloned sheep with the same profiles and same needs.

Perceiving and assessing HRD needs correctly and accurately at an individual level is also critical. Where an individual person has a personal need for learning, the HRD provided is usually a success. Where there is little or no personal need, the HRD, no matter how well designed and delivered, is going to be a waste of time and resources. To reduce waste and concentrate resources on using HRD to improve the performance of the organisation and the individual, the personal-level needs must be accurately identified and worked with. One way to identify individual needs is to compare individuals with standards. If clear organisational, task or occupation descriptions and standards are defined, then individuals can be assessed against them. Some individuals may need more development in some aspects of the task need than in others; obvious occasions being induction and following any major change.

Personal needs can also be identified at various critical gateway points. The first gateway is the exploration of applicants' experience and qualifications during the selection process. The second gateway will be some form of performance appraisal during employment. There is a wide variety of performance appraisal methods, but their common purpose is to identify how far individuals meet expected and desired performance standards. A third gateway might be the use of assessment centres to identify HRD needs, whether for selection, placement, appraisal or career development during employment. A fourth gateway might be the management of career development, up the promotion ladder and across posts and tasks.

As with the organisational identification of HRD needs in a performance management context, some sources and responses to individual performance concerns do not lead into 'training' as the sole or primary HRD response (see Practice 5.2). These are performance issues attributable to other factors. The aim is to analyse HRD needs that connect systematically with personal performance issues over at least an annual cycle, rather than reacting 'as and when' personal issues arise. In the past this depended upon line managers being concerned with HRD provisions as they discussed and planned the work of their staff. Increasingly, employees are being expected to take more responsibility for identifying their own HRD needs through some kind of personal development planning process.

Practice 5.2: Personal Performance Issues and Responses

Reasons why people do not perform	Responses
They've forgotten how to do it	Job aids to remind people how to do what they already know how to do; for example, checklists
They don't know what is expected	Information: clarify what is expected in the job
They do not have the authority, tools, time or space	Give permission to perform, providing not just responsibility for results but also authority to achieve these

Practice 5.2: (Continued)

They don't get feedback	Give feedback – people need specific feedback on how they are doing to help them attain what is desired and expected
Documentation is poorly designed, inaccessible	Improve documentation; manuals and materials to help or non-existent people do their jobs
Work station is badly designed	Change the workplace from being 'just assembled' to being carefully designed for optimum performance
Punished or ignored for doing it right Rewarded for doing it wrong nobody notices if they do it right or wrong	Ensure no 'upside down' consequences; provide rewards for desired performance and punishments for failing to perform. The individuals concerned can see these 'consequences' as upside down if doing it right gets the person 'punished' (embarrassment, ridicule, more work, frustration, boredom) and failing to do it right brings rewards (peer approbation, less work, easier life).
Organisation makes desired performance difficult or impossible	Change organisational structure; to deal with boundaries which are producing 'turf wars' or confusion

Three Dimensions of Learning and Change Need

It is widely agreed that effective performance in work roles requires the development and combination of a number of constituent factors; one long-held view defines the tripartite dimensions of Knowledge, Skills and Attitudes (KSA) as the constituent factors. Kraiger et al. (1993) also recognised three domains, but they defined them as follows:

(1) Cognitive learning – needed for activities to enhance the acquisition and application of knowledge;

(2) Skills-based learning – the ability to execute a sequence of behaviours smoothly;

(3) Affective learning – changes in attitude and motivation.

Kraiger et al. (1993) further recognised that needs in the cognitive domain could have three forms:

(1) Verbal learning, in the form of declarative knowledge (know-what);

(2) Procedural knowledge (know-how);

(3) Tacit knowledge organisation (personal knowledge).

HRD needs, then, can be articulated as 'know what', 'know how' and 'know why'. Defining these factors will shape how HRD needs are defined for a person, role or organisation. There is a common-sense understanding of what knowledge, skills and attitudes mean, which is relatively easy to apply in practice. However, there are also some significant debates on how each of these ought to be defined and operationalised. For example, the concept of 'competence' as a unifying concept for all these dimensions of HRD need has been proposed and used widely (Winterton 2009), instead of tripartite frameworks like KSA. Competence maps tend to cluster HRD needs together around focal behaviours, with a relegation of concerns about 'know what' and an emphasis on 'know how'. Yet, despite the widespread uptake of competence frameworks in organisations, a concern with differentiating different dimensions of HRD need persists. Here the three dimensions will be defined in terms following on from Kraiger's:

(1) Cognitive capacity HRD needs: acquisition and application of knowledge and wisdom;

(2) Skills-based capability HRD needs: the practical abilities involved in work roles;

(3) Affective learning HRD needs: conceptualised in terms of attitude, motivation, values or 'emotional intelligence' (EI) and emotional labour.

These three dimensions of learning and change are present in all kinds of work and organisation, across all kinds of occupation and across all kinds of performance problems that employees may encounter. They are present in the performance of low-skill roles in simple, small organisations and in the performance of employees in the more complex roles in technologically sophisticated, large, multinational firms. More on these will be discussed in later chapters; at this point, a brief exposition of these dimensions and issues in HRD needs analysis is appropriate.

Cognitive Capacity HRD Needs

For Kraiger et al. (1993) cognitive learning has three forms:

(1) Verbal learning, in the form of declarative knowledge (know-what);

(2) Procedural knowledge (know-how);

(3) Tacit knowledge organisation (personal knowledge).

Examining and researching HRD need at this level, then, is to identify what elements of 'know-what', 'know-how' and personal knowledge are significant in a role and for a person to succeed in that role. Effective performance depends upon the presence, development and use of cognitive capacity. A level of intelligence, a kind of intelligence, a degree of knowledge and understanding.

How cognitive capacity is conceived, how intelligence, knowledge and understanding are believed to work, is still subject to debate and theorising. Different theories about the way the brain functions, and knowledge is constructed, lead to different positions on what learning and change entails. There are some highly complex and fascinating technical and philosophical issues involved in understanding this. In a text like this simplification is required (see Perspective 5.4). Models aim to present a simplified version of a complex reality so as to enable purposeful interaction with that complex reality. This is true of models of the brain and cognitive capacity. The issues revolve around debates about how forms and aspects of intelligence are to be operationalised and measured needed in work roles. Some work roles may require specific or specialist forms of intelligence or complex thinking skill because the work is complex and requires the independent use of thinking and judgement in a context of substantial responsibility, where there may be little routine work, and where the person doing the work has to act autonomously. Other work roles may require very little specialist intelligence or thinking skill; all that is needed to perform these roles is an awareness and memorisation of only the most basic of instructions. Such work roles may be fully scripted, with no requirement to do anything other than repeat a series of set behaviours or acts of communication.

Perspective 5.4: Three Models of the Brain

In exploring the change from humans being hunter-gatherers to producing the sudden burst of art, technology and religion that occurred around 30,000 years ago the archaeological record shows an increase in brain size. But the change was not just about the brain getting bigger, being a better 'sponge'. The brain model that assumes the brain is like a sponge (**Model 1**), ready to soak up information implies that the bigger the sponge the more intelligent – and some sponges are better than others. But minds can compare and combine; sponges cannot compare and combine. It was a change in architecture as well.

Model 2   The brain is like a computer; it takes data, runs programmes and provides outputs. The same 'programme' is running all the time; this is a general-purpose learning programme. Different minds are like different specifications of computer, with varying speeds, capacities and software.

Model 3   The brain is like a Swiss army knife: it has a central system like the knife case) and several independent special tools (the knife blades) that can be used for various purposes. These 'tools' are present at birth, built into the brain and are 'opened out' for use if the course of experience requires them. For example, interpersonal abilities are stimulated through the building of alliances and friendships, developing; learning about the use of cunning and deception.

These three different models can be used to explain the development of the mind in historical terms, and as a process that is reprised in the development from child to adult:

- first the sponge, the general-purpose intelligence – the 'soaking up' phase of learning among children;
- then the 'computer', a core general intelligence in central control and using several modules during development into adulthood;
- finally the Swiss army knife – the emergence and use of 'specialised' tools in the right context by experienced mature adults.

Source: Mithen (1996). *The Prehistory of Mind* (London: Thames & Hudson).

Cognitive capacities are most commonly discussed in the context of HRD in terms of developing knowledge and understanding. They are what people gain by studying for a work role before they engage in it, and what they get from experience over time while in the role. Knowledge and understanding both precede performance, and evolve alongside it. As neurological study of the brain and continuing analysis of the nature of forms and aspects of intelligence and thinking advance the modelling of cognitive capacities, and how to enhance them, will continue to exercise and animate HRD both in theory and in practice.

Skills-based Capability and HRD Needs

To perform to the standards expected in employment, individuals and organisations require more than the right levels of knowledge and understanding; they require skills-based capability. Skills-based capabilities are the practical things, or competence, that people need to achieve the required performance. The concept of skill is still present, for example in skills surveys, skills councils, and discussing skills shortages and skill gaps, but the terminology is evolving. In an era of workforce development and lifelong learning, the identification of terms such as skills-based capability can accompany or supersede the discussion of skill alone. Skills are usually measured in terms of occupation or qualification, and perceived on a continuum from low to high skill. Both ways have the merit of being relatively straightforward to measure and readily understood. More recently there has been much greater emphasis on what are variously termed key, core and generic skills, including:

- Literacy and numeracy;
- General management skills;
- Communication and customer handling skills;
- Information handling skills;
- Team-working, etc.

These types of 'soft skill' are frequently emphasised when employers are asked about their skill needs. Thinking about how skills might be linked to productivity and performance also includes these more general and qualitative aspects of skill. Yet these terms are nowhere near as well-established as 'occupation' and 'qualification', either in terms of a consensus about what they mean or on how best to measure them.

Skills-based Capability is the practical performance of a work role. It is either inherent in the person and/or developed through practice. Capability may be considered at three levels, outlined in more detail in a later chapter:

- Underpinning capabilities – for example, literacy and honesty;
- Intermediate capabilities – for example, communication and motivation;
- Overarching capabilities – for example, team-working and customer orientation.

The concept of skill is most strongly embedded in economic theory. To be skilled is, first, to be able to do something basic to an adequate or good standard (see Perspective 5.5). A skill is then a discrete and simple building block of performance and productivity, which exists or is absent. However, skill is often also referred to as 'expertise' in tangible, physical and observable actions: being highly skilled is associated with being an expert in complex physical activities. A craftsman who wielded tools was skilled; a dancer who could complete complex steps was skilled. Nowadays, in economies dominated by knowledge- and service-based industries, much performance at work depends on less tangible 'skills' such as information-handling and interpersonal relations. To classify these as skills is legitimate for some uses but questionable for others. Skill is then a complex of many things associated with expertise and a comprehensive and authoritative level of ability. This multiple sense of 'skill' can lead to confusion; for example, is a skills shortage a shortage of the simple building blocks of performance or a shortage of expertise?

Perspective 5.5: Key Terms in Use: Economics and Psychology

To be skilled is first to be able to do something basic, to an adequate or good standard. A skill is then a discrete and simple building block of performance, which exists or is absent. The concept of skill is one associated with quantification in economically oriented perspectives on behaviour; there can be degrees of skill, from the low to the high. Skill was often referred to as expertise in tangible, physical and observable actions: being highly skilled was associated with being an expert in complex physical activities. A craftsman who wielded tools was skilled; a dancer who could complete complex steps was skilled. Nowadays, in economies dominated by knowledge- and service-based industries, much performance at work depends on less tangible skills such as information-handling and interpersonal relations. To classify these as being skills is legitimate for some uses but questionable for others. But to be skilled can also mean to be an expert. Skill is then a complex of many things, associated with expertise and a comprehensive and authoritative level of ability. This dual sense of 'skill' can be misleading (is a skills shortage a shortage of simple building blocks, or a shortage of expertise?), when the real issue is often a lower level of concern.

The concept of competence, associated with more psychologically oriented perspectives on behaviour, became widely used as an alternative to skills, and many organisations have created sets of competence descriptions for their workforces. Competence in this sense was defined as comprising the key attributes desired and expected of superior performers. It involved setting out a list of core qualities and standards by which all staff in an organisation might be evaluated or appraised, equally and consistently. While many questions have been raised about the validity of the concept of competence it does offer finer detail for describing roles and people than the simpler quantifications of 'low' 'medium' or 'high' skill .

The concept of competence, imported from psychology, became widely used as an alternative to skills, and many organisations have created sets of competence descriptions for their workforces. Competence in this sense comprised the key attributes desired and expected of superior performers. It involved setting out a list of core qualities and standards by which all staff in an organisation might be evaluated or appraised, equally and consistently.

Affective Learning and Change Needs: The Third Dimension

Finally, as well as identifying and developing the cognitive capacity and skills-based capability required for performance, it has been emphasised that there is an important third determinant of performance where learning and change needs may exist. This has been defined and discussed in terms of attitudes, developing 'soft' social skills, and developing EI, and the 'emotional labour' involved in work and employment. Attitudes are settled ways of thinking and feeling about someone or something – positive and negative orientations about the world. Social skills are the 'soft' skills associated with effective interpersonal behaviour. EI refers to awareness and management of emotions in order to act effectively in relationships and social situations (Goleman 1995, McEnrue and Groves 2006)). Emotional labour refers to the 'management of feeling to create a publicly observable facial and bodily display . . . requiring one to induce or suppress feelings in order to produce proper states of mind in others' (Hochschild 1983, p. 7).

What these different constructs have in common is a shared concern with recognising and making transparent the affective influences on behaviour in social situations, in the HRD context, workplace behaviour. To get the desired form of behaviour in the context of work performance, it is necessary to develop the right kinds of attitudes, soft skills or EI, or manage certain aspects of emotional labour. This is because the ways people perform in work roles are determined not only by what they know (explicitly or tacitly) or what they can do (basically or expertly) but also by how they feel. So the way people actually perform can vary significantly, even if they have similar levels and types of cognitive capacity and capability.

Observing HRD Needs: Skills and Issues

The perception and assessment of HRD needs in the context of performance management constitute the first step in initiating HRD so that people can do things well, or do them better, or do new and better things. We can combine these categories of performance concern and levels of HRD into a matrix that maps all the areas where HRD needs may be assessed in order to ensure comprehensive and complete foundations for HRD in the organisation. Effective HRD needs analysis will be based on considering and managing all these aspects. As an activity it requires a range of generic capabilities:

- Process capabilities: setting goals, making plans, and reviewing and evaluating the progress of HRD needs assessment for an organisation, a group or an individual;
- Content capabilities: getting information, analysing it and making sense of it, using tools derived from research methods, such as interviews or surveys, to help collect and analyse objective data about performance;
- Relationship capabilities: maintaining relationships with people during the HRD needs assessment. They are both the skills of being empathetic with learners and managers and others, and the skills of being assertive, to confront and challenge people.

As line managers are increasingly being made responsible for establishing training needs within their company or organisation, their behaviours are important. This reflects a general trend in which line managers are assuming, if sometimes reluctantly, more responsibility across a range of people management and HRM issues. This trend has a number of implications.

First, the ability to assess HRD needs is not unique to HRD specialists: it is a particular application of generic skills, such as benchmarking, surveying the learning climate and relating HRD to strategic change and models of organisation development (OD).

Second, there is much more to observing and assessing HRD needs than merely using standard data collection techniques. The 'technical' aspects of research and data collection are only part of the process; the political and relationship aspects of assessing needs are equally important.

Third, HRD needs assessors often have to make optimal use of limited resources to consider a range of diverse and relevant HRD concerns. Few organisations have the luxury of 'over-investment' in HRD that meets all possible existing and future needs. Instead, most organisations have to struggle with 'under-investment', where resource constraints mean that identified needs are not always met. Nevertheless, it is essential that HRD needs are accurately identified.

Fourth, assessing needs can often be a sensitive issue for the organisation as a whole, for groups in it, and for individuals. These sensitivities arise because the identification of HRD needs always involves investigating gaps between expected performance and actual performance. Anxieties about being judged to be falling short of expected performance can interfere with and offset the forces pushing for gaps to be properly identified and dealt with.

Fifth, the time, effort and skills required to collect data and gather useful information from it are often not resourced properly. The problem is not usually that needs are not observed or assessed at all; it is more likely that there are shortcomings in identifying the gaps that do exist. So there may be good organisational-level analysis identifying strategic objectives and needs, but there may be inadequate operational-level analysis of expected versus actual performance, or assessment of individual needs in personal performance review. Errors can exist in the process of observing and assessing needs at all these levels, as with any observation-based research process. The consequences of errors can be over-training, under-training or meeting perceived needs rather than individuals' actual needs.

The solutions to these potential sources of error are self-evident. They include assessing HRD needs in a systematic way while remaining proactive; having written plans, but also being flexible; having central organisation, but also supporting local action in observing and assessing needs. In the area of occupations and jobs the concern is to keep up with changes, continuous development, standards and certification. In the individual domain the concern is to ensure that there are positive developmental relationships between employees, managers and others so that HRD needs can be analysed and explored openly.

Contemporary Debates

It is not possible to anticipate or observe all HRD needs from an abstract analysis of roles and organisation, no matter how skilled the analyst or how much time is devoted to collecting the right kinds of information. Dealing with and responding to emergent, performance generated needs is equally important. Systems for doing each of these continue to evolve, in the form of whole organisation systems such as 'lean manufacturing' and HRD specific concept such as competence. Alongside this abiding challenge of emergent needs there are other challenges for HRD, two of which are particularly relevant to performance management and the assessment of HRD needs.

First, there is the challenge of either adapting too or challenging a consensus on HRD needs analysis based on the assumption that training and skills should be made responsive to employers' needs for increased productivity and flexibility

(Rainbird 2000). Do the steps being taken to interpret those needs from this perspective have unwanted consequences that will cause tomorrow's problems? In other words, might the solution become the problem, as short-term needs capture investments at the expense of longer term visions? Arguably, it is the needs of tomorrow, which most employers may not be concerned with, or may say that they cannot be concerned with given the short-term pressures to satisfy capital markets, that matter most. So who is going to identify those longer term needs and provide the appropriate HRD to meet them?

Related to this, how far is there an empirical link between training, skills and competitiveness, to justify the focus on defining HRD needs in terms of the needs of current businesses? The emphasis on defining and meeting business needs for HRD through training and skill may be distorting investments in HRD; investing in activities that bolster existing businesses' short-term needs for profitability at the expense of longer term change and the future of the economy. HRD needs might be assessed quite differently if a longer timescale were adopted. For example, consider the marginalisation of employees' needs to operate in an era of lifelong learning as free agents. HRD needs may have to be defined in the context of responsiveness to employers' economic demands, but what about social concerns such as equity and equality? This interpretation of the subtext of relating HRD needs to performance management forms part of the critical approach to HRD that sees the workplace as an arena in which different interests, within a balance of power, are contested.

Second, there is a view that there is a wider context for the direction of HRD needs given the modernisation of work. This needs to be acknowledged and critically analysed, as it sets the agenda for arguments about the content and quality of HRD needs analysis and learning at work. The assessment of HRD needs sits in this wider context, not just within the performance management systems of individual organisations, but also within the wider direction of change in societies and economies. The analysis of HRD needs should not presume that the future will be like the past with, for example, forms of work practice requiring the analysis of jobs into discrete tasks producing profiles of distinctive jobs. Rather, the changing nature of work in a 'post-Taylorist' era, where employee autonomy rather than close control is the hallmark of many jobs, must be taken into account when considering what amounts to a real and important HRD need.

Conclusion

The identification and researching of HRD needs is the initial stage of the HRD process. The quality of what happens in this phase sets the foundation for all that follows; for better or worse. Done effectively, it can determine real needs, clearly and comprehensively, providing a focus for effective HRD. Done imperfectly, it may lead to frustration and waste which could affect individuals, or teams, or perhaps the whole organisation.

This phase of the process takes place within the broad context of performance management in the organisation. Done properly, HRD will be more likely to relate to real and significant performance concerns. If attention is paid to all three levels of needs assessment, then the subsequent phases of the HRD process are more likely to provide positive outcomes for investments in HRD: that is, to address real and important gaps between expected performance and actual performance. Success in the HRD process depends on the quality of analysis of what is involved in organisational performance, task performance and individual performance. It depends upon a coherent and integrated performance management system as a whole. To analyse organisations, tasks, jobs, occupations and professions we must be able to access or develop data sources, business plans or competence profiles of occupations, and/or individual performance reviews. We must also be aware of how changes in structure and culture, or the introduction of new technologies and processes, will change the learning needs of those in the role, both now and in the future.

The design and implementation of effective performance appraisal systems should include the fit with requirements for HRD needs assessment. Bottom-up assessments of need, from individuals in dialogues with their managers, have to be reconciled with top-down thinking about future needs, from the strategic analysis of HRD needs, in planning for optimum use of limited resources to satisfy both individual and organisational interests.

Case: HRD Needs

In a study of 61 hospitals, researchers found a strong association between HRD practices and patient mortality. Greater extent and sophistication of appraisal systems were closely related to lower mortality rates, and there were also links to the quality and sophistication of training and the number of staff trained to work in teams. The survey gathered data on four areas: hospital characteristics, hospital HRM strategy, employee involvement strategy, and HRM practices and procedures. Chief executives and HR directors completed the whole questionnaire, and other occupational groups answered on HRM practices and procedures. Ninety per cent of all these people had training needs assessed annually. Some staff in some hospitals received no appraisal, but more hospitals failed to provide training in conducting appraisals.

Measuring mortality rates was a difficult process: geographical and regional variations might influence these, reflecting factors such as socio-economic status. Hospitals in poor areas might not attract the high flyers. The final results showed that there was a relationship between HRM practices and mortality, with appraisal having the strongest correlation. Why should this be so? How can HRD needs analysis, as found in appraisal, improve the hospitals' performance? The researchers concluded that if an organisation has HRD policies that focus on effort and capability, develop people's capabilities, and encourage cooperation and innovation in teams among most, if not all, employees, then the whole system functions and performs better. Managing all staff well, not just medical and nursing staff, gets good performance.

The researcher's conclusion was that a significant improvement in appraisal, to attain the standards of the best, would be equivalent to 1,090 fewer deaths per 1,00,000 admissions. This does not invalidate the need to employ more and better medical staff, but it does emphasise how much all the staff in the working community affect performance.

Source: West, M. (2002)

Exercise 5.1:

List five signs of poor performance you can think of which might indicate there was a need for HRD.

Examples could be:

- Declining customer satisfaction;
- Low output per head;
- Failure of new products/services;
- Key staff leaving for other organisations;
- Change failing;
- Accidents at work.

These will reflect the issues of organisational concern (control, competition, creativity, collaboration) and underlying causes which can be traced and dealt with.

Exercise 5.2: Answer

- A lack of time and resources;
- Too quick to leap to deciding that training programme is needed;
- Inadequate knowledge of needs analysis;
- Absence of a voice for training in key discussions.

---

3 Key Texts

(1) Ford, D. (1999) *Bottom Line Training, Houston* (Texas, Gulf Publishing Co).
(2) Mager, R. (2000) *What Every Manager Should Know About Training* (Chalford, Management Books).

(3) Rainbird, H. (2000) *Training in the Workplace: Critical Perspectives on Learning at Work* (Basingstoke, Palgrave Macmillan).

3 Key Articles/Reports

(1) Winterton, J. (2009) 'Competence Across Europe: Highest Common Factor or Lowest Common Denominator?', *Journal of European Industrial Training*, 33 (8/9), pp. 681–700.

(2) Gratton, L. and Goshal, S (2006) *Signing up for Competitive Advantage: How Signature Processes Beta Best Practice* (London, EPSR/ESRC).

(3) Muller, N. and Roberts, V. (2010) 'Seven Cures to Skipping the Needs Assessment', *T+D Magazine*, 64 (3), pp. 32–34.

3 Key Web Links

(1) International Society for Performance Improvement: www.ispi.org.

(2) The Society for Organizational Learning: www.solonline.org.

(3) Some European data and analysis on skills and working life: http://www.eurofound.europa.eu/ewco/skills/index.htm.

6

Design for Adult Learning

Learning Objectives

By the end of this chapter you will be able to:

- Plan and design learning activities;
- Write aims, objectives and results;
- Select and use appropriate methods for developing knowledge, skills and attitudes;
- Produce solutions for the design challenges of four forms: the chain, cycle, spiral and Web
- Design learning to support, challenge, engage and stimulate learners.

Exercise 6.1:

What are the typical problems you may have experienced with training that might be attributed to ineffective design?

Introduction

Practice 6.1 shows the time devoted to design in order to deliver an hour of learning in different formats. The time spent on design is a significant part of the Human Resource Development (HRD) process, yet it is often neglected as a skill in itself. The purpose of the design phase in the HRD process is simple; to create experiences which support, challenge, engage and stimulate learners. The purpose is simple, but the artful realisation of it is more difficult. The emulation, or copying, of an existing effective design for learning is always a possible solution. As with any other professional activity though, there are many risks in simply copying what others have done, in an unthinking way. Skill in design, with some original planning and an understanding of the options available, is within the reach of all; there is no need to be a creative genius. Design challenges include of course being effective in developing and giving instruction or facilitation in a training room, but there is more than that. There are challenges in designing in four main forms: the chain, cycle, spiral and network.

Practice 6.1: Design Time Ratios for Estimating Costs		
Design element	**Content-type design**	**Time Ratio (hours of design to delivery)**
Participant manual	Familiar, non-technical	3:1
Participant manual	unfamiliar, technical	6:1
Leader's guide	Familiar, non technical	2:1
Leader's guide	Unfamiliar, technical	4:1
Visuals/overheads	Simple, text based	1:1
Visuals/overheads	Complex, graphic based	5:1
Videos	Simple, voice over, one location	50:1
Videos	Complex, live audio, many locations	150:1
CBT	Simple, text based	50:1
CBT	Complex, graphic based	300:1
Multimedia	Simple, graphic based	150:1
Multimedia	Complex, video based	500:1

Source: Ford (1999).

Planning and designing are generic activities, requiring skills and methods shared with other kinds of planning and design activity. The specific focus and concerns in learning and change planning and design, HRD design, include the following:

- Writing aims, objectives and targets for HRD;
- Understanding and using methods appropriate to learning and knowledge, skill and attitude change;
- Combining methods in integrated episodes and overall programmes of learning and change to engage learners and produce the desired results.

Planning and Design

The time spent on design is a significant part of the HRD process, yet it is often neglected as a skill in itself. The purpose is simple, the artful realisation of it is more difficult (Hansen 2006, Bell and Kozlowski 2008, Bhatti and Kaur 2010). The emulation, or copying, of an existing effective design for learning is always a possible solution. As with any other professional activity though, there are many risks in simply copying what others have done, in an unthinking way. Skill in design, with some original planning and an understanding of the options available, is within the reach of all; there is no need to be a creative genius (Swinney 2007).

Design challenges include of course being effective in developing and giving instruction or facilitation in a training room (Gagne 1985, Rothwell and Razanas 1992, Knowles 1995, Leatherman 1996, Milano and Ullius 1998, Hodell 2000, Carliner 2003), but there is more than that (See Practice 6.2).

Practice 6.2: Design and Design Thinking

What is meant by 'design' can be a bit of a catch-all-term, with different people using it to mean different things. Many concentrate on design's aesthetic aspects, the look and feel of objects. While this is important, it is wiser to view it more as a way of thinking, and hence to use the term 'design thinking'. Attributes of design thinking include; questioning, being creative, being innovation, and communication:

Questioning: designers in all sectors, from engineering to fashion, tend to question things a lot. They tend to 'soak up' information from their environments and store this in a less judgemental/hierarchical way than non-designers. Good ideas being much more than the sum of their parts – combining seemingly 'useless' bits of information can give you a world beating idea). This ability, inherent in all of us, is effectively eradicated from most through the education system. The links between a questioning mind and creative mind are important, and these are skills rather than 'talents'.

Creativity: this is either the combining of existing ideas & concepts in original ways (new-to-the-world/sector/market), or more rarely the development of 'brand new' ideas & concepts.

Innovation: the development of ideas & concepts into something real, new-to-the-world/sector/market i.e. creativity you can do in your head, innovation involves the physical world – and usually other people, too.

Communication: the ultimate element in successful design, as it is through the communication of ideas and concepts, via drawings and specifications, that imaging becomes design. Design can be defined as this act of communication; for while painting your living room is just painting your living room, producing drawings and specifications for how you want your living room painted and you're an interior designer.

Source: Lawson (2000).

There are formula for planning and design, reflecting a set of metaphor for the design of learning experiences. The design, sequencing and supporting material in a learning event, can follow a pattern based on these metaphors. Appreciating which one is appropriate and the issues it involves is the reflective practice challenge. The four main forms are as follows:

(1) A 'chain': a fixed set of events, following one after the other;

(2) A 'cycle': of different kinds of experience;

(3) A 'spiral': from the elementary and simple to the advanced and complex;

(4) A 'network': making connections to compile a system of inter-related parts.

These structures provide a route map of order in which to organise the content of a learning event. The design criteria are that for each part of the structure an input needs to be created. A session is a series of these, and these may provide the building blocks for larger units and courses. A 'chain' will have a set of objectives and a timetable for going through these. A 'cycle' will have a set of experiences, and a way of providing these. A 'spiral' will have a set of levels of increasing complexity, and a process for progressing through these. A 'network' will have some starting points for people to search for connections across other fields of knowledge and skills.

Designers may copy or revise from existing designs, existing chains, cycles, spirals or networks. More often they will adapt, or create, these basic designs themselves. They will think about which stimuli (for example, information, materials, criteria for decision-making) are needed to obtain which desired response (for example, what learners are to be doing, to write, decide upon). This does not mean that professionals in HRD need to be, or become, creative geniuses. It is apparent that more than other areas of HRM, HRD benefits from people with the skills and mindset of a designer, people with design intelligence; and that can be learned.

Earl (1987) defines design as 'The plan, structure and strategy of instruction used, conceived so as to produce learning experiences that lead to pre-specified learning goals' (1987, p. 13). Well-designed learning is

- Effective when the learning goal is met;
- Valued when the learner has found the learning experience worthwhile;
- Appreciated when the learning experience has been enjoyed;
- Efficient when the time and energy spent has been optimum.

For learning experiences to be effective, valued, liked and efficient it is necessary to give time and attention in the design process to design. Given the past experience that is available in the practice of HRD in many organisations over many years, there can be no learning and change need that has not, in some way, been identified and met already. There are many, many chains, cycles, spirals and networks available. There may be an existing programme, and existing template for a programme, for any need identified. If a library of these could be established, then all an HRD practitioner might need to do would be to search that library for the outline of how to meet any HRD need they had identified; for management development, for team building, for communication skills, for customer service and so on. There would be an emulation, a copying, of successful design. And this is indeed the way things can work.

Those who establish a good design, who 'invent the wheel', save everyone else the trouble of re-inventing it; others just learn what a good design has been and copy it. This is realistic. But to extend the metaphor a bit, the kinds of wheel that are needed, and the vehicles or machines they are part of, and even the materials they are made of, may not be the same. HRD is also a field where each person and each episode of learning is individual and unique, and adaptations to individual, team and organisational situations provides for an evolution of methods and designs. Standard designs and original thinking about design in HRD centre on understanding:

- The chain – Learning episodes as a narrative flow of events;
- The cycle – The accommodation of learning styles;
- Spirals – structuring for complexity and progress;
- Networks – searching across existing boundaries.

The Chain: Narrative Flow

The basic design structure of the chain can be thought of as producing a narrative 'flow'; a chain with a beginning, a middle and an end, with many links making up each stage. The chain has a narrative flow. Each of the parts of a chain has its own well-recognised design challenges. To begin learners need to be attracted and engaged; both to commit to learning and then to participate in learning and to engage them at the outset. The chain works with setting the scene, mapping out the logic of the topics to be covered in order, creating and maintaining rapport. Tips on design for the chain include:

- Gaining attention through opening techniques: for example, the use of a question, a quotation, a story, a factual statement, a dramatic statement, a curious opening, a checklist;
- In the middle is where the work is mainly done, to cover the content using a structured approach;
- Maintain learner attention: stress relevance, use visual aids, involve people, be enthusiastic;
- Obtain acceptance: be clear, precise, demonstrate;
- Handle challenges and take questions as each link in the chain is made;
- Use exercises: get people to work as individuals, in pairs, or syndicates within each part of the chain.

To design the 'end' of the chain, and conclude things design tips include:

- Ending on a high note, pulling the session together;
- Identifying action points;
- 'Signing off' with a question, a quote, or a story.

Thus the chain has a recognisable beginning, middle and the end. This provides a design template for a narrative. When done well engages learners, takes them through a topic and concludes with the desired impact. If the narrative is not designed well, then learners will not be engaged, or they will not get much from the learning event, or there may be no impact other than perhaps having had an enjoyable time with the trainer and other learners.

Such a basic narrative structure provides a template and reference point around which different narrative 'plots' may evolve as the HRD process is designed. Originality and creativity in design demands that the following features of how the 'story' is presented through the beginning, the middle and the end are taken into account:

- Involvement: Is this an active or a passive experience, involving the learners?
- Meaningful: Will the learners be doing things that are relevant, within their capabilities and necessary to reach a goal they have?
- Control: Who exercises control? Is it complete trainer control, or shared, or is there some form of complete learner control?
- Constraints: There is always limited time and resources, and finding ways around these is an art; respect, but outwit constraints.
- Feedback: Provide feedback; give information on progress, positive results throughout the experience.

The options for design within this basic narrative structure are myriad, and lots of media are available now to make exciting and professional training sessions; from laptop presentations to all kinds of games and exercises. Training events can become over-designed, busy and that may interfere with learning. Making optimum use of media means always having a careful look at your design, and asking whether you could get the same result if you dropped something. Editing is a design skill too. And double check that what you plan to do will meet the learners' needs; make the learning experience good for them, not just an opportunity for you as the trainer to do something interesting and new. It can be a useful exercise to look at a learning event you have experienced, or are designing, and rank it on a 1–10 scale on these features (see Exercise 6.1). To what extent were these criteria met in the learning experience, with 1 being not at all met and 10 being 'fulfilled as much as possible'.

Exercise 6.1: Event Diagnostic

To what extent was this criteria met in the learning experience, with 1 being not at all met and 10 being 'fulfilled as much as possible'

	1 2 3 4 5 6 7 8 9 10
Involvement An active experience, involving the learners?	
Meaningful Learners be doing things that are relevant, possible, to reach a goal they have?	

Control
Control is shared
Constraints
Outwitted constraints
Feedback
Provide feedback; throughout the experience
Edited
Made good use of media; concise
Not just trainer comfort
Meet the learners needs; not for the comfort of the trainer

Beyond getting the basic structure and narrative of an event right, the aim is to create an environment of stimuli in which learners can respond, are willing to respond, like to respond and as a result of this will learn. Think of each aspect of the design and consider the issues in Exercise 6.1.

A problem that faces the 'chain' design is that it assumes all learners process information in the same way. Yet this is not apparently so. This whole topic is a big one that will be considered in more detail in the chapter on HRD practice. At this point a basic issue can be highlighted using Allinson and Hayes' Cognitive Styles Index (CSI). This distinguishes between those who have a cognitive style that prefer 'Intuition' and those who prefer 'Analysis' (Bunge, 1983). Intuition is the ill-defined ability to spot problems or errors, to 'perceive' relations or similarities; and to imagine, conceive, reason or act in novel ways. Intuition and feeling are, in neurological terms, 'right hemisphere' capacities; operating in a holistic way, with immediate judgement based on feeling and the adoption of a global perspective. To analyse is to consider an object or system's components, environment (or context) and structure (organisation). Sensing and thinking are in neurological terms 'left hemisphere' capacities, logical thinking processes, judgement based on mental reasoning and a focus on detail. Learners may all have functioning left and right hemispheres, but it is believed that one will be more dominant than the other. This means that perceptions of a 'chain', a narrative flow, can be dramatically different. One person may be following the logical sequence, the bit-by-bit delivery of knowledge; while another is bored, confused and adrift from the learning. This differential response has been explored using the concept of learning styles, and has produced the theory of experiential learning and the 'cycle' design.

The Cycle: Experiences and Learning Styles

This idea of learning styles as a factor that informs learners' interaction with learning has proven so popular that, in one study, Coffield et al. (2004) noted that some 70 different models of learning styles had been developed. In practice, only a few dominant models are used for exploring the preferences for learning, and the one proposed by Honey and Mumford (1982), based on Kolb's (1984), is among the more popular.

The logic and language of HRD design has been greatly influenced by the concept of experiential learning was concerned with challenging and reforming big ideas about learning. Learning needed to be seen as a social process based on carefully cultivated and guided experience: this implied a move away from instruction in the classroom to other modes of learning in other circumstances. In this Kolb was adopting the earlier ideas of others about experiences as providing the only firm foundation for developing useful knowledge.

Kolb adapted and applied this with a view to managing learning based on experience. He identified different aspects of what it means to talk about learning from experience, and discussed two dimensions of the way people interact with the world: learning structured as apprehension – comprehension, and knowledge structured as intention – extension. From these dimensions he derived four modes of learning. We have already seen that this had important implications for the reform of delivery, but this sparked a lot of research about another big idea: that a person could have a preference for one or other of these modes of learning.

The concept that people have preferred learning styles derived from the idea that they might have preferences for one part of the experiential learning cycle, and therefore be most comfortable when learning involved activities around that stage.

For Kolb the challenge of learning was one of integrative development; of people who were delivering learning appreciating the need for learners to engage with and deal with all the elements of experiential learning to complete a learning cycle. Learners could also be made more aware of their individual preferences, and therefore understand why some kinds or parts of learning suited them whereas others were more difficult; why some people preferred to read the book first then have a classroom discussion while others preferred to have the discussion before going away to read more about the subject. Learning styles are the key to understanding these different kinds of preferences, and ensure a complete cycle is achieved to ensure learning. Honey and Mumford elaborate upon these.

Learning design biased for activists can become over-active; lots of activities, to the extent that learners never sit still, they are constantly on the go. Learning designed biased for pragmatist can become action-focused; finding an expedient course of action and implementing it with inadequate analysis a tendency to search for 'quick fixes' rather than deeper learning. Learning design biased for the theorist can be under-active; not connecting with first-hand experiences, spend most time talking; learners become embroiled in an 'analysis to paralysis' tendency with plenty of pondering and little action. Learning design biased for the reflector can over complicate; not connecting with first-hand experiences, spend most time thinking, reading more and more; learners become embroiled in complexities and branching onto other references.

The Spiral and the Network

The 'chain' and the 'cycle' are the two most common and dominant modes of thinking, talking and planning about the design of learning events. They have the theories, respectively, of instructional design and learning styles to enable professional practice. The 'spiral' and the 'network' as ways of thinking about learning design are not so well established or articulated for either the training room and individual or group learning. They are more commonly perceived and applied as part of broader HRD processes in an organisation. The 'spiral', moving from the simple to the complex, is, in organisations, seen in the differences in the levels of knowledge, skill and attitude required for learning for operational, managerial and strategic knowledge, skill and attitudes. Operational learning is the simplest, learning the routines and specifics of a role. Managerial learning is more complex, involving several operations and the general knowledge and skill needed to control a team. The strategic is the most complex, involving all operations and areas of knowledge and skill needed to pursue a vision and run an organisation.

The 'network' metaphor for learning design emphasises that learning and change may emerge from connectedness across the boundaries that usually contain knowledge, skills and attitudes. Learning and change does not occur just through managing neat 'boxes' of learning and change, within preset boundaries, or through transmitting well-bounded bodies of knowledge, developing discrete sets of skills and packages of attitudes for work roles and employment. Instead learning and change may emerge from crossing boundaries. Learning could be boundaryless; what people need to know and be able to do may be to combine quite novel, unusual clusters of knowledge and skills. Managing the learning and change required across boundaries, across previously well-defined areas of knowledge and skill, presents a design challenge of a different kind. The rationale for these changes is lampooned in the characterisation of new job titles, such as Director of First Impressions (old job title – receptionist), Digital Music Presentation Coordinator (old job title – DJ), Tonsorial Artist (old job title – hairdresser). In reality work is changing, and organisations are evolving, with more than escalating pretentiousness about adapting to this. Rather than following a 'chain' of learning to become a receptionist, DJ or hairdresser, a network of learning for impression management, digital music and tonsorial artistry would need to be created. As a teacher of many years standing my own role has evolved in the context of technologies, changing student expectations and institutional expectations of more entrepreneurial activity from teaching staff. I do not have a new job title, but the boundaries of knowledge and skill of the past no longer apply. What I need to know and be able to transcends the boundaries that used to exist for teachers in the past.

As other areas of employment are similarly transformed by technologies, and what work roles involve evolve educational institutions face challenges in drawing up new programmes to meet the changing face of employment and work. Some of these might be in new broad areas of employment. Some are in very highly refined and specialist areas of employment. And these are challenges organisations face in developing their workforces. These demands of complexity on the one hand and boundaryless learning on the other combine to require a level of design intelligence in HRD which is greater than ever.

Design Thinking

When organisations cannot just import a solution from already known 'designed courses', or the issues of complexity and boundaryless learning arise, they will have regard to design principles. The design should provide a structure for articulating the form and content for HRD, but the process can dissipate at this point into vague statements rather than focusing attention onto how a need is best met. The same principles of planning and design apply across all design contexts, but each offers special challenges. For, as with all design, there is a general structure for good practice and aspects that are particular to the context and materials being worked with. These can be described in various ways, usually with three levels being specified. In HRD this general context and structure entail developing and specifying statements in the form of aims, objectives and results. This is the good practice structure for HRD design, and has to be seen as an ideal. The rigour it requires may not always be followed in real-life situations.

Design requires analysis and synthesis (see Figure 6.1). Analysis as part of the design process involves starting with the general 'whole', defining an overall aim and then breaking that down into constituent parts, specific objectives, that can be used to structure the actual form and content of HRD experiences. The product of analysis in design is the specific objectives around which the learning and change can be built. Synthesis is also required to contain and place together all these different parts in an integrated learning and change experience from which people will learn. The result of this is the construction of a balanced, practicable and high-quality learning experience, a good off-job training experience, mentoring relationship or multimedia programme.

Any planning and design stage is concerned with the preparation of a blueprint, a draft and outline to guide what will be constructed. Buildings are

Analysis	Synthesis
Breakdown	Integrate
Aim	Unified HRD experience
Set goals	Balanced learning and change
Set objectives	Provide variety in delivery

Figure 6.1   HRD planning and design

designed, clothes are designed, mobile phones are designed, Web pages are designed; we all live and work in a world designed. Planning and design intelligence is the capacity to prepare for and produce plans for constructing with the materials in use in the field of design; bricks and mortar, cloth, plastic, information.

In the field of HRD design intelligence matters for working with the materials of learning and change: knowledge, skills and attitudes. The blueprints that may be prepared may be for a day-long training programme, a mentoring scheme, or a culture change programme.

Planning and design in many areas of practice is highly visual, involving two-dimensional models, drawings, which prefigure the construction of real-world three-dimensional, structures and forms. The design process in HRD is similar, but it is textual. It involves using language and written specifications to produce the two-dimensional models of knowledge, skill and attitude which are to be constructed in the workforce, who are very much three-dimensional human beings. These two-dimensional plans and designs serve the purpose of explicitly making ideas manifest so that they can be discussed and refined in advance of a commitment to constructing and making the learning happen, implementing it.

Designers work out their constructions first in the mind. The capacity to do this, the discipline of doing this effectively is the key to good planning and design in any field, including managing learning and change.

Planning and design tasks in HRD will range from the straightforward to the highly complex: from how to plan and design a single on-the-job training experience for an individual through to developing organisation-wide events and change. Common structures and forms are repeated, so the possibility exists that planning and design is a form of copying what has been done before. Conventional HRD needs and specifications, for example concerns to develop better team-working, can lead to plans and design for learning that is also conventional. However, there is also an opportunity, and increasingly an expectation, that learning and change is best attained by the unusual, innovative and challenging plan and design.

Whether the design outcomes will be conventional forms of HRD, such as a class-based session, or innovative forms such as a computer-based game, the heart of the plan and design stage is the same. It is the establishment of an aim, the specification of objectives and an identification of results. This involves two kinds of design capability. First, analysis for determining and writing aim, objectives and results. Second, synthesis, for balancing and unifying different methods into a learning experience to support the development of cognitive capacities, capabilities and desired behaviours.

Analysis for Aims, Objectives and Results

Planning and design in HRD is, initially, about the preparation and refinement of explicit, written statements to act as foundations for the design process.

These statements provide a public, common and explicit foundation for the further development of form and content, whether of course and lesson plans for classroom-based instruction programmes, or a mentoring programme or of a multimedia simulation. The art of doing this analysis well is to include both the acquisition of skill and understanding knowledge during learning and also the development of attitudes, values.

The first element of analysis is finding the aim that meets the identified needs. Aims are statements of what we want the learning to do: general statements of desired conditions or states which learning and change should produce. Aims are high-level statements of intent which provide the centre and boundaries for further design work. Aims in HRD are not expected to be directly measurable. The use of abstract terms such as 'learn', 'know', 'understand' is acceptable at this level of aim articulation. An aim is often expressed as a single sentence. If the wrong aim is articulated, then whatever design is done subsequently, no matter how good in itself, will not take people on track towards closing the performance gap.

After having identified an appropriate aim for an important HRD need, the next step is to define some objectives. Objectives tell learners what is expected. They indicate what is liable to be assessed. They provide a framework for constructing course content. They are what we expect the learner to get from the course and be successful. In much education written objectives mainly relate to the acquisition of a catalogue of knowledge, and knowing the syllabus. In employment objectives need to be also behavioural: what the learner will be able to do, and the manner and quality of doing, and how that can be assessed in practice.

To translate the aim into discrete parts that can then be associated with results. The concern here is that designing in HRD may produce vague and fuzzy objectives and no results associated with them. If objectives are too imprecise, they will fail to provide a guideline for the further refinement and structuring of an HRD experience, that is, they are not specific enough to drive the next step of setting results. Objective can be classified as three types:

(1) Enabling necessary to be able to perform;

(2) Terminal a consequence of the learning or change;

(3) Application the practical reason there is a concern with this issue.

This way of modelling helps to define prerequisites; the kinds of learning that learners must already have, or which they will need to undertake, before engaging with the focal HRD under design. The focus of planning and design is then first with the enabling objectives, if appropriate, through separate HRD events, then with the terminal objectives.

- Enabling objectives: e.g. appraise, lead, handle conflict, build teams;
- Terminal objectives: e.g. motivate staff;

- Application objectives: e.g. to meet customer requirements for quality of service.

This method of defining objectives can result in a range of statements; from a single set objective for an aim to several interrelated objective statements. The result will depend on the complexity of the performance issue and the scale of the learning and change required. One planning and design rule-of-thumb is to have no more than seven objective statements for any particular aim. More than this is inadvisable, as it complicates communication with others about the learning and change. It also means that the further analysis of specific results becomes a much more complex exercise. Developing a myriad and complex set of objective statements is not an expression of good design; it is a substitute for good design. The identification of up to seven objectives related to an aim can, then, provide the entry point for the third level of analysis.

Defining objectives clearly means stating the objective in terms of what is to be achieved rather than stipulating how it is to be done. This means describing the result of learning, what will tangibly be different as a consequence of learning. Otherwise it is like trying to think about 'how' to get somewhere when no one has specified where 'there' is. For example, if the objective is 'to improve motivation by fixing employee attitudes', specifying how to get from poor to positive attitudes in order to change motivation before defining the desired result, what will tangibly happen if motivation is improved. Phrasing objectives clearly in terms of outcomes, of what is expected, is also essential for communicating with managers and potential learners. They should be able to see how their performance will be impacted by HRD. In setting clear objectives it is also helpful to list the performances that are desired, as they may still be imprecise at this stage. This can be achieved by brainstorming, mind-mapping or any other similar techniques. For example, to develop staff 'to hold a responsible attitude towards their work', these performances might be expressed as:

- Deal with customers courteously;
- Get work done on time;
- Keep work area uncluttered.

Having generated a list of performances, prioritise these to select the primary objectives, then identify and delete those items on this list that are too abstract to be measurable, or revise them until they are measurable. Having gone through this process of listing, selection and refinement, ask the question: 'If someone did all these things (that the HRD event could cover) would that provide the performance that is wanted?' Is there anything more to add? This is a test to see whether you have finished defining objectives.

The final step, the third level of analysis, is to identify 'results' specifying the results desired. Results are statements of the tangible outcomes to be achieved by learning and change, stated from the point of view of the learner. Planning and design results are needed for three main reasons:

(1) To provide the focus for detailed design;

(2) To communicate the purpose of the learning to learners and others;

(3) To establish the context for measurement and evaluation.

Results are the specific statements of intention that define measurable out-comes for the learner. They indicate the specific cognitive capacities, capabilities and behaviours that need to be demonstrated for learning to have occurred. Guidelines for developing HRD results from objectives include the following:

- Specify the target behaviours involved using an action verb:
  not   'understand how to motivate people'
  but   'be able to motivate staff'
- Specify a statement of content using a noun to describe a task:
  not   'to motivate staff'
  but   'to motive staff and reduce customer complaints'
- Provide a statement of conditions and standards; quantity (how much), quality (how well), time (how long):
  'to motivate staff and reduce customer complaints by 10%'.

If it is difficult to identify a direct and apparent, explicit results, this may indicate that the objective involves quite abstract learning. In this case, in employment HRD, try to determine a behaviour that requires performance of an activity show-ing application of the abstract learning; e.g., for health and safety awareness, 'list and explain safety rules'.

The final concern with this level of analysis is that, having generated a num-ber of targets, there is another prioritising process to work through. This is needed to prioritise results into a set and establish a hierarchy defining enabling, terminal and application targets. As a result of this kind of analysis an HRD learning experience could be confidently moved on to a design, based on the enabling, terminal and application objectives and targets. This stage of analysis has established some criteria for measurable evaluation.

Synthesis

Design is not a 'science', based on formulas and guidelines, to be achieved by following set procedures alone. That is evident from looking at other areas of knowledge and practice where design thinking has been recognised as an issue for much longer. In areas like graphic, product and building design, principles have been suggested, but these remain domains for the 'artful'. Knowles (1984) entitled the opening chapter of his seminal text on adult learning 'the art and science of helping adults learn'. What he meant by 'art' was that the process as well as the content has importance; setting the right climate and involving learners. Practice 6.3 shows a set of ideas about how artful aspects of principles for good design in HRD can be suggested as the heart of what is put together, or synthesised, following the analytical phase.

Practice 6.3: Defining Aims, Objectives and Targets	
Terminology	Example
Aim (or sometimes 'Goal'): A general statement of a desired condition or state to which an intervention is directed	To use coaching to develop our talent
Objectives: specific statements that describe what learning and change should accomplish. They connect with the overall aim	(1) Describe and use concepts and methods of coaching (2) Identify and work with three coachees (3) Demonstrate skills in questioning, listening and giving feedback
Results: Each objective should have a specific result associated with it. There should be an indicator that the result has been achieved, and a means of verification. Measuring or observing result can be done either quantitatively or qualitatively	(1) 15 per cent of staff in all stores active as coaches (2) Feedback from coachees on coach capabilities which provides evidence of successful coaching (3) Connection to strategic objectives, to raise customer satisfaction levels by 20 per cent

Meeting All Areas of Need

In achieving a synthesis in learning and change design there is usually an interest in having some balance between each of the key areas of need: cognitive capacity, capability and the affective dimension. These different kinds of learning present different kinds of design challenge.

In determining objectives and targets for 'cognitive capacity', the cognitive categories and levels suggested by Bloom (1965) provide one frame of reference for designing HRD in detail. In analysing capability objectives in learning and performance, a tripartite model of employability, vocational capacities and over-arching capabilities can be referenced. Finally, with regard to analysing desired behaviour objectives in learning and performance, a model of the affective elements involved in performance can be outlined with options to design for changing attitudes, values and/or emotions. These particular frames of reference raise some more general questions about design. We will discuss their shortcomings by using constructivist interpretations of knowing and learning, and the concept of emotional intelligence (EI).

To deal with cognitive capacity design issues first, there are concerns with establishing or improving knowledge as a focus for HRD in the workplace. The term 'knowledge' is used in the HRD design context to mean a range of cognitive capacities. Narrowly defined, knowledge is only one part of a spectrum, referring to organised, factual information. It is clearly misleading to assume that 'knowledge' in this sense contains all possible cognitive capacities. In the effective performance of many roles there are aspects of cognition beyond the possession of organised bodies of fact.

These ideas directly connect the design of HRD with thinking about how people 'know' the world and act in it as accomplished performers. This is not dependent solely on 'knowledge' in the form of organised, factual information. Performance may require people to make judgements and decisions when factual information is uncertain, contradictory or unavailable. And performance may require people to depend on the use and application of 'multiple intelligences', not just an awareness of a few memorised facts. We tackle these issues more thoroughly in Chapter 6 on learning theory. Here we focus on some issues of cognitive capacity as it impacts on design concerns.

Bloom (1965) developed a taxonomy of cognitive capacities for use in designing educational experiences.

- Cognitive Capacity: state, list, identify explain, give examples;
- Knowledge, Comprehension, Application: demonstrate, solve describe, design, create;
- Analysis, Synthesis, Evaluation: appraise, contrast, critique.

This has been a long-established framework for describing a range of outcomes, and as a guide to the form and content of learning experiences, According to one estimate, there are around 35 different frameworks in use, but the classic model has a number of advantages. One benefit is the simple modelling of a hierarchy that can be easily applied to a range of performance domains and learning contexts. 'Knowledge' is the most basic factor, with 'evaluation' being the most complex. In Bloom's taxonomy, 'knowledge' is a term for the baseline or entry-level cognitive capacity involved in human performance: the capture and retention of information as a prerequisite of being able to do something. But the capture and retention of information provide a necessary but not sufficient condition for effective performance. Some kinds of performance rely purely on knowledge; some require the capacity to evaluate. The performance of a call centre operator can be knowledge-based, pre-programmed and scripted; the performance of a surgeon in the middle of an operation will be based more on evaluation (and corrective action).

So, there is more to doing than knowing, and often there is more to performance than the possession of information. Effective performance associated with an increasing degree of difficulty and complexity draws upon other cognitive capacities:

- Evaluation – the ability to judge the value of material for a given purpose: to assess, evaluate, argue, validate, criticise;
- Synthesis – the ability to put parts together to form a whole: to design, formulate, develop, organise;
- Analysis – the ability to break material down into component parts: to analyse, compare, contrast, investigate;
- Application – the ability to use learned material in new and concrete situations: to relate, show, demonstrate;
- Comprehension – the ability to grasp the meaning of new material: to explain, discuss, review, interpret;
- Knowledge – the ability to recall previously learned material: to define, identify, list (see Practice 6.4).

Practice 6.4: A lexicon of objectives

Evaluation	Judge, criticise, compare recommend, determine, measure, assess,evaluate, revise
Synthesis	Compose, plan, construct, design, make, predict, hypothesise, formulate, propose, develop, invent, incorporate
Analysis	Interpret, test, analyse, distinguish, differentiate, investigate, scrutinise, examine
Application	Exhibit, solve, interview, simulate, apply, demonstrate, illustrate, operate, show, calculate, dramatise, experiment, employ, practise
Comprehension	Translate, restate, summarise, discuss, describe, retell, explain, express, identify, locate, report, recognise
Knowledge	relate , know, define, record, name, label, repeat, specify, cite, recount, list, enumerate, recall, tell

In the area of capabilities, 'knowing how' does not always translate into 'being able to'; the possession of cognitive capacities does not ensure effective performance. A person must also have constituent capabilities, which are defined here as the discrete abilities involved in effective performance. In principle the simplest division of capabilities is into three categories: (1) capabilities with data, (2) with people and (3) with things. Finer sets of distinctions can be made. These may elaborate upon differences between types of data, types of people and types of thing. Thus we can make a distinction between quantitative data (numerical) and qualitative data (statements, meanings); between people in external roles (customers) and internal roles (staff); between simple things (use of basic computing applications) and complex things (the control of a complex machine).

Finer and finer distinctions can be made, and there is no obvious limit to this, apart from the practical one of enumeration (Harvey 1999). From a measurement perspective, it becomes increasingly difficult to collect reliable and valid data with increasing numbers and degrees of abstraction of capability categories. One study grouped over 12,000 occupations using highly abstract data and people capabilities, and concluded that only five occupational clusters, five different kinds of capability, existed. However, within each of these mega-clusters of occupations there was a tremendous degree of variability in actual work activities, rendering the description of any specific job using these terms effectively useless for any practical purpose, such as advising people on career paths or developing training plans.

Maps of capabilities are possible at three levels: underpinning capabilities, intermediate capabilities and overarching capabilities. Underpinning capabilities are those that, broadly speaking, are expected as a consequence of primary and secondary education, including literacy and numeracy. As such they may seem to be irrelevant for HRD at work. However, it is widely acknowledged that some people have problems with attaining these underpinning capabilities in education, meaning that they are an issue in many workplace contexts. Many people enter the workforce lacking in numeracy, literacy and certain personal characteristics, such as influencing skills.

Intermediate capabilities are capabilities in occupation-specific roles, and the generic capabilities relevant to most mature adults in employment, and in life generally. These capabilities are most usually associated with training at or for work. They often form the heart of vocational qualification systems, and can be thought of as skills in the traditional sense. Work seen as being either low-skill or high-skill will vary at this level of capability.

Maps of capabilities can be considered in terms of their validity in providing a means of designing useful HRD activities. Determining validity is the process of estimating the extent to which correct and accurate inferences can be derived from the scores or profiles generated by using the model. Such instruments may be classical psychometric tests or more general assessments of capabilities, such as a framework for performance appraisal based on an annual review of objectives by a manager and an employee. The former tend to be subject to formal validation studies, whereas the latter are simply evaluated in terms of their usefulness in getting results. An instrument that provides correct and accurate inferences is valid: for example, a selection test is said to be valid in allowing inferences about the potential job performance of an applicant to be derived from its use. An instrument that does not allow correct and accurate inferences is, thus, invalid. Continuing with the selection example, a psychometric test used in a selection process that does not allow inferences about the applicant's potential job performance is invalid. A similar test can be applied to models of capability.

Overarching capabilities are those attributes associated with people taking on responsibility for their own work and self-development, rather than being instructed to work or develop by others. These capabilities were once thought to be relevant only to people working as supervisors and managers, but they are now seen to be essential to all employees, and to form the core of new and advanced employability. From an HRD design point of view, most importantly, they are capabilities that need to be developed in concrete workplace situations. They cannot easily be learned and developed in other circumstances such as the classroom.

Finally, the identification of aptitudes, or affective factors, as a third dimension of development presents design challenges for HRD. The reason for including this third dimension is that effective performance is a consequence not only of what people know and think, and what they can do, but also of how they actually behave because of how they feel, and how they manage their feelings These affective influences on people and performance can often make the critical difference between good and poor performance, because affective influences on people are the prime controllers or drivers of behaviour. If affective factors are so critical for performance, it is essential that they are addressed in the design of HRD experiences and the setting of objectives. In the HRD context affective factors influencing behaviour are commonly discussed in regard to three constructs:

(1) Changing attitudes: patterns of personal likes and dislikes that can be measured and changed;

(2) Developing values: basic beliefs about right and wrong that will influence what people will pursue and what they will or will not do;

(3) Emotional intelligence: the effective handling of emotions to enable effective interpersonal relations.

To study only an isolated individual, abstracted from his or her social context, or to study people only as parts of systems without any individual agency, is of limited use when analysing performance issues and designing HRD at work. The former is a weakness attributed to the field of individual psychology, and the latter is the weakness attributed to much of sociology.

Social psychology stands between the assumptions and foci of these two sciences, and is defined as the study of human behaviour in interpersonal relations and groups. Social psychology draws on the concept of attitudes, which lies at the heart of much design practice in HRD. Attitudes were established in early social psychology as a focus for research and discussion of the interface between psychological and sociological processes – between interaction and persuasion or group membership and prejudice. Attitudes are enduring predispositions to evaluate objects, people, or institutions favourably or negatively. They provide for patterns of behaviour based on the interaction of three elements:

(1) Cognitive components: elements of perceptions;

(2) Affective components: elements of feelings;

(3) Conative components: elements of patterns of action and experience.

Attitudes are formed either from general experience through exposure to situations in the course of life, or from direct conditioning by which others seek to structure their development deliberately; from parents through peers to educators and then, of course, employers. They are the domain in which the dynamics of balance and dissonance are played out. People are naturally inclined to hold attitudes that are consistent with their perceptions and behaviour, and feel troubled if there is dissonance between what they perceive, what they feel and what they do. These connections open up paths of influence for those concerned to shape attitudes.

In attitude theory, then, shaping or changing attitudes requires us to influence what people perceive, what they feel and what they do, either singly or in combination. Usually, behaviour will tend to be adjusted to remove dissonance. However, there are problems with the concept and shaping of attitudes. First, measurement is difficult: because attitudes are not directly observable it is necessary to use scales and questionnaires to define and explore them. Thus the validity and reliability of these scales and questionnaires becomes an issue. Second, there are concerns based on evaluating arguments about managing attitude change. There is often agreement on the ideal behaviours – for example, it is right to try to reduce attitudes such as prejudices – but there is much less agreement on what is required to effect such change. In order to change attitudes, is it better to use the central route, providing for people to be exposed to and weigh up arguments, or the peripheral route, which involves using emotion to arouse dissonance and change behaviours? Anti-drug campaigns provide a good example of this dilemma: is it better to provide information about drugs and let people weigh up the arguments, or should emotive messages about the dangers of drugs be promoted more forcefully?

Yet it is also the case that people's avowed attitudes may be related only loosely to their actual behaviour: for example, there are those who hold prejudiced views but not actually act in prejudiced ways. Because people's behaviour is constrained by laws and rules, by knowing other's attitudes, by the relative importance of the issue at hand and by perceptions of social pressures, the existence of an attitude may not actually be a good guide to how someone will behave. Someone may demonstrate all the attitudes expected of, for example, a chartered accountant, but then behave in an un-professional way; or they may fail to have these attitudes, but still act in a professional way. These kinds of concern qualify the importance of attitudes as a potential driver of behaviour, and restrict the scope for and usefulness of attitude change as a part of HRD at work.

The concept of values provides another avenue for thinking about the design of HRD, taking into account the role of affect in behaviour that is relevant to performance and HRD at work, and to the setting of objectives. A value can be defined as an enduring belief that a specific mode of conduct or end-state of existence is personally or socially preferable to an opposite or converse mode of conduct or end-state of existence. Values embody basic beliefs about what is right and what is wrong: they both express and control the behaviours of community members for stability within the community.

The community of a specific workplace usually requires people to accept and abide by core values, implicit or explicit. More specifically, explicit values can impact upon organisational, professional and personal performance. It is often considered important that core organisational values should be identified and propagated: organisations define their core values and disseminate them widely to staff and others. These are sometimes called 'Big "V"' values (Leonard-Barton 1995) to distinguish them from 'small "v"' values, which inform interaction and behaviour. Small 'v' values are evident in professional work roles in the form of ethical guidelines: doctors, lawyers, teachers and others must abide by these above all else, or they will be disciplined and barred from practising. Personal values about what is right and wrong, about duty and virtuousness, are invariably at the core of people's sense of personal identity and self (Morris 1965, Davidson 1972).

Values are important because they have the potential to be executive guides for all of a person's actions, attitudes and judgements, with reference to ultimate ends and to issues beyond their immediate goals. While values may be easy to identify and promulgate, they are not necessarily mutually supportive. For example, there are potential contradictions in being both thrifty and charitable. They are both worthy behaviours in the right context and at the right time, but may conflict at certain times and in certain contexts. It is through the resolution of these value conflicts, either consciously or unconsciously, that a hierarchical arrangement is established in a person or group and evolves as a value system. A value system is a rank ordering of values that serves to resolve social and personal conflict and direct the selection of alternatives where choices have to be made. The analytical interest in values has been inspired by exploring different value systems, within specific cultures and between different cultures.

The connection with HRD design is the importance of planning for and designing objectives related to values. Core organisational, occupational and individual values, such as teamwork, quality and creativity, are identified and propagated. Occupational values are relevant and necessary for competent performance of a specific job, and professional values provide ethical guidelines. Personal values, and their fit with the organisation and occupational roles, may be areas where HRD is required.

Finally, the emotional aspects of work and performance have long been acknowledged as important for performance in many jobs and organisational settings, and the topic is now assuming greater prominence in business and management as a whole (see Perspectives 6.3 and 6.4). This has in part resulted from the rise of stress as a prominent health and safety issue in many organisations. An analysis of the kinds of emotional demand being made on staff, and ways of mitigating these, has been seen as highly relevant to responding to the stress epidemic. Concern with emotion is also a reflection of a long-standing concern for human relations within effective teams and relationships at work. Emotion is not just an issue for work and performance in situations where employees may be exposed to high degrees of stress and trauma. All forms of work and performance have emotional contexts. There are emotional aspects of effective performance for holiday representatives in a beach resort, employees in customer call centres, as well as in nursing and care in hospitals.

Operationalising emotion can be done simply: there are four core feelings: 'mad, bad, sad or glad'. These can be expanded upon (Perspectives 6.1 and 6.2). The ways in which performance at work involves experiencing and containing anger, elation, anxiety/fear, disgust, grief, happiness, jealousy/envy, love, sadness, embarrassment, pride, shyness, shame, or guilt can be important in providing areas for HRD design to deal with mindfully (Hochschild 1983, Fineman 1993).

Perspective 6.1: Eight Basic Emotions

Fear

Anger

Sorrow

Joy

Disgust

Acceptance

Anticipation

Surprise

Source: Plutchik, R (1980).

Perspective 6.2: Personal and interpersonal emotions

Personal emotions	Suffering	Pleasure	Pain
Joy			
Content	Regret	Relief	Aggravation
Cheerfulness	Dejection	Rejoicing	Lamentation
Amusement	Dullness	Aesthetic	Taste
Hopelessness	Fear	Courage	Cowardice
Rashness	Caution	Desire	Indifference
Dislike	Fastidiousness	Wonder	Pride
Humility	Vanity	Modesty	Insolence
Interpersonal emotions, feelings in relationship			
Friendship	Enmity	Sociality	Courtesy
Love	Hatred	Resentment	Anger
Sullenness	Benevolence	Malevolence	Threat
Pity	Gratitude	Forgiveness	Jealousy
Envy	Guilt		

Source: Roget's Thesaurus (1987).

Perspective 6.3: Attitude Change Factors

When attempting to design in objectives around attitude change in the context of HRD and work roles, the following variables are all important:

- **Communicator credibility**: Do the people attempting the attitude change have expertise, and are they trustworthy? If HRD experiences are managed by people who are not perceived as experts and trustworthy, any attempt at attitude change is likely to fail.

- **Communicator attractiveness**: That is, their attractiveness to the person whose attitudes are to be influenced. The ability to have rapport with a person or group is essential in HRD.

- **Extremity of message**: Greater attitude change requires more extreme messages.

- **Using one-sided only or two-sided, debate-style, forms of argument**: Many HRD experiences need to be given a structure where either one-sided presentations (of instruction) or scope for debate and discussion is needed. Using the wrong method in the wrong circumstances will frustrate and confuse.

- **The use of fear**: People will change their attitudes if threats can be articulated to favour attitude change.

- **Different social situations**: Group situations are better at eliciting attitude change than interpersonal face-to-face settings, and public situations are better than private. This is one reason why many HRD experiences are organised with groups when attitude change is involved.

- **The influence of prior events**: For example, being forewarned that attitudes will be confronted can lead people to self-inoculation against change. In the management of attitude change through HRD it should not be kept 'secret', but the potential for self-inoculation can mean that time is need to open people up in HRD events.

Source: Albarracin et al. (2005).

Perspective 6.4: Competence Frameworks

Competence can be defined as the capabilities of superior performers. The demand on HRD strategies is to go beyond *doing things well* and move on to *doing things better* and *doing better things*, and this could be based on a mapping and development of competence. Many organisations have subsequently sought to develop their own maps of competence. Competence-based HRD systems were designed to help bind a set of initiatives together with a set of managerial and workforce behaviours that would lead to some future desirable state, usually improved performance. These systems were also often meant to provide a coherent framework for the integration of various HRM processes and initiatives, as well as being the focus for HRD strategy.

Source: Dubois and Rothwell (2004).

Finer distinctions can be made, of variations and expansions on these emotions. In the context of HRD at work the concern is that performance may be affected if positive emotions are not activated and negative emotions are not contained and controlled. In context effective performance may require people to potentially feel angry or embarrassed or disgusted, or to avoid getting angry, embarrassed or disgusted.

There are a range of perspectives (Strongman 1996) on identifying and analysing emotions that are relevant to defining HRD objectives. One is to view emotions as physiological processes: that is, physical changes in the physiology of organisms. This kind of analysis explores the connections between, for example, fear and preparing for fight or flight. HRD design needs to be aware of such issues and aims to help people develop mechanisms for coping with these physiological processes in the context of work roles.

An alternative perspective is to view emotions as an influence on thinking, so that they are studied as a feature of the information-processing brain. Here the concern is the way in which emotions shape perception and thinking. HRD about emotion is needed to make people aware of, and take into account, the way that emotions can influence thinking. The patterns of emotion within social contexts, reflecting conditioning, are also studied as facets of socialisation in patterns of role behaviour. HRD at work can then be about challenging this conditioning, and the stereotypes that go with it. Finally, emotions have been studied in the context of clinical dysfunction: as causes of or contributors to mental dysfunction, for example, depression. While insight about emotion can be found in this domain, HRD design and activity is not the appropriate environment for managing this kind of concern; other professionals are the proper people to investigate and deal with this form of influence of emotion on performance.

In the work and performance HRD context, current concerns arising from all these perspectives focus on the discussion of EI. Intelligence is the ability to define and pursue goals, and to overcome obstacles to achieve them. EI is the ability to appreciate the interpersonal dynamics involved in defining and pursuing goals and overcoming obstacles to achieving them. Performance gaps and HRD objectives can be related to gaps in EI. This suggests that EI requires, as a minimum, some awareness, complemented by personal experiences enabling empathy, and that it further involves being able to express emotions oneself. It therefore, ultimately enables the control of emotions based on awareness, empathy and the ability to express. Without awareness there can be no experience, without experience there can be no expression, and without expression there can be no control.

Finally, connecting how different kinds of emotion can support learning in different phases of a learning experience is necessary. HRD design should include roles for all kinds of emotion to give highs and impact to learning (Reilly and Kort 2003), not just positive emotions:

- Challenge: what dont I know/cant I do? – Anger, confusion, surprise, fear;
- Investigate: how does it work? – Anticipation, curiosity, determination;
- Change: what do I need know and do? – Determination, frustration, disappointment;
- Construct: how can I use this knowledge/skill? – Hope, satisfaction.

Reflections on HRD Design

The preceding frameworks, the chain, the cycle, the spiral and network, are examples of 'content models' to guide the analysis of designing objectives for HRD activities across the three identifiable dimensions of needs. Content models suggest a framework of universal, general, fixed and set hierarchical structures. However they can be misleading, and may even lead to design practices which impede learning rather than supporting it. For example, there are problems with Bloom's taxonomy as a content model of cognitive capacities. The model assumes that, for humans, information is passively received by the senses, and that the more complex cognitive capacities are engaged only during certain kinds of activity, tasks and situations. The overall function of cognition is, thus, to help people discover an objective reality: that is, a reality that exists 'out there', independent of the person sensing it.

However, these assumptions about cognitive capacities are contestable. If people are not just passive cognition machines, passively receiving information through the senses, they may be seen rather as agents actively building up and constructing a view of reality based on their own experience and interests. The functions of cognition can then be interpreted as adaptive sense-making, serving to help manage the person's experience of the world, rather than just accessing an objective reality that is 'out there'. And this kind of sense-making in work is not confined to professionals undertaking difficult and complex tasks; it is an inherent feature of all human action. If that is true, then such a view of cognitive functions implies that learning even the simplest task is always achieved by people as sense-making, active agents, not as neutral cognition machines trying to memorise knowledge. Defining objectives for HRD experiences may impede the natural learning process rather than support it, unless the lessons of constructivism influence design (Debate 6.1).

Debate 6.1: Constructivism

Constructivism has roots in philosophical debates about rationalism and empiricism. Rationalists argue that the individual human has no direct access to external reality, only to impressions of external reality. Thus people can only obtain information and use it through in-built cognitive principles which actively organise their experience, rather than behaving like machines that neutrally process it. The psychologist Piaget, for example, developed a theory of the different cognitive stages through which a child progresses, building up an increasingly complex model of the world. The cognitive principles evident in change during a child's development suggest that there is active construction of information and knowledge. The analysis implies that, when trying to structure and direct learning that involves establishing or developing cognitive capacities, there is much more to doing it well than cramming facts into brains.

With an objectivist view of cognitive capacities, the core proposition is that learning involves obtaining, codifying and packaging the 'truth', whether that means accessing forms of defined knowledge or higher order capacities such as critical evaluation. If cognition is a passive reflection of an external, objective reality learning can be so characterised. This view is then consistent with the idea that, and indeed implies, a process of instruction is the key to effective HRD design; learning about the truth from an authority. In order to obtain an image of reality (the subject), people must somehow receive the right information from the environment: that is, they must be instructed. In learning, people are acting like cameras which capture an image of how the world 'really' is in their brain. Trainers simply present them with the right images in the right sequence, and learning follows.

This characterisation of people is contested. Human brains do not act like mirrors or cameras. People are always actively generating different models of the 'world out there', reinforcing some observations of the outside world while eliminating others. This is a process of selection by the person, rather than a process of mirroring in the brain. The process of personal construction cannot be switched off and on; it occurs all the time. Sometimes it can be productive for learning and sometimes it can cause problems. It can be helpful where it leads people to new insights, as they check and test their versions of the world and come to useful and insightful conclusions. Alternatively it may reinforce mistaken views and delusions, leading people to reject learning, and changes in their cognition, capabilities or behaviour. Cognition itself does not establish one best and true way of perceiving reality.

Contrasting assumptions about cognition are embodied in a constructivist view of learning. Knowledge, all other aspects of cognitive capacity, reflections on capability and behaviour emerge from and are embedded in what is personally constructed by the person, rather than what is impressed upon them by external authorities. Such personal construction matters as individuals seek to control what they perceive in order to eliminate any deviations or perturbations from their own secure, existing and preferred model of the world. Thus people tend to 'see' and consider that which is relevant to their individual goals and actions and their own status quo, but tend to ignore that which they do not feel is relevant. The typical individual does not care about the 'truth' of the knowledge that an expert may try to communicate to them; they are rather more concerned about how much it disrupts their personal constructions. They may face up to and adapt to the changed ideas that come with new knowledge, or they may seek to compensate for perturbations in their existing models of reality by rejecting them.

An example of these ideas related to psychology and learning that is relevant to adults is seen in the work of Kelly and the concept of 'personal construct' psychology. This assumes people are active sense-makers, so it is first necessary to elicit and know people's existing personal constructs in order to clarify why they behave as they do. Only then is it possible to work on what needs to be challenged to change behaviour and help them learn. This is invariably an individual task, and is not about generic objectives.

Constructivist views of learning are suggesting that there is more to the design challenge than effective communication of knowledge as an antecedent of capabilities or behaviours; it can be about overhauling an entire constructed model of the outside world, which the person holds as a whole. An alternative model may be more valid than the learner's own, but still not be accepted. Experts may indeed be right, and their information and knowledge, and prescribed capabilities and behaviours that go with that, may be valid. Yet people may still not adapt or change their own models; their own validated kinds of information and knowledge. The most important HRD design issue is then to help people to open and modify their own constructions rather than impose an expert's external construction on them. This is much more time-consuming and complex; it is easier to try to enforce a correct model, by citing authority, by asserting and by imposing. Yet if this pushing on a locked door, it has not result.

Learners may need to experience dissonance as a starting point of learning, including the experience of thinking or feeling that an existing world-view may be inadequate. It is unhelpful to try merely to pack in more and more new knowledge, because that simply creates information overload. It is also unhelpful because people need time to adapt and adjust their model of the world as they go along a learning and development curve. If they are overloaded, they will almost inevitably reject the new knowledge that others have been trying to instil. On the positive side, a sign of such a qualitative change in a person's constructed model of the world arises with 'Aha!' learning moments, when it seems that they suddenly 'get' something that previously had eluded them.

Conclusion

To plan and design for effective HRD it is necessary to establish aims, objectives and targets. These need to relate in a balanced way to the cognitive capacities, capabilities and behaviours required for effective performance in roles and organisations. Particular models for identifying these are available and used in practice, though they are all partial and biased in some respects, and we need to handle them with care.

To plan and design HRD well requires design thinking, which faces challenges in three areas: (1) analysis, (2) synthesis and (3) communication. The challenge of analysis is to break needs down into discrete 'developable' units of learning. The challenges of synthesis are about balance and variety in putting together designs for dealing with cognitive, capability and behavioural dimensions of learning. Communication is central to the whole process, requiring clarity and simplicity in definitions and statements. The structures suggested by an improved consciousness of design will help support personal change. It can be developed in various ways: intellectually exploring ideas such as the constructivist framework for thinking about the nature of learning and HRD design, and familiarity with general design principles and concern (Practice 6.5).

A pragmatic interpretation of the constructivist view is that it alerts us to the ways in which the process and adequacy of learning requires more than an authority specifying information and knowledge profiles. In some areas where HRD design arises there may be expert-validated and accepted bodies of information and knowledge, and the kinds of cognitive capacities required for jobs and tasks. It is, nonetheless, often difficult to get people to learn, partly because of their pre-existing model of the world. The learning may act to perturb, so that new information and knowledge, or changes to behaviour, are resisted.

Practice 6.5: Design Principles

Principle	General issues	Applied to HRD design
Balance	What is to be made will need to be balanced, and design should be the time when the right balance is gauged. How much of one thing, and how much of another, to ensure balance?	What proportion of cognitive capacity, capability and behaviour is going to be right?
Contrast	Powerful images use high contrast. These may use high contrast, of dark and light, shapes or materials. Another way to show contrast is with contradiction This can provide muscle to get a message over.	Powerful learning can use high contrast: before and after, bad practice and good practice, light humour and serious stories.
Direction	Peoples experience through a newspaper, a building or anything else that is designed has to be 'directed' clearly, or they will feel lost.	Trainers need to lead learners through their HRD experiences, without getting them lost or confused. Direction in learning is about managing going in circles, but still making progress.
Economy	Getting down to the bare bones of the design, once all extraneous elements are eliminated, are you sure the message is clear?	If you are not, then the learners will not be either. And sometimes it is essential to send a large message with a small voice; there is no time or resource for anything else.
Emphasis	People are always telling stories that end with them saying 'And my point is this . . .' Although the story might be interesting, the point could be made with less embellishment and more structure.	If everything is emphasised, nothing is emphasised. When you create a HRD event, what point are you making? Where does the emphasis need to be?

Rhythm	Following a rhythm, a pattern, is central to all forms of communication. Without rhythm, communication is lifeless and drab. The principle of rhythm is as unavoidable as the element of contrast.	Good learning experiences have rhythm, a 'beat' that people can feel and which allows them to feel comfortable.
Unity	If form and content don't match goals, it all ends up an agony of self-defeat. Unity sounds like the crowning achievement of all the principles of design, but it's really no better than emphasis, no less than rhythm. Unity is judged on how well the event is received.	Elements must be employed effectively within a format. A success depends on the appropriate relationship of content within the format.

Source: http://www.graphicdesignbasics.com.

Individuals' criteria for selection of the kind of information and knowledge they will accommodate may be 'coherence'-related; that is, the new information and knowledge agrees with their existing patterns of information and knowledge, what they already know. Or their criteria may be 'consensus'-related; that is, the extent to which they believe it is widely accepted in significant groups. This consensus dimension connects learning design with broader social construction ideas, which see more than intrinsic, personal cognition factors as shaped by social processes of communication and negotiation, part of the person's larger social construction of reality as the member of a group. HRD always occurs in and contributes to a social context.

Case Study: Transfusion

A company producing and bottling alcoholic drinks at various sites employed around 1,500 people. There was a history of adversarial employee relations in the company. In an increasingly competitive environment they adopted a strategy based on what they called a 'change agenda'. This involved a change to flexibility, shared responsibility, continuous improvement, more customer focus and team-working. These were the characteristics that they needed to be a pioneering and innovative organisation. Associated with this was a process of intensive and extensive HRD. 'Transfusion' was the name given to the major HRD event they planned and designed to meet the demands of their broader change agenda.

The HRD was planned and designed as a series of three-day workshops for all staff. These workshops would use dramatic techniques to challenge and break old norms of rule-following and task orientation. They were designed to help staff develop a more holistic view of and commitment to the new organisational culture, along with a new entrepreneurial ethos in the company. This training event was seen by staff as almost evangelical, requiring them to confess their weaknesses before moving on to embrace the new values. At each event up to 50 people drawn from various locations attended. On day 1, as participants entered the room, loud music was playing, and during the day learning points were illustrated with clips from major motion pictures. These were intended to stir up a quasi-religious fervour, providing a quite different experience from the way that previous company seminars had been run. The other sessions included guided fantasy exercises, Tai Chi exercises, and the use of forms of dramatised group interaction.

It was an event that was planned to engage with the whole person, not just limited elements of knowledge or skill. The days started at 7.30 am and went on until late at night. Only healthy food and drinks were made available for refreshment. There were 'spotlight sessions', where participants were put on a stage in the room in darkness; they were then asked to tell the group their values, hopes and fears. This encouraged many to reveal astonishing disclosures: items discussed included divorce, deaths and serious illness. And at the end of each day there was a 'ho' session, mimicking traditional North American Indian practices. Participants sat cross-legged and had to access a symbolic stick to be able to talk; when they were finished they called 'ho' to signal it, and everyone else had to respond likewise.

At the end of all this, the directors of the company felt that Transfusion had 'done it': it had broken down barriers, taken away inhibitions, and given people a real buzz. Young team leaders were more ready to talk and interact. The HR manager commented that 'people who would have been seen as cynical were jumping and singing and dancing and whooping because they thought it was brilliant.' Apparently no one had a negative view. Research done 18 months later confirmed this overall positive assessment of the HRD event. The planning and design had worked. The need to meet the demands of the change agenda, in a company having had severe employee relations problems, had been met.

(*Source*: Beech et al. 2000)

3 Key Texts

(1) Carliner, S. (2003) *Training Design Basics, American Society for Training & Development* (Alexandria VA, ASTD Press).

(2) Lawson, B. (2000) *How Designers Think: The Design Process Demystified* (Oxford, Architectural Press).

(3) Rothwell, W. and Razanas, H. (1992) *Mastering the Instructional Design Process: A Systematic Approach* (San Francisco, Jossey-Bass).

3 Key Articles/Reports

(1) Bhatti, M. and Kaur, S. (2010) 'The Role of Individual and Training Design Factors on Training Transfer', *Journal of European Industrial Training*, 34 (7), pp. 656–672.

(2) Bell, B. and Kozlowski, S. (2008) 'Active Learning: Effects of Core Training Design Elements on Self-Regulatory Processes, Learning, and Adaptability', *Journal of Applied Psychology*, 93 (2), pp. 296–316.

(3) Hansen, J. (2006) 'Training Design: Scenarios of the Future', *Advances in Developing Human Resource*, 8 (4), pp. 492–499.

3 Key Web Links

(1) Guidelines for Training Plans OnLine: http://managementhelp.org/trng_dev/gen_plan.htm.

(2) Training Journal: http://www.trainingjournal.com/?gclid=CKDKqea19qYCFUoKfAod_nCIDw.

(3) Trainers Library: http://www.trainerslibrary.com/?gclid=CKi18t-79qYCFUoKfAod_nCIDw.

7

Methods and Practice

Learning Objectives

By the end of this chapter you will be able to:

- Describe the theory and practice of instruction and facilitation in delivering HRD;
- Describe and analyse other forms of performance support relevant to HRD;
- Critically evaluate the strengths and weaknesses of instruction and facilitation as methods of managing HRD; adopt and adapt and use instruction and facilitation methods in HRD.

Introduction

In a professional context the major method, practice and skill issue is perceived to be about delivering training, including presentations and exercises, in the training room. Underlying this are skills in instruction and facilitation, and engaging with the learning styles of adult learners. These methods of instruction and facilitation are practised not just in training room environments, but also in other contexts, from managing one-to-one learning to delivering large-scale change programmes in work. The significance and balance of instruction and facilitation in an organisation's Human Resource Development (HRD) strategy will also reflect the overall approach to the HRD process which is present in the organisation.

Introductory Case

CapitalAirport was a large, busy airport in a country that had become increasingly dependent on air travel. It served the nation's capital, and was run by a state-controlled company. In the previous 5 years there had been a virtual doubling of passenger numbers, and a big increase in freight. Staffing had not increased at the same rate, however, and there was strain on existing resources. Senior managers saw some key problems. Managers were concerned that many staff were not going out of their way to help customers; customer service did not seem to be a high priority. Increasing competition with services offered by other travel companies, both ferry and train, was a factor. Customer surveys presented a reasonably positive picture, but with a near-monopoly people could not vote with their feet. But the real threat was of privatisation if poor service was not improved. The company wanted to provide a quality service for passengers and other customers, but was not making any significant investments in training. It was known that some workers felt themselves undervalued, and were at best a 'necessary evil'. For example, the airport police service felt this; yet they were the biggest employee group in the organisation, and played a big day-to-day operational role. There was conflict between the police service and the operations department. Management felt that this whole situation needed changing.

It was decided that an HRD strategy aimed at improved handling of increased levels of service had to be set up. Three key activities were organised. First, consultants were hired to run a course on 'the human factor'. This off-site company-wide course involved getting employees to think about their careers, and life–work balance, and also included role-playing for dealing with customer service problems. Then, new customer service teams were introduced, based on quality circle principles to look at continuous improvement. Despite initial successes with these teams, relations in them deteriorated; two years on they had ceased to function. Finally there was another training programme: an event called 'the winning factor'. This was a one-day, organisation-wide event run at a nearby hotel. It consisted of a film presentation on dealing with customers, a workshop on identifying competitors and how well they delivered customer service, a play performed by airport staff, a question and answer session with the Chief Executive and awards given at a ceremony to 'outstanding employees'.

Managers and employees had strong views about this last aspect of the training, and it failed to have any positive impact. They thought of it as a demeaning programme, because it treated managers and staff like fools and insulted their intelligence. The people responsible for organising and running the programme were seen as two-faced: saying one thing and doing another. Some expressed very strong views that the event had been fraudulent and a disgrace. This reflected general discontent.

There were a number of interconnected reasons why the managers and staff were so irritated and provoked by this aspect of the training. However, the key issue seemed to be that the message being promoted in training was that all employees could be 'winners' and 'heroes' in the course of undertaking their day-to-day work. And, of course, winning should be accompanied by loud celebrations and applause, reminiscent of many US companies' employee-of-the-month schemes.

This portrayed a romanticised view of their work situations that bore no resemblance to the day-to-day reality, which, for the most part, was routine and hard work. Even on the training day itself only a few actually received awards. In fact employees struggled to meet customer needs. They were involved in exhausting and difficult interchanges with customers, who projected their anxieties and frustrations onto staff. They saw themselves very far from being winners in any sense, and could not see any way in which they might be winners in the future. Even the airport firemen, the most likely 'heroes', were struck by the incongruity of the idea of being 'winners'. Much of their time was spent in extreme boredom waiting for things to happen. What was so irksome was that the whole idea of the HRD strategy denied the reality of their day-to-day work. It seemed that managers did not want to know, and therefore did not care about, the employees. The managers seemed unable to acknowledge the realities of stress and boredom that characterised the employees' work. The HRD strategy of instilling in everyone the thought that they were 'winners' was at best deluded and patronising and at worst dishonest.

Methods and Practice

HRD development and delivery may range from providing to a single person a brief, one-off activity to delivering complex courses many times to thousands of people as a part of larger organisational projects. Whatever the scope and scale of delivery there are common challenges around practice, connected with practicability, costs, quality and time. There are also practice challenges in adult learning at work to do with blending methods that represent instruction and facilitation (Sheehan 2004, Ellinger and Cseh 2007, Owen 2009). Methods of instruction involve a directive, standardised and 'closed' approach to learning knowledge, skills or capabilities. In contrast, facilitation methods involve using participative, personalised, non-directive delivery methods. These methods aim to encourage change by learning that engages learners emerges from that in the form of knowledge, skill or capability change. Instruction means 'telling'; facilitation means 'selling'. These are the ends of the spectrum of acting to deliver effective HRD (see Perspective 7.1), and are described in this chapter.

Perspective 7.1: The Practice and Methods Spectrum	
Instruction	**Facilitation**
Directive	Participative
Scripted	Improvised
Standardised	Personalised
Giving answers	Questioning
Support	Challenge

Approaches to methods and practice can reflect contrasting sets of assumptions about learning: deficiency assumptions or potential assumptions. The deficiency assumption is that the adult learner to be deficient in some aspect of knowledge, capability or behaviour, and therefore an intervention to remedy the deficiency is necessary for performance to be achieved. The alternative assumption is that adult learners have growth potential and resources in some aspects of knowledge, capability or behaviour, and they are willing to be helped to discover how their latent abilities can help them fulfil their potential. Methods and practice challenges reflect the management of learning as a process that is at times 'outside-in' and at times 'inside-out'. In other words, it can be with the former directed at instilling what is new and with the latter at drawing out what is latent. Managing the combination of working 'outside-in' and 'inside-out' is a balance in methods and practice. In some circumstances one approach or the other may fit the need and structure the design. In many circumstances it is blending these which matters.

There are a range of practical contexts in which blending instruction and facilitation for supporting learning in work will be necessary, including:

(1) On-the-job learning experiences at the workplace;

(2) Organisation-based short training courses;

(3) External short courses or learning events;

(4) e-learning – computer-based or learning in a 'learning centre';

(5) One-to-one learning relationships, coaching and mentoring.

Instruction

Instruction works through the direct development of predetermined and programmatic kinds of knowledge, standardised capabilities and explicit behaviours. The principles of programmed instruction (Eitington 1984, Forsyth 1992, Mager 2000) reflect behaviourist theories of learning, and the structuring of guided practice to shape and influence human development through instructional steps (Practice 7.1). These influence action and delivery, ranging from systems to enable the memorisation of basic knowledge (including mind maps), trial-and-error practical learning for developing capabilities and reinforcement of desired attitudes and values. A four-phase model of HRD delivery by instruction in the classroom outlines the most common recipe. For effective instructional practice the emphasis is initially on providing a learner with knowledge (guidance), then supported practice (trial), with affective dimensions associated with reinforcing desired responses (correcting errors).

Practice 7.1: Phases of the Development and Delivery of Instruction
Exit-level performance Evaluate; Apply, Observe, Feedback Review; Check standards, Check skill transfer Practice; Simulate, Coach, Trial and error

---

Practice 7.1: (Continued)

Present; Demonstrate, Explain
Orient; Motivate, Assess, Prepare
Specification

Types of instruction include; direct verbal instruction from managers and others in the course of work; self-instruction, using workbooks and learning packs; or instruction provided in specialist learning environments by trained instructors. The success of action and delivery depends on a well-sequenced experience. Principles for instruction, whichever mode is to be used, can be prescribed.

Specifications for learning events are established in detail, aiming to outline in full what learners have to know and be able to do, and how they should be able to act. Learning is then delivered, with these elements presented in a logical sequence. The instructor is required to play the roles of showing and telling. Learners are then directly and formally tested on whether or not they have developed the knowledge, capability and behaviours required.

The development and use of professional instructors is an essential and integral part of organising learning. The professional development of trainers, the training of trainers, has been associated largely with proficiency in the process of instruction, and delivering formal training programmes. Professional instructors are people who have a thorough knowledge of the skill or subject, and an understanding of what is required for performance in work; they understand the 'know what' and 'know how' of the skill or subject that trainees are experiencing. They also understand and use the principles of structured and programmed instruction in design and delivery. They are able to perform consistently over many learning events, and over time as instructors, to deliver instruction sessions and objectively assess learners. The challenges facing instructors across sectors, contexts and kinds of adult learner are universal (see Practice 7.2). Good instructors are generally seen to be consistent, meticulous, patient and observant. Consistent in their ability to manage repeated delivery of the same/similar HRD processes; meticulous and obsessively organised in order to ensure that all aspects of instruction are effective; and sympathetic to learners of different abilities; patient with the process of showing and telling, trial and error; objective in assessing others' knowledge, capabilities and behaviour.

Practice 7.2: Delivery of Instruction and Adult Learners

Instruction	Adult learners
Get attention	Have different kinds and degrees of experience
Motivation	Can already perform many skills; get bored

Modelling	Seek to avoid pain and embarrassment; dislike feeling exposed
Timing	Pacing for different abilities; some bored, some lost
Practice and feedback	Feel exposed and vulnerable
Relevant practice	Through experience judge classrooms or cases are unrealistic
Reinforcement	Have own experiences to reflect on; dislike being 'taught'

Facilitation

The core meaning of 'facilitate' is 'to make something easy or easier'. In the HRD context, what we are 'easing' is a change in knowing, doing and/or behaving (Leigh 1991, Berry 1993, Bentley 1994). 'Easing' can be necessary and appropriate because of the widely recognised nature of HRD for adult learners. Facilitation is both a general concept, and a process associated with the clusters of methods that have evolved for supporting active adult learning. Adult learners engage and learn best when those supporting their learning approach the relationship of learning as one occurring between adults, and often straight and pure instruction is perceived as what will later be examined as being like a 'parent–child' relationship. Reacting to perceptions of a 'parent–child' relationship can produce disengagement and conflicts rather than trust and rapport in learning at work environments. Straight and pure instruction may also be deficient because of the nature of some of the kinds of objectives and targets that are significant in HRD at work. Where 'soft' skills, such as leadership and team-working are the focus, methods of instruction may not be the appropriate way to engage in and advance learning and change.

Finally, facilitation is also seen as appropriate because the value and logic of experiential learning is broadly accepted as the paradigm of workplace HRD. Facilitation is argued to be valid and useful as it helps those supporting HRD to use an experiential cycle model of learning covered in the previous chapter. People are eased into discovering and learning by and about themselves rather than being 'told' what to do or think. For some (Daloz 1999), the heart of adult learning is often a change in perspective, in how things are perceived. The theory of experiential learning suggests that for successful HRD delivery to occur learners need to work through every part of the experiential cycle.

Much traditional education, for example, has been critiqued because its delivery is based on abstract conceptualisation, teaching around theories. When it comes to 'real world' applications, much that is learnt in school, college or university seems to have been delivered ineffectively. Much training, in contrast, was critiqued for being only based on classroom concrete experience. Again, when it came to delivery, the training had not been enough preparation for the 'real world' of actual work, with the contingencies and circumstances found there. There was, thus, a need to build in time and opportunity for reflective observation and active experimentation, as well as providing concrete experience and abstract conceptualisation or theory.

Facilitation is sometimes perceived to be a more recently evolved delivery method in HRD, compared with instruction. In one respect the interest in facilitation is more recent, emerging as it does from the growth of values and systems of experiential learning that have permeated learning institutions and workplace learning in many cultures since the 1960s. The origins of the principles and practice of facilitation are more ancient. Socrates, the Greek philosopher, was renowned for responding to learners who came to him seeking his wisdom by questioning them rather than giving answers. He insisted to those who came to hear his great 'wisdom' that, far from being a font of all wisdom who could instruct others, he knew nothing. All that he could do was question those who thought they did know the answers. And, by having them examine their own thinking, he eased them into a state of 'productive confusion'. This had a greater impact than dispensing wisdom directly, as it helped provide an opportunity and space for the critical exploration of ideas through dialogue, to ultimately improve their understanding and develop better knowledge and behaviour. Balancing support and challenge is still the key to understanding how facilitation can impact on adult learners.

Daloz (1999) suggests we should map the extent to which 'challenge' and 'support' are present in a development partnership to promote growth. Where there is neither much support nor challenge, learners will experience 'stasis', or no growth. Where there is much support but only little challenge learners will experience only 'confirmation' and limited growth. Where there is much challenge but little support, learners may choose to 'retreat', and consequently not experience growth. Only where there is both support and challenge will adult learners potentially experience real growth and change.

Rogers (1969) was a major influence on those who perceive that facilitative practice and methods are central to learning in work. They believe that environments where 'space' for facilitation, questioning and challenge, mattered as much as providing direct instruction. This approach was not just desirable for ethical reasons, but was increasingly essential for promoting learning in workplace environments. The instructional approach was stifling, approaching learning as a task of filling up empty vessels with prescribed and standardised bodies of knowledge, discrete predetermined capabilities and behaviours. In such learning people were to be controlled, confined to fixed paths and subject to the authority of the instructor. Alternatively, Rogers argued, people who were 'free to learn' would be more likely to engage with and benefit from learning. Those responsible for learning had to engage not control, to inspire not dragoon, and to work with rather than 'on' the learner. This all meant that learners had to experience learning and change by encountering significant experiences that were meaningful to them, not instructor-driven programmes of skills development. If this was not done, there was little hope of engaging learners with learning in any meaningful way.

The challenge for Rogers was that learners were not engaged with learning, they were in what Daloz termed 'stasis' or 'retreat'. Classrooms in schools did not provide a positive learning environment; nor did training programmes in organisations. Schools, colleges and other learning environments had to be reformed to allow for and enable the freedom to learn. Like the philosopher Socrates, Rogers perceived a deeper purpose in the methods and practice of learning: to provide for and manage effective learning relationships that could overcome the challenges stifling participation in learning. In Socrates' time that stifling was grounded in the acceptance of unexamined assumptions about the world and what it was like. In Rogers' time the stifling was grounded in a climate where there appeared to be an endemic lack of purpose, lack of meaning and lack of commitment on the part of individuals; a climate where people were alienated not just from learning and educational environments, but more broadly from their societies. Facilitating learning was one way of breaking with these broader problems of alienation rather than perpetuating or exacerbating them.

Rogers concluded that there was a need to create communities of learners, where the 'educator' was facilitating change and learning, not instructing. This vision of learning communities is an abiding one, and it has flourished in the workplace learning context in various forms, up to contemporary interests in knowledge management. The practical challenge is for those promoting HRD to provide resources, develop learning contracts, organise groups and stimulate enquiry to get employees as learners to work together on real problems. In educational contexts this has produced movements to reform formal classroom teaching, examinations and grading systems. Facilitators set the mood and enable learning, moving away from formal teaching roles to being in learning relationships. In HRD and workplace learning, facilitation as a delivery method is reflected in the use of action learning with people together on real problems rather than sitting in classrooms (Megginson and Pedler 1992). To date facilitation methods seem to have found a more favourable reception in the workplace than in education, which still remains largely structured around classroom-based, teacher-led systems.

The major point of facilitation is that practice and methods should involve actions across the full learning cycle, accommodating all learning styles and drawing upon facilitative methods as well as instruction. For example, an organisation may seek to build more effective teams because problems with an absence of teamwork are causing performance concerns. It may seek to facilitate the development of teams by sending a group of people on an outdoors experience. This may involve the following:

- Cognition: knowledge about how effective groups work. This will come from an experience of being in a group and reflecting on its developments;

- Capabilities: exploring what it takes to be a leader in a group by giving people an opportunity to experience it for themselves. As they practise it, issues are raised about options for leadership and about their own abilities;

- Behaviours: exploring how to encourage and maintain communication even when difficulties with handling conflict in the group arise.

Styles and Delivery

Those delivering HRD, whether trainers, managers of others such as coaches and mentors, develop preferences which make them more comfortable with certain aspects of practice in learning than others. These preferences can, in some situations, lead to a systematic distortion of the learning process as greater emphasis is placed on some aspects to the detriment of others. Here are some typical examples, using the terms of Honey and Mumford (http://www.learningbuzz.com) which will be discussed further in Chapter 10:

- Preferences for experiencing can mean that delivery will include lots of activities, to the extent that learners never sit still but have to be rushing about, constantly on the go. This results in plenty of experiences and the assumption that having experiences is synonymous with learning from them.

- A preference for theorising will mean that delivery includes lots of discussion and debate. Delivery may shy away from dealing with first-hand experiences, and most time might be spent in promoting thinking; learners postpone reaching conclusions for as long as possible whilst allowing for more and more data to be gathered. This results in an 'analysis to paralysis' tendency with plenty of pondering and little action.

- Preferences for pragmatism can mean delivery focused on finding an expedient course of action and implementing it with inadequate analysis. This results in a tendency to go for 'quick fixes' by over-emphasising the planning and experiencing stages to the detriment of reviewing and concluding.

Facilitators will aim to motivate and manage learning through the use of participative methods, and reflections on experiences that they nurture or arrange with the learner. The learning happens as the experiential cycle is running, not in relation to a preset and fixed agenda scripted entirely by the trainer. Learners are not empty vessels to be filled up; they come with pre-existing cognitive capacity and ideas, capability and behaviour. Changing these through HRD involves either adding ideas, capabilities or behaviour, or displacing erroneous ideas, bad habits or dysfunctional behaviour.

The use of facilitation principles and methods with adult learners can create an environment in which the key issues are dealing with questions and responses, handling problem people and maintaining rapport. Rather than having a set sequence like instruction, facilitation requires an awareness of principles:

- Establishing the right environment;
- Ensuring participation;
- Confronting difficult issues;
- Maintaining a focus on achieving objectives;
- Managing the pacing of tasks and exercises.

For a facilitator, one of the challenges is handling 'difficult' people. If the goal is to 'ease' learning by actively involving learners in the delivery of HRD, treating them as participants not passive spectators, a number of challenging kinds of behaviour can emerge that may interfere with facilitated learning. Identifying and managing these can be essential to successful facilitated HRD (see Practice 7.3).

Practice 7.3: Facilitation and Adult Learning

Behaviour	Issues
Showing off	Hogging the limelight, impeding others' contributions
'Heckling'	Undermining the trainer or others who try to participate
Rambling	Going on and on, wasting time and losing focus
Griping	Taking the opportunity of being asked to speak up to moan
Fighting	Discussions become a space where conflicts surface in the group
Whispering	Once speaking up is sanctioned, some may begin a constant low-level chatting, distracting others
Struggling	Those unable to express themselves will struggle to contribute
Silence	Those who are unable or unwilling to participate in activity and discussions

There are inherent challenges in delivering either pure instruction-based or facilitation-based learning. Such problems are sometimes due to inadequate resourcing, with poorly prepared instructors or facilitators who are inexperienced. But even given adequate resourcing and effective needs assessment and design, there are still inherent challenges in using pure instruction or facilitation.

The demand is to combine them in delivery, to have a balance, with structure and process incorporating elements of instruction and facilitation.

The perceived disadvantage of facilitation is, it seems, that more can go obviously wrong with trying to 'ease' learning than with instruction. Poorly delivered instruction may be hidden on the day because the learners are passive, only when it transpires that they have not learned what was desired, back at work, does the inadequacy of a learning experience emerge. And poor instruction can be countered or redeemed by further learning in practice. With poor facilitation it is evident immediately in the learning environment. The underlying challenge with facilitation is knowing about learners as individuals, getting and using information about them before and during the learning process. The 'trainer' or manager using facilitation may also have professional anxieties about not being in control of the learning process. The lone facilitator has challenges in managing to coordinate small group work, and in providing effective and useful feedback to many individuals; the gains are greater, and the risks are higher as well.

Facilitation also demands that learners approach learning in a way that they may be unfamiliar or uncomfortable with, given how much education and schooling is still managed. But facilitation is worthwhile where existing knowledge impedes assimilation of new knowledge; where habits that are already well-established impede practising new ways of doing things; and where values and attitudes are already deeply entrenched. These can all survive the most intensive periods of instruction untouched and unchanged, but some good facilitation can make a difference. The most common problems with the delivery of instruction are given in Practice 7.4.

Practice 7.4: Instruction Issues

Problems	Causes
Dull (tell, tell, tell)	Too much information
No buy-in from trainees	Mandatory courses
Not real life	All theory, no practice
Falling behind or racing on	Goes at instructor's pace
Only get instructor's point of view	Only one instructor
Little chance to question and consolidate	Time and nature of instruction
Pitched at one level	Lack of preparation
Not adapting to different styles	Lack of time
Too authoritarian	Not knowing audience
Boring; stand and deliver	The structure too rigid

One-way; teacher–class	Include interactivity
Limited/no feedback from audience	Check and get feedback
Lack of preparation/knowledge	Train the trainers
Poor presentation style and material	Improve styles, OHPs and handouts

For better instruction the focus is on the following:

- Define and convey clear aims and objectives;
- Improve materials (ensure up to date), prepare, make time, know audience;
- Vary styles within the learning environment;
- Encourage intervention;
- Encourage participation (ice-breakers, room layout, facilitation);
- Work on presentation style.

The more common facilitation delivery problems and solutions are given in (Practice 7.5).

Practice 7.5: Facilitation Issues

Problems	Solutions
Group dynamics	Need to know all types prior to start and be able to listen/observe
Some over-talkative	Tactfully stop talkative people
Some very quiet	Get all to contribute
Fears, personality, attitudes	Create a safe environment for learning
Perception of the learning	Will not be the same for all
Experience and opinions can hinder agreement on solution	Accept and deal with different experiences, managing conflict
Keeping it focused on objectives	Can involve questions before and at end of course
Facilitator is not competent	Facilitate for them, leadership in the group
Difficult to keep on track	Prior planning prevents poor performance; think about timings

Practice 7.5: (Continued)	
Objectives not clear enough	Define clear objectives
Different levels/ kinds of needs	Respond flexibly to these
Lack of control	Ensure that the learning rather than personal agendas prevails
Motivation	How does this translate back to work?

Connections to HRD Process

The practice and methods of HRD will also fit with different approaches, Systematic Training (ST), Performance Improvement (PI) or Continuous Development (CDP) processes outlined earlier. With ST instruction is often the core approach, though even well-conceived, designed and delivered formal training programmes may fail, with a pattern of regression to pre-training skill levels of performance. Initial learning and improved performance after training may lapse, with performance problems again coming to the fore.

In PI approaches instead of concentrating on delivering more and better training the focus shifts to thinking about the work context, and analysing more closely expected behaviours and the environments that reinforce these. The logic is that organisations have perhaps not defined expected behaviours clearly enough or built an organisational environment conducive to attaining these behaviours. This argument rested on a view of behaviour as human activity that can be seen, measured or described. There is a concern with identifying and dealing with specific behaviours, rather than generic or abstract issues of cognitive capacity, capability or affective factors. Thus results and the cause of results were not given equal weighting. A few vital behaviours can be seen to account for effective performance and results, not a wide span of cognitive capacities, capabilities and emotional intelligence.

The application of behaviourist concepts is seen then not only in instructional training but also in the need for more effective analysis of human performance problems, based on identifying and reinforcing key behaviours, and designing and developing environments that reinforced such behaviours. This core basic insight has been elaborated upon and 'reincarnated' in several forms, such as those models of 'excellence' articulated in some competency frameworks and the advocacy of movements such as Neuro Linguistic Programming (NLP) and, more recently, 'Positive Psychology'. In its most basic form it can be thought of as at Behaviourist's ABC, and in one guise or another it plays an important role in thinking about and delivering HRD in many PI contexts:

- Antecedents: identify the causes of behaviour;
- Behaviours: describe people's overt and actual actions;
- Consequences: analyse what then happens as a result of the behaviour.

For example, staff might be instructed during health and safety training to wear hard hats on construction sites. Following such instruction, they might then wear the hard hats when returning to a normal work situation, only to be derided by their peers who do not wear them. This feedback does not reinforce the required behaviour, and indeed undermines it. It may then make sense to the person not to wear the hard hat in the first place to escape the derision of their peers.

This kind of outcome was taken as a paradigm for what was wrong with even the best-delivered training: it could not alter the dynamics of 'ABC' in the real world of the workplace, which undermined the transfer of learning. The antecedents that were most influential were not the instructions people were given in the classroom or their facilitated learning, but the environments in which they worked. These antecedents were seen to be the principal causes of the behaviour, and not the learning being provided on courses. So even the best-designed and carefully thought-out training programmes were seen to fail because they were not supported on the job. The consequence of this finding was a change in focus in dealing with performance gaps by developing interventions aimed at analysing and rearranging the outcomes of desirable or undesirable behaviours – for example by using reward systems to reinforce effort or output.

Behaviourists are renowned for eschewing the possibility of scientifically studying mental states – effectively, what goes on in people's heads – as a cause of behaviour. The notion of the 'ABC' reinforces this because it does not require any overt analysis of thought processes. It assumes that people behave the way they do because it 'makes sense' to them, even where it may not make sense to others who may actually see their behaviour as dysfunctional. The consequences of behaviours may be understood through the eyes of the beholder. Yet the nature of such perceptions and sense-making is less important for influencing behaviour than reinforcement of desired behaviours; by managing consequences. It is the way that consequences exist and are managed that has to be seen from the perspective of the learner, not from anyone else's point of view. If, for example, the payment outcomes of learning and changing particular behaviours are valuable to them, then they will learn, change and behave consistently with what is desired; if the outcomes are of little or no value to them, they are unlikely to learn, change and behave differently.

Problems for an 'ABC' form of delivery in PI interventions can arise in various ways. One is when organisations send mixed signals. For example, there may be an assertion of new values and aspirations, but failure to alter existing systems of consequence. This can be a deadly combination. For example, organisations may attempt to reorganise the work environment to elicit innovative behaviour by using performance-related pay; but at the same time they may maintain bureaucratic adherence to existing ways of doing things and the promotion of people who are bureaucratic. Or organisations may seek to promote 'empowerment' by training their managers to involve teams in decision-making, which is often aimed at improving long-term performance. Yet they may keep rewarding these managers for achieving short-term targets. Under these circumstances, managers are likely to interpret their jobs and make behavioural choices in terms of what matters most to them, usually those behaviours that are actually measured; in this instance short-term targets. The likely result is that managers would become directed to achieve targets rather than empowering, which was the aim of the HRD aimed at learning and change.

Other kinds of problems exist where there are positive consequences for the same behaviour in some conditions, but negative consequences in others. For example, new ways of army training were tried, based on self-instruction rather than instructor-led instruction. The trials of this new system went well, with learners completing the courses they were taking much faster than had previously been the case. But when the new system was put into more widespread use, the results were the opposite. Learners were taking as long, if not longer, to complete the training. The situation was investigated, and it was found that, when the learners finished, they were moved on to other work details. It was in their interest to delay finishing to avoid being sent on those other work duties. So the nature of consequences did not, from the trainees' point of view, elicit the desired behaviour those providing the HRD had wanted, which was to complete training more quickly.

One other common problem in the work environment that undermines the 'ABC' delivery is the distance between behaviours and consequences. The further in time a consequence is from a behaviour the less impact the consequence will have. So, for example, many employees are held accountable for performance not immediately after an episode of performance but only at their annual performance review. The time period between much of their behaviour and the consequences emanating from these reviews is too great for there to be a consequence of any impact, even if the feedback they get is accurate and clear. The ideal is to provide consequences at the time of behaviour; small doses of positive or negative rewards at the appropriate time, rather than large doses of feedback much later. In particular, positive consequences ought to arise on an immediate basis.

If the 'ABC' delivery approach is to be used in the workplace in PI approaches, feedback must be given frequently. Feedback is about providing information regarding performance on goals; reinforcement is the desired effect of effective feedback. Performance gaps may be closed by appropriate reinforcement of desired behaviours using reinforcers rather than providing training. Effective feedback should be as follows:

- Immediate;
- Goal-specific;

- Expressed positively not negatively.

Feedback on performance problems will not work if:

- It is used as punishment;
- It is delayed or too late;
- Given to someone not in control of the problem;
- Given on the wrong variable, e.g. quantity not quality;
- It needs too much effort to record it.

Even so, the use of feedback and reinforcers will not have overnight effects. Shaping people's behaviours to be consistent with what is desired is about changing in the right direction, reinforcing improvement in the right direction, building upon success, and noticing and reinforcing improvements. Intermittent reinforcement is, in theory, the best strategy. Non-existent reinforcement or continuous reinforcement both fail to shape behaviour effectively. Non-existent reinforcement fails because, without consequences, the desired behaviours will diminish. Continuous reinforcement is not only impracticable and costly, but fails because the apparent certainty of consequence means there is no credibility for it as a reinforcer. The symbol of classic intermittent reinforcement is the behaviour of playing slot machines: the people who play them know that they will pay out some time, but they do not know when. The trick in designing machines that engage people is to reinforce their playing with intermittent wins. The work environment is similar. People should want to play the performance game because they know they will get positive consequences, but they are not sure exactly when – that way they keep playing.

Reinforcement of desired behaviour has to be complemented by the punishment and extinction of undesired behaviour. Punishment focuses on reducing or eliminating undesired behaviour, which is a more problematic concept than the provision of feedback for positive consequences. This is because the use of punishment creates long-term problems in relationships, and can lead to their disintegration. Moreover, people learn to tolerate punishments, and it has only temporary effects; on the other hand, it can extinguish other desired behaviours. Its use also generates a culture of excuses, and escape and avoidance behaviour. The intermittent reinforcement schedule effect also arises: if punishment is intermittent, the behaviour continues at a higher rate. Above all, it cannot lead to the desired behaviour being established. In CD approaches the interest is in facilitating learning through coaching and mentoring. These are dealt with in more detail in a subsequent chapter.

Conclusion

The methods and practice of instruction and facilitation are both significant for delivering workplace learning. Skills with the elements of each are essential parts of professionally providing learning at work. These skills can be applied across a wide range of possible contests for HRD, from one-to-one development to whole organisation change. Instruction is most associated with ST approaches, instruction and facilitation are blended in PI approaches, and CD tends to depend more on facilitation.

3 Key Texts

(1) Daloz, L. A. (1999) *Mentor: Guiding the Journey of Adult Learners* (San Francisco, Jossey-Bass).

(2) Eitington, J. (1984) *The Winning Trainer* (Houston, Gulf Publishing Company).

(3) Mager, R. (2000) *What Every Manager Should Know about Training* (Chalford, Management Books).

3 Key Articles

(1) Ellinger, A. and Cseh, M. (2007) Contextual Factors Influencing the Facilitation of Others' Learning through Everyday Work Experiences, *Journal of Workplace Learning*, 19 (7), pp. 435–452.

(2) Owen, C. (2009) Instructor Beliefs and Their Mediation of Instructor Strategies, *Journal of Workplace Learning*, 21 (6), pp. 477–495.

(3) Sheehan, M. (2004) Learning as the Construction of a New Reality, *Journal of Workplace Learning*, 16 (3/4), pp. 179–197.

3 Key Web Links

(1) BLOG on Workplace learning: http://www.brandon-hall.com/workplacelearningtoday/.

(2) A Graphic Overview: http://www.fugitiveknowledge.com/PDF/Learning_Infographic.pdf.

(3) Training Manager Job Descriptions: http://www.bls.gov/oco/ocos021.htm.

8

Quality and Improvement

Learning Objectives

By the end of this chapter you will be able to:

- Describe the main themes and challenges commonly used to support quality management in HRD;

- Analyse the methodologies available for the review, evaluation and improvement in learning and change;

- Critically evaluate the use of rational-economic models of evaluation in the employment context;

- Design and construct valid and reliable ways of reviewing, evaluating and improving learning and change activities.

Practice 8.1: A Quote from Practice

'The real world is characterised by imperfections, probabilities, and approximations. It runs on inference, deduction, and implication, not on absolute irrefutable hard-wiring. Yet we are constantly asked to measure and report on this fuzzy multidimensional world we live in as if it were a cartoon or comic book, reducing all of its complexity and ambiguity to hard financial "data.". . . Putting a monetary value on training's impact on business is fraught with estimation, negotiation, and assumption – and putting a monetary value on the cost of learning is often even less precise. Yet when was the last time you saw an ROI (return on investment) figure presented as anything other than an unqualified absolute? If you tried for statistical accuracy and said something like, "this project will produce 90% of the desired ROI, 95% of the time with a 4% error margin," you'd be thrown out of the boardroom.'

Source: http://www.trainingzone.co.uk/item/143544, accessed 4 September 2006.

Exercise 8.1: Evaluation Information

Identify a Human Resource Development (HRD) initiative you are familiar with, either in professional practice or from a case study. To what extent can you find information of Baseline indicator development (see Figure 8.1).

Baseline indicators	What information do you already have?	What additional information do you need?	What methods will you use to gather additional information?	Who will take responsibility for gathering this information?	When do they need to do it by?
1					
2					

Figure 8.1   Baseline indicator development

What would be the problems of completing the analysis grid given in Figure 8.2 for this case?

What have we tried	
What have we learned	
What are we pleased about	
What are we concerned about	
What will we do now	

Figure 8.2   Analysis grid
Source: Evaluation Scotland (2011).

Introduction

The concepts used in discussing and managing the quality of HRD are defined. The functions and contexts in which evaluation is managed are described. The challenges of evaluation and quality management in HRD are identified, and methods for managing these explained (see Practice 8.1). The metatheories which shape evaluation in HRD are described, reflecting the rivalry between quantitative and qualitative mindsets in HRD as a whole.

Quality Management in HRD

The quality management phase of learning and change involves review, evaluation and improvement. Quality management refers to the activities involved in determining the merit, worth or value of learning and change processes in the workplace. This fulfils important functions for significant stakeholders in HRD in employment: employers, learners, product and service users. This stage of the process may involve determining the extent to which identified needs have indeed been met, whether aims, objectives and results have been achieved, and how the delivery of HRD has gone in practice (Hamblin 1974, Newby 1992).

Practice 8.2: Definitions

Quality: the effectiveness of a programme of learning, given the needs of the learner in the context of defined learning outcomes.

Quality assurance (QA): writing down what HRD is aiming to do and checking periodically that this is being done.

Quality enhancement (QE): finding out what those who have an interest in and use HRD systems say about them, and amending systems accordingly. This has four different functions:

- to shape or implement strategic policy;
- to meet regulatory requirements;
- to develop services and provisions based on learning from external sources;
- to develop services and provisions based on learning from internal sources;

Quality audit: keeping records to prove that QA and QE are being managed well.

A common language for discussing quality management of learning and change (Practice 8.2) is given by McGhee (2003). There are then multiple functions of exploring quality (Scriven 1991) which are given in Debate 8.1.

Debate 8.1: Functions of Quality Management

There are recognised to be several functions for quality management in HRD, reflecting the interests of different stakeholders;

- Pragmatic functions: Identifying the 'bad', eliminating costs and waste, resource concerns;
- Ethical functions: Ensuring good service, fairness and justice for those involved in HRD;
- Intellectual functions: Providing useful information via valid tools and avoiding bias and prejudice;
- Social and business functions: Directing limited resource and effort where it is most needed, costs and benefits;
- Personal functions: Providing a basis for those offering HRD to have self-esteem; knowing that what they do works.

This is an integral phase of the HRD process, though a phase which many see as a major challenge. As the quote in the introduction suggested there are perceptions that quality management in HRD can be displaced by 'quants' management; that is by measurement that seeks to prove training and development have had a direct, immediate financial return using quantitative methods and figures.

In the context of workplace HRD there are frameworks for quality management that provide basic methods to more robust and sophisticated systems of continuous improvement. From the use of end-of-course evaluation surveys, often called 'happy sheets', to formulas for calculating costs and benefits, the domain has its widely used frameworks. Quality management is also of greater concern than just reflection on the previous stages of a specific instance of learning. Assuring and improving the quality of HRD, learning and change across the organisation, while controlling and reducing the cost of providing workplace learning systems, is perhaps the biggest challenge, and is one of the most often debated and discussed.

For Phillips (1991) the challenge is the prevalence of myths that interfere with and impede evaluation, which include the following:

- The results of training cannot be measured.
- It is unclear what information to collect.
- Return on investment (ROI) cannot be calculated, so it's not possible to evaluate.
- Measurement works only in production and finance.
- If the chief executive officer (CEO) does not require it, why bother?
- There are too many variables affecting behaviour change.
- It will only lead to criticism.
- The trainers have a proven track record.
- Measuring progress towards objectives is enough.
- Evaluation costs too much.

Source: Phillips (1991).

Dispelling myths is one way to focus on the discussion of evaluation, but there are substantial and abiding challenges in evaluation (Likierman 2009):

- A lack of enthusiasm for measuring among all parties, including managers, trainers and learners;
- A skew towards what can be measured, that is activities rather than outcomes;
- It is difficult to recognise and align different interests and views of success; HR, Management, and learners;
- Objectives tend to be poorly defined, where it is not clear what success looks like.

These expose evaluation to the risks and errors of 'common sense' rather than enlisting the methods of normal science to support and improve HRD, an issue explored in the earlier chapter on theory.

For Holton and Naquin (2005) the challenge is greater than that. Evaluation models developed and commonly used in HRD, which will be described later in this chapter, can all be considered products of a particular kind of thinking; rational-economic, decision-making thinking. Yet the use of rational-economic evaluation thinking may be futile or counterproductive in quality management in HRD. If stakeholders in organisations do not make decisions in the manner envisaged by the rational-economic model, determining value by considering all the costs and benefits and coming to a view of the optimal alternatives by gauging that information rationally, then quality management systems based on this can be part of the problem, not a solution. The OECD (2003), for example, has emphasised that the economic arguments for people to engage with learning does not often win over people or organisations. People and organisations are often not attracted to learning even with free access, or having potential economic gains in the longer term spelt out for them. They need to be persuaded that learning is appropriate for them in the 'here and now', that it will satisfy real needs they have. And central to that is having good, even great, experiences of learning when they encounter it. The concern to ensure good HRD and improve it to 'great' is central for sustaining and expanding the impact of HRD in the workplace.

Holton and Naquin question whether the rational-economic thinking that informs much of the debate around evaluation in HRD is realistic. As stakeholders generally use bounded rationality when making decisions, they use standards other than economic utility. These are more subjective, about expectations and utility or probabilities, to inform thinking about what is possible and probable, and guide the decision-making of learners, trainers and managers. People form and hold aspirations, and if these are met and satisfied, then conclusions are positive; if not, conclusions are negative. Understanding what satisfies not what optimises is the key to quality management in HRD; away from data ion four levels and towards balanced scorecards or stories/cases (see Practice 8.3).

Practice 8.3: Evaluation Connections: Strategic Objectives and Participant Outcomes

One simple method for structuring evaluation is to identify Strategic Objectives (SOs) and Learning Objectives (LOs). Strategic Objectives are set by Management and Leadership, and shape the HRD programme. Learning Objectives, the knowledge skills and attitudes desired are set by Participants who do the HRD; they specify for themselves what the aim to learn. Impact Measures and Targets for these SOs and LOs, can be derived by Managers and Participants respectively. Participants record the impacts of the programme at its conclusion. These, taken together, can be cross referenced to SOs.

These concerns with quality management and the impact of quality improvement systems exist in all areas of management and work, so in this regard learning and change are no exception. Looking at the systems in common use for managing quality in learning reveals a very mixed picture of robust basic frameworks but limited delivery across all these functions. The first step is to review the quality of the delivery of the HRD experience and the planning and design process (see Perspective 8.1). Have the specific objectives been met? Did the learning happen according to plan? Was that the right plan? These all seem straightforward matters, and depending on the evidence either the HRD intervention may be judged a success or the intervention may have to be re-run in order to deal with any shortfalls or continuing gaps.

The long-standing and well-known framework of levels of evaluation in HRD is a way of fulfilling at least some of the functions of evaluation. This levels of evaluation framework has an enduring appeal, though it curtails rather than engages with new and fresh thinking and debates over quality methodologies, and theories of quality of HRD (Wang and Spitzer 2005).

Perspective 8.1: Levels of HRD Evaluation; Dominant Framework for Quality Management

Evaluation level	Focus and concerns.
Reactions	What are the learners' reactions to the HRD they have experienced; in their estimation was the learning experience helpful and useful? This generally involves post-course or intervention feedback to the developers.
Learning	To what extent have the objectives of the HRD intervention been met? What have the learners learned? This can involve tests and assessments of knowledge, skill and abilities.
Performance	To what extent has the performance gap been closed? This is generally seen as the extent to which learning is or is not transferred to the workplace or is manifest in improved performance.
Organisational	What were the costs and benefits of the HRD? Is it confirmed that the HRD has provided value for money?

Ultimate value	What are the overall tangible and intangible outcomes of having provided HRD? Are staff more committed, are they more flexible? Is the organisation better placed to realise its strategy, to compete successfully?

The most evident activity in workplace learning quality management is at the 'learner' level, with the use of end-of-course or event evaluation forms. This is, at least, done as a ritual and possibly with more serious intent, although the design and use of such surveys, for they are a form or survey, is not of much focal interest. Beyond the conventional use of learner evaluation forms, there are underlying and deeper concerns engaging with the other functions of quality management. As the final stage in the HRD process, quality management can be expected to fulfil at least one, and often several, of these functions. That requires much more than asking learners to complete an end-of-course evaluation form. To determine the value of HRD in these contexts we need some form of evidence, and measurement and judgement of the achievement of objectives, to confirm that the initially defined HRD need has been met.

Quality management is often taken to be the hardest phase to do well, and often makes for the weakest link in the whole HRD process. This is partly because of the multiple functions it may be required to achieve. Because of its nature, coming at the end, it is the step most likely to be neglected in practice or be least satisfactorily accomplished. All the other phases will have had to be completed to some extent, but it is possible to neglect or avoid evaluation; without apparent consequence. The failure to think about needs would show when people contemplated participating but did not because what was on offer did not interest them. To fail to design would show as the absence of a balanced set of objectives and use of methods. To fail to deliver would show as people turning up to an empty room! But to fail to evaluate does not necessarily show so clearly so easily. Over time it would have a cumulative and powerful impact, but not immediately or evidently in the short term.

Quality management is a challenge to both the theory and practice of HRD. In theory terms, the main framework for debate, which encompassed a wide range of concerns, are that the key failing in practice was not demonstrating clear cost-benefit analysis (CBA) and meeting business needs.

It has been a long-established concern that most organisations find it difficult to analyse their HRD in clear cost-benefit terms (Russ-eft and Preskill 2005). As has been emphasised for each phase of the HRD process, quality management is not just about using tools and techniques to determine how effectively the HRD process is managed; it is also about working in a broader management and political context, here about review, evaluation and improvement.

Quality in the HRD Context

In the HRD context, quality management is an umbrella term, one that covers a wide range of activities with various purposes. These include the following:

- Obtaining information about learners: testing them to evaluate their cognitive capacities, their capabilities and their behaviours;

- Obtaining information from learners: how they rate their HRD experiences, and how much they feel they have learned or developed;

- Reviewing whether the right objectives and targets have been met, and whether the overall benefits of doing that warrant the costs that have been incurred.

These various activities all seek to address the same basic questions: was the HRD that was identified as necessary planned, designed and delivered effectively, and was it worth doing?

In the evaluation of HRD at work, there is an interesting contradiction. On the one hand, basic methods have been formulated and widely used for some time (Kirkpatrick 1975).

Perspective 8.2: Potential Indicators of Quality to Measure

Measures of learners' success

- Successful completion of qualifications;
- Value added and distance travelled;
- Extended existing value-added measurement;
- Non-accredited learning;
- Equality and diversity and a framework for analysis of measures.

Measures of providers' success

- Learner satisfaction at provider level;
- Learners' destinations at provider level;
- Measuring the capability of providers' staff;
- Measures of employer engagement;
- Giving value for money.

These methods are still in use today, and provide reference points that structure HRD quality management in theory and in practice. The main method is one that defines and explores set levels of evaluation for HRD at work (see Perspective 8.2). The continuing influence of methods embedded in the popular 'levels of evaluation' model is also seen in recent major surveys on training in

Europe, where the information on and analysis of evaluation of quality is based on data on the levels of employee satisfaction, test results, certification, transfer to the workplace and impact on performance. These are different ways of conceiving the same old levels.

On the other hand, there is no single, agreed, standard, universal system in use. Greater concern with quality in the present and the future, driven by forces from various contexts, has put a spotlight on the evaluation phase of HRD. These forces include strategic policy and funding reviews, regulatory organisation concerns, developmental agencies' concerns, and research for quality enhancement. What is measured, how it is measured and who measures it appear to vary greatly among countries, contexts of learning and different kinds of learner.

In most countries quality management of learning is something of interest to many agencies are involved in aspects of workplace HRD; for colleges, universities and work-based learning, adult learning, community learning and independent, private and commercial colleges and training organisations. Agencies vary, and the approach adopted may be based on a method such as total quality management, or just be concerned with the outcomes of a specific programme. We can accept this diversity, and simply continue to use a variety of different approaches to managing quality in HRD, or we can seek to remove diversity by developing standardised systems of best practice that can be used across different contexts.

One survey (LSC 2004) of learner satisfaction showed that the quality of teaching/training accounts for the most deeply held views of satisfaction or dissatisfaction: one in ten learners have made complaints about their course or their experience. The aspects of teaching and training that fall into the priorities for action, according to this survey, are as follows:

- Making the subject interesting or enjoyable for the learner;
- Understanding the learner and how they like to learn;
- The support they give the learner, for example in improving their study techniques or time management;
- Planning their lessons;
- Setting clear targets to help the learner improve;
- Providing prompt and regular feedback on progress;
- Managing the group of learners.

The abiding popularity of the 'levels of evaluation' framework should not preclude deeper and broader diversity in evaluation. At present, evaluation is perceived to be stuck with what amounts to little more than a basic recipe for evaluation (the levels of evaluation model) with no more fully developed quality standards or models emerging. Seeking more rigorous and mature systems of evaluation is a major concern (see Scriven 1991, Perspective 8.3).

Perspective 8.3: Maturity of Evaluation Systems

Mature and established; framework for evaluation
Metatheories proposed;
Debates about Methodologies; Rational-Economic vs Naturalistic
Basic recipes established in early practice; Kirkpatrick 4 levels

Source: Scriven (1991).

The search for more sophisticated and robust systems to drive up quality triggers debate about methodologies of evaluation. Methodologies are coherent frameworks for guiding the identification, collection and analysis of data and sense-making. There are several methodologies available, ranging from those which embody positivist assumptions and principles about collecting and investigating 'hard' facts to those embodying naturalist assumptions and principles about collecting 'stories' and cases whose interpretation underlies effective sense-making. This is where HRD appears to be presently. One example is offered by McGhee (2003). He suggested a review of quality management in learning that offered a general framework for taking analysis beyond a 'basic recipe' into debates about methodologies, and metatheories. In going beyond basic levels of 'evaluation as inspection', McGhee further suggested that there should be a conscious attempt to encourage a culture for quality in the way that HRD is evaluated. McGhee identifies five important features which are common to good learning cultures, and contends that if these features are all present and dealt with effectively then a good culture for quality will exist:

(1) The foundations: basic systems for gathering and using information about learning quality.

(2) Cognitive: generating and nurturing ideas for innovation and change in quality.

(3) Emotional: that people involved in learning are able to discuss and deal with sensitive issues raised by openly exploring quality.

(4) Interpersonal: there exist open and inclusive relations among all those concerned with evaluating quality.

(5) Organisational: there are clear roles and a project management approach to quality.

Why these factors matter has been highlighted again by Sherlock and Perry (2008) who provide an overview of the origins and changes in quality management in learning. Early 'Inspection' concerns were about learning from shortcomings – even disasters and accidents – in order to stimulate improvements in the provision of adult learning for work. This was an agenda which cast the inspector as a figure independent of the government of the day; the citizen's expert representative and advocate. Inspection became an accepted and respected part of civil society. This matured into a fixed inspection regime and cycle, with institutions inspected regularly; prompt re-inspection of those found wanting, with the prospect of severe sanctions for a second failure; a requirement for regular self-assessment by every institution; the introduction of numerical grades to summarise performance in every significant area of activity; and publication of inspection reports. This new regime mainly affected publicly owned institutions, and was often given statutory force.

However, traditional approaches to inspection – which entail steps to collect evidence, pronounce judgement and walk away – were perceived as inadequate. Progress was achieved only slowly and the atmosphere created by hawkish and highly confrontational. This might be tolerable in educational institutions like schools, but was counterproductive in workplace HRD where training was only a part of the whole quality picture. Quality management needed to clearly add value in terms significant to the organisation. And evolution of inspection systems led to thinking about how quality should be judged by the level of benefit that training brought to each learner which opened up more sophisticated avenues of inspection. Inspectors could do more than criticise management practices; they could cite evidence of ill-effects on learners.

This moves away from making evaluation something which is essentially rooted in having learners complete an end-of-course evaluation form. It is about opening up debates around methods for evolving a quality-aware culture supporting HRD. Instead of just collecting data on how training courses have gone, new concerns emerge. Such a quality-aware evaluation culture for HRD could have powerful effects on the effectiveness of HRD as a whole. It could act to reinforce change by legitimising new capacities, capabilities and behaviours among those who have changed, and by identifying effectively those who have not changed. It could also act to ensure that all other stages of the HRD process – from needs through design and delivery – are protected, sustained and enhanced. In promoting such a quality-aware culture the assumptions and perceptions of stakeholders about HRD may be clarified. Managers who do not really commit to supporting HRD, or employees who are reluctant to participate/succeed in HRD, or even HRD professionals used to the 'old ways' and systems who are averse to changing, will be more clearly visible.

This is how an apparently straightforward process of seeking to collect information to enable more quality-awareness about HRD systems, and its contribution to improving performance can lead to much more interesting and challenging things. Because many stakeholders may be aware of this, one consequence can be that advocating and promoting a more quality-aware evaluation of HRD is resisted – either actively opposed or 'passively' sabotaged. In the worst case, effective HRD review and evaluation can more or less entirely break down in an organisation. This approach connects interest in evaluation with the higher maturity metatheories level suggested by Scriven.

Methodologies of Quality Management

Recognising different levels of maturity frameworks for quality review (see Perspective 8.4) and analysis, it is possible to look in some detail at how HRD quality management may be done when evaluating reactions, learning, transfer or ultimate costs and benefits. Basic questions are as follows:

- How will the data be used? Should the instrument be tested?
- How will data be analysed? Is there a standard instrument?
- Who will use the data? What are the consequences of errors?
- What facts are needed?

Perspective 8.4: Maturity of Evaluation

Maturity (and Car Metaphor)	Focus	Objectives	Evaluation Process
Basic Trabant	Immediate reactions	Aims unconnected with organisational objectives	No preparation or follow up
Enhanced Smart	Goes A to B economically with no extras, feedback from participants	Overall direction given by senior managers/HR but no systematic objective setting	minimal preparation and follow through (more detailed work done by participants and line managers)
Improved Volkswagen (NTA?)	Efficient but not extravagant; completed by HR	Changes against objectives	Overall development strategy and connections across these
Prestige Bentley	Luxury model with complex machinery Comprehensive, detailed and continuous involving all stakeholders	Comprehensive description of objectives linked to organisational priorities	Preparation and extended follow follow-through and learning systematically shared

Source: Likierman, A. (2009).

A system needs to be practicable in the organisation: easy to administer, simple, brief and economical, taking into account the costs of design, development or purchase, and the time taken to get and analyse the data. Solutions include common activities such as:

- End-of-training-course 'happy sheet';
- Rationales for standard tests;
- Models to analyse training costs.

But these are only a basic and not very sophisticated means of quality management. In the area of HRD, some have argued that the levels of evaluation model have not provided organisations with a means for attaining robust evaluations. Organisations using these activities often still do not know what they were getting for their money (see Practice 8.4). This is not just because some aspects of the evaluation recipe are being ignored or done in an unprofessional manner. It is not easy to identify HRD costs and benefits properly, and the risks of not doing HRD. In the final analysis for professional practice, few really value absolute forms of quantitatively sound evaluation. In this situation there are two possible paths, reflecting a choice in beliefs and methodology; quasi-scientific or humanistic. Each provides a gateway to different methodologies for HRD quality management.

Evaluation Instruments – the Questionnaire

Questionnaires are the most common evaluation tool at the level of 'reactions'. They are easy to design, develop and administer. They are familiar to most people, and provide data that can be summarised easily.

(1) Determine the information needed;
(2) Select question type:

- o Open ended
- o Checklist
- o Two-way question
- o Multiple-choice
- o Ranking scales

(3) Develop the questions;
(4) Test the question for understanding;
(5) Develop the completed questionnaire;
(6) Prepare a data summary sheet.

Practice 8.4: ROI – How is it Done?

(1) To measure ROI, start by isolating the impact of training as much as possible. To do this it is necessary to have a control group. Train one group several months ahead of another, so that you have a control group to test against. Alternatively, narrowly focus the training so that a before-and-after comparison can be made.

(2) Decide the impact the training should have. If learning a computer programme is expected to shorten each customer service enquiry, then attach a cost to that extra productivity.

(3) The bottom line is: calculate the productivity effect. For instance, will each customer service person be able to handle 10 more phone calls a day? Calculate the money associated with that: say each phone call represents £6 of the employee's time. Get a final value, for example that 20 employees each save an average of £60 a day: therefore £1200 per day, multiplied by 280 annual days. Divide that by the cost of the training. The result is the ROI.

Tests

Pre-course and post-course tests are used to evaluate the 'learning' level – to evaluate changes in knowledge, skill or ability. Tests can be classified in a number of ways, but the main divisions are by media and design:

(1) By media:

- Written, paper and pencil tests
- Simulations or actual performance
- Computer-based tests

(2) By design:

- Essays and exams: the most common in formal education
- Objective tests: specific and precise answers in relation to programme objectives
- Norm-referenced tests: compare participants with each other or other groups, rather than attainment of objectives
- Criterion-referenced tests: an objective test with a predetermined cut-off score for a minimum standard
- Performance tests: to exhibit a skill, whether manual, verbal or analytical.

Other Instruments

In a narrow way these methodologies are about the process of measuring how far objectives and results have been achieved. Beyond accumulating and presenting facts about the achievement of HRD objectives in cognitive capacities, capabilities and behaviour to make judgements, there is also evidence relating to standards and changes in organisational performance as a whole.

(1) Interviews: to secure data not available through other means, and probe to uncover stories useful for evaluation.

(2) Focus groups': if other quantitative methods are not adequate, to get at judgements about 'quality'.

(3) Observations: before, during or after an HRD event. Need to be prepared and trained, be systematic, know how to interpret and report what they see, and their influence should be minimised. Use of behaviour checklists, coded records, video recording or delayed report.

If it is challenging to identify and use objective standards to identify performance gaps which warrant HRD in the first place, then evaluation mirrors this challenge at this stage; the extent to which performance gaps have been closed is a challenge at the other end of the process. Quantitative information provides 'quick and dirty' data about the kinds of areas that are measurable in the immediate period after HRD experiences. Other, more robust and 'clean' assessments of cognitive capacity, capability and behavioural change can be more difficult to collect and analyse.

The feature of the methodology is that quantitative and objective standards provide a means of gauging what has been of value. The determination of objective standards may mean a range of things. Is it defined in terms of ROI (Flynn 1998) or some other description of expectations about what HRD can achieve or some other way of defining results or outcomes? CBA has been proposed as a means of structuring the evaluation of HRD. The costs are known in advance, but the benefits can only be estimated; they cannot be fully known. In a business and management context the common sense underlying such estimation is widely used, so why should it not be applied to HRD? One good reason is set out in Debate 8.2. It concerns the 'tyranny of numbers' when applied to intangible assets and benefits.

The idea of ROI is at the heart of this methodology, the pursuit of an absolute number, a neat package that shows the exact value returned for an exact value invested in training. This is a seductive idea as calculating the ROI of HRD can be simple and objective, and fits into the business context. However, it can also be complex and would never displace the role of more subjective judgements (Flynn 1998). Sometimes it is seen as the Holy Grail for many involved in HRD in order to prove their worth; and some are willing to go to great lengths to do so. Sometimes it is not worth the effort.

If it is a possibility in some form, the first question is 'Is it worth doing?'. Before embarking on any ROI quest, it is wise to estimate the ROI for calculating an ROI. Will it be worth the time and money that it will take? The answer depends more on the type of HRD that is planned than the cost as such. The type of training best suited to calculating ROI is one-time training on a specific skill; for example, in customer service staff training on a new software tool. This is a discrete module in which few other factors will affect the outcome, and in which the outcome can be readily tested in a before-and-after scenario. This is the easiest and most clear-cut way to calculate an ROI. In other circumstances – although HRD potentially may have a greater effect on the company – its effects will be more difficult to quantify. It's hard to do a before-and-after test, for example, on leadership skills training, as other factors will come to play in managers' performance.

Debate 8.2: An Alternative Description of Cost-benefit Analysis:

'A procedure by which the higher is reduced to the level of the lower, and the priceless is given a price. It can never therefore serve to clarify the situation and lead to an enlightened decision. All it can do is lead to self-deception and the deception of others' (Boyle 2001).

This is a sceptic's definition, of course. Those who agree with it argue that the concern should be with analysing the qualitative benefits – the 'higher' things – but this gets driven out by concerns with quantitative benefits. The number-crunching of exam pass-rates preoccupies the compilers of school league tables, for example, but it is the quality of development that really matters, and that is not easy to quantify. This measurement obsession is more to do with standardisation and control (and with establishing control given a lack of trust among the people involved in HRD at work). Some managers and functional specialists insist on measuring others every step of the way because they believe that the more rigorously people are observed against impersonal 'objective' criteria the better they will behave.

Boyle, D. (2001) *The Tyranny of Numbers: Why Counting Can't Make Us Happy* (London: Harper Collins).

To believe that perfect, objective, non-political decisions can be reached through number-crunching and that human prejudice and error can be eliminated, is the hope. Yet a fixation with quantification embroils people in a paralysis of analysis. Instead of pursuing pseudo-scientific precision – the impression of dealing objectively with things – people should measure less. Instead of analysing HRD costs and benefits why not trust HRD professionals to identify needs, design activities and deliver them professionally?

In more complicated scenarios, attention is better placed on value and results than on a number-based ROI. Once the move is away from an objective 'x more bolts sold' scenario into more vague managerial skills, it is necessary to use more subjective judgements to determine the effectiveness of the training. This involves making assumptions which can be difficult to defend; that there is a connection between spending on leadership training and the impact of leadership on performance. But bear in mind that HRD is not unique in this, and anxieties about ROI weaknesses may show over-sensitivity. For in other areas of management, such as advertising expenditure or internal auditing practices, these kinds of issues also exist; assumptions are also made about the impact of resources expended on advertising and audit, and these are not usually challenged. It is assumed to be worth spending money on advertising, it is assumed to be worth spending money on internal auditing; so why not make the same assumption for HRD instead of expecting those concerned with the least ROI-friendly domain to come up with an ROI case?

An alternative proposal for calculating return on investments is to measure return on expectations instead. In this kind of approach, those who are involved decide what they expect to achieve from the HRD. This set of expectations becomes the baseline for determining success. After the HRD is complete, the stakeholders review their agreed expectations. They then decide whether the results are in line with them. This approach allows for more anecdotal and less arithmetic analysis. For example, where a group of managers complete a communications training course, stakeholders can discuss the ways they feel communication has or has not improved. This provides a more realistic picture than if HR staff were forced to place a convoluted financial figure on the value of improved communications. It is 'softer', but it is not false rigour.

Another concern which can lead to ROI calculation being sidelined is a conscious decision to focus on the long-term value of HRD rather than a simple ROI for individual events. HRD is to be seen as an investment, and all investments have risks associated with them. A company may not find a direct correlation between specific costs and helping their workforce to develop, but the company can treat HRD as one key piece in an overall business strategy.

Given the pressures to adopt this broad methodology – to quantify and 'speak the language' of ROI in organisations – it is a methodology challenge to shift the focus from an ROI obsession in the field of HRD. As the old saying has it, many things that count in quality HRD can't be easily counted, and many things that can be counted don't count. The change in attitude can be achieved by demonstrating that these demands aren't as much for a clear ROI as they are about making providers of HRD more accountable, and for HRD to be more applicable to jobs and organisational needs. Recognising and meeting these demands by showing some form of cause and effect for HRD can be good enough. It is, though, the case that the fewer hard-and-fast ROI numbers there are to work with, the more anecdotal information will be needed. This kind of information can be better means of communicating with line managers about HRD because the managers may see workforce changes from HRD, thus giving credibility to HRD without an ROI.

Methodologies, such the quantitative and objective one associated with ROI, aspire to use scientific or at least quasi-scientific principles to evaluate HRD objectively. They evaluate as if they were looking 'from the outside in'. The concern is to keep a methodology of evaluation 'results-oriented', with methods that enable and speak about that. Courses should be results-oriented, and investment in them can be measured by financial returns, with senior and line managers' involvement and concern. If the ultimate level of evaluation is to compare the financial benefits with the costs of the HRD, then some (Phillips 1991) conclude that HRD should be managed in organisations by converting training departments to 'profit centres' to ensure that they are contributing effectively to the organisation.

Critics of the quasi-scientific approach argue that this kind of conclusion is more ideological than practical. As an alternative methodology they offer a more marketing-oriented or even humanistic approach (Talbot 1995). This attempts to manage better subjective evaluations of HRD 'from the inside out'. This means that learners are to be involved in the evaluation process rather than subjecting them and their learning to the evaluations of others through the use of quantitative measures. In practice, it means seeking to manage user surveys and focus groups, to investigate learner satisfaction, customer attitudes, job impacts, attitudes and manager perceptions. These methods can produce great insights and save money and time. This makes sense because the problems with attempting to foresee and calculate returns in advance of actually investing in HRD are immense. No amount of ROI analysis can determine whether or not it is right to invest in HRD at work, and indeed it can distract from focusing on what can be done to establish and improve HRD contributions to performance.

The logic of this methodology is to see HRD as 'profit centre', running as a small business inside the organisation. This aligns with the thinking of those using financial lenses to make sense of HRD activity in the organisation. The alternative is to wean the organisations themselves away from seeing HRD through these financial lenses and convert the organisations into learning organisations. In learning organisations even the 'softest' of 'soft skills' and informal kinds of development can be valued as much as specific investment in training for specific results. HRD is to be seen as an integral part of working life, not confined to what happens in a separate activity called 'training' managed by a few training professionals in the organisation. If a learning organisation philosophy is followed, then its results cannot be separated out and discretely measured; it is an organic part of the whole organisation and its performance. The point can be illustrated by analogy with a decision, on the basis of a person's low blood pressure, that the heart was not working efficiently and that, if it were cut out, the removal of a poorly performing part would allow the rest of the body to work better. Of course it is a step to make things look better according to one measure that would kill! So with evaluating HRD; if signs indicate that it is not contributing to ROI as might be expected, then it ought to be stopped – though that too could 'kill' the organisation, but it would be logical enough.

As an example of the potential relevance of a humanistic methodology of evaluation, consider the provision and evaluation of interpersonal skills training. HRD on interpersonal skills will often entail interventions with variable content: the same course – say on communication, or on handling conflict – will be experienced differently by different groups. This is because each course will evolve differently and flexibly as it is experienced. There is also great resistance from learners to formal assessment in areas such as interpersonal skills: people may want to be given feedback, but in no proper sense do they want to be tested and judged on their interpersonal skills. Quantified evaluation of such HRD is then neither possible nor desirable. Talbot (1995) suggests that the best that can be done is some form of joint evaluation, with collaborations between the learners and the trainers to explore what has been learned and what might remain to be done.

Metatheories of Evaluation

Debates about and rivalries between different methodologies of evaluation are often a symptom of more basic and deeper differences about theories which need to be considered and dealt with. For effective evaluation to be achievable, these theoretical matters and rivalries can be clarified. Scriven's term 'metatheories' implies that, although there may be many theories or answers to basic questions about how and why to value an area like HRD, these can be clustered together into a few 'higher order' explanations. It is these metatheories that can be seen to offer coherent, comprehensive explanations of evaluation, and to be rivals in this.

The idea of higher order metatheories in HRD is easy to apply in one sense, as these may simply be taken to be the theories of the constituent human science disciplines in use in HRM: economics, psychology and sociology. These theories will be explored in more detail in Chapter 9. Here, when developing or drawing upon metatheories to evaluate HRD and its value, the higher order theories of economics, psychology and sociology can provide the frameworks for investigating and explaining what is of value and merit. In HRD the current state of play is that these metatheories all have a role: psychological theories shape individual evaluations; sociological theories shape social policy evaluations; and economic theories inform cost and benefit evaluations.

There is some interplay among different kinds of theory in HRD evaluation. This may be seen as healthy and productive because there is both rivalry between and synthesis of theories that makes the evaluation of HRD more robust and balanced than if it were governed by one discipline, either economics, or psychology or social theory. However, others take issue with the adoption of such an unproblematic view of drawing upon these human science theories in evaluating HRD. They argue that, even though these different domains of theory differ in their backgrounds, their dominant forms share a common philosophy that is based on a realist perspective, or paradigm. A paradigm can be defined as a traditional body of coherent theoretical and methodological belief that guides research and action. The realist perspective as a paradigm can be seen to dominate across the disciplines.

The Characteristics of Effective Evaluation Instruments

Effective evaluation instruments for learning experiences need to be both valid and reliable. A valid instrument measures what it claims to measure. Validity is defined with respect to four aspects, here illustrated with reference to a student taking an exam.

- Content validity: does the instrument represent the content of the learning? The evaluation instrument should test a sample of what has been covered. All key items should be covered, with no imbalance. For example, does an exam cover all of the course, with equal weighting for equal parts of the material covered?

- Construct validity: does the instrument represent the construct it purports to measure? In this case, is the good exam answer a reflection of all of the student's abilities, skills or knowledge in performance? These are generally defined and defended by citing expert opinion or correlation with other constructs. For example, here, does a good exam answer actually measure the real differences in people's capacities?

- Concurrent validity: does the instrument agree with the results of other similar instruments at approximately the same time? If assignments or other tests are done, do they provide the same results as the exam? Are the other exams a person is taking consistent with results in the exam in question?

- Predictive validity: does the instrument help predict future behaviours and performance? For example, does performance in the exam predict anything about that person's abilities in professional practice?

Reliability

A reliable instrument is one that gives consistent measures. There are various sources of error with reliability in any instrument:

- Fluctuations in the alertness of the participants;
- Variations in conditions of administering;
- Random effects caused by participant motivation;
- The length of the instrument;
- Differences in interpreting the results of the instrument.

For example, learners often complete post-course evaluation questionnaires, or 'happy sheets'. But are these reliable instruments for evaluating that course? Several factors can create errors, leading to an inaccurate evaluation, whether that be favourable or unfavourable. With some learners focused on the course and others thinking about getting home quickly, with some evaluations completed there and then and others taken away and perhaps never returned, with some learners who did not care about the course and others who cared deeply, the results of such happy sheets can be unreliable. And, even if not, when trainers pore over them thereafter, they can interpret selectively what has been measured and said. Some may see them as just a 'beauty' contest ranking, and take some pride in rationalising away any bad evaluations as representing the learners' inadequacies in failing to engage with a 'complex and difficult' subject. Whether they are defended, reformed or replaced can alter the way that valid evaluation is seen and practised. Stewart (1999) takes issue with what he argues is the dominant realist paradigm. But, as Stewart's critique and alternative conceptions illustrate, it is largely practitioners alone who subscribe while academics disagree with it. It is arguable that a paradigm of any kind, whether of this quasi-scientific or other variety, may never be established. If that is so, then the evaluation of HRD will remain beset by the inadequacies of basic recipes, and be subject to cycles of debate and rivalries without progress.

Limits of Valid and Reliable Instruments

Quality management challenges us not only to go beyond common sense in evaluation but also to understand the limits of valid and reliable instruments. Mazlish (1998) characterises all the human sciences as uncertain. The promise of predictive and certain scientific knowledge to solve problems has not been fulfilled: either in regard to individual behaviour, social relations or economic development. Mazlish concludes that:

> Common sense tells us that a result emerges from people's passionate and political actions, not from predictive scientific knowledge. Many, if not most, problems are too delicate and disturbing to the actors involved to resolve clearly and rationally, even if a solution is available. An example might be the allocation of resources, where the attempt to impose a rational plan often leads to a violent conflict of interests or to an unacceptable authoritarianism... what solves social problems is social interaction... rather than a science that pretends to deal with social interaction. Actions, in turn, constitute a never-ending sequence of solutions that create new problems.
>
> If, in general, what solves problems is social interaction, and people taking actions that in their turn create new problems that others have to solve, then why should HRD be any different? (Mazlish 1998)

Rather than seeking a rational science of HRD evaluation, it is the realities of people's passions for or against HRD that will determine what happens and what the results are. There is an impasse at the level of metatheory in the quality management of HRD. This means that the final and highest phase of the evolution of quality management in HRD is far from being achieved. For Scriven the mature phase would be an evaluation system with which it was possible and scientifically practicable to deal with primary value claims. If this is true, and if such a quality management system is required to validate claims about what is, in fact, meritorious and valuable in a scientific and rigorous way, then the conclusion is that the evaluation of HRD is far from being the robust activity that many want it to be, and which different groups claim to be able to achieve. Until there is an agreed metatheory or paradigm within which people concerned with quality in HRD can work and communicate, the prospects for improving the evaluation of HRD are poor.

Conclusion

Quality management, review, evaluation and improvement constitute the final link in the whole HRD process. This has traditionally been seen as a problem area and a challenge in HRD at work, as quality management can fulfil several functions for various stakeholders, and this makes it complex. Recent improvements in methods and thinking are evident, but the basic debates and concerns are still very much present. HRD quality management is now done more widely than ever before, at the most basic level possible, with levels of evaluation routinely addressed. In practice there are popular and common models: the levels of evaluation relating quality management to the different aspects of the HRD process itself, to learners and the resolution of performance gaps. The prospect of producing more quality-aware HRD cultures and scientifically valid analyses of claims about HRD remains a matter of debate and argument. Becoming more 'quality aware' is probably the current major focus for improvement in this area.

Debates take shape around the use of either quantitative or qualitative measures, and how the major metatheories influences and impact on sense-making in HRD quality management; particularly psychology, economics and ethics. In the end, the formulas and techniques for evaluations of HRD have to balance the demands of scientific rigour with the practicalities of professional practice. And the theoretical demands of 'truth seeking' have to be reconciled with the practical goals of 'pragmatic management'. To apply only the standards of scientific rigour and truth-seeking to the quality management of HRD would be to invest so much in evaluation that there would be little time for action. To only trust in the expertise of professional practitioners in the name of pragmatic management would be to leave the evaluation stage of HRD, acknowledged as a critical phase and a weakest link, as a weak link in the process.

Exercise 8.2: Cost-Benefit Analysis

In each of the following cases based on examples given in Flynn (1998) identify:

Whether you would or would not use cost-benefit analysis (CBA)

and

if you were to use CBA analysis, what would be involved.

or

if you were not to use CBA analysis, what else you would evaluate and how.

Case 1. A manufacturer of office and school supplies, with products ranging from paper clips to binders and computer-related supplies, intends to provide training for new hires to its production lines.

Case 2. A company with 7,000 employees intends to spend a multi-million amount on a programme to give staff a one-week course on the company's new computer desktop environment.

Case 3. A group of managers is to be trained on a course about communication skills to help cross-functional teams communicate and work with each other better.

Case 4. A photocopier manufacturer aims to shift to multifunctional products, where its copiers are no longer just copiers but also scanners, printers and fax machines, and its dealers need to be retrained.

Case: Working in the Horse Industry

The following describes the quality of adult learning provided in one company in the Horse industry, which has been reviewed by the countries learning inspectorate and received the highest ratings possible. What they do is perceived to be very effective, and of outstanding quality. Further background is available at http://www. stubbingcourttraining.com/.

The case has the following sections:

- Company background;
- Individual case;
- Training inspectors report.

Read these, and reflect on the extent to which you believe all the necessary informa-tion to justify this as a robust example of an outstanding example of HRD practice is present.

Company Background

Stubbing Court Training Ltd. enables learners to gain the skills, qualifications, opportunities and experience to be an effective, educated and competent worker in the horse industry. Stubbing Court Training Ltd. work with employers in the United Kingdom to provide:

- Individual, flexible support, training and assessment;
- Highly trained, qualified and experienced staff;

- Excellent success and achievement rates;
- Top-class training locations;
- The SCT Masterclass Series – training from world-class professionals for Apprentices and Employers.

There are two levels of Apprenticeship available: Apprenticeship and Advanced Apprenticeship. An Apprenticeship includes:

- Working towards and gaining a National Vocational Qualification (NVQ);
- Improving your key skills, including Communication, Application of Number, Working with Others and Information and Communication Technology;
- Gaining a Technical Certificate;
- Other qualifications to help in your career, including First Aid and Health and Safety.

As an Apprentice the learner is employed with a wage. The Apprenticeship takes approximately 12 months to complete and leads to NVQ level 2 in Horse Care. The work is mainly practical, and learners will gain technical skills as well as valuable work experience. There is also the opportunity to progress onto an Advanced Apprenticeship. As an Advanced Apprentice the learner will be in full time employment with an appropriate wage, aiming for a supervisory or junior management role. The Advanced Apprenticeship lasts approximately 18 months, and leads to NVQ level 3 in Horse Care and Management. Achievement of the Advanced Apprenticeship accredits the learner with points which may enable them to progress to Higher Education. The benefits of Apprenticeships are great – with hands on practical experience in the workplace to prove capabilities, a real wage and a recognised qualification which will dramatically increase future job opportunities.

Individual Case; Ben McClumpha – My Road to the Advanced Apprenticeship

I am 18 years old and have recently completed the Advanced Apprenticeship with Stubbing Court Training. I have been interested in horses for as long as I can remember, growing up through the Pony Club, competing to Area level in both show jumping and eventing. It was when I left school after my GCSEs that I first got involved with SCT.

It was through SCT I was fortunate to get a placement with International show jumpers Andrew and Emma Saywell, based in Nottinghamshire. Riding the horses, travelling to shows and keeping the yard maintained, it was a very exciting experience, as it was the first time I had lived away from home. Whilst I was there I completed the Apprenticeship. I also had the opportunity to spend a week with Ian Stark at his yard in Scotland, which was a great experience.

I was with the Saywell family for around 15 months and thoroughly enjoyed the experience.

I then started working for the leading International lady event rider and Grand Slam winner Pippa Funnell. I spent the season preparing horses for International events such as Badminton and Burghley, as well as preparing the young and novice horses for more low-key events. This was also the start of the Olympic year, with a lot of work going into the preparation of Primmore's Pride, such as increasing fitness work and galloping in a full-length rug covering the neck to tail, to help the horse adjust to the sweltering temperatures of Athens.

Towards the end of the eventing season, shortly after Burghley, I changed sides and went on to ride for Pippa's husband, International show jumper William Funnell.

William's show jumping yard has a totally different routine to the eventing yard. We currently have 18 horses in at the moment, and 4 young horses out in the field, who will shortly be coming in to be broken. I have the opportunity to ride the top international horses as well as getting to work and jump the other horses on the yard. We have a lot of young homebred horses that are broken and ridden away. I also have a few horses that I am able to compete; they are currently jumping the 5-year old and Performance classes, Newcomers and 1.10m. I have also jumped my first Young Rider's class at Ardingley, South of England.

If it were not for the help of Stubbing Court Training, I would never have had the opportunity to get on the ladder and start to work my way up, with such top people. Not only have I had the hands on experience that future employers look for, but I have also achieved qualifications, including Key Skills in Communication, Application of Number, Working with Others and Information and Communication Technology, all of which are needed in the industry today.

Outline of Training

The Training offers:

- Qualifications while learners work;
- Experience and qualifications employers really want;
- Placements with professional riders up to International level in show jumping, eventing and dressage yards;
- Placements in Riding Schools and Livery Yards;
- Opportunities to ride and care for performance horses here and abroad;
- Training to teach and gain teaching qualifications;
- Residential placements available.

Stubbing Court Training apprentices and employers have the opportunity to take part in the Masterclass Series with World Class professionals including Ian Stark OBE, four times Olympic Silver Medallist, European Champion and three times winner of Badminton Horse Trials. He is also a selector for the Great Britain Team for the Olympic Games. Ian is also the judge of the Stubbing Court 'Apprentice of the Year' – a reward for excellence and commitment to achievement of the qualification during the year.

Other Masterclass trainers include Olympic show jumper Michael Whitaker, Team manager for the British Olympic team and world renown coach Yogi Breisner and Irish Olympic, World and European rider Mark Kyle. Ofsted has recognised the SCT Masterclass Series as 'best practice' in training. Stubbing Court Training has won a National Training Award for the Masterclass Series.

Training Inspectors Report

Stubbing Court Training (SCT) is a limited company established in 1982. The company provides land-based training in horse care. The majority of training takes place at equine centres throughout Derbyshire, Nottinghamshire and West Yorkshire. However, the company also works with a small number of centres located outside these counties. SCT provides training at 11 centres throughout these areas and works with approximately 66 employers. Programmes are funded through a single contract with the Skills Funding Agency.

Currently 93 learners are on programme with SCT. Of these, 32 learners are advanced apprentices, 60 are apprentices and one learner is on an Entry to Employment programme. Forty-seven per cent of SCT's learners have additional learning needs. In addition to government funded apprentices, SCT provides training for employers and learners in equine transport.

The overall effectiveness of SCT's apprenticeship provision is outstanding. Learners enjoy their training and speak highly of their programmes. The chief executive of the company provides excellent leadership, promoting high standards. Targets for improvement are set and monitored effectively. The previous outstanding provision has been maintained with further improvement since the last inspection. Outcomes for learners are outstanding with learners developing a high level of practical and work-related skills. The number of learners who successfully achieve their qualification in the planned timescales has improved significantly.

Teaching and learning are good overall, with practical training being outstanding. The extent to which the programmes meet the needs of learners is outstanding. Enrichment activities are outstanding, with good opportunities for learners to participate in courses run by international riders. Support for learners requiring additional help to develop their literacy and numeracy skills is good.

SCT has developed very effective partnerships with employers, colleges and external agencies, which improve the provision and benefit learners. Arrangements to ensure learners are safe are good. Learners feel very safe and effectively utilise their health and safety training to ensure safe working practices. SCT's promotion of equality and diversity is outstanding. The company engages with a range of community groups and external agencies to promote its programmes to groups traditionally underrepresented within the equine industry. All groups of learners achieve equally well.

Main Findings

- Outcomes for learners are outstanding. Success rates have been consistently high and are well above the national average for this area. Success rates within the planned timescales have improved significantly and are well above the national average. Most learners gain employment at the end of their training.

- Learners develop excellent practical skills, in most cases exceeding those required for the qualification. Learners have a good understanding of health and safety; they take responsibility for their own well-being and the safety of others.

- Teaching and learning are good overall. Practical training is outstanding, with learners receiving instruction in show jumping, training of young stock and the use of the very latest equipment. In some theory sessions, teaching lacks inspiration. Information and learning technology (ILT) is not used sufficiently to support learning.

- Assessment is generally good; however, the company has recognised that it needs to improve the way in which this is recorded. The use of photographic evidence needs to link better to specific assessment criteria. In most cases the internal verification process has identified this, and plans are in place to further improve the internal verification process.

- Target setting and monitoring of learners' progress are good. Learners are clear about what needs to be done to help them progress. SCT sets employers clear targets for what they need to achieve with their learners. In most cases targets are sufficiently challenging; however, there is insufficient challenge for some advanced learners.

- The range and content of provision meet the needs of learners and employers exceptionally well. Learning is well planned, flexible and highly individualised. Enrichment activities are outstanding with good opportunities for learners to work with international equestrian trainers.

- Care, guidance and support for learners are good. Support with the development of numeracy skills is particularly good, with individual training sessions that link to the vocational area. Tutors use excellent visual aids; learners enjoy these sessions and make good progress.

- The strategic planning of learning at SCT is very effective with a clear focus on improving provision. Development plans are clear with challenging targets that are frequently monitored to assess progress. The strategic plan has a strong focus on safeguarding and the promotion of equality of opportunity and diversity.

- SCT's approach to promoting equality and diversity, tackling discrimination and narrowing the achievement gap is outstanding. SCT has a clear strategy to engage with learners from groups traditionally underrepresented in the equine industry. All groups of learners achieve equally well.

- Employer engagement and work with external partners are outstanding. Highly effective and productive links have been made with colleges and other external partners to develop projects that improve the provision and benefit learners.

- SCT have a strong focus on quality improvement. The self-assessment process is a very effective tool for quality improvement. Data are used well to indentify strengths and areas for improvement. Very effective use is made of learner and employer feedback. Quality improvement planning has maintained and improved the high standards from the last inspection.

- SCT's self-assessment process has been successful at identifying and implementing strategies to improve some aspects of teaching, assessment and internal verification.

3 Key Texts

(1) McGhee, P. (2003) *The Academic Quality Handbook: Enhancing Higher Education in Universities and Further Education Colleges* (London, Kogan Page), pp. 71–86.

(2) Scriven, M. (1991) *Evaluation Thesaurus* (Newbury Park, CA, Sage).

(3) Sherlock, D. and Perry, N. (2008) *Quality Improvement in Vocational Adult Education and Training* (London: Kogan Page).

3 Key Articles/Reports

(1) Kirkpatrick, D. L. (1978) ' Evaluating In-House Training Programs', *Training and Development Journal*, September, pp. 6–9.

(2) LSC (2004) *National Learner Satisfaction Survey* (London, Learning and Skills Council).

(3) Wang, G. and Spitzer, G. (2005) 'Human Resource Development Measurement and Evaluation: Looking Back and Moving Forward', *Advances in Developing Human Resources*, 7 (1), pp. 5–15.

(4) Russ-eft, D. and Preskill, H. (2005) 'In Search of the Holy Grail: Return on Investment Evaluation in Human Resource Development', *Advances in Developing Human Resources*, 7 (1), pp. 71–85.

3 Key Web Links

(1) Evaluation tips and guidelines: www.evaluationsupportscotland.org.uk.

(2) UK Agency for quality management in workplace learning: http://www.ofsted.gov.uk/Ofsted-home/About-us/Adult-learners-and-employers.

(3) Training Zone discussion: http://www.trainingzone.co.uk/item/7260.

9

Talent Management

Learning Objectives

By the end of this chapter you will be able to:

- Define talent management;
- Describe the 'pipeline' metaphor;
- Explain and uses of a common structure for mapping performance and potential;
- Critically analyse key themes and challenges in talent management.

Introduction

Talent Management is now a term widely used to describe learning and development at work. It is a possible evolution beyond Systematic Training, Performance Improvement and Continuous Development approaches to the Human Resource Development (HRD) process. To most talent management is concerned with improving the calibre, availability and flexible utilisation of exceptionally capable, high potential, people who can have a disproportionate impact on business performance especially leaders and key professionals, or 'clever' people. Mapping performance and potential in this way has implications which bring some HRD challenges. Managing the problems that can be caused by 'smart people' in work and employment contexts has been a challenge in the past, and maybe more prominent in the future. These include providing effective feedback, managing diversity and enabling status shifts as people move through the talent development pipeline. In either sense there are three practical concerns: (1) defining talent, (2) developing talent and (3) structures and systems to support talent management. Or it may be a 'fad', a superficial change of fashion rather than a substantial evolution.

Talent Management

Since the idea of a 'war for talent' was floated in the late 1990s (Chambers et al. 1998, p. 44), a concept of talent management has been evolving. Attracting and retaining talent, assuming it was in limited supply, became increasingly important (Michaels et al. 2001). Much activity and discussion in HRD has since been couched in terms of talent management and development, and it has become a key area of interest for practitioners and academics (Blass 2009, CIPD 2010, Stewart and Rigg 2011).

It may be a widely used term in treatments of development at work (Cheese et al. 2008, Parry and Unwin 2009, Schiemann 2009) but its definition can be loose and vague. Broadly used talent management is concerned with developing the talents of all the people who are contributing to the growth and success of organisations. More narrowly defined it is concerned with improving the calibre, availability and flexible utilisation of exceptionally capable, high potential, people who can have a disproportionate impact on business performance (Tulgan 2001, Michaels et al. 2001, Rothwell and Kazanas 2003, Tarique and Schuler 2010), especially leaders (Work Foundation 2010) and key professionals, or 'clever' people (Goffee and Jones 2009). Blass (2007) concludes

> By using a segmentation strategy for their talent, an organisation is not identifying the rest of the workforce as talentless. Talent management is about doing something additional or different with those people who are defined as talent for the purpose of the organisation – be it top performers, high potentials, senior managers suitable for director positions, or people suitable for critical roles in the organisation. (2007, p. 7)

As the term HRD is used here for what some authors are meaning by the broad sense of talent management it is the latter, narrower sense of talent management that is of significance here and is worthy of further consideration. Talent management is about the additional learning and development involved in identifying and producing future and consistent 'stars' (see Perspective 9.1).

Perspective 9.1: Mapping Performance and Potential

High Performance Low	High performer in role	Utility Performer	Consistent star
	Average performer in role	Capable and experienced	Future star
	Low performer	Inconsistent	Diamond in the rough
	Low Potential High		

Source: Based on Smilansky (2007).

Iles et al. (2010) identify three streams of study current in the field of HRD around talent management in this sense. One is talent management as a normative prescription, another is about talent management as empirically informed review of policy and practice, and the final stream is about the development of concepts. Normatively talent management is prescribed as an integrated set of corporate initiatives (Smilansky 2007). The rationale and justification for this is that talent has become a key strategic priority, most emotively summed up in the idea of a 'war for talent'. The argument, or assumption that became accepted as true, was that talent is limited in supply and in high demand. Most especially, but not solely, that top graduates who formed the future generation of key professionals and leaders, were in short supply. This was an argument proposed in part by industries, including the consulting industry, whose business was premised in part on the sale of 'talent' to organisations. Consulting firms and others also developed products and services to create a 'talent management' industry to complement this. That centred on developing the 'pipeline' which took new entrants to organisations and groomed them through promotions from entry to management to senior leadership roles. This was branded as being more than succession planning. It extended to include external scouting and hunting for talent. It involved establishing new 'feeder populations' in organisations for fast tracking through the pipeline. And it was promoted as being both hard and soft on talent. It was hard as people in the pipeline, being fast streamed, either moved on and up or they would be moved out. Business teams were to be treated like sport teams; the stars delivered or they were dropped. It was also soft in the sense that personal development and support to help those in such pressurised environments was purported to be at the heart of developing talent. That meant that support in forms like executive coaching and mentoring were to be a key part of the talent management process.

That was the normative and prescriptive picture. Empirically, what was actually happening? Blass (2009) in one study identified 18 dimensions which were common to all the organisations he studied, within three areas: (1) defining talent, (2) developing talent and (3) structures and systems to support talent management. The evidence was that in large and complex organisations talent management did show as a practical focus on the 'pipeline' involved in developing key professionals, managers and leaders whose performance and potential was meant to be critical for success and was therefore under increasing and greater scrutiny. The 'pipeline' issues, in sequence, are as follows

- Entry: Self-managing in relation to one's own work;
- Progress 1: from 'self-managing' to 'managing others';
- Progress 2: from 'managing others' to 'managing managers';
- Progress 3: from 'managing managers' to 'managing divisions';
- Ultimate destination: from 'managing divisions' to 'managing organisations'.

At all these pipeline and progress points it was a challenge to identify potential and nurture the professionals' or managers' strengths to get them to the next level, and possibly beyond. HRD could help bring on potential and performance in these various situations to provide future stars. HRD needed to help professionals, managers and leaders better process their experiences, encourage reflection, release strengths and work on emergent obstacles to development and success.

Conceptually a number of issues came into the frame. One was concern about the 'leaky' pipeline, and whether talent management was helping to establish greater diversity, with previously under-represented groups making progress, or if talent management was perpetuating, and perhaps even compounding, barriers to progress given the affects it might have on, for example, work–life balance. Another issue was exploring the process of developing and managing 'smart' people, with the perception that the challenges this entailed were distinctive, and for developers to engage with supporting and challenging such people were also distinctive.

Another underlying issue was that of generational relations and differences. The workforce always contains distinct generations (Puybaraud et al. 2010), but the concern was that upcoming generations had such different sets of values and attitudes that to manage talent required understanding and responding to these. Depending on national contexts these generations can be defined in various ways. For example, Parry and Urwin (2009) have named the different generations in the United Kingdom today as the Veterans (born 1925–1945), Baby Boomers (born 1946–1964), Generation X (born 1965–1980) and Generation Y (born 1981 onwards). Yi et al. (2010) define generations in China as the 'cultural revolution' generation (1960s), the social reform generation (born in the 1970s), and the millennial generation (born in the 1990s). The premise is that generations differ significantly in their goals, expectations and work values (Cennamo and Gardner 2008). These differences in characteristics are said to be caused by each generation's life experiences, such as the state of the economy and labour market, family values and political events while they were growing up (Parry and Urwin 2009).

The multigenerational work environments can breed misunderstanding and conflicts that can be a source of positive challenge, opportunity and significant growth if managed effectively (Paul 2010). One area where this is perhaps most evident is in talent management, where the different generations may be seen to meet and interact in aspects of the HRD process. Talent management in this sense defined and with the practical concerns identified meant thinking about and exploring key concepts and tasks in and across generations:

- Creating an honest and open performance and potential map of talent in the organisation;
- Using different kinds of development relationships to nurture talent;
- Take development beyond the routine and the obvious;
- Providing great feedback, as this has the biggest impact on development, and tackling bad habits.

Implications

Placing professionals, managers and leaders on a performance and potential map is the start of talent management, and systems for mapping talent are now common in larger organisations. Putting the 'stars' in the most critical jobs, and focusing on their development is the primary, though not exclusive, purpose of talent management. Those who are not positioned as current or potential stars are not to be neglected, but the ethos of this is to create a transparent system that invites an appraisal of potential as well as performance. To the traditional challenges of performance management and improvement are added the challenges of determining potential. As the organisation grows and evolves a sense of what potential entails, and who has it, can change.

Development Relations

Once identified and located in a position on a talent map there is an expectation and a responsibility to help and encourage people to look for and respond to different kinds of development relationships and experience, or working alliances to develop their talent. What HRD can offer, and where others might need to be involved can include, by analogy, some or all of the following archetypal working alliances (de Haan 2005), involving specialist HRD staff, managers, peers and others:

- Master–apprentice like relationships; dealing with practical issues and offering direct, meaningful responses;
- Doctor–patient like relationships; allowing the person to turn themselves 'inside out', revealing uncertainties and emotions – to be interpreted and resolved;
- Midwife–mother like relationships; helping to anticipate problems and provide the strength to tackle themp
- Peer review relationships; look together at day-to-day practice, a mutually critical approach, insight-focused;
- 'Old boys/girls' relationships; being a sparring partner to exchange and try out ideas.

Access and involvement in all these kinds of relationships are seen to be necessary to develop talent. One of the challenges of being 'talent' is engaging in a set of so many and diverse development relationships. One of the characteristics of any effective set of working alliance is achieving the right the balance between the rational and the emotional. The interrelationship between changing thinking and feeling as new and greater responsibilities are encountered will fluctuate. To learn and be more effective it is sometimes desirable to address the 'analytical' or the 'emotional' side of development. The ideal is to develop people who combine high levels of knowledge and skill in analysis and emotional intelligence together. This fits with the greater demands made as people progress through the pipeline to greater responsibilities.

Feedback

Giving feedback is a critical part of ensuring and sustaining effective talent management over time, across over several working alliances and in the course of the often major programmes initiated to develop professionals, managers and leaders. If talent is going to develop and learn the most from their development and practical experiences, they need feedback. This is a critical feature of the HRD process. There are well-known cognitive and emotional barriers and challenges to giving and receiving feedback in general (Carroll and Gilbert 2008), which are encountered and need to be carefully managed or they can be amplified in systems designed for developing talent. These general challenges include the fear of causing hurt, disrupting relationships, embarrassment, rejection of the feedback or conflict arising from it, the difficulty of re-evaluating self-image, and the need to follow through and change behaviour. One of the challenges of talent management is that these challenges are heightened and more significant than is normally the case. On the one hand, people are being developed because they possess great strengths. On the other hand, they are being subject to a level of degree and scrutiny of their behaviour which many may be very uncomfortable with (Practice 9.1).

Practice 9.1: Feedback

- **Set ground rules** in advance; agree what feedback will be focused upon
- **Consider its value** for the receiver before offering any feedback; if there is none, keep quiet
- **Select relevant priorities**; you may see a lot of things, but identify and concentrate on the most important few first.
- **Try to ask questions rather than make statements**; open up issues by asking for example 'how else could you have reacted when . . . ' rather than 'you should have . . . '

When giving direct feedback

- **Stick to observed behaviour**; not inferred attitudes;
- **Describe what you see**; don't give it second hand or as a judgement;
- **Talk about specifics**; 'I liked the way you kept good eye contact and a relaxed posture during the negotiation' rather than 'you created a friendly atmosphere';

- ***Observe limits and do not overload***; offering too much can be as unhelpful as offering too little;

- ***People sometimes 'see' it better than they hear*** it, so make notes about what they say and do and lay it out and let them ask questions.

The prescriptions of good feedback are at the heart of talent management; focusing on behaviour, sticking to what is observable and the effects that has on others, while always looking to solutions for doing things differently.

Feedback to support learning is also critical as even the most talented of professionals, managers and 'smart executives' can fail to properly perceive reality. This failure to recognise and face up to reality, often associated with information and control systems in organisations being mismanaged, and 'unsuccessful habits' being unchallenged can combine to have drastic consequences (Finkelstein 2003); major and dramatic organisational failure. Talented people, stars with strong egos, can act as ineptly as anyone else. If the average employee gets defensive, doesn't face reality, has difficulty dealing with change and sometimes choose not to respond even when they know they should, the outcomes can be a local problem. If talent managed stars act that way, it can mean organisational failure. Talent management systems and processes are potentially the environments in which to recognise and deal with this. There is a risk that, unintentionally talent management systems may sometimes promote attitudes then become part of the problem (see Perspective 9.2);

Perspective 9.2: Possible Signs of Talent Management-Induced problems, and Talent Management Challenges

- People who see themselves and their companies as dominating their environment
  - Keep a sense of perspective
- People who identify completely with the company
  - Keep clear boundary with personal interests
- People who seem to have all the answers, speedily and decisively dealing with issues
  - Take time to reflect
- People who make sure everyone is behind them, eliminating anyone who might undermine them
  - Encourage different views
- People who are consummate company spokespeople, devoting efforts to developing company image
  - Be careful about buying your own PR

Perspective 9.2: (Continued)

- People who underestimate major obstacles
  - Be realistic
- People who do not hesitate to return to strategies and tactics that made them successful
  - Avoid trying to repeat past fixes in different times.

The underlying issue for Finkelstein is the tendency to an 'illusion of personal pre-eminence', believing that personally they know more than others and as a result can dominate others in terms of their decision-making, thinking and behaviour. There is an inability or unwillingness to learn new things, so that if faced with a challenge they tend to go back to the same ideas they have previously followed, even when it is no longer appropriate. When things do start to go wrong, many of the people in this situation truly believe they have all the answers, and they impose their perspective on others with the result that the organisation ends up with inferior decision making. Executives with this mindset often fire or remove people who disagree with them. They go out of their way to close down alternative points of view within the organisation. They get locked into a path and lose adaptability and flexibility. Meetings happen where people tend not to push back or challenge.

The practical conclusion is that leaders themselves, and those managing talent development systems, need to be aware of and can identify cautionary signals and the common pattern by which mistakes spread through companies. The warning signs can be seen early and there are opportunities to step in. Talent management experiences can be the environment in which these warning signs may become apparent.

Talent Management and Diversity

A final challenge is that if talent management aims to do more than replace existing kinds of talented people with clones or copies of themselves, then diversity issues matter. The challenge is less about committing to bringing in people who might have been previously overlooked, it is more about managing the status shift involved in people progressing from groups that were historically 'out-groups' to the 'in-group' of people employed in senior roles and posts. For even having identified diverse kinds of people as potential, and provided working alliances in which good feedback is given, there can still problems with moving talent on to realise their potential and to higher and better performance as part of higher level teams. Status shift interference can be an inhibitor (Pawson 2004). A challenge in talent management can be helping manage shifts in status. In general this may mean a change in the pipeline stages from the status and mindset of being an 'employee' to being a 'manager', and from being a 'good professional' to being a good leader of an organisation as a whole. For people from traditionally under-represented groups the challenge is amplified.

A person's response to, and even interest in, having their potential and talent developed can be understood with reference to their status group affiliation. Status issues emerge where the following situations exist:

- Outsiders with aspirations: people looking to progress, to move on and up and who are ready to change look to the higher status destination groups yet may still feel like an 'outsider' as they move on and up.

- In-betweeners: people may feel caught, even stuck, between commitments to an old 'in-group', with its norms and behaviour, and destination group norms and behaviours. They can experience conflicts of norms which make them feel uncomfortable at times and may interfere with realising their potential.

- Peripheral antagonisms: people who have potential and could progress may seem to be resistant to being enrolled into talent management processes, perhaps seeing the destination groups as an 'out-group' they do not want to join and belong to. Employees with potential may refrain from progressing into management, and effective middle managers may refrain from progress into leadership; not due to a lack of talent, but because they have other commitments or concerns which preclude joining talent management systems in work.

Perspective 9.3: Status Journeys

New	Status Current Reference group		
Reference group		Outsider	
Insider	Marginal	3	Aspirational
		2	Acquiescence
		1	Antagonism

Considering the different journeys to be made from a current reference group to being a insider in a new group (Perspective 9.3), most 'developers' are insiders who can act as advocates. Most learners are aspirationals.

Developers may also have to deal with other situations:

(a) Identity talent management: from antagonism to aspiration;

(b) Achievement talent management: from outside to insider;

(c) Engagement talent management: from antagonism to insider.

Long moves across status and identity positions are hardest to manage; to support longer moves developers need additional resources in advocacy, skills, direction setting and dealing with the affective. The following aspects of HRD then arise as challenges to deal with these and help people to either progress to become insiders, remove uncertainties or deal with antagonism:

• Advocacy: offering positional resource, networking and promoting the person to achieve and consolidate development;

• Skills: offering aptitudinal resource to encourage and coax in skills needed to make the change;

• Direction setting: offering cognitive resource, choices and decisions to make the change and develop;

• Affective contacts: emotional resource, hand of friendship, support feeling different to make the change and develop.

One challenge in this is encouraging authenticity as well as developing skill (see Perspective 9.4). Talented people can be perceived as effective 'stars', or they may be perceived as 'stars' who are clumsy, role players or even mavericks (Goffee and Jones 2006). Effective leaders are both authentic and skilled. Authenticity and 'being yourself' is the foundation of effective leading, not mimicking another person, or a set of traits or self-knowledge in itself. However, authenticity without skill can be seen as mavericks; people determined to 'be themselves' in ways that can have a negative impact on others. Understanding and respecting origins and weaknesses, and an awareness and knowledge of these which is suitably disclosed, underpins effective talent development.

Perspective 9.4: Authenticity and Skill

High		
Authenticity	Maverick	Effective 'Star'
	Unaware and clumsy	Role-player
Low	**Skill** High	

Source: Based on Goffee and Jones (2006).

Conclusion

Talent management is a common term for development focused on progressing and advancing key talent or the workforce as a whole. It is currently popular, with critics of both the 'talent myth' (Gladwell 2002) and those seeing in it no more than a 'fad' (Iles et al., 2010), a focus of attention for a period rather than a foundation for reconfiguring policy and practice. As a concept it appears to fulfil the criteria for being a successful fad (DiMaggio and Powell 1983, Abrahamson 1996). It sounds good and modern; and trend setters have convinced key adopters, large and high-profile organisations, that it is a rational and progressive response to a perceived gap, the 'war' on talent. Alarming scenarios about the impact of this war for talent are argued to exist, and positive cases show how talent management is the solution. The trap is that fads meet the psychological needs of adopters rather than practical HRD needs of organisations. Those psychological needs are defined as; a need for novelty, innovation and to symbolise that HRD is being progressive. Even the best fad, though, contains the seeds of its own destruction; as it has to be vague and ambiguous to meet the adopter's psychological needs, it is not a very sure foundation for practical management. This does not stop others emulating high-status organisations who act as the initial adopters of fads. After a time the early adopters will move on to another fad, and the process begins again.

The cycle of fad replacing fad can be seen in HRD, as in management more generally. It can be hard to break that cycle in HRD. If talent management is to be more than a fad, the practical implications and benefits have to become evident. Identifying critical talent development targets and opportunities means taking the time to develop robust performance and potential maps. It involves also developing flexibility in the organisational approach to HRD for talented people, and how key stakeholders can become involved in that. The abiding challenge, underneath and surviving any fad, is to have and take conversations with key people and leaders beyond the obvious; providing useful feedback which changes behaviour and supports learning. Doing that can be challenging as it means working with strong egos, and building confidence in people but not colluding with unchecked illusions of personal pre-eminence. This is a criticism that was levelled at HR given the emergence of problems for economies grounded in the behaviour of 'talent' and leaders in the banking and financial services sector; where unchecked illusions of personal pre-eminence played a role in creating the financial then wider economic crisis (Lanchester 2010) which had such a impact.

Talent management may be more effective where attention is given to status shift dynamics, enabling or blocking talent development. Looking more closely at the person and at the social aspects of talent development the result can assist with more potential realised and improved performance. In talent management there are balances to achieve; between personal and professional development, between growing ad progressing a person's analytical rationality and their emotional intelligence or authenticity, and between support and challenge. Getting the balance in these right can be make a major difference to both organisational and industry success, and not only the growth of more effective professionals, managers and leaders but all members of their teams.

Case: P, Global Brand Director

WhiskyCo manufactures and distributes whisky. P is a Global Brand Director based in sales and marketing office. P has been employed with the Company for just over 10 years and was previously Brand director for a particular drink brand. P was promoted to the Global Brand Director role. Ps strengths lie in strong project management skills and she has a reputation for delivering results. P is very task focused and is known for her determination and hands on approach, which result in lengthy hours at work and on travel. P is responsible for a key brand and has exceptionally challenging objectives.

She also has a new team of which all three of her key brand managers have no more than a few months service. P has recently been having performance challenges with two of her team. One of her employees has capability issues, and there is a real concern that he will not be able to achieve his objectives. There are issues with his interpersonal effectiveness, which is having a detrimental effect on his relationships with internal and external customer base. What is of more concern is that he does not recognise that he has capability gaps. The second employee does have potential, however she requires more confidence in her ability. The role she is in requires her to be decisive and self-assured.

Issues

A key issue for P was effective leadership. P was not creating the space in her working week to coach and support her team. P was asked two simple questions: 'What is keeping you from getting the results you want?' and 'do you have any sense of your part in not getting these results and what do you find personally challenging about leading this effort?' These questions allowed P to open up a whole raft of personal challenges she was facing. This was the start of talent management for her.

She was allocated a coach to help her develop. The coach sensed some scepticism in their first session. P had had a meeting with her boss the day before around the performance issues in her team and her ability to manage these issues. P had it in her mind that the coaching partnership was being set up as a remedial approach to help her deal with her team. The coach spent most of our first session explaining what executive coaching was all about and the benefits that would be derived from this development intervention. P is very conscious of the fact that she has been promoted into a big role and that there are many in the organisation who have high expectations of her and some sceptics who feel she may not be up to the task. Being assigned a coach, with her level of understanding of the benefits of a coach could be seen as a negative.

After the first session, P agreed to establish a coaching partnership. The coach agreed to draft a formal contract of engagement, which would also include what the roles of coach/coachee and her boss would be. The issue of confidentiality was a big issue for P, and the coach satisfied her concerns by explaining how they would approach the relationship with strictest confidence and only agree what information would be shared with her boss. It was also important to outline 'rules of engagement' with P because of her stringent travel arrangements.

In the second session they were able to start focusing on goals and objectives of the partnership. The coach asked P what she through her team's perception of her as a leader was. What would they be saying about her? Then the coach asked her what behaviours she thought she needed to enhance or change to be more effective. Interestingly enough, P found it difficult to articulate what she thought her team thought of her. However P did say that she thought she could create more space and time for her team and be more 'people centric'. When she was under pressure, she became more directive and very task focused. The coach asked P how she thought she could get some honest feedback from her team on her style. She felt that her team would not be as open as she would like if she had to ask for the feedback. The coach asked her what message she got from this. P was not creating an environment of openness. They agreed that the coach would elicit informal feedback from her team. Key pieces of feedback from P's team were as follows:

- Hard working and focused sometimes to the detriment of what's going on around her;
- Behaviour becomes directive and dictatorial when the team is under any pressure;
- Team would like more direction from her;
- Team would like to see more of her;
- Team would like more 1:1 coaching conversations.

P and the coach met to discuss the feedback from her team. They agreed on what the reality of the situation was, and P was not surprised by her team's feedback. She quantified this by how busy she was and that she was trying to make a good impression in the business. Her travel itinerary was pretty rigorous and this was not allowing her to get more time with her team. One other insight that did come out of our session was that P admitted that she was more comfortable managing a project than managing a team. The coach probed a little deeper and established that P did not have the confidence to coach members of her team. She was afraid to let go and felt that it was easier to make the decisions. It was a great moment once P articulated the above that she had an 'AHA! Moment'. It was clear what they needed to do. P identified the following goals:

- Request more 1:1 time with her boss to ensure that P has the adequate direction and support;
- P agreed to build in an hour for each of her three team members every 2 weeks. Therefore it equates to at least 6 hours per month dedicated 1:1 sessions. P also agreed that the 1:1's would be 50 per cent task focused and 50 per cent soft skills focused;
- P will reduce her travel by 10 per cent every month to allow her to be more strategic instead of tactical;
- They will identify a coaching programme for senior managers, which will provide P with the skills/tools and experience of coaching her team. She will also work with the coach to develop her coaching skills;
- P will have a look at her work–life balance and readjust accordingly. P has indicated that her long hours in the office and travel commitments were placing strain on her home life. They agreed that an appropriate work life balance was a fundamental goal.

Conclusions

It's important to have a results orientation to any leaders challenges. Both the coach and coachee should feel that it is a partnership. The coach needs to be aware of all the factors affecting the leader and not just focus on the leader him/herself. Consider more than the leaders traits, goals, challenges and motivations; consider also their teams and other departments, organisational politics and the environment the leader is working in. Then providing direct and just in time feedback can help talent development more effectively.

3 Key Texts

(1) Blass, E. (2009) *Talent Management: Cases and Commentary* (Basingstoke: Palgrave Macmillan).

(2) Finkelstein, S. (2003) *Why Smart Executives Fail* (New York: Penguin Group).

(3) Smilansky, J. (2007) *Developing Executive Talent: Best Practices from Global Leaders* (Hoboken, New Jersey: John Wiley & Sons, Inc.).

3 Key Articles/Reports

(1) Abrahamson, E. (1996) 'Management Fashion', *Academy of Management Review*, 21 (1), pp. 254–285.

(2) Iles, P., Preece, D. and Chuai, X. (2010) 'Talent Management as a Management Fashion in HRD: Towards a Research Agenda', *Human resource Development International*, 13 (2), pp. 125–146.

(3) Parry, E. and Urwin, P. (2009) *Tapping into Talent: The Age Factor and Generation Issues*: *Research into Practice* (London, Chartered Institute of Personnel and Development).

3 Key Web Links

(1) Blog with discussion of Generation issues: http://blogs.freshminds.co.uk/talent/?cat=5.

(2) Finkelstein on YouTube: http://www.youtube.com/watch?v=SFGCV8L5lxM.

(3) Representative assembly of themes and resources for talent development: http://talentdevelop.com/.

10

Professional Practice

Learning Objectives

By the end of this chapter you will be able to:

- Describe and analyse aspects of individual personality that influence learning and change, including the MBTI framework;
- Describe and analyse aspects of relationships that influence learning and change using Transactional Analysis;
- Describe and aspects of group that influence learning and change;
- Critically evaluate challenges in organising learning in work addressing personality styles, relationships and group dynamics.

Introduction

Human Resource Development (HRD) professional practice is not a simple and repetitive completion of a common journey; there are diverse and complex paths and experiences. That diversity is attributable to three factors that can be explored in more depth: (1) individual personality differences, (2) relationships and (3) groups. Individual differences and personality type will impact on how people engage with learning and change. The Myers Briggs Type Indicator (MBTI) framework provides one option which is widely used. The dynamics of relationships also provide both opportunities and challenges in the practice of HRD as people engage with people in learning and change; these may be relationships between the learner and the HRD professional, or among learners themselves. The framework of Transactional Analysis (TA) (Hay 2009) provides one perspective on this. Finally the dynamics of groups also affects practice and these can be analysed using various frameworks; one derived from the psychoanalytical tradition is given here.

These perspectives on people, relationships and groups provide knowledge that can be useful when managing, professionally and ethically, the development of other people, supporting learning and change that will have impact and make a difference.

Professional Practice

The general emotional profile of learning and change (see Perspectives 10.1 and 10.2) sets the context for much HRD professional practice, traversing optimism and pessimism as engagement with learning both rewards and challenges the learner, moving from contemplating change to establishing and sustain new knowledge, skill or behaviours.

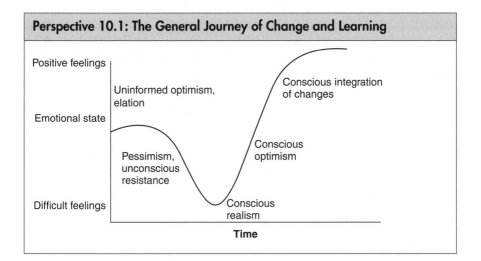

Perspective 10.1: The General Journey of Change and Learning

Positive feelings

Uninformed optimism, elation

Conscious integration of changes

Emotional state

Conscious optimism

Pessimism, unconscious resistance

Difficult feelings

Conscious realism

Time

Perspective 10.2: Stages of Change

- Precontemplation: developing awareness of issues where learning and change is needed;
- Contemplation: exploring the issues which merit learning and change;
- Preparation: committing to learning and change;
- Action: making behavioural changes, modifying behaviour;
- Maintenance: continuing change and consolidating learning.

HRD professional practice is not a simple and repetitive completion of a common journey; there are diverse and complex paths and experiences. Individual differences, relationships and group experiences will have an impact on how people become aware of learning and change needs and engage with learning and change, or present challenges that can interfere with learning and change. They provide the concrete and unique challenges of the abstract and general journey that learning and change entails.

Individual Differences

Understanding individual differences among learners and the challenges of organising learning among diverse personality types is one aspect of professional practice. A baseline for this is be aware of and recognise the 'Big 5' personality factors and their primary characteristics. According to Gosling (2010) these are as follows:

- Openness – (inventive/curious vs. cautious/conservative). Appreciation for adventure, unusual ideas, curiosity and variety of experience;
- Conscientiousness – (efficient/organised vs. easy-going/careless). A tendency to show self-discipline, act dutifully and aim for achievement; planned rather than spontaneous behaviour;
- Extraversion – (outgoing/energetic vs. shy/withdrawn). Energy, positive emotions, urgency and the tendency to seek stimulation in the company of others;
- Agreeableness – (friendly/compassionate vs. competitive/outspoken). A tendency to be compassionate and cooperative rather than suspicious and antagonistic towards others;
- Neuroticism – (secure/confident vs. sensitive/nervous). A tendency to experience unpleasant emotions easily, such as anger, anxiety, depression or vulnerability.

In HRD practice, organising learning in formal learning or developing informal learning systems, these individual differences will be present and shape how people engage with learning. They produce a range of challenges for guiding and helping people to learn and change. Awareness of these, and attending to them and accommodating them (see Practice 10.1), is a skilled part of HRD practice.

Practice 10.1: Individual Differences and Learner Characteristics

Type 1	5 Factors and Possible Behaviours	Type 2
cautious	conservative distracted	curious
easy going	careless fussy	efficient
shy	withdrawn loud	outgoing
competitive	outspoken chatting	friendly
sensitive	nervous domineering	secure

An awareness of the 'Big 5' is one window onto thinking about individual differences. Many other psychometric instruments for capturing individual differences are available. A commonly used framework is the MBTI personality type. This model is based on making a core distinction between people who are extravert (E) and people who are introverts (I). For extraverts attention is naturally oriented to outer world of people and/or activities. They tend to feel energised when engaging with the outer world, and their behaviour reflects that; they mix a lot, and enjoy being in company. For introverts attention is naturally orientated to inner world of thoughts and reflections. Their behaviour reflects that; they feel energised when engaging with their internal world, being on their own and enjoying that. The extravert gives greatest interest and value to objects: people, things and external accomplishments. They are most comfortable when active in the external world and human relationships. They can be restless and ill at ease when alone, without diversions. The introvert is characterised by a tendency to orient inwards, connecting with the subjective, inner world of thought, fantasies and feelings. Greatest interest and value is given by them to the subjective: inner reactions and images. The introvert prefers their own company and may be reserved or uncomfortable in large groups. Both introvert and extravert have their strengths, and associated challenges. To the extravert, the introvert appears self-centred and withholding. To the introvert, the extravert appears shallow and opportunistic (Edinger 2010).

MBTI further distinguishes between personality types who are sensing (S) or intuitive (N) in their preferences for processing information. It distinguishes between people who are Thinking (T) or Feeling (F) in their decision-making. And finally it distinguishes between people who are Judging (J) or Perceiving (P) in their lifestyle. Combined this gives four dimensions with which to produce a profile of 16 different personality types. For example, I am profiled as an 'INTP'. A personality who is an introvert, intuitive, thinking and perceiving. This is a profile that might be predicted for someone who is an academic, and who is interested in ideas, and systematically exploring them, then writing about them. The opposite to my profile would be a person who is extravert, sensing, feeling and judging. Such a person would flourish more in roles where there was much more social interaction requiring and involving emotional engagement with people. These differences affect how people prefer to gain information, make decisions, behave around others, communicate, and handle conflict and change.

Perspective 10.3 outlines the factors that the framework identifies and explores. It should be evident that the 'journey' which learning involves will be seen and approached differently by the different MBTI types. If in a learning group there were representatives of all 16 types, it would be a real challenge to engage with them all. Usually, given the fit of certain types with certain kinds of organisation and roles, a group will have similar if not shared profiles. Generally, for example, sales people are more likely to be extroverts; information technology specialists are more likely to be introverts.

Perspective 10.3: MBTI Categories

	Facets	Mid-zone											Facets	
		5	4	3	2	1	0	1	2	3	4	5		
E	Initiating												Receiving	I
	Expressive												Contained	
	Gregarious												Intimate	
	Active												Reflective	
	Enthusiastic												Quiet	
S	Concrete												Abstract	N
	Realistic												Imaginative	
	Practical												Conceptual	
	Experiential												Theoretical	
	Traditional												Original	
T	Logical												Empathetic	F
	Reasonable												Compassionate	
	Questioning												Accommodating	
	Critical												Accepting	
	Tough												Tender	
J	Systematic												Casual	P
	Planful												Open ended	
	Early starting												Pressure Prompted	
	Scheduled												Spontaneous	
	Methodical												Emergent	

Relationships: Transactional Analysis

Transactional Analysis (TA) is a perspective on understanding relationships (Berne 1964, Allen and Allen 2005, English 2005) which has been used for some time in HRD. It has been widely used by professionals supporting learning and change in employment contexts (Hay 1996, 2009). It is discussed here to illustrate how a description and analysis of relationships can assist organising learning in work. Further reading and understanding is possible, particularly with the work of Hay. TA has evolved overall as an alternative to extended forms of therapy, with concepts and methods adopted and adapted to training trainers and supporting coaches and mentors in HRD.

For an extended exploration of these dynamics, a source on TA such as Hay's (2009) is invaluable. TA's characteristic assumptions (Hay 2009) are that:

- People encounter change challenges not because they are 'broken' or deficient but because they are growing;
- People don't need fixing; they need nurturing;
- People think as they do because they have made their own minds up; they can change their minds too;
- People encounter barriers to learning because they are often discounting what they can do to change, and keeping hold of problems; they can be helped to become more aware of this and act differently.

Some of the key concepts of TA are given in Perspectives 10.4. They range from the very simple and clearly relevant to HRD, such as the analysis of 'strokes', to the more complex and perhaps more contentious concept of 'life scripts'. A version of what life scripts can entail in the employment and learning context is provided in TA by a discussion of 'working styles'.

Perspective 10.4: Transactional Analaysis Terms

Transactions

Transactions refer to the communication exchanges between people. Transactional analysis is recognizing which ego states people are transacting from and to follow the transactional sequences so they can intervene and improve the quality and effectiveness of communication.

Ego States

Complex interpersonal transactions are made up of three 'ego states'. Each ego state is an entire system of thoughts, feelings, and behaviors from which we interact with one another. The Parent, Adult and Child ego states and the interaction between them form the foundation of transactional analysis theory.

Strokes

TA emphasises that people need strokes, interpersonal recognition, to survive and thrive. Understanding how people give and receive positive and negative strokes and changing unhealthy patterns of stroking are aspects of transactional analysis.

Perspective 10.4: (Continued)

I'm OK – You're OK

'I'm OK – You're OK' is probably the best-known expression of the purpose of transactional analysis: to establish and reinforce the position that recognizes the value and worth of every person, capable of change, growth, and healthy interactions.

Games People Play

TA defines certain socially dysfunctional behavioral patterns as 'games.' These repetitive, devious transactions are principally intended to obtain strokes but instead they reinforce negative feelings and self-concepts, and mask the direct expression of thoughts and emotions.

Source: http://www.itaa-net.org/ta/keyideas.htm.

Transactions refer to the communication exchanges between people. These transactions will reflect the three ego states each person can have and are triggered in relationship as they unfold. Each ego state is a system of thoughts, feelings and behaviours with which people can interact with one another. Transactional analysis is a method of recognising that ego states people can intervene and affect the quality and effectiveness of relationships and communication.

The essence of a TA approach is to understand how ego states can influence behaviour and relationships, and especially how certain kinds of transaction can interfere with learning and change. These ego states are threefold: an 'adult', 'parent' and 'child' ego state. When in each ego state people tend to think and feel, respectively, as an adult, parent or child. The adult can be seen as logical or unfeeling; the parent as caring or critical; and the child as adapted or wild. Of course any partner in a relationship also has their own ego state; they too may be thinking and feeling as if an 'adult', 'parent' or 'child'. Where these are matched appropriate to a relationship and situation, then that relationship is underpinned securely. However, the behaviours of ego states can be overdone, perceived negatively, or be inappropriate. That can undermine rather than underpin a relationship. If overdone, perceived negatively or inappropriate the behaviours of the adult, parent or child ego state become, respectively, domineering, smothering and disruptive.

In HRD contexts, organising learning at work, the relationships that trainers and learners or managers and learners have, it is expected that behaviours be matched and complementary and effective as each party adopts and behaves in an appropriate ego state; adult to adult, or the positive aspects of parent and child ego states and relations. If this is not the case, and relationships evolve in the negative forms, they may become crossed and problematic. If for example, a trainer has behaviour that is 'critical parent' like and learners have behaviour that is 'wild-child' like, then the behaviour and relationship which occurs is likely to be problematic.

Departing from adult–adult relations is relevant where firmness or playfulness is appropriate. There are risks in sustained departure from the adult–adult relationship. First is that the dependency of the child on the parent interferes with engaging in adult learning methods; learners are passive and respond only to instruction, where HRD professionals seek active involvement and for learners to respond to facilitation. The second risk is that HRD professionals are perceived as 'critical parents' and learners adopt behaviours of 'wild children'. This can create dynamics which significantly interfere with learning.

In TA compliments and general ways of giving recognition are called strokes. Stroking can be verbal or nonverbal. There are a great variety of stroke needs and styles possible and present. TA proposes that people all have particular strokes they will accept and those they will reject. Appreciating one's own stroke patterns, and those of others, can assist with creating an environment in which learning and change is possible. TA in general advocates an awareness of and practice in 'stroking' which translates well into HRD contexts where learning and change are sought:

- Give strokes when we have them to give;
- Ask for strokes when we want them;
- Accept strokes if we want them;
- Reject manipulative strokes;
- Give ourselves positive strokes.

The concept of 'drivers' is more complex, the idea that people form and then hold to a story about who they are and how they should live from very early on in childhood. They then stick to this thereafter, responding to and making sense of events in relation to this driver. In the employment context the abstract notion of a driver is modified to produce the idea of 'working styles'. These are approaches to work that people have, formed around a core 'rule', and which they use to guide orient, understand themselves and others. The five drivers or working styles TA identifies are as follows:

(1) Be Perfect;
(2) Try Hard;
(3) Be Strong;
(4) Hurry Up;
(5) Please Others.

The 'Be Perfect' working style and script has the Motto; 'If a job is worth doing – it is worth doing well.' People create a rule about what perfection is, and then they don't meet up to it they have a go at themselves. This may also mean that they expect others to be perfect too which can be hard on the colleagues they work with. This type has strengths in work and learning environments in the form of:

- Accurate work;
- Checking facts and preparing thoroughly;
- Liking to get things right at the first attempt;
- On a quest for no errors.

As with any style these are qualities which can be positive. They may also produce problems, in work and in learning situations and relationships.

- Can't be relied on to produce work on time;
- Reluctant to issue drafts – prefer the finished article;
- May miss the opportunity to include the ideas of others;
- Misjudge level of detail that is required and include too much;
- May do everything themselves.

The 'Try Hard' working style is often that of those who are great pioneers. They are people who love new projects and new things to do. They usually have a great wealth of information as they like to gather different ideas together. They are best working under pressure. When stressed they may start too many things. This type has strengths in work and learning environments in the form of:

- Energy peaks with something new;
- Valued for their motivation;
- Enthusiastic about problem-solving;
- Often volunteer to take on new tasks.

They may also produce problems, in work and in learning situations and relationships.

- More committed to trying than succeeding;
- Interest wears off before they finish the task;
- Volunteer for new projects before they have completed current tasks;
- May be resented by others for lack of follow through;
- May spread their interests too thinly;
- May over complicate issues.

The 'Be Strong' working style is known for being calm under pressure, energised by having to cope, and great to have around in a crisis. This type has strengths in work and learning environments in the form of:

- Emotionally detached;
- Can make unpleasant decisions;

- Seen as reliable and steady;
- Even tempered.

They may also produce problems, in work and in learning situations and relationships, as they do not like to admit weaknesses. Failure to cope is seen as a weakness – so they may become overloaded at work. They can be highly self-critical, and in development contexts can appear:

- Standing apart from playful activities fearing they may look stupid;
- Disguise difficulties by 'hiding' work away;
- Colleagues may feel uncomfortable due to their lack of emotional response;
- Hard to get to know.

The 'Hurry Up' working style is the person proud that 'If you want something done – give it to a busy person.' They work quickly and get lots done. They look for the most efficient way to do things. This type has strengths in work and learning environments in the form of:

- Energy peaks under pressure;
- Work quickly – get a lot done in a short time;
- Respond well to short deadlines;
- Good at juggling several things at the same time.

They may also produce problems, in work and in learning situations and relationships. In their haste they can make mistakes, and the quality of work is not what is expected. The urge to save time may be inappropriately applied to everything they do, including engaging in learning and development:

- May miss deadlines;
- Going back to correct mistakes can take longer;
- Tendency to speak quickly and interrupt;
- They are likely to be impatient with others;
- They make only superficial changes as they are so quick to get on with things and not take an in-depth perspective;
- They might select priorities so quickly that a significant area is overlooked.

The 'Please Others' working style has the aim to please and encourage harmony within relationships and the group. They like to please people, perhaps without even asking them how they can do this. They can see both sides of an argument and attempt to calm things down. They will be keen to do things for others, often to the point of 'rescuing' them. Decision-making is not their strong point and they may frustrate people by not expressing their own opinion. They may be perceived as good team members, as they show genuine interest in others, and are recognised as inviting quieter members into discussion. They may also produce problems, in work and in learning situations and relationships.

- Concerned about the approval of others;
- Reluctant to challenge the ideas of others even when they are wrong;
- Over cautious;
- May seem to lack commitment as they tend to over qualify everything;
- May lack assertiveness;
- Hesitate to question as they feel they should have the answer.

An awareness of as well as appreciation of working styles can help organise and manage learning and learners. It helps to make clear and provide options for dealing with the behaviours encountered in development situations, such as the training room, and relationships, such as coaching. In employment it may be that an awareness of the strengths and weaknesses of working styles, and modifying it, can be a key to improving performance and realising potential. If development environments are the place in which this awareness first emerges, then they provide a catalyst for this broader review of working style.

Group Contexts

Understanding personality and appreciating relationship behaviours can both assist by giving 'lenses' with which engagement in learning or disengagement from learning and change can be seen and understood (London and Sessa 2007). They provide options for the facilitator of learning and change to seek to engage all in learning and change. The value of these is clearly present in one-to-one support for learning and change, such as coaching and mentoring. It is also present when people are gathered in groups to learn, and people in groups provide the most common context for learning and change. One widely used and reviewed model (Aritzeta et al. 2007) is that of team role types, developed by Belbin (1996) which describes how diverse roles may be fulfilled if groups are to perform well as teams.

It is evident in such contexts that further factors can be in play, influencing what, how, and indeed if, people learn and change. The factors in play are neither solely about the collection of personalities present, nor the character of the patterns in their interrelationships. They are about the group as a whole. Just as individuals have personalities, and interrelationships have patterns in them, so groups can be analysed. These include the following:

- The shaper, an aggressive achiever who helps drive the team in action;
- The plant, the innovator who provides creative ideas to the group;
- The monitor-evaluator, the critical thinker who queries the feasibility of plans;

- The implementer, hardworking member who takes practical and efficient action to achieve group goals;
- The coordinator, who facilitates and organises the efforts of others;
- The completer-finisher, who pays attention to detail and ties up loose ends;
- The resource investigator, who liaises with others outside the group;
- The specialist, the technical expert who supplies the group with specialised knowledge.

Having individuals who will assume complementary informal roles within the group can dramatically improve group performance, as well as the satisfaction of group members. It is, for example, much better for a group to include a plant, a monitor-evaluator, an implementer and a specialist rather than four plants or four monitor-evaluators. The trainers and the learners can be aware of this and act accordingly.

Learning and change group contexts for learning and change range from people being members of informal meetings of peers, occasionally sharing experiences, to being members of groups which meet regularly over years as part of structured and formal learning processes. A group can be defined as consisting of at least two individuals, who:

- Interact with each other;
- Are psychologically aware of each other;
- Perceive themselves as a group;
- Are recognised as a group by at least one other group.

All four conditions need to be met for an aggregation of individuals to be considered as a group (Tuckman 1965, Tuckman and Jensen, 1977). Group dynamics then are the combined psychological processes and social interaction processes at work among group members; affecting how (and if) groups form, their structure and processes, how they function and how they are experienced by individual members, other groups and the organisation.

To manage learning and change an appreciation of group norms, roles and stages of formation can be helpful (Bonebright 2010). Significance is attached to characteristics such as group size, cohesiveness, groupthink, social loafing and team qualities on learning and change. Beneath these tangible characteristics are deeper aspects affecting group formation and working; emerging from the authority relations between learners and instructors and facilitators managing groups.

This matters in HRD in a variety of contexts; Garavan and McCarthy (2008) identify several forms of collective learning context (Perspective 10.5).

Perspective 10.5: Group Learning Contexts		
Type	**Concept**	**Challenge for HRD**
Organisational learning	processes enhancing the actions of organisations through better knowledge and understanding	Making mistakes; single loop and double loop issues, espoused and in use theories
Leaning organisation	best practices in communication, team-working, participation which produce effective and pleasant organisations	Ideals to strive for or political prescriptions?
Team learning	Teams act and reflect locally, meeting needs of members	Going beyond the local
Communities of practice	How communities form and interact to create and share knowledge and understanding informally	Managing formally
Collaborative learning	people discussing their experiences and networking to do this	Building networks spanning boundaries

Group Norms: Role and Formation Stages

Groups impose norms and roles on their members. Group norms serve four main purposes:

(1) They express the central values of the group so they can inspire group members and project the nature of the group to others;

(2) They simplify and make more predictable the behaviour of individual group members;

(3) They prevent situations where group members may be offended or emotionally hurt;

(4) They increase the likelihood of group survival (e.g. by rejection of deviant behaviour that poses a threat to the existence of the group) and group success.

Roles are sets of tasks that group members are expected to complete to justify their group membership. In learning groups these will encompass the obvious roles of trainer and learner. But there can be different kinds of formal trainer and different kinds of formal learner role. Group members have informal as well as formal roles. These roles vary widely and relate to the way a member interacts with other group members and the benefits he/she brings to the group.

Group Formation

Formal and informal groups in learning situations are never totally independent, and it is a mistake to think of formal and informal groups as distinct entities. The formal organisation is connected with, and largely determines, the informal one. Every formal organisation has informal groups and many informal organisations eventually evolve some semblance of formal groups. Learning situations are the same.

Formal and informal groups can be thought of as both progressing through a series of stages. The way in which a group does this will largely determine the extent to which it will succeed in its tasks. These stages are generally known as the forming, storming, norming, performing and adjourning stages (Tuckman and Jensen 1977). If groups fail to progress successfully through one or more of these stages, they may encounter difficulties in completing tasks. In the case of learning groups the task is to learn. They may rather become groups that do not deliver their objectives and/or impose psychological stress on some or all of their members. Steps can be prescribed to improve the likelihood of the group forming, storming, norming and performing, though challenges will always occur and groups may experience episodes of dysfunction. The ideas of Bion can be used to explore features of this in more detail.

Group Stages

Forming: Group members get to know one another and understand their roles, as well as defining goals and expectations and developing procedures for task accomplishment. Group members tend to be reserved at this stage, in which case there may be uncertainty and even confusion. The use of 'ice-breaker' and introductory activities eases this.

Storming: Resolution of issues, such as methods for task accomplishment, definition and allocation of tasks, goal prioritisation and leadership, often involves conflict and confrontation, which may cause member withdrawal or isolation. Clashes and disagreements over fundamental issues (goals, performance standards, roles) may hamper the group. Not resolving this will decrease the likelihood of the group succeeding in its mission, and progression through subsequent stages will also suffer.

Norming: The stage in which group norms are established, including intended or acceptable performance standards. Cooperation among group members is a dominant issue during this stage and ideally a sense of shared responsibility should develop, with high cohesion, shared group identity and camaraderie.

However, sub-optimal norms may be established in groups that have not successfully progressed from the previous stage.

Performing: The stage where the group reaches the peak of effectiveness and efficiency in task accomplishment, with the work roles of individual members, trainers and learners, accepted and understood. The persistence of covert conflict between group members from the storming stage will inhibit group performance. Performance can also be affected by members' pre-occupation with their individual performance and goals, the degree of functionality of norms, and the quality of leadership.

Adjourning: Once the group has achieved its intended objective (e.g. the learning is complete) it may be adjourned, and social relations are terminated but in a healthy way. Adjourning can be 'natural' or timed to happen at the appropriate point, as with the planned break-up of a formal group after accomplishing its role. Untimed adjournment represents a sub-optimal case. In certain ongoing, permanent groups this last stage will never be reached.

Team learning championed as an ingredient for success. Kasl et al. (1997) suggested four learning modes:

(1) Fragmented: individual learning that is not hared;
(2) Pooled: individual learning that is shared among some;
(3) Synergistic: in special events group as a whole creates knowledge mutually, integrating diverse perspectives;
(4) Continuous: habitual kinds of synergistic learning.

With appreciation of teamwork, individual expression and team-building principles combined there is scope for team learning, people are open to and listen to others, invited to express inputs and objections, and helping each other learn is highly valued (Yorks and Sauquet 2003).

Characteristics of Effective Groups

The characteristics of effective groups, in general rather than specifically in learning contexts, have been studied. The conclusions from these studies can be applied to thinking about learning in groups. The size of the group is a factor. When groups rely on direct relationships between their members, size plays an important role in performance. The functional size for a group ranges from 3 to 12 members, and optimal performance seems to occur with a membership of seven to nine. Researchers have found that increasing group size above nine has negative effects on verbal participation of group members, quality of decision-making, speed of communication and satisfaction of group members. At 12, interaction between members becomes difficult and the group 'naturally' splits into smaller sub-groups.

The cohesiveness of the group is a second factor. Cohesiveness refers to the strength and quality of interpersonal ties among group members. It depends on the frequency and quality of contact between group members, the degree of interdependence of members' roles, and the demographic and ideological (attitudinal/value) similarity of the group members. Group cohesiveness is strengthened when group members perceive external threats and the group has a history of success. Cohesiveness is a highly desirable quality for group performance. It serves as a motivator for the group or the team, to work towards the advancement of the common objectives. Cohesiveness functions as a form of implicit control on group members in their activities, so these activities are compatible with the interests of the group. In most cases, cohesive groups will outperform their less cohesive counterparts. More cohesive groups are likely to perform better than their less cohesive counterparts (Evans and Dion 1991).

A history of success for the group builds cohesiveness. However, this can lead to complacency, with negative consequences for the quality of group decisions and group performance. This is because past performance creates the 'illusion of invulnerability', which impairs future decision-making. Group cohesiveness is one of the antecedents of the well-known phenomenon called 'groupthink' (Janis 1982). 'Groupthink' is defined as a deterioration of mental efficiency, reality testing and moral judgement that results from in-group pressures on individual members to conform and reach consensus.

Measures to counter groupthink include allowing free expression and even encouraging minority sub-groups and legitimising unpopular viewpoints. Clearly, it can be difficult to establish a climate of healthy debate and even conflict among group members, while at the same time aiming for a strong focus on learning around a consensus-based curriculum. Firms that operate in simple and relatively stable markets should benefit most from consensus while firms that operate in diversified and uncertain markets will benefit most if they encourage dissent and healthy conflict (Cosier and Schwenk 1990). So learning groups in simple and stable domains benefit from consensus, those in diverse and uncertain domains require dissent and healthy conflict.

'Social loafing' refers to the apparent reduction in the effort that individuals exhibit when they are required to accomplish a task as members of a group. However, although social loafing and coordination problems are obstacles in learning group performance it is still possible for a group to produce more than the cumulative productivity of its members. This is achieved when we instil coherence and purpose into the group. Coherence and purpose lead to a 'process gain' in a group situation. The implication is that the arrangement of work around groups, or teams, can have beneficial effects on performance, provided that there is appropriate planning and implementation.

A team can be distinguished as an evolution of the group; a group with some additional characteristics. A simple way to distinguish a team from a group is by defining a team as 'a group with a high performance ethic' (Katzenbach and Smith 1993). Hence, teams are groups whose norms include high performance standards. Other differences identified by researchers include:

- Shared leadership in the team, rather than a clearly focused leader in the group; team members have complementary roles and shared objectives, so different members are able to assume leadership roles depending on the circumstances;

- Mutual accountability of team members for team outcomes, in contrast to individual accountability of group members;
- The products of a team are collective, and cannot be produced by individuals alone, while the products of a group are accumulations of individual rather than synergetic work;
- Team meetings are active and focus on resolving problems and producing innovative ideas, while group meetings simply focus on efficiency;
- Performance measures for teams are direct, that is, they assess the collective products of the team, while performance measures for groups are indirect, that is, they focus on overall organisational or departmental performance.

Inter-team competition can be a major threat to the success of team-working in organisations (Mohrman et al. 1995) because it promotes interest in and commitment to the team rather than to the organisation. In learning situations teams that compete with each other may withhold vital information from other teams or be unwilling to provide them with specialist help and support.

Group Formation, Working and Authority

The importance of factors interfering with group relations and their impact on learning is often underplayed in the study and professional development of trainers and educators. Performance in handling instruction and facilitation groups, particularly the latter which are increasing in use, requires deeper analysis. To be able to facilitate learning in groups effectively requires an understanding of the nature and challenges of group formation and group working. Practically, the aim is to nurture an environment demonstrating positive signs of being a good environment for learning, without the negative features that can indicate an environment for learning is absent (see Practice 10.2).

Practice 10.2: Positive and Negative Signs for a Learning Group Environment

Positive signs	Negative signs
Relaxed and friendly	Tense and stressed
Open exchange of information	Lack of exchange
Providing suggestions and solutions	No suggestions or solutions given

Willing to participate	Unwilling to participate
Staying focused on learning	Not focused on learning
Feeling of comfort and enjoyment	Uncomfortable
Working with the instructor/facilitator	Conflict with the instructor/facilitator

Source: Derived from Hardingham (2000).

The leadership and authority demands on those acting as instructors or facilitators of learning groups in formal adult education settings can be explored in more depth. The group and social context of most adult learning and education has attracted some 'method'-oriented analysis, with tips and techniques for facilitating groups. Adult learning has tended to stick around a prescriptive approach to facilitated learning that favours a menu of participative methods and action learning-like techniques. The learning contexts vary widely, from large lecture theatres through groups of around 30 learners and down to small teams of 3 or 4 learners. Accordingly the leadership and authority issues vary. Many professionals will have encountered a range of stresses and problems in seeking to fulfil the role of facilitator of a group in many different situations. There have been few theoretical advances, making some of the original thinking on group environments in this field by people like Bion (1977) of continuing significance.

Bion was a pioneer in applying ideas and concepts from psychodynamic theory about individuals and their problems to groups and their dynamics. His original motivation was to establish better therapy systems, based on people experiencing analysis in groups. Since he discussed and outlined his thinking, his ideas have migrated in various ways to thinking more generally about group processes and group relations in other contexts. For Bion a healthy group had certain characteristics for these healthy characteristics to be present and be sustained in a group, whether supporting therapeutic tasks or other tasks, required leader–follower relations to nurture them. This was easy to describe and prescribe, but often presented immense difficulty in practice. For Bion this was attributable to a fundamental ambiguity about being in a group. While people need to be in groups to satisfy various individual needs, they also find them a stress. Each of the positive characteristics signalling a good environment can be undermined and interfered with as the natural stresses are worked out. Alongside the potential of any group to satisfy an individual is the potential of group membership to present challenges to each person. People in a group may have diverse purposes, they may not recognise the same boundaries to the group as others, they may not respond well to losing old members or absorbing new ones, they may evolve sub-groups, they may devalue some members and they may be unable to confront discontent in the group. Each of these possible problems emerges organically and naturally from the group experience. They are not attributable to error on the part of a facilitator or leader. Central to the way that these problems may be encountered is how people form an idea of how they are being 'perceived' by the group, via a sense of its collective 'group mentality'. That may seriously jar with the individual's own sense of self.

Leadership and authority in groups involves appreciating the existence and role of dynamics emerging around these characteristics and perceptions of group mentality. Managing a learning environment is about helping people achieving things, cooperatively, using skills, with purposeful activity and cognitive processing engaging with reality. Tensions around group mentality and the individuals' sense of self apply equally to the leader, the facilitator, as well as the followers. Any group of adults assembled to learn will be subject to these kinds of dynamics under the leadership and authority of a group instructor or facilitator. How group relations might be best managed can be considered by following Bion's thinking about the leadership issues that present problems for groups, and thinking about what might be encountered in learning settings. The questions that a facilitator needs to be aware of and answer to support the positive and avoid the negative are as follows:

- What are the group's needs?
- What are the danger signs?
- How to keep the negative group dynamics at bay?
- How detached from the group should I be?

Exercise 10.1: Ideals and Interference

Consider a group you have been a member of. To what extent did it succeed? To what extent was it an ideal group, in these respects? Were there signs of drift or interference?

Ideal group	Signs of drift	Learning interference
A common purpose	Different purposes	Competing purposes
Recognition of boundaries	Confusion of boundaries	Conflict on boundaries
Absorb new/lose old	Tensions on new/old	Disruption of new/old
No sub-groups	Elements of sub-groups	Definite sub-groups
Individuals valued/free	Most valued/free	Few valued/free
Discontent managed	Discontent ignored	Discontent erupting

As people come together to participate in learning they typically face a set of interpersonal issues which they will need to work through, address and resolve:

- Inclusion needs: the facilitator of learning needs to give them a place and accept their identity in the beginning, during the experience and in concluding it.
- Control needs: the people in the group seek to understand who is in control, what their responsibilities are and how others will be exerting their control? There are power issues, as control may lie with different people at different times. As learning experiences are unfolding people in the group may be divided and re-composed into sub-groups. It is important to avoid trainer–trainee power confrontations, and defuse trainee–trainee conflicts in group work.
- Affection needs: in any kind of group people have affection needs, served by openness and closeness, with personal worth being validated.

For instructors or facilitators a concern is to satisfy their own needs in these areas while maintaining some detachment, because the instructor or facilitator is not part of the learning group. They are in the learning environment, but they belong to other groups which are not present; for example, to external groups such as the HRD department or their professional group. The instructor or facilitator seeks conformity with positive norms and values, and model behaviours.

Functional Signs and Interference Signs

Bion provides a framework for thinking about why and how negative group dynamics can arise, despite the best efforts of a skilled instructor or facilitator. He argued that groups aspired to be functional work groups, but that underlying 'basic assumptions' might emerge and interfere with that. A functional work group would be one that is getting on with the tasks in hand; in the case of learning, the learning tasks. A 'basic assumption' is a form of group mentality that expresses a primitive emotion about what the group exists to do. As an assumption it is often never consciously perceived by people in the group, but can be traced and seen in behaviours. A group with interference from a 'basic assumption' would not be a functional work group. They would be subject to interference and be 'losing the plot'. It would be spending time and energy on things other than the functional task (see Practice 10.3).

Practice 10.3: Functional Group vs. Interference Effects	
Signs of a functional work group	**Signs of a basic assumption interfering**
Clear about what needs to be done	Lose focus, or too intense and rigid

Practice 10.3: (Continued)

Signs of a functional work group	Signs of a basic assumption interfering
Output high	Low standards
Ready to disband at the appropriate time	Time wasted on relations not working
Open to the outside	Hostile to outside
Reviews itself and improves	Sees feedback as a threat
Acknowledges failure and analyses it	Denies failure, ignores it
Tolerates differences	Unspoken rules, in-jokes, covert activity

Examples of the differences between a functional group and one experiencing interference are plentiful. Much 'reality television' is based on showing groups experiencing such interference for entertainment. Some to think about would be:

Functional group	Basic assumption interference
Football team in a challenging game	Same team in the pub after, disparaging their opposition
Yacht crew sailing a stormy sea	The yacht crew arguing about who is to cook dinner
Management team discussing budgets	The same management team paralysed in contemplation of a changing world
A learning syndicate group brainstorming	A learning syndicate group just having a gossip

In learning groups, as in groups generally, the foundation is that people ought to be given relevant and interesting work that is achievable. The instructor or facilitator ought to keep groups organised and structured. Even then groups may experience basic assumptions and interference. The first signs may be:

- Coming to depend excessively and unrealistically on the instructor or facilitator;
- Seeing the instructor or facilitator as an 'enemy' in some way;
- Looking to members of the group to ally with and/or take over from the instructor or facilitator.

Underlying these signs and behaviours the following may be active issues to deal with:

- Transference: where negative feelings about a significant person or people in authority are being transferred from the original source into the current relationship. The instructor or facilitator is an innocent agent on the end of negative feelings in a group. In learning groups these may occur in straightforward ways as people consider the instructor or facilitator to be like an archetypal authority figure such as a 'teacher' or 'parent' and respond accordingly.

Response – clear up any contamination of transference from other experiences.

- Projection: learning group members can have sensitive or negative traits or beliefs that they are uncomfortable with and anxious about. They may come to see these sensitive or negative traits and beliefs in others, recognising they exist but keeping a clean and positive view of themselves as 'good' people. This helps them to avoid owning the 'bad' traits themselves. Instead they can be seen to appear as qualities in others, allowing the members of the learning group to release tension about the sensitive or negative trait or belief. In learning groups projection may occur around being assessed. People are subjective in their reactions to this but like to think they are being objective, while the assessor is seen to be subjective if they do not get a brilliant mark.

Response – clear up misunderstandings.

- Splitting: under stress people tend to perceive things in black-and-white terms; they adopt extreme positions, being either for or against ideas, suggestions and so on. Learning can be stressful if the demands it makes exceed the capabilities of the learners and if, instead of reviewing that accordingly, the stress builds discussions can become polarised and the instructor or facilitator and group members may end up in extreme positions.

Response – reduce stress, bring learning back within capabilities.

- Managing learning in groups is the environment for much workplace learning and development. Prescriptive 'best practice' on this for instruction and facilitation is useful, but limited. When there are difficulties with a learning group the underlying sources of that can be hard to see and deal with. One framework for exploring this is an analysis of the basic assumptions, derived from Bion, that may interfere with the functioning of a group. To keep on, or get back on, track to a positive learning climate and attaining group ideals to achieve learning means understanding these basic assumptions and their dynamics as they emerge in mild forms, or even 'erupt' very strongly.

Interference from these basic assumptions can be hard to work through. One reason for that is that they may provide a rationale for the group to feel fulfilled even when the members are not actually learning. At the other extreme, the group may produce situations that make the group punishing for at least some individuals, including the leader, the instructor or facilitator. This reverses the satisfactions of group membership, and produces dissatisfaction. While this is to be seen as something to avoid it is also an organic part of group experience, and cannot be excised. Such dissatisfactions are never going to be eradicated as long as people continue to be ambivalent about being in groups. The more realistic aim is that people will still want to continue in membership rather than leave a learning group.

The 'solution' is not for the leader of the learning group to eradicate the prospect of interference. It is for the group to work with and through interference and strive to sustain the environment of a healthy group, which, to reprise, is:

- A common purpose;
- Common recognition by members of the boundaries;
- Capacity to absorb new members and lose old ones;
- Freedom from internal sub-groups with exclusive boundaries;
- Individuals all valued and with 'free movement';
- Able to face and cope with discontent.

3 Key Texts

(1) Berne, E. (l964) *Games People Play* (New York, Grove Press).

(2) Hay, J. (2009) *Working it out at Work* (Watford, Sherwood Publishing).

(3) Briggs Myers, I. and Myers, P (1995) *Gifts Differing: Understanding Personality Type* (Palo Alto, CA: Davies-Black Publishing)

3 Key Articles/Reports

(1) Aritzeta, A., Swailes, S. and Senior, B. (2007) 'Belbin's Team Role Model: Development, Validity and Applications for Team Building', *Journal of Management Studies*, 44 (1), pp. 96–118.

(2) Garavan, T. and McCarthy, A. (2008) 'Collective Learning Process and Human Resource Development', *Advances in Developing Human Resources*, 10 (4), pp. 451–471.

(3) Tuckman, B. W. (1965) 'Developmental Sequences in Small Groups', *Psychological Bulletin*, 63, pp. 384–399.

3 Key Web Links

(1) Myers Briggs tool website: http://www.myersbriggs.org/my-mbti-personality-type/mbti-basics/.

(2) Transactional Analysis: http://www.itaa-net.org/ta/.

(3) Resources and links on Group dynamics: https://facultystaff.richmond.edu/~dforsyth/gd/.

11

Development Partnerships

Learning Objectives

By the end of this module you will be able to:

- Describe practices associated with HRD partnerships;
- Explore the use of coaching and mentoring as HRD practices;
- Compare and contrast coaching and mentoring, sharing some common characteristics and distinctive functions;
- Reflect on the theoretical and practical trends affecting the use of development partnerships in workplaces.

Debate 11.1: Who Needs Compliments?

One study of the behaviour of adult learners in three different occupations (teaching, police services and financial services) found that much learning occurred during normal work and interaction with peers or managers which supported learning. Across all these occupations one strong finding was clear; in each area of work there was a clear pattern of learning occurring based on interaction partners (peers or managers) communicating negative reactions and feedback to the learner, with very few learners reporting that learning entailed being complimented or given positive feedback.

Why do you think this might be so?

Source: Koopmans et al. (2006).

Introduction

Development partnerships, especially coaching and mentoring, are widely used methods for supporting adult learning in work. The nature and functions of these partnerships, ranging from developing skills to managing careers, can be described. The skills they entail, and the situations in which they are used, can be identified and analysed. The challenges of adopting and improving the use of coaching and mentoring are a major part of the Human Resource Development (HRD) landscape.

Case: Coaching in RetailCo

RetailCo is a high street retailer with many stores in its chain. It prides itself on having weathered some hard times recently to regain a prominent position as a prestigious retailer of fashion, food and other lines. As a part of attempts to improve customer service it has implemented a coaching programme into the organisation as a result of the new pay structure introduced at the beginning of the financial year. Previously, there were over 200 different pay levels within the company as a result of performance-related pay. The company decided to try and dramatically reduce this number to only six pay levels. These proposed levels include roles for:

(1) Trainee;

(2) Customer assistant;

(3) Coach;

(4) Section coordinator;

(5) Trainee section manager;

(6) Section manager.

As a natural progression from customer assistant, the role of a coach has been implemented within the company offering increased responsibility and a revised pay level. The company aims to have 15 per cent of the workforce in each store as a coach. The process is voluntary so employees who are interested volunteer to begin the training process.

Implementation

In preparation for their role as a coach employees are sent on a two-day training programme with other prospective coaches from other stores. This programme is aimed at providing the employees with ideas and incentives to implement this way of working, supporting and teaching within their role. During this programme, the employees learn new skills by discussion, role-play and presentations. They are given a folder containing each component part of the course allowing them to view what they will have achieved at the end of the programme.

The employees are firstly required to take part in ice-breaker tasks including an informal chat and asking each other questions. Each employee is then asked to give a prepared presentation to the group on any hobby or interest. This is seen as another way for the employees to get to know each other but also as an opportunity for the instructors to analyse their interaction and speaking skills to evaluate how well the employee presents themselves and appears to others. The employees receive feedback from the group and instructors and are required to learn from this feedback and discuss how they would improve in their role as coach.

In order to become familiar with the requirements of the role and display characteristics needed to be effective in the role, the employees discuss what they think a coach is and what the role entails. Following this, they take part in a role-play exercise playing both a coach and coachee and the instructors observe their behaviour. At this stage again, the employees give and receive feedback on their performance and discuss any new skills and behaviours they regard as being important for the role. By this stage the employees have experienced the practical side of the course and progress on to the theoretical elements involved in coaching.

The programme ends with the employees reading about what they are expected to do in their role. The two-day session leaves the employees 'half accredited' as a coach. The other half of the accreditation process takes place in store from observation of the employees by their line manager. It is the decision of the line manager if the employee becomes fully accredited as a coach. The line manager then conducts continual assessment of the coaches in store.

Process

Once accredited the coaches are actively involved in the training process within RetailCo, training new employees by incorporating what they have learned during the course. The new employees are regarded as 'coachees' whom the coaches train and develop at this initial stage to prepare themselves for employment with RetailCo. The coach continues to work with the new employees throughout the early stages of their employment by the ongoing training and development coaching process. The use of 'coaching cards' in RetailCo allows for a universal means of employee learning and development in addition to the support network they obtain through their coach. The coaching cards allow employees to learn the services, values and functions of their role and the role of the organisation. Each coachee must demonstrate learning of all elements of the coaching card before they can move on to the next card. The coach must therefore record successful completion and provide feedback to the coachee and line manager. This process enables new staff to develop their knowledge of the company and its functions. It is also an interaction process between coach and coachee, developing a working relationship that embodies support and encouragement.

Strengths and Weaknesses of Introducing Coaching

As a process, coaching enables all employees to be involved in the organisation and interact with fellow colleagues. This allows new employees to have a good support network from the moment they enter the organisation that does not end once the initial training stage is over. The continuous training and development means new employees do not have to partake in on-the-job learning by themselves but can learn at the beginning and as they go along with someone to support and encourage their learning. The process also allows experienced employees to give back to the organisation some of the knowledge and expertise they have gained throughout their time with the company. The role also gives employees the opportunity for career progression through a large established company which may not be experienced frequently.

The role requires time and energy from the coaches and a weakness is that there needs to be more time allocated to the process so it can be carried out more effectively. The process can be time consuming and so this needs to be recognised by management. The process has not been fully accepted by the workforce due to resistance to change incorporating aspects of age and experience. It is a commonly known problem that older employees who have been present in an organisation for a long time are resistant to new changes that may benefit younger employees more than them. RetailCo, in particular, has employees who have been present for many years, and it is more common for an employee to have been employed for over 20 years than not. An additional weakness of the process is that due to the new pay structure implemented in the organisation, the pay level for the coach is less than some customer assistant roles as a result of performance related pay. These financial issues are a reason that some employees did not volunteer for the role as coach which should have been taken into consideration at the time by management at RetailCo so as to ensure the best employees volunteered to become a coach. However, this has implications as customer assistants on a low level of pay may volunteer having been attracted by the large pay rise generated to cover the high levels of pay already obtained through performance-related pay.

Development Partnerships

The RetailCo case illustrates how development partnerships like coaching are being integrated into working life in leading organisations. This is a trend which emerges from recognising an important feature of HRD practice; that formal training can account for less than 10 per cent of employee learning (Tannebaum 1997). Much HRD in the other 90 per cent is apparently being practised in the context of development interactions and partnerships. Capability and expertise is acquired through development partnerships. Developmental partnerships can be defined (Eddy et al. 2006, p. 60) as:

> Interactions between two individuals with the intent of enhancing personal development or growth. They may address a variety of personal or professional topics, such as career advice, work-life support, and job or task.

Common topics discussed in development interactions may be classified as career advice, work-life support and job/task development. Career issues may range from discussing specific assignments to networking support. Work-life and psychosocial support may encompass a broad range of subjects. Job and task development is about getting guidance and instruction. There can be a long list of different kinds of development partnerships in the workplace. One study on a range of developmental interactions (D'Abate et al. 2003) mapped 13 types (see Theory & Research Box 11.1).

Theory & Research Box 11.1: An Initial List of Development Partnerships

- Action learning
- Apprenticeship
- Coaching
- Distance mentoring
- Executive Coaching
- Formal mentoring
- Group mentoring
- Informal mentoring
- Multiple mentors
- Peer coaching
- Peer mentoring
- Traditional mentoring
- Tutoring

These are typically describing different forms of coaching and/or mentoring. Often these are roles which managers in organisations are expected to fulfil. Some believe that research shows that the quality of manager–employee relation (Hay 2002) is the biggest factor in employees leaving their jobs, where moves are not related to a lack of satisfaction with pay, but a lack of satisfaction with how a person's skills and talents are being developed. Here we can look at what makes the different roles of coaching and mentoring distinctive, the skills they involve and when they should be used in their various forms. This represents a substantial and growing theoretical and practical area of analysis in workplace learning. In this chapter the conceptual issues around these different kinds of development interaction; look in detail at the core aspects of coaching and mentoring; identify some key characteristics of effective and ineffective developmental interactions; and conclude by mapping core development interactions against a set of competencies and indicators. As these issues are explored it is worth bearing in mind the findings of the study referred to in Debate 11.1; that in practice much development partner support for learning seems to be about giving negative feedback rather than compliments.

Conceptual Issues

The D'Abate et al. study (2003) highlighted some issues with research on developmental interaction constructs. To begin with there are significant variation across authors use of the terms of coaching and mentoring about meanings. Conceptual confusion exists about these constructs. It is not possible to depend on authors meaning the same things by them across different studies. Eddy et al. sought to seek some clarity on this by mapping existing uses of these terms in the literature, using a nomological network approach. A nomological network approach seeks to relate theoretical constructs to each other, and to relate theoretical constructs to observable measures, and observable measures to each other. Defining a theoretical construct, such as different kinds of development interaction, is then a matter of elaborating the nomological network in which it occurs.

This kind of analysis shows how constructs are conceptually and empirically related. At the same time, such an analysis may 'net' ties that help define these constructs in terms of key construct variables. If that is done, it is possible that constructs which appeared to be qualitatively very different, as kinds of coaching and mentoring often are, may come to be seen as 'overlapping' or indeed to be, in effect, measuring the same thing. The nomological network approach in this instance entailed distinguishing and considering measures of developmental relationships given in Perspectives 11.1 and 11.2.

Perspective 11.1: Key Variables in Distinguishing Different Kinds of Development Interaction

- Demographics

  - Age, experience, career

- Interactions

  - Duration, medium, span

- Distance/directed

  - Direction, reporting, location

- Purpose

  - Object, time, beneficiaries

- Structure

  - Formality, choice, matching, procedures

- Behaviours

  - Learning, emotional, career progression

Perspective 11.2: Expanded Variables in Development Interactions in the 'Behaviour' Domain

Learning	Emotional	Career
Collaborating	Affirming	Advocating
Directing	Befriending	Introducing
Goal setting	Aiding	Sheltering
Assignments	Calming	Socialising
Modelling	Confidence building	
Observing	Counselling	
Problem-solving	Encouraging	
Practical application	Supporting	
Sharing information		
Teaching		

D'Abate et al. produced matrices which showed the percentage of articles citing one of the 13 named constructs they began with, using any of these items as a defining characteristic of the developmental interaction. There were four possible categories for any defining characteristics to be found cited in the literature:

- A. A characteristic cited in 76–100 per cent of the articles
- B. A characteristic cited in 51–75 per cent of the articles
- C. A characteristic cited in 26–50 per cent of the articles
- D. A characteristic cited in 1–25 per cent of the articles

The main finding was that there are inconsistencies in the use of variables to define these development roles. There are very few indicators in the A and B category, most being in the C and D category. There were, for example, no 'A' ratings (76–100 per cent) ratings for literature discussing 'mentoring' at all. This strongly suggests that there is indeed inconsistency and wide variation in the use of these development partnership terms. There are, indeed, contradictions; with experts citing opposite characteristics for mentoring or coaching. With this level of disagreement present it is impossible to summarise and build on knowledge from existing studies.

It was also possible to see in the literature, however, certain characteristics that were more in the spotlight overall than others. Eight characteristics dominate out of the 23 that were analysed. These include factors such as; span, object and time, formality and behaviours. The tight focus in the current literature on these factors may be helpful. Or it may mean that other characteristics are being overlooked, or not thought about at all. In subsequent work (Eddy et al. 2006), other factors that may help us differentiate between effective and ineffective developmental interactions. These factors include personal, relationship and communication factors (see Perspective 11.3).

Perspective 11.3: Factors Potentially Involved in Successful or Unsuccessful Development Partnerships

Personal factors	Demographics; gender, age, ethnicity
	Adviser style; directive . . . self-discovery
	Adviser focus; own needs or advisee's needs
	Adviser expertise; in development area
Relationship factors	Initiation
	Choice in participation; voluntary or not
	Frequency and duration;
	Time known
	Source of relationship; superior, friend, peer
Communication factors	Location; face-to-face or distance
	Primary mode; medium used

Eddy et al. (2006) conclude that for effective development interactions the following is important for advisers (providing development), advisees (learners) and organisations to behave in certain ways (see Practice 11.1).

Practice 11.1: Behaviour for Partnerships

Advisers

- Have a goal of self-discovery: advisers should encourage advisee self-discovery rather than being highly directive;
- Frame interactions as voluntary and mutually initiated;
- Focus on advisees needs, not mediating the organisations needs;
- Be accessible for multiple conversations over time, not one quick-fix.

Advisees (Learners)

- Seek advisers with relevant experience, not just those already known and convenient;

> **Practice 11.1: (Continued)**
>
> - Actively seek out people to get advice and feedback;
> - Do not rely on one-off interactions.
>
> **Organisations**
>
> - Not safe to assume development interactions can be handled without some preparation;
> - Meetings with direct supervisors are the hardest, most likely to be ineffective;
> - Prepare supervisors for job/task-related development interactions; uncover needs and promote self-discovery.

Having considered the basics of what might be common factors in 'good practice' in general for development partnerships, there are important questions to be thought through about different kinds of development interactions, and their uses in the workplace. Central to these, and illustrative of the themes that emerge, is the comparison and contrast of mentoring and coaching. This central area of study and debate can be explored in more depth.

Mentoring

Mentoring can be defined as:

> a learning and developmental relationship between two people. It depends on essential human qualities such as commitment, authenticity, trust, integrity and honesty. It involves the skills of listening, questioning, challenge and support. (Garvey and Garret-Harris 2005, p. 9)

There are a diverse number of kinds of relations and activities being included under the generic construct of mentoring. Mentoring is a construct which is 'close to hand' in a number of contexts, and thereby comes to feature in diverse discussions. Different types of people, in different types of relationships, in different organisational circumstances, are all 'doing' mentoring. Thus mentoring appears to occur, for example, between; different sets of people:

Masters		Apprentices
Senior managers	-	Middle managers
Managers		Employees
Teachers		Students

Senior students		Juniors
Professionals	-	Aspirants

Mentoring first grew to some contemporary prominence in the USA. This was a result of two main catalysts. Firstly was the influence of developmental psychology (Levinson et al. 1978), which 'discovered' and highlighted mentoring as a natural, ubiquitous and highly beneficial relationship for men. It was a relationship formed between adults in their 'mid-life' stage and young adults. The former were searching for a constructive role in the lives of others and the latter were trying to 'realise their dreams'. Mutual benefits could arise from forming and having a mentoring relationship (see Practice 11.2).

This framework struck a number of chords. It related to the problems faced in 'mid-life' and late career by older adults; the search for purpose given the passing of previous purposes, such as attaining career success for themselves. It spoke to the problems of socialising/inducting young (increasingly independent) adults into the adult world of work and family responsibility. Was it coincidence that these concerns were becoming prominent as an age of change and uncertainty in career and life success was about to be experienced? Was the concern with mentoring an early indicator of what was to come?

Secondly there was the influence of studies (e.g. Roche 1979) which claimed to show that 'everyone who makes it has a mentor'. People who had attained the most senior positions in their organisations attributed at least a part of that success to having had a mentor. Mentoring was then a specific and necessary condition of ultimate career success. This articulation of mentoring as a variable in the achievement of ultimate career success clearly stimulated both individuals concerned with such ultimate career success and organisations seeking to manage the development of future leaders to explore the possibilities of mentoring in the context of growing and developing senior managers.

There was also a third environmental factor in the USA which helped to promote the growth of contemporary mentoring; the rise of active policies on equal opportunities (Shapiro et al. 1978). It was argued that one key form of support for positive action in enabling women and ethnic minorities to progress up the career ladder, particularly in professions and management, was mentoring. This led to a growth of formal mentoring schemes.

Practice 11.2: Mentors Are Characterised By:

- Setting high expectations of performance and offering challenging ideas;
- Building self-confidence;
- Encouraging winning behaviour, confronting negative behaviour and attitudes;
- Offering friendship and listening to personal issues;

Practice 11.2: (Continued)

- Teaching by example, offering quotable quotes;

- Providing growth experiences;

- Standing by mentees at all times, offering wise counsel;

- Triggering self-awareness;

- Inspiring, offering encouragement and assistance;

- Sharing critical knowledge;

- Listening deeply, asking tough questions;

- Respecting and maintaining confidentiality, honesty and integrity.

Mentees, as partners, find mentoring more effective when they tell the mentor what they want from a mentor; can identify who would make them a good mentor; know the questions they want answered; establish a trusting relationship; are prepared to work; can take the lead.

Exercise 11.1:

identify a mentor–mentee relationship in a movie or novel you are familiar with; use the analysis framework at the end of this chapter to review the extent to which that mentoring relationship shows all the characteristics of effective mentoring.

Mentoring continued to ride upon a number of powerful waves of change in the USA through the 1980s; some practical and others cultural. Practically, an increasing concern with HRD as an essential part of Human Resource Management (HRM) meant that innovations like mentoring were looked upon favourably and embraced. Culturally mentoring made sense in circumstances where people believed in the possibilities of close personal relationships as a means to an end; the achievement of power. Mentoring attracted a lot of attention and provided a concrete instance of the exercise of power in organisations. In this cultural context, given the type of relationship involved it was inevitable that equal opportunity issues would not only help generate interest in mentoring; they also provided a research focus in themselves. Thus there was a concern about whether mentoring between men and women could be as effective as same gender relations, or whether it invariably involved sexual tensions/issues. There was the issue of whether people of different ethnic backgrounds could develop effective mentoring relationships.

Finally there was a debate about the strengths and weaknesses of organising mentoring in formal schemes. Some (Zey 1991) saw the formalising of mentoring, through organised schemes, as essential. This may be to ensure an effective scheme actually exists, or to ensure that there was equal opportunity to access mentoring. Others (Clawson 1985, Kram 1985) argued that mentoring could not be effectively organised through formal schemes. It could only emerge from broader Organisational Development (OD) initiatives which promoted an environment in which mentoring relationships would 'naturally' arise.

By the time that mentoring became an issue in other contexts, in the 1980s, there was then a well developed agenda of concerns. These can be summarised as:

- The contribution of mentoring to career success;
- The nature of mentoring as a 'significant' relationship;
- The equal opportunities debate;
- The costs and benefits of formally organising mentoring.

To an extent mentoring as it grew elsewhere developed as a mirror of the agenda set in the USA, with some modifications.

> Rather than simply focusing just on career success for those at the 'top' there was a broader concern with developing talent (Clutterbuck 2004). It was not just about those who 'made it'; everyone needed a mentor.
> The focus on mentoring as a non line-manager activity was stressed. The problem of being entangled in conventional command and control relations was to be circumvented rather than confronted.

While there had been some interest in Britain since the early 1980s (Mumford 1989, Storey 1989), it was only really in the 1990s that there was a significant profile for mentoring. During the early part of the twenty-first century that growing interest has accelerated, with publications, institutions and qualifications concerned with mentoring increasing dramatically.

This growth of mentoring does not occur in isolation; it has been part of the growth of other formal and organised systems. For example:

- Structured 'Personal Development Plans' derived from experiences at Assessment Centres;
- Performance Management systems being introduced or reformed;
- Workplace learning qualification systems being developed;
- Continuous Professional Development (CPD) initiatives;
- Revised Degree and Postgraduate programmes in Higher Education.

It has taken the development of these initiatives to create the conditions in which mentoring in Britain becomes a more central activity. One effect of these kinds of contextual trends was that the context seemed to be one in which mentoring was becoming more prevalent in formal and organised schemes (see Practice 11.3).

One of the underlying problems of a formally organised approach to mentoring is that it requires a degree of policy-making, instruction for participants and evaluation which involves a clearly prescriptive view of what mentoring is. To develop policy it is necessary to spell out what mentoring is.

To train mentors and advise mentees on a large scale it becomes convenient to spell out what mentoring is. To evaluate mentoring it is, according to convention, necessary to set objectives; requiring a close definition, up front, of what mentoring is.

Practice 11.3: Conditions for Success in Mentoring Schemes

Agreeing the scope and purpose of the mentoring and identifying the factors that will support mentoring and those that will inhibit it is essential when devising a scheme.

In doing that a range of issues that need to be considered are as follows:

Voluntarism – mentoring is essentially a voluntary activity. The degree of voluntarism will depend on the situation and the circumstances.

Training – both the mentor and the mentee will need some orientation towards the scheme. This may involve a skills training programme for both mentors and mentees. Sometimes this can be done with them together in the same programme.

Ongoing support – Mentors often need support. This may take the form of a mentor support group or one to one mentoring supervision – a mentor to the mentor.

Matching – It is important to have a clear matching process to which the participants subscribe. It is also important to establish a 'no fault divorce clause' after say, the first three meetings.

Establishing reviewable ground rules – It is important to clarify the boundaries of the relationship at the start.

Ongoing review – The most important factor in successful outcomes to mentoring is regular feedback and review within the relationship about the relationship. Establishing ground rules at the start can facilitate this process.

Whose agenda? – Mentoring is for the mentee. The research suggests that attempts to impose the agenda within mentoring on the mentee result in manipulation and social engineering. The benefits of mentoring to all stakeholders result from broadly following the mentee's agenda.

Evaluation and monitoring – Ongoing evaluation of the scheme is important also. There is little point in evaluating the scheme after say, two years, to unearth problems, which could have been resolved at the time

Source: Garvey, B. and Garrett-Harris, R. (2005) 'The Benefits of Mentoring: A Literature Review', The Mentoring and Coaching Research Unit, Sheffield Hallam University.

Rather than encouraging and enabling people to develop a diverse set of activities in an organisation which may all be thought about as 'mentoring' like there is an institutional process of standardisation. One framework for conceptualising and standardising mentoring sees it as serving a set of vocational and psychosocial functions (see Perspective 11.4). A relationship that serves these functions is mentoring, whatever it may actually be called. If it does not serve these functions, then it is not mentoring.

Perspective 11.4: The Functions of Mentoring

Vocational Functions

- Sponsorship: a senior individual's public support is critical for advancement.
- Coaching: enhancing a person's knowledge and understanding of how to effectively navigate in the environment.
- Protection: shielding the protégé from untimely or potentially damaging contact with other senior officials. Taking credit and blame.

Challenging assignments: building of critical technical skills, leading towards greater responsibility. Psychosocial functions

- Role modelling: senior person's attitudes, values, and behaviour become model to emulate. Desirable example-setting; mutually beneficial.
- Acceptance and confirmation: validation of the individuals' self-worth; appreciation and support.
- Counselling: enables an individual to explore personal concerns with mentor; sounding board.

Source: Kram (1985).

Friendship: mutual liking, understanding; enjoyable informal exchanges about work/non-work.

The phases of a partnership are also important in conceiving of mentoring and the issues it raises (see Perspective 11.5). These phases, in what many would consider real mentoring, will occur over a period of years, whereas in formal workplace schemes they may occur over a period of months. The key point is that mentoring involves both career and psychosocial functions. Though mutuality is necessary for effective mentoring to take place, the mentor's openness to serve as such must be made known to prospective protégés. A dual commitment, both to the individual's growth and to learning in the workplace, is at the core of mentoring relationships. Effective mentoring will involve some vulnerability and discomfort. It involves commitment on both individuals' parts. It involves not only supporting but also challenging ones protégé.

The underlying process in mentoring has been characterised as one of individuation. Individuation is about becoming your own person, making choices at different stages and transitions. It arises as a big issue in making particularly significant choices, such as those about occupation, career and relationships like marriage (Levinson et al. 1978). Levinson et al. were specifically concerned with the choices that men make and then have to build upon – living within them, or enhancing them or moving to make new choices at times of change and crisis. Within this context mentoring features strongly as a role that older men can play with younger men. In terms of the choices being made by the younger man they are to do with identifying and establishing their own personal dream: the mentor is, most crucially, there to support and facilitate the realisation of the dream. Subsequent work applied the same kind of analysis to women, and the development pathway concerns they share with men but also their distinctive individuation issues.

Perspective 11.5:

- **Initiation**: a potential mentor is admired and respected by the protégé. The potential protégé is seen as someone with potential, interest in work, easy to work with. Mutual benefits are perceived.

- **Cultivation**: generally, career functions emerge as the first focus, then, psychosocial functions emerge. There are wide variation around the nature of functions, depending on individuals' needs.

- **Separation**: an outcome as a function of change in one or both individuals' confidence. Involves both psychological and structural aspects, which can be stressful, but also exciting. This allows the protégé to demonstrate mastery of skills without support.

- **Redefinition**: the relationship, where one continues, often manifests itself as friendship. It may involve counsel and coaching from a distance. This can be uncomfortable as protégé becomes peer, and the mentor may view this development as threatening.

For either men or women in early adult life, individuation involves working through dependences on others. Mentors are ambiguous figures here; they are people on whom the young adult will depend, but their primary role is to help the young adult overcome such dependences. Combining the concept of individuation and the hypothesised stages of adult development as they saw it in the course of their research, Levinson et al. arrived at a view of the mentoring process as a key, if highly problematic, resource for young men, and as a fulfilling role for older men. Thus they saw the mentoring process as highly significant for both parties, and crucial to effective adult development, by facilitating continuing individuation for both parties. They stressed that the mentoring process may be either difficult or highly problematic in its eventual outcomes for both parties. This was not a rosy view of a perfect, mutually beneficial partnership; it was a realistic appraisal of a partnership that, like all partnerships, can be fraught with difficulties and challenges.

This focus on being person-centred rather than being the giver of advice/wise counsel assumes that, for people to become happy, they need to understand themselves. Faced with pressures at work and home, problems with work–life balance, and uncertainties in terms of personal and career goals, this need seems to be real, meaningful and pressing in modern society. The mentoring process is no longer about a wise figure giving counsel to heroes, or even necessarily a master in any field developing an apprentice. The legacy of this view of the mentoring process is that to the constellation of family, peers, formal educators and superiors we must add the mentor as someone who provides a person-centred counselling and supporting role for an adult.

Recent growth has been evident in formal mentoring schemes, but that has not stopped a persistent questioning of the value of institutionalising mentoring in organisations. It may, in theory, be more attractive to argue for broader organisation development initiatives to support mentoring rather than developing a formal scheme. But, in practice, the development of a formal scheme is an essential first step.

The qualities of mentors are listed by Megginson and Clutterbuck as wisdom, experience, questioning, listening, patience, networking, being oneself, process and content balance, dependable. The relations with a mentor may be triggered by a crisis, though they will require long term trust, overcome isolation, chemistry, respect bases, both plan and prepare. Organisation issues which matter are aligning this with change management, CEO support, and internal and external relations. Issues around the learner are often acknowledging a need for help with the role, isolation at the top, not accepting they can be told, little scope for role modelling.

The duality of career and/or psychosocial functions or purposes are often given as defining terms here. The controversy is about the duality of career or psychosocial development and the role of mentoring is often interpreted in terms of North American versus a European views of work and human relations. But it is possible to discern a different kind of division being used in debates in this aspect of mentoring; a duality of values. In this case these are liberal and the conservative values and conceptions of mentoring. Liberal values are associated with a conception of mentoring that emphasises its progressive and modernist functions; the utility of mentoring in opening up careers for disadvantaged groups and promoting humanistic ideals through improved psychosocial development. Conservative values are associated with a conception of mentoring which is about its contribution to the continuity of the status quo and its utility in legitimising and replicating patterns of behaviour; control through the influence of the 'old guard' on the career and psychosocial development of new generations.

Viewing debates through the lenses of these archetypal conceptions of value provides one way to explore discussions about mentoring as exemplifying the broader dynamics of intellectual controversy, which follows and extends a complex history (see Perspective 11.6).

Perspective 11.6: Historical Contexts for Mentoring				
The contexts	**Process & role**	**Process in context**	**HRD themes**	**HRD legacy**
Classical mythology	Development interactions as a role in the drama of the patriot-warrior	Heroes on quests and adventures The archetypes and symbols of wise, the young, the villains	From timidity to resourceful-ness Good vs. evil	The role of wise 'counsel' The ascension to power
Craft guilds	Development interactions as the lynchpins in the economics and society of small, independent businesses	Communities in emerging towns Masters-apprentices	Craft regulation The community ethos	The role of masters The correlation with community
Humanist psychology	Mentors supporting the development of the individual	Development throughout adulthood Counselling	Transitions in adulthood Helping 'processes'	Self-development issues for adults Human relations

Coaching

While mentoring has had much of the spotlight in development interactions and partnerships attention is now turning, it seems, to coaching. Coaching is used for improving individual performance, productivity and skills (Practice 11.4).

Practice 11.4:

The popularity of coaching is apparently fuelled by factors, including:

- Modern organisations features: flatter, pace of change;
- Employee demand for training;
- Lifelong learning;
- Targeted and just-in-time development;
- Focus on performance (larger leaps on new roles);
- Individual responsibility for development.

Coaching is associated historically with sports and performance improvement at work. In sports dedicated experts working closely with a performer or team to manage and direct their development. In work, remedial activity on skills, where someone is failing. Now it is applied to more developmental activity in work. Coaching in the workplace can involve internal staff, managers or external specialists who work one-to-one with a person on identifying and attaining specific goals for learning and development which will impact on performance. Coaching in the workplace is about improving individual and team performance, productivity and skills (CIPD 2009):

- 90 per cent of organisations use coaching by line managers;
- 64 per cent of organisations use coaching by external coaches;
- 74 per cent or organisations expect to increase their use of coaching.

Coaching is about working with and alongside people in the workplace and their teams in complex, sensitive and changing environments to support leadership and talent management. It is about looking to support problem and solution-focused thinking, strategic insight and personal development. That means using a combination of skill, knowledge and attributes to develop and have impact, mainly one-to-one, with limited peer support and feedback. Coaching has emerged strongly in an era of talent management challenges and demands. The classic client-coach entering into a relationship which is used for the benefit of the client and their organisation is evolving. Coaching give the client an opportunity to explore, discover and clarify ways of leading and developing resourcefully and effectively.

Development of capability in coaching reflects key drivers in HRD:

- Aim to be helpful and supportive for learners in developing their talents;
- Taking human sciences perspectives on deepening awareness of relationships in organisations;

- Reflect on and investigate trends and demands in talent management in organisations;
- Respectfully and rigorously work with paradigms, tensions and conflicts to generate understanding about clients and coaching.

Coaching Methods

Coaching can be described as a structured approach to questioning people in order to help them improve their awareness, and take actions to achieve goals. A common framework for this is called the 'GROW' model (Practice 11.5).

Practice 11.5: The GROW Framework and Questions

Goal – What do you want?

What do you want to achieve in this discussion?

What does success look like if you were there?

What would be a milestone on the way?

When do you want to achieve it by?

Is your goal positive, challenging and attainable?

Reality – What is happening now?

What is happening right now with this goal?

Who else is involved?

What have you tried so far?

What results did that give you?

What does your own intuition say is going on?

Options – What could you do?

What are three alternative things you could try to reach your goal?

What else?

What if you . . . . .(had more time, power, money, etc.)?

If you asked your wise man/woman, what would they advise you to do?

Will – What will you do?

Choose an option.

What are the first two steps to delivering this option?

When will you start and finish each by?

Whose support do you need?

> Who do you need to inform about your plan and when?
>
> What commitment do you have on a scale of 1–10 of taking action?
>
> What can you change to raise your commitment level to 10?
>
> Is there anything else I can help you with?

In coaching a concern is to either follow the persons thinking or comment and introduce other lines of thought; to follow or to lead. And also whether the coach is reinforcing strengths or overcoming weaknesses. Critics can find ammunition. Finding high-quality external coaches is a problem. Much of the research base for coaching is in sports and education, not the business context. Coach training tends to focus on specific tools and techniques. There are 'cowboys' around, and a lack of regulation, and alongside that emerges 'professional' body in-fighting as a response.

Exercise 11.2: Coaching

Identify someone to have a coaching conversation with.

Explain you will coach them by discussing a performance issue, asking them questions about it. The conversation will be confidential.

Ask them to identify an issue they want to improve their performance on.

Then go through the GROW questions with them.

What worked well?

What might you do differently the next time you have a coaching conversation?

On the more positive side it is expected that the interest in coaching will be sustained because there is a shortage of skilled leaders and the use of coaching in leadership development is expected to increase. The main area of growth, mangers as coaches, will keep interest high. There is a need to organise and integrate coaching internally; to develop coherent strategies for doing that. There is a belief in benefits but little formal evaluation; the scope to reveal value is great.

There are currently no publicly available surveys on the demand and supply dynamics specifically around coaching.

Common Factors

Those who see a difference between mentoring and coaching are represented by Clutterbuck and Megginson (2000), who advance a concept of mentoring, defining mentoring as 'Off-line help by one person to another in making significant transitions in knowledge, work or thinking' and contrast it with coaching as shown in Figure 11.1.

	Mentoring	Coaching
Source	Internal	External
Foci	Diverse	Behaviour
Structure	Less structured	Structured
Centre	Person centred	Performance
Duration	Lengthy	Short

Figure 11.1   Mentoring executives
Source: Clutterbuck and Megginson (2000).

Mentoring is for whole person development and periods of rapid change and big challenges, whereas coaching is an activity to help people along 'level ground', in a short-term relationship concerned with skills. Mentoring in the specific context of leadership development, for executives, is increasing as pressures at the top, the balance and quality of life, a continuing need to learn and transitions involving radical change increase. These people need a reflective mentor for an intensive and holistic relationship, akin to looking in the mirror with someone else, an experience in which an emotional release of energy may also occur. Indeed this creation of 'Personal Reflective Space' (PRS) is the 'power' of mentoring, which is never a stark science, or technique driven, but a role whose essence is ideal for executives. This is because Executives are not a law unto themselves, in a self-contained world; they operate in teams, cannot 'know it all' and need to keep learning. What they are often missing is PRS and

> An opportunity to develop personal insight through uninterrupted and purposeful reflective activity. (p. 8)

The typical relationship goes through recognisable phases in which initial concerns to problem-solve or make a decision are suspended in order to consider deeper questions about purpose and behaviour; leading them to reframe their understanding of themselves and others and thereafter make a choice. Executives experience three potential kinds of challenge warranting such mentoring. These are given in Practice 11.6.

Practice 11.6: Executive Mentoring Challenges

Curtain raisers

- Get noticed
- Get experience and understanding
- Manage politics and projects
- Develop networks

Once in an executive position

- Continue to learn and grow
- Stimulate challenge from others
- Manage performance and stress
- Influence rather than command, credibility

If also a director

- Distinguish roles, develop skills
- Know what, and strategic thinking
- Collaborative independence
- What about my career now?

Several other kinds of development partnership as well as coaching and mentoring can be mapped against a set of features (Perspective 11.7).

Perspective 11.7: Common Process for Development Partnerships

Outcomes: an explicit outcome or goal that both parties, coach/mentor and client, are collaboratively working towards.

Rationale: a sensible rationale or explanation for how coaching/mentoring as a process fits the client's needs and situation.

Procedures: a procedure or set of steps that is consistent with the rationale and requires both the client's and the coach's/mentor's active participation.

Relations: a meaningful relationship between the client and the coach/mentor such that the client believes the coach/mentor is there to help and will work in the client's best interest.

Development: A collaborative working alliance in which the coach's/mentor's explicit role is to expand the client's development, maintaining challenge and facilitating change.

Change: a focus on the client's ability and willingness to change.

Personal: recognising and dealing with often personally poignant issues during helping the client create change.

Any role, or approach to roles like coaching and mentoring, can be profiled with these features. Developing development partnerships, like coaching or mentoring entails these common core challenges:

- Suitability: becoming a 'best fit' coach or mentor;
- Focusing: addressing the tougher questions in contracting for development;

- Matching: addressing the deeper issues of a partnership early on;
- Connection: also managing senior manager/others interest and participation;
- Quality standard: high standards, validity and reliability, for the approach adopted.

Finally, development partnerships emerge from and help extend networks. One model suggests there are five dimensions of networking (Cross et al. 2004). These can be analysed to review how complete and well balanced a person's network, including coaches and mentors, is. These five dimensions are as follows:

(1) Vertical dispersion: connections with those having more experience, at the same level and less experience than you;
(2) Horizontal dispersion: relations inside and outside your 'home' network;
(3) Experiential proxemics: how close in terms of background you are;
(4) Intentional interactions: time outside routine scheduling of interactions with them;
(5) Time known: balance of well known and newer.

Exercise 11.2

The following exercise allows you to map your own existing network against the five dimensions given above. First identify the three key people you see as being present in your current network for professional development. If you cannot identify three people, list as many as you can. Then map these people against the criteria given in the first network analysis table (see Table 11.1). You should see that there are gaps in your network; perhaps gaps in terms of the experience levels of your network

Table 11.1 Mapping your existing network

Existing network					
Name of person	**Experience** 1 = more experienced 2 = equal 3 = less experienced	**Hierarchy** 1 = peer 2 = senior 3 = junior	**Background** 1 = Same background 2 = Similar background 3 = different background 4 = Very different background	**Contact** 1 = Irregular 2 = Monthly 3 = Weekly 4 = Daily	**Time known** 1 = less than 1 yr 2 = 1–3 years 3 = 3–5 yrs 4 = 5–10 yrs 5 = 10 + yrs
Existing network					

Additions to your network?					

contacts (all with similar levels of experience?), or in their backgrounds (too similar to your own?) or in the kind of contact you have with them.

Now you can then identify what a re-balancing of your network would look like. To do that you can identify profiles that represent the gaps in your current network, for example if your network is mainly made up of people in the same unit, seen daily then who you have known a long time then you might want to develop links with new contacts, people in other countries you see only infrequently. Once you have identified these profiles you are then in a position to identify search for people who fit them.

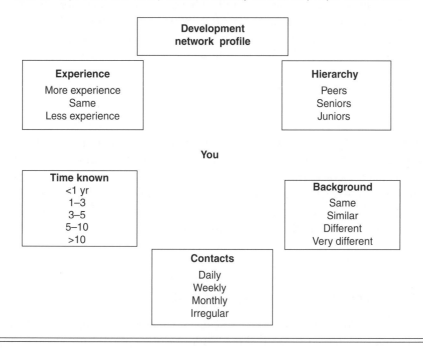

Debate 11.2: Who Needs Compliments?

Very few learners reporting that learning entailed being complimented or given positive feedback.

Why do you think this might be so?

Are compliments and positive feedback simply not part of the organizational climate?

> **Debate 11.2: (Continued)**
>
> Are they less recalled than negative reactions?
>
> Or are they something that does not foster employee learning?
>
> *Source*: Koopmans et al. (2006).

Case: Line Managers as Developers

Increasing line manager involvement in Learning and Development (HRD) at work is one important part of the broader changing relations between line managers and Human Resource Management (HRM). The advantages of increasing line manager involvement in HRD at work are frequently highlighted. However there are challenges as well, outlined here, which raise questions about the overall impact on HRD at work. Evidence about the practice of HRD at work depending on line manager involvement is limited. Instead of having an evidence base to evaluate it there is only scope to reflect on the significance of the trend to line manger involvement in HRD at work in context. Two principal interpretations are possible; one that the trend is of minimal significance, the other that it is of much greater significance. For the latter increasing line manager involvement in HRD at work is both part of the means of attaining, and also one of the ends of, broader changes in work, organisation and HRM. Even so there are legitimate concerns about increasing line manager involvement in HRD at work, where that prejudices the provision and use of specialist HRD at work resources. However, these concerns are outweighed by the greater concern to re-align work, organisation and management for an era where knowledge management is predominant. The issue of line manager involvement in HRD at work will continue to be an important part of the corporate agenda.

Line Manager Involvement in HRD at Work

Mapping of clusters of research themes in Human Resource Development (HRD) in Europe highlighted 10 key themes. While one of these explicitly identifies the role of line managers in Learning & Development (HRD) at work, suggesting the issue is of some importance, most of the others also have implications for line manager's involvement with HRD at work; the concern with integrating learning and work, for example, must have implications for the role of line managers. This mapping of research clusters emphasises the specific and general interest in the role of line managers in HRD at work, in contrast with past perceptions where the focus was on HRD specialists.

Some emphasise the need to include line managers in planning for HRD, and to 'hand over primary responsibility to the line'. But it is the more general way

Ten Key Themes in HRD Research
National employment and training patterns shaping HRD
Tackling the problem of skill shortage in the work force
Specific HRD strategies in medium/ small organisations
Adjusting continuing training to organisational flexibility
Notion of 'flexible worker' challenging 'professional identity'
Changing role of HRD professionals (from trainer to consultant)
Sharing responsibility for HRD between professionals, managers and employees
Shift from skill building to performance improvement and competence development
Integrating work and learning in organisations
Knowledge sharing as both managerial and participatory approach *Source*: Manning (2002).

that, in the name of changes in work, management, organisation, and HRM, greater involvement of managers with HRD has been proposed that sparks most contemporary interest for example, argues that the reason most people leave their jobs and move is not related to a lack of satisfaction with pay, but a lack of satisfaction with how a person's skills and talents are being developed. HRD at work is always an aspect of the whole HRM of an organisation, not an isolated, stand alone activity. The strategies and policies organisations have for attracting and retaining staff, and the ways that stakeholders define their different and common interests at work can have a great impact on how HRD at work is managed. However, the scope of this article is to consider HRD at work and the involvement of line managers in it.

Evidently in many conceptualisations of changes in work, organisation and HRM in theory, and in many companies in practice, there are perceived to be advantages in making greater use of line managers as developers of people, as a part of one or a combination of these kinds of initiatives. The advantages of greater line management involvement in helping others to learn can be related to four main areas; the quantity of HRD at work, the quality of HRD at work, the value for management in the organisation, and the re-alignment of HRD activities with human relations changes in an organisation as a whole.

Advantages of Greater Line Manager Involvement in HRD

First is the belief that there will be more development for a wide range of people if line managers are more involved in HRD at work. Long-standing criticisms of what have been called the 'sheep-dip' and 'injection' models of HRD at work have existed (Lynton and Pareek 2000). The idea that employees would, at regular intervals, be given doses of HRD had become institutionalised in organisational systems and workplace training practices. But the workplace now requires the promotion of positive attitudes towards continuous and lifelong learning. HRD at work is not something that happens periodically in formal classroom-based settings. It needs to be an integral feature of working life. To get a job, to retain a job or to develop a career people need to become more involved more often with HRD. This prescription applies to people in all situations. It applies to those who have no qualifications, and who may lack basic skills. It applies to those who have either academic or vocational qualifications, but not a balanced skill/knowledge base. It also applies to those who are highly trained professionals in occupations where keeping pace with new knowledge and skills has always been desirable but is now even more essential. To help promote such lifelong learning those in the workforce currently in work rather than those in formal education need to be reached and changed. There would seem to be a key role here for line managers to become more proactive about development. Line managers should expect and help to support the efforts of employees to learn and develop.

The second argument is that there will be a better quality of HRD at work for organisations and individuals if line managers are more directly involved. Criticisms of the quality of organisational learning interventions, such as classroom based courses and traditional instructions/facilitation have stressed problems with the operation of the systematic training cycle (Allen 1994). The gap between organisational performance needs and individual performance can be closed where those who are familiar with both the organisational need and the individual play a greater role. That means it may be line managers rather than training specialists who best understand the organisational need or the individual's needs.

The third argument is that requiring line managers to be more involved in the HRD of employees will lead to a transformation of managers themselves. The need for such a transformation is justified by a critical estimation of line manager's generic people management skills. The belief is that by taking developmental responsibilities on board line managers will have to change more generally, ultimately becoming more competent in interpersonal interactions in work teams. There are then benefits to line managers as they become more competent at managing people because they have to take responsibility for their development. These benefits help to enhance management in the organisation as a whole.

The final advantage often identified is that enlisting line managers as developers of people can contribute to broader organisational change and transformation of human relations at work. Broader change and transformation of human relations at work can be characterised at many levels. It may be focused on human relations being aligned with being more quality oriented, or with being more innovative, or with being more efficient and giving greater value for money. However it is characterised the contribution of HRM skilled line managers, and the enhanced interpersonal relationships that are thought to develop with HRD partnerships, is considered to be significant. People will be more inclined to and more able to talk to each other, to trust each other and to work together in periods of change.

Challenges in Greater Line Manager Involvement in HRD

The criticisms of greater line management involvement in helping others to learn at work can also be considered in relation to each of these claimed benefits. First there is a belief that there will be less development for many if line managers are made more responsible for staff development. Current learning at work systems are based in some way on systematically enabling people to participate in learning, despite pressures in the working environment to focus on productivity by continuously being busy working rather than away learning. If this element of the system is weakened, or indeed is done away with, then HRD might be neglected. Other pressures in the workplace, principally the need to deal with immediate tasks and short-term priorities, will take precedence. Without the option of taking time out to go and learn, learning will decline. Even if time is still set aside for learning it may be that, in the absence of well-structured training plans and courses, employees will not get a complete and coherent package of HRD at work.

Second, there is no reason to believe that line managers can be better skilled developers than specialists trained in HRD at work, no matter how much development they receive as 'coaches' or 'trainers'. Inevitably most line managers will not be able to organise and evaluate as high-quality HRD processes and practices as specialists. Line managers will not be as accurate as others can be in objectively determining HRD needs. Line managers will not be as good at instructing, coaching or facilitating development as specialists. And line managers will not be as adept at evaluating HRD in order to validate it, and/or highlight further HRD needs.

Thirdly, depending on line managers to fulfil these roles may mean marginalising specialists in HRD at work. Some argue that the specialist role will become transformed as line managers take more responsibility, rather than being marginalised; with specialists evolving to act in roles like an internal consultant or change agent, and being advisors to the line manager. In practice, others fear it will often mean the actual or practical exclusion of specialists from the HRD process; as they and their facilities, whether those be humble training rooms or grand training centres, disappear from the scene. If relatively powerful HRD specialists are an important factor in ensuring that HRD is taken seriously, then making managers more responsible may be a backward step. Outsourcing HRD facilities, requiring the use of the buying in of consultants to provide HRD products and services, may prejudice effective HRD support.

Finally, many would argue it is naive to assume that relationships between line managers and staff can be the key relationship to guide an employee's development (Lynton and Pareek 2000). While managers need to evaluate performance and help out where they can, the responsibility for an employee's development should lie in part with a neutral third party. This is because the line manager–employee relationship may involve clashes of interests that the manager may not be in a position to resolve effectively. Lynton and Pareek characterise part of the range of line managers responses to being 'learning partners' as ranging from hostility and reluctance, through to being critical and sceptical, to being supportive but little involved. That range of responses can be mirrored on the part of employees. In many organisations the traditional problems of managing career and personal development are compounded by the pace and scale of change, workforce restructuring and harsher internal labour market regimes. Surviving in such a tough climate is a problem for everyone. What happens to the line manager as developer when, for example, the managers are asked to make decisions about the development needs of staff who might in a few months be competing for that line managers job?

To simplify, in the absence of substantive evidence, a balanced view about these questions would be that there are clear links between using line managers for HRD and broader changes in HRM on the one hand while on the other there are justifiable reservations about a greater role for line managers in this area of HRM. In that case the question is perhaps better conceived as being about evaluating the implications of increasing the line manager role in HRD at work, rather than just contrasting it as a displacement or takeover of the conventional HRD specialist's role.

3 Key Texts

(1) Garvey, R., Stokes, P. and Megginson, D. (2009) *Coaching and Mentoring: Theory and Practice* (London: Sage).

(2) Stober, D. and Grant, M. (eds) (2006) *Evidence Based Coaching Handbook: Putting Best Practices to Work for Your Clients* (Hoboken, NJ, John *Wiley* & Sons Inc).

(3) Kram, K. (1985) *Mentoring at Work; Developmental Relationships in Organizational Life* (Glenview, Il, Scott Foresman & Co).

3 Key Articles

(1) CIPD (2009) *Taking the Temperature of Coaching* (London, CIPD).

(2) Koopmans, H., Doornbos, A. J. and van Eekelen, I. M. (2006) Learning in Interactive Work Situations: It Takes Two to Tango: Why Not Invite Both Partners to Dance?, *Human Resource Development Quarterly*, 17(2), pp. 135–158.

(3) Eddy, E., D'Abate, C., Tannenbaum, S., Givens-Skeaton, S. and Robinson, G. (2006) Key Characteristics of Effective and Ineffective Developmental Interactions, *Human Resource Development Quarterly*, 17(1), pp. 59–84.

3 Key Web Links

(1) European Mentoring and Coaching Council: http://www.emccouncil.org/.

(2) Institute of Coaching: http://www.instituteofcoaching.org/.

(3) National mentoring network example: http://www.scottishmentoringnetwork.co.uk/.

12

E-Learning

Learning Objectives

By the end of this chapter you will be able to:

- Describe the evolution of technologies and e-learning in HRD;
- Discuss the strengths and weaknesses of various forms of e-learning in HRD;
- Analyse the cost, quality and other features of e-learning in HRD;
- Critically evaluate the changes and challenges involved in e-learning.

Introduction

Technologies are developed to enable people to do new things and things they already do more easily, more quickly, more cheaply, more efficiently and more widely. Digital technologies are at the heart of more of what we do, not just in work but also in recreation, entertainment and communication, in reading and shopping, in politics and culture, in education and learning. As this change occurs the institutions and social relations around all these activities evolve and change too. In Human Resource Development (HRD) there is no need to be a technological expert, but to appreciate what technologies can do. The social and technological aspects of e-learning both evolve, reciprocally enabling and constraining each other. In HRD this raises questions in six areas:

(1) IS in the organisation: effectiveness of HRD relations;
(2) Technological change: new behaviours;
(3) Refine learning processes: expand and deepen capabilities;
(4) Intranet: participation and contribution;
(5) Internet/Web 2.0 options: beyond the 'trainer' channel;
(6) HRD specific presence: learners using multiple sources.

In sum, e-learning can be critically analysed as a new set of tools for distributing information differently, or a transformation in the forms of communication and relationships in HRD as a whole.

Exercise 12.1: Introductory Activity

Which of the following have you done as part of a learning experience?	Done this . . . not done
Check an existing book mark for information Used a search engine to locate a resource	
Set up a alert in a search engine Set up a news feed	
Accessed a forum/blog related to the topic Started a forum/blog related to the topic	
Used an existing social/professional networking site to ask or answer questions Joined a social/professional networking site to ask or answer questions	
Used instant messaging to connect and communicate with tutors/other learners Use Skype or other video-based communication to connect and communicate with tutors/other learners	
Found an online resource that provided substantial knowledge on the topic you were learning Found an online resource that provided skills development on the topic you were learning	

Case: E-learning in Context

A large pharmaceuticals organisation was going through a period of major change, introducing new ways of working. The purchasing function in the organisation, which bought supplies and materials, was to be changed. It was to shift from having 'do it all' purchasing units based on each of the several sites that the company had, to being organised in units dealing with discrete categories of expenditure for all sites. This purchasing function involved 500 people in 41 different countries. The goal for the company as a whole was to make better decisions and cost savings. The business objectivefor the purchasing function was to make it the 'best in class' for the industry. To achieve this it needed to develop core competences in new ways of working and in technical skills. Without this HRD the organisation believed it faced a mass exodus of staff, with the implications that entailed for more recruitment need and induction training.

The first step it took was to develop a new competence framework, based on the changed organisation, in which several levels of management had been stripped out and many people's jobs had been changed. This also required a clear career map showing how individuals could progress in the different roles of buyers, budget-holders and senior managers. Technical competences, such as negotiating skills and financial analysis, had priority during this stage.

The organisation used courses, on-the-job development and 'development zones'. The last of these were delivered by self-contained multimedia modules and intranet-based materials. The organisation developed an online career and development planning tool. This enabled staff to identify their own competence requirements and gaps. There were also links to development activity suggestions, from courses to self-study modules. This was a flexible way of providing HRD across the globe for all their staff. However, they faced a number of problems with:

- Different technology infrastructures in different parts of the company;
- Variations in bandwidth capacity in different countries, causing problems with accessing Internet materials;
- Variations in levels of computer literacy among staff;
- Building in effective HRD; existing instruction material could not just be transferred online. Interaction had to be built in;
- Costs: it took around 300 hours of development to create 1 hour of content, at a developer's fee of £100 an hour. This meant a cost of £30,000 for 1 hour's learning material.

E-Learning

E-learning refers to the use of a collection of learning methods using digital technologies, which enable, distribute and enhance learning (Fee 2009) in work and employment. The umbrella term 'e-learning' includes a range of technologies and of uses. The technologies themselves include all of the following:

- Computer and multimedia software;
- The Internet and company intranets, including their use for computer conferencing;
- Video and audio tapes;
- Television and radio broadcasting;
- Telecommunications;

- Satellite communications;

- Videoconferencing;

- Virtual reality.

Since the 1980s and the development of computer-based training (CBT), the prospects for learning have been much vaunted. The use of multimedia, text, graphics, animation, film and audio mixed together to provide information and enable interaction, was heralded as a way to 'turbocharge' learning. But in practice there were problems with these developments. First, there were technical issues associated with different kinds of platform and operating system, not only those provided by vendors but also those found within the user organisations. Second, the material that was created was, in the view of many, deadly dull. The content comprised textbooks on screen, but more difficult to read, and interaction that was restricted to un-stimulating drill and practice exercises. Third, there was the problem of content stability. This refers to the inherent dating of material: high content stability material does not change quickly; low content stability material has a short shelf-life. CBT cost a lot to develop, but often its content was quickly rendered obsolete. This fact alone curtailed interest and investments, regardless of the technical and quality problems. It was only any good as a medium in circumstances where many people needed instructing in a short time in a subject that had a short shelf-life.

The current question is: is the evolution of e-learning replicating this pattern – the cycle of hype, fad, failure and eventual integration – or will this medium be genuinely different, with a different and high-impact transformation of HRD at work because it fundamentally challenges the socio-technical system? It changes and challenges the classroom, the trainer and conceptions of what being a learner means from root to branch. For some the uptake of e-learning through the characteristic ICT simply replicates the benefits and problems of distance learning systems. As distance learning has been used for a long time there is no transformational change with e-learning. For others the use of ICT and e-learning is a genuine step change in the management of HRD. This is because it goes beyond improving the delivery of instruction via a trainer to establishing the 'learner handling information' as the core of the HRD process.

The current question is whether the evolution of e-learning, and especially developments around Web 2.0, is replicating this pattern, the cycle of hype, fad, failure and eventual integration; or will this media be genuinely different, with a different and high-impact transformation of HRD at work because it fundamentally challenges the socio-technical system. It changes and challenges the classroom, the trainer and conceptions of what being a learner means from root to branch. For some the uptake of e-learning through the characteristic ICT simply replicates the benefits and problem of distance learning systems. As distance learning has been used for a long time there is no transformational change with e-learning. For others the use of ICT and 'e-learning' is a genuine step change in the management of HRD. This is because it goes beyond improving the delivery of instruction via a trainer to establishing the 'learner handling information' as the core of the HRD process.

There are many positive stories and champions, of e-learning as a platform for learning in the workplace, a way of providing good learning resources and experiences for all the workforce 24 hours a day, 7 days a week. Understanding and engaging with the use of e-learning as part of the toolkit for workplace learning is part of the HRD landscape.

It is important to keep in mind three related issues here: (1) the technology, (2) the pedagogy and (3) the social dimensions of technologies in learning. The technology component is the most volatile element of the three. With the latest changes in digital technologies there is continuing rapid change in web-based and other platforms. With higher bandwidth, smaller 'screens', mobile access and innovation in multimedia communication there is much that can and will change almost daily.

The pedagogy element is more constant; there is nothing 'new' regarding adult learning revealed by technological change, or approaches to organising learning in work. Ideas about managing learning can be helix-like, though: they circle in and out of fashion, and can be differently combined or formulated as they come around again. The evolution of the third strand, social relations, is about how change in employment and workplaces, as knowledge economy emerges, also alter how social relations in organisations look and feel. This can impact on managing learning in an era where the old standard model of 'expert trainers' controlling the learning of 'deficit learners' is receding into history, to be replaced by a model of networked partnerships.

E-learning can provide greater realism, retention and relevance, and harness the power of social networking (Li and Bernoff 2008). More than that though, some (Alan 2007, Tapscott 2008) argue that what is evolving is more than a new set of tools for distributing information differently, but a transformation in the forms of communication and relationships in HRD as a whole. Digital technologies put power and control, and the dynamics of collaboration, in the hands of learners as well as HRD professionals. Web 2.0 systems represent a movement of people using online tools to connect, take charge of their own experiences and get what they need from each other, unmediated; information, support, ideas, products. The prospect, and desirability, of such transformation is disputed. As Web 2.0 learning is being done 'informally' what learners are actually doing, the systems they are actually using to help them learn, may not be under the control or even awareness of HRD strategy and professionals.

The organisational context for adopting and applying technologies in learning can be considered from a practical perspective and a socio-technical perspective. From a practical perspective for organisations to make use of e-learning in HRD they need reliable access to technologies and partnership with IT professionals inside or outside the organisation. They should aim to create a learning portal; a single point of access that serves as a gateway to a variety of resources. Organisations also need to consider establishing a Learning Management Systems (LMS) to manage e-learning; for example, recording who is learning what. There are both social and technological aspects to this, so a socio-technical perspective is desirable to appreciate that changes in technology that might bring benefits in some ways while this may also disrupt existing social relations (see Perspective 12.1). Unless attention is also given to evolving the social system of learning with the uptake of e-learning the system can become problematic, even chaotic. As new technical systems are adopted the way they impact on aspects of the social system have to be thought through if the changes are to support effective learning relations; to encourage people to try new things rather disengage from learning; to expand learning in capabilities; to inspire more people to join in learning; to get beyond dependency on the trainer; and to add to the reputation of HRD. If the uptake of e-learning and change does not consider these aspects, the advantages it may bring may not be realised.

Perspective 12.1: Social and Technical Aspects of Technologies in Learning

The social system for learning

Effectiveness of HRD relations	New behaviours	Expand and deepen capabilities	participation and contribution	Beyond the 'trainer' channel	Learners using multiple sources
Cost	Innovation	Execution	Relationships	Channels	Brand
IS in the organisation	Technological change	Refine learning processes	Intranet options	Control Internet/ Web 2.0 options	HRD specific presence

E-learning technical system for learning

Source: Derived from Finkelstein et al. (2006).

The following review of e-learning explores the six areas of socio-technical analysis in sequence:

(1) IS in the organisation: effectiveness of HRD relations;
(2) Technological change: new behaviours;
(3) Refine learning processes: expand and deepen capabilities;
(4) Intranet: participation and contribution;
(5) Internet/Web 2.0 options: beyond the 'trainer' channel;
(6) HRD specific presence: learners using multiple sources.

IS in the Organisation: Effectiveness of HRD Relations

The Information Systems (IS) an organisation possess and uses can enable HRD relationships, relationships between people learning at work. These systems will include the hardware that is used, from worktop computers and laptops, network systems, to mobile phones and other devices. They will also include the software that is used, the programmes and facilities that the hardware offers. Relationships between trainers and learners, managers and learners, and between learners themselves are all potentially mediated by these IS in the organisation as whole, including HRD specific IS for administering and providing HRD.

Traditional 'push' learning strategies have declining relevance and effectiveness as these systems are more widely used and user-generated content, openness, sharing, collaboration, interaction, communities and social networking all replace the traditional controlled learning environment. The changes associated with Web 2.0 are significant because they result from the displacement of conventional boundaries (Kerres 2006). Users, for example, may be able create content or change it, from adding commentary or revision, thereby becoming authors themselves.

This represent major advantages for effective HRD relations, potentially, and also policy and security issues for corporate HRD. The initial rationale for e-learning was, typically Practice 12.1:

Practice 12.1: Conditions for E-learning

- Learners are dispersed;
- Difficult to assemble at same time;
- Blocks of time are hard to schedule;
- A computer-related task is involved;
- Consistent messages are absolutely essential;
- Systematic test marking is required;
- Instructors are in short supply.

More effective relations were to be enabled by IS, and computer-based learning, to deal with these problems (Practice 12.2). Instead of conventional media there were e-learning alternatives (see Practice 12.3).

Practice 12.2: Organisational Resources

Course catalogues

Registration system

Up-front competency assessment

Assessments

Library of materials

Point-to-knowledge resources

Provide reports

Support knowledge communities

Integrate with other IS

Practice 12.3: E-learning and HRD

HRD through Conventional media;	HRD through IS;
Instruction	**E-learning**
Based on a diagnosis of user needs	Based on people searching for knowledge in the course of their work
Purpose and direction of learning	Purpose and direction of learning defined by instructional designers is defined by users as they experience problems in work
Focused on a defined learning outcome	Focused on providing contents that can be accessed in varying combinations
Sequenced for optimum memory retention	Sequenced for optimum reference in the 'here and now' then can be forgotten
Contains presentations, practice, feedback assessment relating to learning	Centred on effective presentation and of many kinds of information set outcomes relevant to performance

With diverse tools and systems emerging it was challenging to develop a clear and coherent analysis and evaluation of advantages and disadvantages in e-learning. A model of learning which makes these matters more transparent is provided by Laurillard (2002). She considers effective learning to be an outcome of several kinds of experience for a learner being enabled by various methods which typically require a range of different media forms to be used (see Perspectives 12.2).

A matrix can be derived which enables the capture and consideration of the elements of the aspects of relations from the learners point of view, and the e-learning alternatives that might be introduced (see Practice 12.4).

Perspective 12.2: Laurillard's Concepts

Learning experience	Methods	Media forms
Attending, apprehending	Print, lecture, video/DVD	Narrative
Investigating, exploring	Library, DVD, web	Interactive
Discussing, debating	Seminar, conference	Communicative
Experiment, practice	Lab, field trip, simulation	Adaptive
Articulate, expressing	Essay, product, model	Productive

Practice 12.4: Relations Issues

Learning design factors		HRD options analysis	
Elements of learning	**Behaviour of learner**	**Conventional course elements**	**E-learning options and alternative**
Narrative	I get information	Print, lecture, video/DVD	Web base
Interactive	I explore	Library, references, DVD	Learning centre, TBT, Internet
Communicative	I discuss	Seminar, conference	Videoconferencing Chat rooms
Adaptive	Then I try out	Lab, field trip, simulation	TRS
Productive	I can now do . . .	Essay, product, model	Virtual reality Immersion

To introduce and use e-learning is an exercise in change management; overcoming resistance to change, establishing the skills and abilities to engage in e-learning, and providing resources. (Practice 12.5) provides the background for doing this.

Reviewing e-learning at this level, the advantages are all the advantages of flexible/open learning, of consistency, flexibility of place and time. In addition there are the benefits of interactivity, immediate feedback and high realism.

Exercise 12.1:E-learning Options Analysis

Identify a training programme or activity to meet a learning need that is currently organised without any e-learning. Identify the e-learning options for it. Then consider what impact this has on social relations; who has the power, is in control and needs to be engaged/involved

Elements of learning	The current HRD	E-learning options
Narrative		
Interactive		
Communicative		
Adaptive		
Productive		

Practice 12.5: Business Concerns and E- learning	
Cost	What will it cost and how can that be managed? Savings create higher profits or resources for investment. What will training cost to get or develop? E-learning is more efficient; conveys information quicker. Costs more on development, saves on the delivery. Particularly opportunity costs
Quality	Are we meeting customer expectations? Reactions; proper surveys built in Learning; use for feedback not assessment Performance; Results; for the business; intellectual capital
Service	Do we respond to needs? Access and availability (24 hours a day, 7 days a week) Tailored to individuals
Speed	How fast change strategy, bring in a new product, respond to customers; this is the key criteria To get up and running? To reach everyone Be altered due to changes

Source: Rosenberg (2001).

Training time, it is claimed, is reduced by 26 per cent, excluding the gains from reduced need for travel to locations of HRD. Direct costs are dramatically reduced; premises, travel, course fees. E-learning is more enjoyable than paper based. Checking progress is easy, as is practising in safety.

The extent to which the evolution of HRD alongside developments in IS in organisations has produced all these benefits is still under researched. Enhanced computer-based training (Enhanced CBT) is still the largest single application of technology in training; this is the delivery of learning through CBT or multimedia, most typically as self-paced open learning. CBT seems to offer all the advantages of flexible and open learning. This includes consistent presentation of material, the flexibility for the learner to work at his or her own pace, and the opportunity for the learner to study at a convenient place and time. CBT may be used as a self-study resource, with or without tutorial support and/or mentoring, for small groups or as part of a larger course or training event. Learners may study at a single CBT workstation in the workplace, in a learning centre, on the premises of an external training provider, or at home, if they have the right equipment. Organisations are increasingly delivering CBT via networked computers, intranets and the Internet, but these do impose some limitations.

A CBT approach may entail a significant investment. Decisions on hardware will depend on the software applications that will be used. For some applications, a standard PC will be sufficient; for others a higher-specification multimedia PC will be essential. A wide range of off-the-shelf software is available for CBT HRD. One key lesson is that buying an off-the-shelf package, if a suitable one exists, will normally be much cheaper than commissioning new material.

There are specific advantages of CBT over paper-based open learning. These include: interactivity, which can improve motivation and retention; immediate feedback to completed question and practice exercises; and the greater realism that results from including graphics, photographs, sound and moving images in simulations. There are also disadvantages of CBT compared with paper-based open learning. These include the need for a power supply and specialist equipment, equipment that is not easily portable, and learning material that is more costly to prepare. The relative costs of technology-based and paper-based open learning depend on a number of factors. In general, CBT has higher origination costs, lower production and packaging costs, and higher delivery costs. Advantages and disadvantages have to be recognised in the context of learning style issues as well (see Debate 12.1).

New Behaviours: Technological Change

The uptake of IS for HRD did not necessarily fit with or require any significant change in HRD professional or learner behaviour. Different media could be sued, mediated by e-learning, without substantially altering the nature of the relationships involved in organising learning. Trainers still trained, managers still coached/mentored and learners still communicated with each other under the

---

Debate 12.1: For and Against CBT

For computer-based systems	Against computer-based systems
Fun; mimics games	Less than inspiring systems
Multimedia presentation	Mainly text based
Self-control order of presentation	Pre-structured
Choose activities	Required activities
Pace self	Being on your own
Able to monitor and assess on your own	Celebrate success with other people
Use of simulations (experience)	Quality of 'realism'
Links to tutors or groups	Limited feedback
Access Internet	Not available

---

control of trainers and managers. With more extensive use of e-learning, and Web 2.0 systems, there are more issues raised about changes in behaviour for learning (see Figure 12.1).

As the options and realities for learning shift, systemically, from non-Web 2.0 2 systems to web-based systems there are new risks and challenges:

- Learners never start, never finish;
- Learners make the wrong choices about what to learn;
- Learners make no contributions;
- Learners access and recycle flawed resources;
- Interaction is not related to learning, it is social.

The challenges are to consider the learning process as a whole, not just providing 'e-reading', and engage the learner. Systems should relate to the goals of the

	Non-Web 2.0 E-learning	Web 2.0 E-learning
When and where to engage in learning	Passive – starting and finishing controlled by someone else	Determined by the learner
Choices and priorities	Pre-determined- designers control	Learners control more of what they learn
Contributions	Designer led	Can contribute themselves
Access	Resources provided	Broad and rich resources in multiple domains
Interaction	Designer centred	More opportunities for interaction

Figure 12.1   Changes in learner behaviour

organisation and learning, with new options for managed programmes, not the fragmented accumulation of bits and pieces of learning online. And these should be more entertaining learning; friendly and humorous, and micro design tips matter; navigation. HRD professionals become purchasers/developers/facilitators of 'e' materials and services. Learners can experience learning in such systems as part of their working life, rather than being confined to the classroom.

Refine Learning Processes: Expand and Deepen Capabilities

Technologies are the means of delivering learning and change, and evolve alongside social relations and systems for HRD. The potential of technological developments to drive wholesale changes in learning, and challenge the social relations and practices has been a major theme in contemporary HRD. In the contemporary context HRD is evolving in an increasingly digital economy, where organisations and employment are based on extensive networked telecommunications and individuals have access to ubiquitous computing power. Learning is just one area of practice among many which is being challenged and changed by the ubiquity of networked computing and computing power. For some (ref), the potential net effects on HRD of developments in information and communication technologies (ICT) are of an order that herald the wholesale transformation of learning in the workplace. This is because the use of ICT promises to make learning more accessible, more enjoyable and better aligned, with self-directed, more realistic work-based learning and all at less cost. The technical platforms for such a change exist now, and continue to evolve at a rate which reduces costs considerably.

- Learning centres;
- Task replication systems;
- Virtual reality systems.

Learning Centres

To date the most visible and popular use of e-learning, the greatest new version of a revised socio-technical system for learning, has been through developing learning centres, rather than providing access to network-based systems on their own. Learning centres are physical spaces devoted to providing resources for learning in organisations, usually with PCs that have intranet and Internet access. The benefits of these are as follows:

- A good learning environment, away from the workplace;
- A secure place for often expensive materials;
- A focal point for providing learner support;
- The provision of a physical presence, for image and marketing;
- The use of existing standard hardware.

The process of developing a learning centre involves steps that will be new to the trainer in the workplace: researching what will be supplied in the centre, planning the administration of the centre and marketing it on launch and thereafter. Retaining some of the social aspects of learning on courses can be important in the success of a learning centre (see Practice 12.6).

Practice 12.6: Learning Centres

- A welcoming environment
- Suitable opening hours
- A distraction-free study environment
- Equipment and materials which would be uneconomic to provide for one individual
- Access to a range of high-quality open learning materials
- Access to a range of other learning services (e.g. conventional courses)
- Access to information and communication technology
- Advice and guidance
- Information about learning opportunities
- General and specific support
- Mentoring
- Communication with other learners to share experience and gain peer support
- Loan of materials to facilitate home or work place learning
- Loan of computers and other equipment
- Accreditation

Small Learning Centres are essentially an information point which provides access to information about learning opportunities, taster materials and advice. A Standard Centre usually provides: Computer facilities linked to the Internet, A range of courses, General learning support. A Major Learning Centre; a substantial centre which provides: Substantial computer facilities with multiple links to Internet, Access to a library of open learning materials, e-mail and/or face-to-face access to advice and guidance service. A Virtual Centre can provide access to the service from home or public locations.

Networks of centres have been developed in most large companies, cities and countries. Many centres do not offer a comprehensive range of services but are customised to meet the host organisation needs. The success of a centre is clearly related to how well the centre serves the needs of its customers. Appropriate support is critical to the success of a learning centre. Support can take many forms and it is not always necessary to provide immediate face to face subject specific help. A trained generalist who understands learning can provide significant assistance. The availability of expert subject support is only required occasionally and can be provided by e-mail or telephone access or the occasional tutorial. Learners may find it far easier to approach each other with questions than to contact an expert. Many students need a balance of general and individual help.

Task replication systems (TRS) simulate work tasks, apparatus, systems and processes to support learning. They may involve the development of large-scale business systems, modelling the way something works, replicating operation or decision-making exercises. The benefits of such simulations are the ability to practise in a safe environment, to measure learning as it occurs and to control situations to various degrees of difficulty. They are popular, because they can substitute for on-job training, and they involve the trainee in the learning. There have now been over three decades of experience in the design and development of learning materials for. Despite guidelines for doing this there have been many problems:

- The content was not good; courses were not revised and updated to take into account changes in policy and procedures.
- Exercises were not 'authentic'; people did not believe the steps they completed were realistic, and simulations were not believable.
- They were great looking, but awful to use.
- Users are at the mercy of rapid changes in technology, making their technical platforms redundant.
- TRS learning packages are useless after the initial use, because they are not searchable.
- Learning was not being reinforced.
- There was no support for it within the organisation; TRS was not really cared about.
- It went against people's views of what training should involve – what 'real' training should be.
- It was plain boring.
- It was just 'shovelware', delivering old material in virtually the same way, just moving the delivery to TRS or the web.

Virtual reality systems (VRS) and games are special case of a TRS. They involve people experiencing a 'fully immersive' environment. The classical example is that of the flight simulator, which is used to train and test pilots. The pilots are exposed to simulations of flights that are fully immersive because they are in a model of a cockpit, with the plane responding to their actions. The logic of this is obvious: the costs of errors using the 'real' environment are so high that the costs of developing simulators make sense. The advantages are the possibilities of controlling complex tasks, to provide situated learning and monitor learners closely as they learn.

Perspective 12.3: Digital Game-Based Learning, McGraw Hill

Learning Content	Examples	Learning activities	Possible game styles
Facts	Laws, policies, product specifications	Questions Memory Association drill	Game show competitions Flashcard games Mnemonics Action, sports games
Skills	Interviewing, selling, operating equipment, project management	Imitation, feedback, coaching, continuous practice, increasing challenge	Persistent state games Role-play games Adventure games Detective games
Judgement	Management decisions Timing, ethics, recruitment	Reviewing cases, asking questions, making choices, feedback, coaching	Role-player games Detective games Multi-player interaction Adventure games Strategy games
Behaviours	Supervising, exercising self-control, setting examples	Imitation, feedback coaching, practice	Role-playing games
Theories	How people learn	Logic, experimentation, questioning	Open-ended simulation games Building games Construction games Reality testing games
Reasoning	Strategic and tactical thinking, quality analysis	Problems, examples	Puzzles

Perspective 12.3: (Continued)			
Process	Auditing, strategy creation	System analysis and deconstruction, practice	Strategy games Adventure games Simulation games
Procedures	Assembly, clerical	Imitation Practice	Timed games Reflex games
Creativity	Invention, design	Play, memory	Puzzles, invention games
Observation	Moods, morale, problems	Observing, feedback	Simulation games
Communication	Appropriate language, timing, movement	Imitation, practice	Role-playing games Reflex games

Source: Prensky (2000).

Fully immersive simulations and environments have been developed and used for many purposes. Entertainment is probably number one, with architectural design, sales and prototyping functions also important applications. Learning environments have been low down the priority list for the application of virtual reality simulations, perhaps with the exception of the military, though the scope for the evolution of learning environments can be glimpsed. Perspective 12.3 provides a set of options suggesting how computer game formats can be adapted or applied to work-based learning.

The problems with all these kinds of e-learning-based methods have all the disadvantages of flexible/open learning; individual isolation, motivational problems, the quality of help and support. And the use of e-learning is not right for all kinds of learning and HRD. It is seen as the best option in certain circumstances (see Debate 12.2).

There are also opportunities and challenges presented by the changing roles which the use of e-learning in HRD raises. Trainers become purchasers/developers/facilitators of hardware and software. Providers have to shift to be online and producing multimedia materials; which takes a great investment. Government has to be concerned with infrastructure development, and the extent to which government should play a role is open to question and divides different stakeholders. Users too have to change; to being learners live at the screen-face. And, once again, it seems that connections with managers are removed from the HRD loop.

Debate 12.2: Evaluation of E-learning in HRD	
Reactions	learners are positive about using e-learning
Learning	The use of e-learning makes no significant difference?
Costs	Lower costs at volume; so big organisations can use it, the smaller cannot?
Transfer	If it is 'IT' learning itself the learning transfer to performance is high; if it is other kinds of learning transfer is still an issue
Ultimate	Organisations need to be on the wave or be left behind? It is becoming the norm to at least 'blend' e-learning into HRD at work, if not to rely on it entirely

Intranet: Participation and Contribution

Intranets are internal networks within organisations that use web browsers and web protocols. Because they are internal networks they are faster than the Internet. They are also more secure than the Internet, and provide a controlled environment for communication, accessing resources and publishing resources. Intranets can also be more assured of standardised software/plug-ins required to access web pages. These systems not only enable new approaches to instruction, they also open up new possibilities with the provision of information to support performance improvement and knowledge management.

E-learning can help people do something better, faster or cheaper, without having to learn it completely in the conventional way. Some roles and tasks require full and formal training, and cognitive capacities and capabilities must be internalised and kept up to date – for doctors and pilots, for example. But for other roles and tasks people can become 'expert' through finding and using information rather than being formally instructed and trained. For example, new managers in an organisation do not need to know all the HRM policies immediately to perform well. Performance support provides the means for supporting HRD as it is needed, in the course of accomplishing tasks, without having to learn chapter and verse. ICT job aids are either external aids to work or intrinsic aids to a computer package. External aids require the user to stop work to get support from job aids, documents or help desks. Intrinsic aids can be accessed while work continues: software help, wizards or cue cards provided as part of a computer package. Summing up presents the pedagogic advantages of adopting e-learning in performance support (Practice 12.7).

Beyond the 'trainer' Channel: Internet/Web 2.0 Options

E-learning also includes the use of web technologies to deliver a broad array of solutions that enhance knowledge and performance. It is network-based and

Practice 12.7: Performance Support and the Advantages of E-learning

Social system issues	Old technical system	New technical system; e-advantages
The learner as knowledge producer	Learning is controlled by the providers of training. Intellectual capital is distributed by them to passive learners	Knowledge is constantly changing, and the training department is not equipped to cope with constant update. Have staff capture, organise and disseminate knowledge; value learners as knowledge producers contributing to the organisation's intellectual capital.
Supporting performance	The problem of 'transfer' has to be managed as learning is not done in the actual performance environment	Improve performance while reducing time spent in training. Electronic performance support systems, an integrated electronic environment that is available to and easily accessible by each employee and is structured to provide immediate, individualised online access to the full range of information, software, guidance, advice and assistance, data, images, tools and assessment and monitoring systems to permit job performance with minimal support and intervention by others
Integrating individual and organisational learning	Not integrated as learning is targeted at individuals, not about reciprocal exchange	Make training experiences direct contributors to the organisation's intellectual capital gain? Transform individual training events into organisational learning events; design learning activities where learners produce meaningful results that contribute to the organisation's knowledge base; put less emphasis on 'instructionally designed material' and more on 'instructionally designed activities' using primary resources

Enhancing learning experiences	Unrealistic environments in which to learn.	How to provide a realistic, non-threatening learning environments supporting the practice of critical skills; use simulators
Customising learning	Not customised, mainly sheep-dip, the same for everyone	Improve the link (efficiency) between skill-gap analysis (learning needs) and learning activities; link learning activities and resources to competence database; provide skill-check and 360° assessment facilities

therefore capable of instant updating, unlike other CBT platforms. It is delivered using a computer and standard Internet technology. E-learning can then be seen to involve a broader set of activities in HRD at work, not just an interest in conventional training and instruction.

It is the use of the Internet and intranets that has most caught the imagination and which represents a step-change in the socio-technical system. The Internet is a global web of computers interconnected with each other. It enables three functions relevant to and important for effective HRD.

- It enables communication: one to one, one to many, many to one;
- It enables the search for resources;
- It enables the publication of resources.

Delivery technologies will continue to evolve, and this will have an impact on the design and delivery of e-learning. Until recently distance learning and e-learning services were available either via dial-up access to the Internet or via broadcast TV. The Internet is the obvious choice for hosting interactive digital courseware, but available only to those networked and with a PC. Countries leading the way with high levels of households online have high Internet 'readiness'.

There are other options, with intriguing implications for how HRD at work could evolve. Most households have a TV set, but these to date have only provided access to broadcast educational programming and limited analogue interactive educational services. Only limited numbers of educational programmes are available, and no interactivity is possible without cable or satellite. The development of technologies around the TV could provide simpler and cheaper access devices. This would encourage those who do not now have access at home to look into learning. Meanwhile the quality and reliability ofInternet access will evolve. Broadband technologies will provide much faster download times, and facilitate new services and applications that simply could not be supported by dial-up connections.

Other technologies may have a role, including mobile phones. The use of wireless data applications is predicted to take off when the wireless interface to the Internet becomes more user-friendly and the transmission speed increases. In addition to an improved interface, other enhancements are envisaged. Mobile telecommunications will bring mobile networks significantly closer to the capabilities of fixed networks. It will provide mobile users with full interactive multimedia capabilities and make full video streaming possible, allowing people to watch 'broadcast' materials on their handsets. All these developments may provide new means to provide instant performance-support HRD for people in all kinds of work situations – or perhaps all that will happen is that people will text each other more or surf the Internet for non-work related reasons!

HRD Specific Presence: Learners Using Multiple Sources

But the widespread use of ICT, other communications media and Internet-based and multimedia training is still far from being the norm. It appears that only a minority of organisations use any kind of ICT for HRD in any significant way at all (ref). Surveys also suggest that those with access to these technologies would prefer to use older technologies such as paper- and person-based versions of learning materials, because these are easier to use or provide more detail. The early heralding of the advent of e-learning as the new platform for HRD at work seems to have been more hype than substance. The debate about transformation does not displace, but does overshadow the more fundamental question about the value of e-learning in the HRD toolkit in most of its current forms; for there is scepticism and doubt, certainly among learners, with experiences of e-learning being negative.

Why this might have been so leads to looking at unclear thinking about how and what HRD practices can be enhanced by technologies, and which are better kept apart from technical change. It also means recognising that HRD is embedded in a socio-technical system. Certain sets of social relations evolve to fit the use of a certain kind of technology; masters and apprentices in work-based learning, trainers and instruction in training rooms, coaching and mentoring in continuous development and lifelong learning are all examples. As technologies change in HRD they may disrupt existing social relations, as they do in work more broadly. That might usher in a period of transition and change to new social relations, or it might just lead to confusion and poorer HRD, or even degeneration of the system as a whole. If technologies evolve quicker than the social relations around them can, managing to adapt roles and change relations becomes a bigger and bigger challenge for the providers and consumers of learning.

Quality issues have always been raised about the impact of technologies. In the United Kingdom, for example, when a University for Industry (UfI) was established as a clearinghouse for providing e-learning resources to companies. Learning packages from over 700 organisations were submitted as samples of work for inclusion as resources. But no more than a quarter of these were deemed to have achieved quality standards during the first stage of assessment by a panel of experts. The main reason for this failure seemed to be a tendency to use presentational spin rather than informed learning design, producing e-learning materials that were strong on glossy presentation but weak on pedagogy.

Conclusion

E-learning's promise of greater access to and potential cost savings in HRD has generated a lot of hype. And this is big business for hardware and software suppliers and companies. But there are difficult and complex issues surrounding platforms, technologies and the organisational realities in using e-learning (see Practice 12.8). Even e-learning advocates have to counsel care rather than unbridled enthusiasm. They have sought to brand 'blended learning' as a way of accommodating critiques of e-learning that threatened to swing the pendulum back against them. For e-learning's potential to be realised, the classic four Cs of technology evolution in HRD still matter: that is, a need for the right culture, for champions, for communication, and for change management.

Practice 12.8: Practice: An Evolution

Maturity		Socio-technical systems concern
Entry level	Convert some existing provisions to CBT or purchase CBT	Experimenting
Stage 2	Develop a Learning Resource Centre and HR web site	Unifying around new relations
Stage 3	Develop network provisions and/or make use of 'e partnerships' for up to 25 per cent of HRD needs	Expanding new relations alongside the old
Stage 4	Full integration of all elements of development between learners-managers mediated by ICT (from ITN to evaluation)	Integrating HRD around the new
Stage 5	Electronic performance management; integration with other Information and HR systems (appraisal, career development)	Integration of HRD in business in new ways

At present many organisations use e-learning for HRD, or have an e-learning strategy; some have websites, or use courseware and other e-learning artefacts (see Practice 12.9). This reflects three important factors:

1. Internet technology may be the key to a profound revolution in learning, but technology is just a tool.
2. There is an enduring and important role for classroom instruction; it is misguided to think otherwise.
3. Learning is a continuous process, not a series of events; it is not just formally organised provisions and training.

If e-learning's potential is to be realised, organisations must have an overall business- and people-centred strategy, alongside their e-learning strategy. This message is reinforced in all areas.

If e-learning in HRD is to flourish, then it is crucial who develops it. The infrastructure and the content can be created by market forces, by special institutions and organisations, or by governments. This can give rise to fears that it is all infrastructure driven: because the delivery mode exists, and it can be done, so it *must* be done – so e-learning takes over even if it is not wanted. There is a need for mature systems with clear standards (see Debate 12.3).

The uptake of e-learning provides an opportunity to rethink and redesign learning experiences, and resolve apparently intractable problems such as access, flexibility, quality and cost (see Practice 12.10). But this still presents challenges as much as solutions, and it is still the quality of basic needs analysis design, delivery and evaluation that matters. Equally, the management of implementation matters as much as, if not more than, the management of the medium itself. It is still important to retain the benefits of the 'old ways' of learning in groups and in positive personal relations. The concept of 'blended' leaning, where e-learning offers something in addition to conventional media and methods rather than a substitute for them, goes some way to meeting these concerns.

Practice 12.9: Oilco Exploration and Production

Oilco Exploration and Production (OEP) were concerned with global team-working, recruitment and staff retention, competitiveness, and what the company terms 'faster time to competence'. In fashioning a formal and informal learning culture, in which the acquisition, distribution and enhancement of expertise have acquired growing business status, OEP has sought to link personal career development for the professional 'lifelong learner'.

Participation in knowledge-sharing and learning support structures was immense: with 10,000 active members on the various technical and cross-business networks regularly participate in exchanging solutions, ideas and learning. These networks, along with a new 'guru' class of global consultant from within OEP's ranks and several designated 'centres of excellence', have helped move knowledge out of people's heads into oil field operations. Engineering and technical support staff at any one location can depend on peer assistance throughout the world, often at the touch of a button, to support and enhance their efforts locally. The personal challenge is to seek and grasp the opportunities to learn, to create knowledge and, most importantly, to apply it day to day. In this way the company can build a highly competent workforce ready to face new business challenges.

The second critical part of OEP's model for achieving 'competence faster' was life-long learning provided through its corporate university (CU). The CU was launched and within 6 months some 6,500 students had signed up to take courses, growing to the 10,000-plus strong student body of today. The CU represents an integrated education framework comprising regional learning centres, online learning materials and libraries and a network of accreditation links to degree-validating third parties. Both internal and contractor 'students' can use this blended learning model, seeking to match various styles of learning with appropriate access channels and opportunities for self-driven personal development.

With so many complex operations running globally, the organisation sees knowledge sharing and lifelong learning not as options but as necessities to improve its competitive edge, through being able to realise a higher standard of technical and operational excellence. Being 'in the know' through learning or the transfer of knowledge clearly makes good personal, professional and corporate sense. These advantages have become mission-critical: the future depends on OEP's ability to harness the diverse talents, experience and creativity of its people, and it emphasises the capacity of its worldwide professional network to share learning and disseminate knowledge rapidly. It succeeds by being both global and local, applying the experience of worldwide operations through locally rooted organisations sensitive to the needs of its customers and communities.

One qualification: it is valid to emphasise this type of e-learning, but it can also be misleading. Much recent and current e-learning growth has been in the context of the development of learning centres in workplaces, not in systems networked to isolated/lone learners or to workstations as such. Among the main technical problems with e-learning are wasting time on searches, computers crashing, poor quality of materials and gimmicky web sites.

Practice 12.10: Learning Technologies: A Full Costing Model	
Research and development	staff time, reports and reviews, administration, research activities, displacement costs, briefing meetings
Initial Investment (non recurring)	building or refurbishment, electrical work and cabling, furniture, fittings, hardware and peripherals

---

Practice 12.10: (Continued)

Initial investment (recurring)	replacements for hardware, software, insurance, staff training, TBT development, support staff, admin support, telephone charges
Operating and support	hardware, software, peripherals, security, rentals, materials, staff and evaluations
Disposal and salvage	sale of hardware, disposal cost, retraining

---

Debate 12.3: E-learning: Areas to Debate

Claims	Counter claims
New multimedia is relevant everywhere	Limited to some kinds of instruction
Lower costs	Higher initial costs
Greater access and volume	People switch off
More effective learning	No difference
Replicates situated learning	Cant replace situated learning

Case: Finish Bookstore

Read this Case, and Consider the Benefits of E-Learning Described

A Finnish Bookstore wanted to improve the quality of their sales force's customer service skills. Most employees had been taught generic sales skills in a two-day immersive sales training programme. The existing classroom training, which the Finnish Bookstore ran from time to time for all sales personnel, was already ten years old, so there was need to develop a new kind of training programme. With major help from external vendor specialised in digital solutions, the Finnish Bookstore developed a simulation-based online programme that engaged participants in solving real-world sales situations. The training comprised one day working online with a live coach and a group of peers, then the possibility to continue working alone with the oneline programme later over the intranet. The general goal of the training course was to focus on building on practical skills rather than merely on delivering information.

A simulation-based programme was designed based on dialogue between a salesperson and a customer who visits the store twice. At various points in the dialogue the learner, as salesperson in the dialogue, had to select one response among a series of responses offered by the programme. The virtual customer was a difficult one, prone to walk out of the shop if the salesperson did not offer a response that satisfied her. The programme was divided into two customer dialogues. The first dialogue provided the sales person the chance to try their hand at approaching the customer, probing for her needs and positioning the product. The second dialogue concentrated on practicing taking orders, managing counterarguments and closing the sale.

The content of the dialogues as developed together with the group of experienced in-house salespersons and professional scriptwriters. Careful attention was paid to creating authentic interchanges between a demanding customer with many arguments and a salesperson whose role the learner would adopt. In contrast to the previous classroom-based course, this course aimed to provide opportunity and training to coherently integrate initially disconnected information. The dialogue exercises challenged the learners to reason over the different alternatives and their consequences. The learners' task was to handle all customer arguments politely and find the best solution to the customer's need. Feedback was provided immediately all the way through the course by a virtual coach. He told employees to back off when they got too aggressive, and said encouraging words and useful tips when they got too passive or strayed from key messages.

Introducing the online simulation with a live coach was designed to enhance the social aspects of the learning. First, all sales directors were provided a one-day train-the-trainer session to prepare them to act as coaches for their own store. The session provided the directors with the chance to go through the simulation in small groups, discuss the best ways of serving customers and some theoretical background about the topics in the simulation. Thus, the directors were trained to use the online simulation and facilitate an associated learning process. The intention was that they would first experience the possibilities of the online simulation-based course, and subsequently present a similar way of working in small groups with the simulations for their own sales personnel.

The online programme was introduced with a live coach in all individual stores in the Finnish Bookstore chain. The coach assisted participants to engage with the online simulation, evaluate their own prior experiences and construct individual understandings before defending and discussing those understandings with their colleagues. This blended approach was intended to motivate the learners to initiate and continue the discussion with their colleagues during and after the one-day session.

User Views

The most commonly expressed compliment for the simulation course was about the challenging customer dialogue with which participants easily identified. For example, one participant admitted that it was a wonderful feeling to succeed and close a sale with a busy and acrimonious lady. Many of the comments in this category of compliments emphasised the need to stop and carefully consider the various possible lines of discussion with the customer, as the chosen customer service situations were just challenging enough. It was good, in many instances, to have to think about the alternatives. You don't necessarily always come to think how you can influence customer's attitude with just a little alternation in what you say to them. Many situations seemed to be self-evident, but they were presented in a tricky way.

The second largest complimentary category (47 comments) indicated that the simulation-based programme was 'engaging' and 'cheerful'. In the words of one participant: 'Nice method that is much more effective than reading PowerPoint slides in the classroom.' Another learner considered that her interest remained through the course and she realised 'how important it is to listen what the customer says'.

The third common line of reasoning (31 comments) for complimenting the course relied on the possibility to 'try again without the threat of getting the sack'. At the same time, the majority of comments highlighted the importance of getting feedback – both proper reasons for why a particular answer was wrong, and encouraging words to proceed with the demanding customer.

In addition to the perceived benefits, the respondents offered some critical feedback for the simulation-based course. Among these responses four themes were found: the course was technically too inflexible, some answer alternatives did not fit a realistic selling situation, there was not enough variety in the dialogue process and the course was experienced as too easy. The comments regarding technically inflexibility were mainly related to the need to return, in certain points of the simulation dialogue, a couple of steps backwards to repeat the dialogue. The usability was, however, based on the idea that if users have once learnt the principle of how to serve customers in a right way, it should be easy and quick to choose the correct answer again. In the case that it would be difficult for them, the programme provides the learner a new chance to practise with a virtual customer instead of the real one.

One participant pointed out that in her opinion the virtual coach's view of ideal sales was rather forward, pushy and obtrusive. Another criticised that she did not agree with the course designer that the successful customer service situation would always end up with a sale.

The course has been very successful as, practically speaking, all learners reported that they could recommend the simulation-based course to other colleagues and they would like to study other courses with the same method. Furthermore, a majority of participants' expressed their overall level of being able to apply the customer service skills to their own work task had improved.

3 Key Texts

(1) Fee, K. (2009) *Delivering E-Learning* (London: Kogan Page).

(2) Gibson, D., Aldrich, C. and Prensky, M. (eds) (2007) *Games and Simulations in Online Learning: Research and Development Frameworks* (Hershey PA, Information Science Publishing).

(3) Aldrich, C. (2005) *Learning By Doing: A Comprehensive Guide to Simulations, Computer Games and Pedagogy in E-learning and other Educational Experiences* (San Francisco, Pfieffer).

3 Key Articles/Reports

(1) Bondarouk, T. and Ruël, H. (2010) 'Dynamics of E-learning: Theoretical and Practical Perspectives: Introduction to Special Issue', *International Journal of Training & Development,* 14 (3), pp. 149–154.

(2) Tsai, A. (2010) 'An Integrated E-Learning Solution in Hospitals', *Journal of Global Business Issues*, 4 (2), pp. 85–93.

(3) Wang, G. (2010) 'Theorizing E-Learning Participation: A Study of the HRD Online Communities in the USA', *Journal of European Industrial Training*, 34 (4), pp. 344–364.

3 Key Web Links

(1) Serious Games Institute: www.seriousgamesinstitute.co.uk.

(2) E-learning network: http://www.elearningnetwork.org/.

(3) Analysis of the Impact of E-learning in Work: http://www.towardsmaturity.org/.

PART III

Contexts

In this section the contexts within which HRD concepts and methods are applied are described and reviewed. These include the context of organisation strategies, and knowledge management; national policy for learning and change in employment; comparative HRD which is about exploring HRD systems and practices in different countries; and finally critical HRD, with reflections on the nature of HRD as perceived by 'realist' and 'constructivist' perspectives.

13

Strategic HRD

Learning Objectives

By the end of this module you will be able to:

- Define the concept of Strategic HRD (SHRD);
- Identify the key themes and issues raised by SHRD;
- Define and analyse Knowledge Management;
- Critically evaluate the theory and practice of SHRD.

Introduction

There are three kinds of specific framework for thinking about the possible nature and evidence for a role for Human Resource Development (HRD) in the strategic context here. First is the modelling of special kinds of process and products associated with strategy. Alternatively in a broader analysis of developments in the strategy literature, an evolution of five distinct eras, the five C's can be described. Finally, SHRD may be thought of as a cluster of activities which fit and enable the cost, innovation, execution, relationship, channel and brand concerns organisations have to, respectively, optimise value chain, exploit R&D, refine business processes, leverage networks and alliances, develop market access and manage customers. The interface with Knowledge Management is significant.

SHRD

HRD can be thought of as a strategic activity with a contribution to overall organisation (Garavan 1991, McCracken and Wallace 2000, Grieves 2003, Garavan 2007) and national success. In any of its forms the concept of SHRD is subject to questioning. Identifying and analysing the links between strategy, HRD and effectiveness has proven to be conceptually and practically complicated. It is equally difficult to prove that HRD was not 'strategic' in the past but is 'strategic' now. Meanings, evidence and value judgements are unclear. In general there appears to have been a shift from the equilibrium model of HRD to a concern with change: and activity to redress perceived weaknesses with HRD in order to compete or improve service standards. Rather than direct attention to proof for any definite link between strategy and HRD, it is necessary to analyse this both the status, functional tasks and power of HRD.

It has become commonplace to argue that 'people make the difference' in ensuring corporate and national success and company mission statements abound with the sentiment that 'people are our most important asset'. The status of people management relative to other aspects of the organisation, such as financial management or technological innovation, would seem to be high. Yet research in even an evidently heavily people-dependent sector such as the health services is ambiguous. Some conclude that people management is considered to be peripheral, whereas others claim to show that effective HRD is central to key performance, such as reducing post-operative mortality rates. Nevertheless, evidence suggests that the traditional higher status functions of finance and marketing continue to overshadow HRM and HRD: people with an accountancy background and skill make good senior managers, whereas people with HRM/HRD backgrounds and skills do not. This echoes the findings of those who found a negative correlation between managers' concern with HRM/HRD and their career success.

In traditional approaches to HRD, there was a tendency to equate effective people management with the development of specialist personnel and HRD departments. Consequently, there was no great premium put on people management skills for general managers. General managers were the decision-makers who needed to be clear about business aims and manage budgets effectively. Management development in general, and the development of 'soft' people skills in particular, was not a high priority for supervisors, middle or senior managers.

Yet the management of people is both an integral part of all managers' work and a distinctive field of professional practice. These sentiments are best expressed in the aphorism that 'managers achieve results through people', even when the reality of much managerial work would seem to contradict this. Some attention has been given in the past to the development of a specialist role for HRD practitioners, and more recent research continues to highlight the changing nature of the specialist role. There has also been a growing literature on the way that general management has changed. Here the emphasis on the quality of management generally, and the need to develop better managers, has been important. In addition, the impact of restructuring and delayering has been emphasised. The role of senior managers has been reviewed, middle management has been squeezed, and the supervisory role has been transformed.

This area of balance between specialist and line manager responsibilities across the spectrum of HRD activities is attracting a lot of interest. The net effect seems to be that the devolution of people management responsibilities from specialists to line managers has an impact on the number and roles of specialists, while managers need increased development to manage their new responsibilities. Specific agreements to clarify responsibilities can be made. The association of changes in this sphere of activity with new HRD approaches is often highlighted. Given the thrust of new HRD ideas, there is clearly a greater need to have managers who are able to create and develop the committed, flexible, quality workforce required for success. The feeling that personnel specialists and departments were not up to meeting and driving the changes necessary led to a reinforced emphasis on the role of managers. Although this view of personnel has been disputed, the quantity and quality of management development concerned with HRD have become major issues and a priority for many organisations.

The popularity of this delegation and devolution to line managers is hard to gauge. Specialists may lose their jobs, or core parts of their workload. Managers may see the devolution as simply added responsibilities at a time of increasing stress and work intensification, rather than an opportunity to become better managers. Resistance to change is likely to occur on the part of both specialist and manager.

In addition to the changing balance of responsibilities, there is the issue of the changing content of responsibilities. HRD has been characterised in the past by agreements and procedures that reflected a mixture of legal, social and professional best practice. Change or improvement meant revising those agreements and procedures. This often happened in an *ad hoc* way: as an issue came up, it was dealt with.

New approaches to people management have a substantially different set of emphases. First, the idea is that the foundation of effective HRD is culture rather than procedure. Having a culture in which human resources are valued, in which commitment is expected, and where all managers are highly skilled and trained can be seen to preclude the need for collective agreements and procedures. Second, the use of levers such as teamwork is much more important. Overall, there is a concern to restructure employment patterns, jobs and organisations. In this context, training and development assume a greater role, which involves more than the level of technical training being given and extends to initiatives such as empowerment. This is a difficult construct to pin down, but it refers, at a minimum, to a significant reconceptualisation of roles by both managers and employees.

In sum, the organisation as a unit of analysis has changed and the national context as a unit of analysis has changed. As a result of these changes, the roles and activities of management and personnel specialists appear to be changing. Stable structures and systems administered by specialist staff are perhaps necessary, but they are not sufficient.

Now that HRD concerns are more prominent and potentially strategic, has this changed? Is HRD an integral part of the process of strategic analysis, a feature of strategic choices? Where the flexibility, quality and efficiency of human resources become major concerns there are concerns with both the macro environment that influences human resources (including labour markets and education systems) and with the internal environment, where past practices need to be reviewed and changed in order to align and/or integrate HRD practices with strategic aims.

As well as this link of HRD to traditional strategic management, HRD can also be in the forefront of developments in thinking about strategic management itself. This is because the trend is away from the use of wholly quantitative models and planning techniques in strategic thinking towards attempts to draw on human creativity and learning as an organisation makes and pursues its strategy. That means a greater concern with 'vision' rather than planning, and with mobilising human resources to achieve that vision. Strategy is not just a preconceived and detailed set of steps for achieving a coherent package of concrete goals within a given timescale. Rather it is the outcome of a process of decision-making and resource allocation that is embarked on in pursuit of a vision. This is the changing model of strategy into which thinking about strategic HRD needs to fit.

The Strategic Context: Three Options

Finkelstein et al. (2006) offer a way of organising and advancing thinking about how HRD can be a feature of strategy development and practice for the whole enterprise. There are three kinds of specific framework for thinking about the possible nature and evidence for a role for HRD in the strategic context here. First is the modelling of special kinds of process and products associated with strategy (see Perspective 13.1). These identify aspects of strategy as a series of possible processes and products constituting SHRD.

Perspective 13.1: Strategy Processes and Products

Process	Product
Strategic Thinking	Vision
Strategic Definition	Value Proposition
Strategic Alignment	Business Model
Strategic Enactment	Projects and Programs

Source: Based on Harvey et al. (2006).

If HRD were to be part of strategy, it would need to contribute to vision, value propositions, business models and key projects and programmes. When a case is described and these connections are present, then there is meaning to the concept of SHRD. A concern here about the reality of SHRD would be that such visions and value propositions were superficial rhetoric rather than real commitments enacted in practice.

Alternatively in a broader analysis of developments in the strategy literature, an evolution of five distinct eras, the five C's (see Perspective 13.2) can be described. SHRD may be glimpsed in each of these eras, with the contemporary concern on change and learning clearly making HRD a very prominent feature of strategy.

Perspective 13.2: The five C's Typology

Changing   Learning, Culture, Complexity
(Argyris, Schein, Eisenhardt)

Constructing Networks, Capabilities, Reputation
(Kay, Hamel, Prahalad)

Competing   Positioning, Innovation, Technology
(Schendel, Rumelt, Porter)

Coordinating Scale & Scope, Managing, Globalizing
(Chandler, Mintzberg)

Controlling   Planning, modelling, forecasting
(Ansoff, Beck, Drucker)

Source: Harvey (2006).

The different eras affecting definitions and practices in strategy each have their major thinkers and themes, with HRD coming more to the heart of this over time. If change is at the heart of strategy, then so must HRD be.

Finally, SHRD may be thought of as a cluster of activities which fit and enable the cost, innovation, execution, relationship, channel and brand concerns organisations have. This model was previously used in the discussion of e-learning, and is also appropriate here to, respectively, optimise value chain, exploit R&D, refine business processes, leverage networks and alliances, develop market access and manage customers (see Perspective 13.3). These cluster of activities would include the following:

- Improve work practices;
- Create protected space;
- Expand and deepen capabilities;
- Inspire trust and loyalty;
- Enhance knowledge and communication;
- Promote ideas and identity framed.

Perspective 13.3: Strategy and a Socio-technical Framing

Organisational social-system					
Improve work practices	Create protected space	Expand and deepen capabilities	Inspire trust and loyalty	Enhance knowledge and communication	Promote ideas and identity
Cost	Innovate	Execution	Relationships	Channels	Brand
Optimise value chain	Exploit R&D	Refine business processes	Leverage networks and alliances	Develop market access	Active customer managing
Technical-system					

Source: Harvey et al. (2006).

The key dimensions in this, as far as HRD is then concerned is providing the interfaces between the social and the technical systems taking into account:

HRD and cost;

HRD and innovation;

HRD and execution

HRD and relationships;

HRD and communication channels;

HRD and brand.

SHRD may exist then in many forms reflecting differing organisational value propositions (see Perspective 13.4), ranging from cost leaders (the cheapest) offering the basic functional product/service through to the organisations operating with premium prices offering the most prestigious products and services. This framing of SHRD goes beyond special and particular kinds of organisational circumstance, and offers the entire range of organisational circumstances for consideration.

Organisations are concerned to generate a value proposition, and they can consider six areas for doing that. In each area they can seek to locate themselves on a scale. At one end are organisations whose value proposition is that they are price leaders (cheap), basic, with acceptable quality, providing minimal support, restricted availability and with a functional reputation. At the other end of the spectrum are those organisations whose value proposition is premium pricing, original features, excellent quality, comprehensive support, universal availability and prestigious reputation. Any industry sector will contain

Perspective 13.4: Generating a Value Proposition as a Context for SHRD

Price	Features	Quality	Support	Availability	Reputation
Premium	Original	Excellent	Comprehensive	Universal	Prestigious
Premium/ Competitive	Original/ Customised	Excellent/ Average	Comprehensive/ Standard	Universal/ Selective	Prestigious/ Respected
Competitive	Customised	Average	Standard	Selective	Respected
Competitive/ Leader	Customised/ Basic	Average/ Acceptable	Standard/ Minimal	Selective/ Restricted	Respected/ Functional
Leader	Basic	Acceptable	Minimal	Restricted	Functional

in organisations with value propositions across this spectrum. For the purposes of considering SHRD the implication is that HRD would support and in some way mirror the value propositions; being a contributor to it and being consistent with it. So one organisation's Strategic HRD would be premium priced, excellent and prestigious; another organisation's strategic HRD might be cheap, acceptable and functional. Management development in a major financial services company might fit the former, and customer service posts in a fast-food outlet might fit the latter. Each in their own way is Strategic HRD.

Where these connections are of interest and managed SHRD can be meaningfully said to exist. The presence of SHRD is not simply the existence of an explicit and special articulation of explicit mission around and including HRD, nor just in an organisation concerned with 'changing'. HRD is an integral part of all organisations work around these issues and developing, managing and keeping optimal both the 'hard', the technical system, and the 'soft', the social system.

Issues and Themes

So how strategy is defined shapes what Strategic HRD can mean. It may be defined in terms of the strategy process, or in respect of an era or activities associated with constructing an organisational social system to fit with technological system and value proposition of the organisation.

An empirical link between HRD and organisational success, the quantitative key to SHRD, has yet to be demonstrated consistently and rigorously in any meaningful sense. Whether it is invoking HRD in strategising, or partnering it with change or seeing its connections to value propositions there is limited evidence. The reality remains one where HRD and the initiatives associated with it can be seen as an additional cost that is vulnerable to being cut, whether that be by reducing HRD staff numbers (downsizing), by reducing the resourcing of certain critical activities (such as appraisal systems), or by trimming specific budgets (for example, training).

An underlying problem for the case for SHRD is the extent to which the visions that ostensibly frame the long term for HRD can be criticised as culturally bound, managerial 'fictions'. The knowledge bases and disciplines that underpin research and practice in employment and SHRD are just not secure enough to influence strategising substantially. They are not influential in providing a framework for thinking about the future, and consequently for including concerns about HRD at the elite level of strategising. It is restricted to informing the world-views of practitioners and researchers defining and exploring human resource problems and solutions.

The tensions among the demands of short-term problems when seeking to 'play the longer game' provide major challenges. Reducing the workforce, controlling pay and rewards for performance, and working a reduced workforce harder in a tough climate does not sit easily with longer term visions of the benefits of 'win–win' HRD. The erosion and decay of HRD commitments because of organisational change is an issue. The cultural dimension is resistant to this erosion. The role of culture, beliefs and values in shaping performance remains important for individuals, organisations and societies in the field of SHRD is important: it ranges from individual expectations of a career, through the management of corporate cultures, to different national or regional versions of capitalism.

An underlying problem for the universal approach is that SHRD is shaped by the structural dimensions of employment and people management, leading some organisations to be much more concerned with HRD than others. These differences reflect the nature of the employment environment and work organisation in different sectors and kinds of situation. The employment environment is traditionally analysed in terms of the economic, social, legal and political contexts. Changes and developments in these contexts will also affect interests in HRD. Changes and developments in organisations will affect HRD. Rational and empirical analysis of the employment environment and of work organisations provides a necessary perspective on developments in HRD.

Further, the innovations made possible by information technologies and the social changes accompanying the embracing of diversity, for example, can be seen to alter the whole picture. What was ideal and desirable in employment, what value propositions entail in terms of interface and interaction, has altered fundamentally; and this raises questions about the meaning of SHRD. It is important to distinguish three different units of analysis when reviewing this and the universal case for SHRD. The first unit of analysis is the individual organisation; the second is the broader environment, usually taken to be the nation-state; and the third is relevant supranational contexts, such as the European Union (EU).

If we look at the organisation as a unit of analysis, then the universal case for SHRD is based on the structure of work and people's experience of standard or typical employment in traditional organisations. This applies to both the private and public sectors at a general level. It assumes management to be a mix of classical command and control functions, integrated with human relations activities and processes. In practice, SHRD centres on a number of discrete employment systems. These would include human resource planning systems, appraisal systems, reward systems, and systematic training and development.

If we consider the environment, the universal case is informed by traditional approaches to the employment relationship within capitalism, albeit possibly in different forms of capitalism. Freedom to contract in labour markets meant that the contract of employment between an employer and employee binds them in a standard employment relationship. People management themes and concerns reflect issues about management as a controlling function in production systems and bureaucracies. The concept of labour was analysed as a factor of production – as a commodity subject to market relationships. The role of large organisations within a national framework was predominant: both enterprises concerned with profitability, and organisations providing public services.

Combining the units of analysis – the organisation and the environment – a standard approach to good employment was identifiable. As part of this in HRD, in enterprises and organisations there was a status quo, an equilibrium established upon key economic and social realities and standard organisational practices. Crucially, it meant a relatively secure full-time job for life, with fair wages, with full employment an accepted aim of HRD.

Such a universal case is no longer relevant: the standard enterprise or organisation and the standard workforce employed in standard employment relationships have gone. Internally the search for efficiency and effectiveness, getting more from less, has meant change in jobs, flattened hierarchies and transformed organisations. Further flexibilities in employment practices, and changes in workforce composition, have also altered the technological and social interfaces considerably. Job security and full-time work for the many are gone, or at least threatened. More generally, the decline of old sectors and the growth of new sectors have transformed the basic infrastructure of work. Information and knowledge are now fundamental to that infrastructure.

The structural certainties have changed at the level of the organisation and at the level of the nation-state. An old equilibrium has passed, but a new stable system is yet to be determined: hence the continuing experimentation with employment and career flexibilities inside organisations and the political debates around levels of skill, wages and employee representation. As this takes shape, there are many who emphasise that HRD cannot be seen in isolation, but must be located within the power relations that affect organisations as a whole.

Employment Relations and SHRD

The employment relationship between employee and employer. In some cases this developed around a system of industrial relations where collective bargaining provided the main framework, whereas in other cases a more direct relation between managers and employees was sought. The other set of beliefs was about relationships within employment: this can be described as the psychological contract – the unwritten expectations that individuals and organisations bring with them into their employment.

It is also argued that the nature of psychological contracts is changing. Attitudes to work and working life, to what is desirable and possible, have changed. At one level this is reflected in surveys that chart the transformation of traditional frameworks such as the 'British industrial relations' system. It is also reflected in the growth of approaches to employment, where commitment rather than compliance is argued to be the primary framework. There is a degree of harmonisation within organisations, with old values being, apparently, transcended. Employee attitudes appear to have changed as well. It is not possible to identify a single direction of change. There seems to be a polarisation. On the one hand, there are groups who expect more from work. Work provides a 'community' within which creativity and personal growth is possible. On the other hand, there is a group whose attitude to work is entirely instrumental, and where the notion of job satisfaction is not entertained at all. There is, of course, a further group who are, in effect, excluded from the experience of work at all: the socially excluded, including single parents, the long-term unemployed, disabled people and ethnic minorities.

Knowledge Management

Ours is still an era in which organisations are seeking to become more effective in knowledge management (KM). The idea of KM has come to provide a major perspective on understanding organisations as a whole, and on HRD and learning in the workplace. The rapid rise of 'knowledge management' era has been ascribed to six causes:

(1) Wealth. This is demonstrably generated from knowledge and intangible assets. An often-cited example is Microsoft, which has been assessed as having 94 per cent of its market value based on intangible, knowledge-related assets.

(2) The rediscovery of people as the locus of organisational knowledge, rather than written guidelines and procedure manuals. As organisations downsized and made people redundant, they soon found they had to re-hire them as consultants, because they still needed their knowledge and know-how in addition to the guidelines and manuals.

(3) Accelerating change. This requires increased attention to be paid to continuous learning: the need to create, absorb and assimilate new knowledge, skills and behaviours rather than rely on existing knowledge.

(4) Recognition of innovation as the key to competitiveness, as innovation depends on managing knowledge. This involves a high degree of risk, both

in managing current knowledge to innovate and in seeking the new, the untypical and the creative.

(5) The importance of cross-boundary transactions. There is a need to recognise the dependence on crossing internal organisational boundaries and on drawing upon external sources, to have more complete and full knowledge. Yet doing either of these things represents a real challenge; the walls between units, organisations and potential partners can be quite a barrier to knowledge transfer.

(6) The limits of technology. The potential of information technologies to make organisations and their businesses more effective and efficient in their basic tasks has been a major hope. Alongside the increasing use of information technologies came the additional hope that more transparent and easier access to information might have pay-offs in other ways. For example, it could enable more knowledgeable management, as all kinds of information could be easily accessed and shared. Indeed for some this is exactly what KM means. But it is knowledge, not information, that is the issue. And much knowledge in organisations is hard to codify, since know-how and know-who are often tacit. There are no truly effective software or hardware solutions to tapping these kinds of knowledge.

KM in firms or sectors that are part of the knowledge economy is focused in practice on a set o concerns (see Practice 13.1).

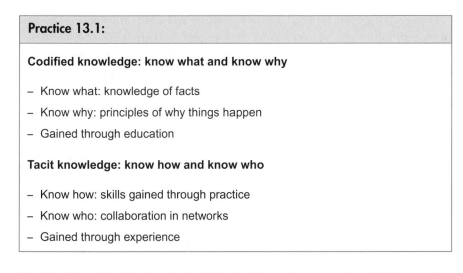

Practice 13.1:

Codified knowledge: know what and know why

– Know what: knowledge of facts
– Know why: principles of why things happen
– Gained through education

Tacit knowledge: know how and know who

– Know how: skills gained through practice
– Know who: collaboration in networks
– Gained through experience

The significant implication is that the key to greater current and future performance is how well knowledge workers can create and sustain knowledge-based organisations that are capable of competing in a knowledge economy (Foray 2004). One of the principal means for creating and transferring such knowledge in organisations is through developing Communities of Practice (CoP). CoP (see Practice 13.2) are informal, self-organising networks of people dedicated to

Practice 13.2: Kinds of Groups Compared With CoPs				
	Purpose	**Members**	**Cohesion**	**Lifecycle**
Operational team	Work	Assigned	Common task	Permanent
Project team	Task	Roles in project	Project	Project goal attained
Informal Network	Get and give help	Friendship basis	Personal need	Evolves with career
CoP	Create and exchange learning	Self select	Identify with learning issue	Till learning cycle is completed

sharing knowledge in an area of common interest or expertise. The advantages and attractions of nurturing such learning groups are illustrated by the introductory case. These advantages and attractions are about CoP as a complementary method of providing HRD functions. CoPs

Thus a strategic task for HRD is how to capture and codify the evolving knowledge, capabilities and behaviours as they engage in daily work and learn (see Practice 13.2). This is in addition to transferring knowledge to employees so they can perform effectively. CoP can be seen to function to attain this newer HRD role, and to do so at various maturity levels. These will range from groups which are informal gatherings where people exchange knowledge and learn through telling stories to managed and directed groups under a style of leadership which nurtures CoP in the whole organisation.

In the more mature versions the issue is to capture and codify new knowledge from employee learning, the process has to be managed. Phase 1 of this process is to acknowledge and recognise the existence of these, often informal, CoP, in which new knowledge, capabilities and behaviours are often produced and shared by employees as they work. Phase 2 is to capture or map such knowledge, capabilities or behaviours. In phase 3, mapped knowledge, capabilities or behaviours have to be made available to others who may need it, in the organisation and beyond. The end of this process might signify the end of the CoP. But as new issues and experiences are encountered, new off-map problems arise, once again requiring a CoP.

The kind of learning – learning from each other through sharing each other's experience – is universal, and occurs naturally in all kinds of organisation, group and job. The issue for managers is to convert this CoP learning into a structured form that fleshes out and expands the knowledge map so that all employees can perform effectively. Advocates of knowledge management suggest that the main job of senior managers in modern organisations can be reconceived as being better able to capture and use knowledge from CoP.

Although such a view of management may be desirable and attainable, there is no doubt that the implications of supporting KM and nurturing CoP radically alter the way that the function of HRD is seen. HRD is no longer to be thought about as a process whereby trainers or managers remove deficits in knowledge or skill; rather it is about managing and enhancing the naturally growing knowledge assets and skills emerging in practice. This increases the intellectual capital of the workforce. The challenge is that organisations can be environments which can either help or obstruct sharing knowledge and learning (Ipe 2003). What appears to matter is recognising how knowledge sharing arises in contexts where it is

- Mediated: by stakeholders with different perceptions and understanding of organisational goals;

- Situated: in concrete interpersonal and group, power-based relations;

- Contested: among the common and different interests which exist in any organisation.

Co-operation and knowledge work is more feasible when participants have choosen their community based on reciprocal attractiveness, passion, involvement and identification with each other's expertise.

Activity: Think about an organisation you are familiar with. To what extent are there 'communities of practice' among employees that provide for the creation and dissemination of learning from experience, leading to new or different ways of working? Are there equivalents to the 'reps' breakfast' where employees share learning with each other, but not necessarily with managers?

Three Currents of Thinking in KM

As models of KM develop, with concerns about how to develop and manage CoP, there have been three important currents of thinking. These are as follows:

(1) The information systems perspective, which emphasises the potential of information management tools for the capture, storage and retrieval of knowledge for CoP;

(2) The organisational learning perspective, which emphasises the way CoP in organisations are embedded in and influenced by the internal organisational structure and culture;

(3) The intellectual capital (IC) perspective, which emphasises the value of IC and the worth of knowledge as embodied in patents and strategic core competences, and raises issues about ownership and control of such assets.

The Information Systems Perspective

For some people the Information Systems (IS) perspective on capturing and cod-ifying knowledge in organisations is the most important. One model suggests a tripartite structure for HRD: instruction through training, performance support through information provisions and KM. KM can be seen as the pinnacle of a hierarchy of IS and performance management concerns, up to being concerned with creating what some term the intelligent enterprise.

Resources such as job aids have always existed, and IS technologies enable an online central repository that people can access by downloading manuals and guidelines. CoP could use these to input their knowledge, and operate more effectively, using access to such information-sharing systems. In addition, activ-ities such as company suggestion schemes have always existed, seeking to tap workforce knowledge; what IS enables is more extensive and faster sharing of such knowledge. Finally, in one sense enterprise intelligence is a question of integrated enterprise resource planning (ERP) systems, where IS-enabled systems monitor and analyse the performance of all aspects of the organisation's func-tioning – including people. In another sense it is more that the organisation has the equivalent of a 'brain', a master governor in control of the whole. The exper-tise of people is embedded in this system, and it is possible to access ideas and analysis relevant to any issue. Thus IS-based KM issues and concerns in perfor-mance support range from enabling better access to existing and already-mapped knowledge in the organisation to the wider sharing of newly captured knowl-edge and the attainment of enterprise-wide intelligence, enabling innovation and rapid change.

Organisational Learning

The essence of organisational learning (OL) is that the complex interactions that are involved in organisations require continuous learning and re-learning for the system to survive. Learning is not a discrete function, restricted to trainers providing training. It is more like the brain of organisation as an organism, essen-tial for continuing existence and performance. OL has often been a forum for applying systems thinking to HRD, for exploring the complexes of connections and feedback loops in organisations that are believed to govern and regulate human behaviour. Behaviour and performance cannot be magically improved by providing some training courses. Instead, we need to explore the whole sys-tem and the factors inhibiting or enabling the kinds and level of behaviour and performance desired. Interventions involving HRD, working on cognitive capac-ities, capabilities and behaviours, cannot be properly conceived or implemented without analysing these factors. Therefore a systemic rather than a systematic approach to KM and learning is appropriate.

This leads, undeniably, to a different, more elaborate and more sophisticated way of thinking about HRD and KM. It is also potentially confusing. We have got used to thinking about HRD at work as a systematic process of identifying needs, planning, delivering and evaluating, and the tasks seem to make sense: run training courses, provide on-job coaching or design multimedia software packages. But the OL perspective plays down such activities and replaces them with another, more difficult-to-grasp set of concepts and activities: systems thinking, action research into problem-solving, trying to map and tap the knowledge of the workforce and developing CoP. OL analysis often runs into problems because it vacillates between two perspectives. On the one hand, it seeks a substitute recipe of prescriptions – a new toolkit – to help manage systemic learning; on the other, it denies that these are useful, and says that OL is more of a way of thinking in holistic and systemic terms about organisations. From our perspective, however, OL perspectives see learning as an integral part of the organisation going about its day-to-day business.

An interpretation 'industry' has grown up around the various models proposed for OL. KM has attracted experts in management from many academic disciplines, including psychology, sociology, economics, anthropology, political sciences and history, and it now provides an interdisciplinary focus for them similar to the way that strategy did during the 1980s and 1990s. This is also true for the newer fields of study (we cannot really call them disciplines) in management – information management, strategic management, change management, HRM and innovation management – that are all interested in OL. In this sense OL provides an altogether new way of thinking about management and organisations. The problem for practitioners is that these disciplines all have their own way of looking at OL, whereas what is needed is a truly transdisciplinary perspective.

Currently we have many models, and no one has yet claimed to have identified the perfect 'learning organisation'. There are no templates equivalent, for example, to the Ford motor car production line, which exemplified a certain kind of management and organisation practice. Proponents of OL suggest that they can see glimpses, or suggest practices and tools. One concern, though, is that the first-generation prescriptions have not helped achieve the large-scale reform of organisational structures and cultures explicitly embraced by OL proponents. New methods have to be developed, beyond conventional HRD methods such as team-building and personal development. Such 'frontier' issues represent a continuation of the constituent fields that have led to OL as a construct.

OL can also be seen to have emerged from classic concerns in three areas of concern to management:

(1) Identifying and dealing with problems while they are still small;

(2) Drawing on internal resources and tacit knowledge;

(3) Using systems thinking about snowballing and balancing feedback loops.

Identifying and dealing with minor, fragmented problems is the stuff of everyday organisational life. It happens all the time in healthy organisations, so that people hardly even notice it. From afar the organisation appears a seamlessly efficient operation. Close up, the organisation is seen to be a hive of activity around large numbers of errors being noticed and dealt with.

Identifying and remedying small problems at source as a strategy for ensuring organisational effectiveness has been addressed primarily by the quality movement for over the last 50 years. One way of summing up this movement is to say that it represents a desire to identify and eliminate all errors that can be eliminated, by continuously improving systems and processes. The oft-acknowledged barriers to the detection of small problems are often related to human communication failures:

- Managers claiming 'but nobody told us there was a problem';
- Employees claiming that 'nobody listened to us when we told them';
- Information available and communicated, but overshadowed by other concerns that took precedence.

Second, there is the question of making the best use of internal resources – the intelligence and knowledge of people inside the organisation. The questioning of the effectiveness of professionals in modern organisations remains a contentious issue. Professionals are meant to be the solution: developing and using experts with the knowledge and skill to ensure organisational effectiveness in all kinds of areas, highly educated and specialist people. Whether it is doctors in hospitals, engineers in manufacturing or personnel managers in work organisations these are often perceived as being less effective than they could be. One source of this ineffectiveness was thought to lie in the education of professionals, suggesting a need for reform of this education. However, researchers argued that it was the climate within organisations themselves that hindered the use of professionals. There was little point in simply reforming education for professionals; organisations needed to appreciate the ways in which they presented barriers to professionals using their knowledge and capabilities.

It was in this context that the researchers Argyris and Schon (1974) outlined and modelled two types of organisational learning. The first was what they called single-loop learning: this occurs when an organisation detects errors in performance that will compromise the achievement of its preset goals. For example, productivity may be too low to meet an important order on time. The organisation will have to adopt a new strategy to meet its goals: for example, organising extra shifts or increasing productivity. Identifying and correcting these kinds of error is single-loop learning. The organisation is acting, by analogy, like a heating system governed by a thermostat: as long as it acts to maintain the temperature set by the thermostat it is said to be single-loop learning. Many performance management systems are elaborations of this kind of learning: to set goals, to get feedback on them and then to take corrective action to attain those goals.

But there is also another form of learning. This occurs when an organisation can detect errors in its overall master goals, and respond to those. Argyris and Schon called this double-loop learning. Extending the thermostat analogy, it is the ability to determine that the preset temperature is wrong: that it is no good trying to run the system to meet that set temperature, as the thermostat setting – the goal itself – must be changed. If the environment is too hot or too cold, it needs a new temperature to be set. Following the productivity example, there is little point in increasing the productive capacity if either the market is declining or a new market is emerging in other products. The overall goal must be reviewed: new product development must be introduced. Double-loop learning does not supersede single-loop learning; it complements it.

According to Argyris and Schon, the problem with many organisations, and the problem for professionals in organisations (see Perspective 13.5), is that they are not at all good at this double-loop learning. They find it hard to question the appropriateness of the governing variables they have adopted – their key goals and assumptions. Hence they continue adopting new strategies to try to reach preset goals when what they actually need do is question the goals and assumptions themselves. Argyris and Schon went on to describe and analyse the ways in which organisations could be seen to be inhibiting professionals' contributions

Perspective 13.5: Organisational Learning Climate Issues

	The Ideal	But...	So the problem is	The solution is
When defining goals...	Collaborate with each other to set goals; review collectively as well.	Act unilaterally, set own goals, or only with own group/peers; have own goals attained rather than others.	No commitment among various parties to shared goals. People are used to acting unilaterally.	Build trust; maximise acting with commitment to common goals
When problem solving...	Mutual problem-solving and adopt a win-win outlook;	People adopt a maximise winning and minimise losing position in the course of problem solving	Playing a blame game; to assure winning and avoid 'losing'	Be able to accept/explore failure without 'blame' cultures

Perspective 13.5: (Continued)				
The culture should be	Everyone should speak up and be open	People want to minimise provoking others, eliciting negative feelings	Protect yourself by keeping quiet,; do not take the risk of aggravating others	A climate aware of and discuss feelings, as well as ideas
Conflict should be handled ...	Rationally; people in formal roles should interact rationally	People act politically; the workplace is political	Behind closed door 'politics', is seen to be necessary to succeed	Get 'politics' out from behind closed doors

Source: Based on Argyris and Schon (1974).

to double-loop learning. They concluded that professionals' behaviour in organisations is characterised by what they called espoused theories and theories in action. An espoused theory is the explicit reason that people give to describe their behaviour; a theory in action is a description of the beliefs that underpin their behaviour, regardless of the 'espoused' reasons that they give. Theories in action reflect what people really think rather than what they say they think.

The net effect is that, without careful management, professionals and others behave competitively and are mistrustful. Those supposed to ensure learning and success are complicit in obstructing it. Either they are stuck in cycles of compliance with goals they do not believe in, or they find themselves pursuing goals that they know are no longer right but which they seem powerless to change. Even though people may be aware of impending disaster, they cannot use their internal resources to break free and stop it happening. Individual awareness of these dynamics, and professional development to provide individuals who can manage to support double-loop learning – people who can confront its challenges with what would now be called 'emotional intelligence' – is needed. This is the key to creating an environment that supports OL.

Finally, there is systems thinking. Systems thinking investigates the principles common to all complex entities by developing abstract models that can be used to describe them. Systems analysts emphasise that systems are open to, and interact with, their environments. Because of this they can acquire qualitatively new properties through emergence, resulting in continual learning. Rather than reduce an entity, for example the human body, to the properties of its parts or elements, the organs and cells, systems thinking focuses on the arrangement of and relations between the parts that connect them into a whole. The body works as more than the sum of its parts under the influence of active learning. Socio-technical work organisation can be explored as this kind of system.

Being a system implies that something other than simple cause-and-effect relations is involved. Rather than A affecting B, there is the possibility that B may also be affecting A. From the mutual interaction of the parts of a system, there arise characteristics that cannot be derived from any of the individual parts or one-way causal relations between them. The phenomenon is synergy: the whole is greater than the sum of its parts. We can characterise systems as either closed or open. A closed system is one that does not need to interact with its environment to maintain its existence. Examples of such systems are atoms and molecules. Mechanical systems are closed systems. Open systems are organic, and must interact with their environment in order to maintain their existence. People are open systems: they must interact with their environment in order to take in food and water. An open system will interact with its environment in a growing or in a balancing fashion.

Two types of loop occur within systems: they either grow or are balanced. First are reinforcing loops. In a reinforcing loop the interactions are such that each action adds to the other: what happens to A adds to B and what happens to B adds to A. Any situation where action produces a result that promotes more of the same action is representative of a reinforcing loop. The 'snowballing' metaphor represents the reinforcing loop. Typical examples of 'snowballing' reinforcing loops are population growth or decline, uncontrolled nuclear reactions, or panic runs on banks in times of financial crisis. It is, for example, what happens in a savings account. The principal in the savings account interacts with an interest rate and the principal is increased. This reinforcing action happens regularly, depending on the period over which the institution computes the interest.

The other form of loop is the balancing loop. This is one in which an action attempts to bring two things to 'agreement': what happens with A reduces B, and what reduces B also reduces A. As the system state gets closer to the desired state, the gap gets smaller and smaller between A and B, so the action adds less and less. Once the action has moved the current state to a point where it equals the desired state, the gap is zero and there is no more action. A typical example of a balancing loop is closing a gap in space by making a journey from location A to location B. The desired state is to be at B, the actual state is at A: the further from A, and hence the closer to B, the less action is required to get to the desired state. Another example is developing from being incapable (A) by trial and error (action) to become competent (B). The more that the action (trial and error) reduces A, the more it also reduces what is needed to get to B.

These effects of actions, leading to snowballing or balancing loops, can combine in many ways that result in all manner of typical situations in daily and organisational life: the escalations that run out of control, or the reaching of states of satisfying equilibrium. Sometimes snowballing is wanted; sometimes it is not. Sometimes equilibrium is wanted; sometimes it is a form of paralysis.

The point of this systems perspective is that it opens up insights into the pitfalls of obvious solutions for apparent problems. Obvious solutions are those that have a short-term effect, and may improve situations temporarily, but make the situation worse in the long run: for example, safeguarding crops against insect infestations by using insecticides, dealing with crime by greater levels of imprisonment or encouraging economic growth by investing in the 'new' economy rather than the old. These obvious solutions seem to work. But these actions occur within systems, with snowballing loops. Using insecticides causes pollution, which makes the land useless, or balancing loops as insects evolve immunity. Prisons become schools for criminals, and fail to rehabilitate. Investment in the new economy peaks, the bubble bursts, and subsequently slows general economic growth or causes a recession. Where obvious solutions are seen to fail, we must seek to understand the apparent 'system' in operation, which has not been changed – or may even have been made worse – by the intervention.

This is the approach of Senge (1990). Situations in organisations exist where systems are in balance, are stable and persist, or they are reinforcing growth and escalation, or they set limits to success and can cause decline. Senge sees organisations as needing to develop a networking culture in which everyone engages in dialogue in order to question their own assumptions and to expose and deal with these kinds of systems problem.

Systems thinking is synthetic, expansionist and non-linear. It is synthetic and expansionist in defining problems in terms of clusters of variables, and the interactions within and between them, and not in terms of discrete variables. It is non-linear in envisaging both cyclical and mutual interactions among the elements of a system – the inputs, processes, outputs and feedback elements. The net effect is to argue that to solve problems we need a way to understand interconnections and interdependence, producing a set of interacting solution ideas simultaneously. In terms of management and organisation, HRD and performance, the key conclusions are the following:

- Human systems are 'open' systems: they involve internal and external relations with regulation. People and organisations can always be learning.
- There are both wholes and constituents: individuals, groups, organisations, societies. Trying to change one part may not work if the other parts of the system are not in favour.
- There are always clusters of problems.
- Real problems are ill-structured and ill-defined; they are 'wicked'.
- The subjects must be included in any study of a system.
- There can only ever be tentative, incomplete solutions.
- Ethical issues matter in redesigning systems.

There are many challenges with using systems thinking to explore organisations. If problems cannot be reduced so that it is possible to solve them piece by piece in order to remedy larger problems, then all problems are probably beyond the capabilities of one group of specialists to grasp. This is because, to understand the whole, it is necessary to understand every part – in other words, to possess some kind of transdisciplinary awareness. If there is a need to understand interconnections and interdependence, and produce interacting solution ideas simultaneously, then every enquiry is about systems change. Any enquiry is then potentially 'boundless'. In the context of what is practicable and pragmatic in management and organisation, there is a preference for analytical, reductionist and linear causal thinking. That is inconsistent with systemic approaches to management.

Intellectual Capital and Strategic HRD

The connections between KM, CoP and HRD have become associated also with the concept of Intellectual Capital (IC). This implies the idea of measurement using the infamous and cliched 'bottom line'. Capital is thought of as money or other assets owned by a person or organisation that can be used to control economic activity. IC represents the development, possession, ownership, control and use of knowledge by people or organisations as a part of that economic activity for profit. This means that knowledge, as well as natural resources or technological advances, provides a basis for competing, and indeed for wealth creation and prosperity as a whole. Knowledge has always been an integral part of capitalism, and an intellectual ferment of research and development of market, products and services is a feature of its dynamism. But the concept of IC suggests something beyond that. Part of this idea was captured with the dot-com boom (and bust): investors believed that some IC, based on Internet-based business, was all that was needed, as there had to be potential for growth with the uptake of Internet services. In most cases this was incorrect, and substantial losses were incurred as many dot-com businesses failed to generate any money at all, never mind profit. However, there were developments, such as the human genome project, that posed questions about IC. Two groups raced to map the human genome. One sought to benefit mankind as a whole; the other sought to map the genome in order to control, and have the right to control, the use of that knowledge. The medical implications of knowledge of the human genome were immense, and the issue of IC was at the heart of the story.

So IC was not just a hyped element of the rise of the Internet. It represents a real concern, and provides both new accounting problems and challenges for organisations, as it is less tangible than other forms of capital. As a construct, IC challenges the dominant, conventional, financial and legal modes of thinking about value in organisations and societies, and about economic activity as a whole. This opens up many debates, but what matters here is that people and organisations with IC have a market price: they can supply what is in demand. As owners of the means of knowledge rather than the means of production they can also 'walk out of the door' with their IC at any time. This problem applies to regions and nations if their knowledge workers leave to take up jobs elsewhere. There are also problems with renewing IC if people or organisations are prone to 'walking away', causing investors to be wary of investing in companies where the assets are invisible and highly mobile.

The evolution of IC ideas and practices presents challenges for organisations. These centre on the classic issues for organisations and HRD: loose–tight control and empowerment, communication, and creativity. There are also wider social issues. The prospect is often raised of creating a new underclass of people without capacities in or involvement with IC. There would be a boom in employment for highly knowledgeable and skilled people and organisations, who will be dispersed and mobile throughout the globe, but further unemployment and urban decay for those who are excluded from a share in IC.

How far does an era of wealth creation depend on IC and the management of tacit knowledge? This is questioned by those who point out that employment growth is often in low-skilled personal services, not high-tech and high-knowledge jobs and industries. Some believe that IC is relevant only to a minority of organisations, whereas others see it as universally relevant. In some sectors – software development and biotechnology, for example – the creation, ownership and protection of intellectual assets are central. Yet even these sectors depend on conventional physical infrastructures and explicit knowledge as much as on the tacit knowledge of their employees.

An application of IC as an element of general and strategic management is provided by Leonard-Barton (1995). Her model is broad in its concerns, but quite straightforward. She sees knowledge as the core capability of organisations. This capability is found in four forms: it is embedded in physical systems and technologies, in managerial systems, in skills and in values.

(1) Core capability in the form of knowledge may be in a physical form. It may be, for example, in a design a company has protected by patent. This is knowledge you can see and touch; it is tangible.

(2) Knowledge may be embodied in managerial systems. It can be embodied in learned ways of doing things most effectively.

(3) Knowledge may be embodied in the explicit skills bases and tacit knowledge of employees: the individual competences that have been brought into the organisation or developed within it through experience.

(4) Finally, knowledge is to be found embodied as values. These may be explicit 'big' values of the company: for example the values of a bureaucracy, which emphasise following all guidelines rigorously, or the values of an entrepreneurial firm that emphasises a bias for action. It may also be found in what Leonard-Barton terms 'little values', to do with the norms of behaviour in the workplace, or what others would call organisational culture.

Leonard-Barton's concern is to analyse how knowledge embodied in these forms can be the foundation for knowledge-inhibiting activities. Knowledge-inhibiting activities are experienced as limited problem-solving, an inability to innovate effectively, limited experimentation and the 'screening out' of new knowledge in organisations. These problems, in Leonard-Barton's terms, are caused by an over-commitment to the current knowledge base and recipe as embodied in existing physical forms, management systems, skills and values. The practical focus is on overcoming old recipes, which act as inhibitors of experimentation, problem-solving, innovation and the inclusion of new knowledge.

The purpose of this analysis of knowledge management is to emphasise that inherited knowledge is everywhere in an organisation, embodied in many different forms. To change and renew knowledge may require new physical systems, new management systems, new skills or new values. It is necessary then to understand how to ensure and enhance changes in physical systems, management systems, skills and values in order to manage knowledge effectively and maintain a core capability. Values as a form of embodied and fixed knowledge provide the form that is most difficult to change and develop. The evolution of new physical forms, products or services, facilities or technologies is inherent in market capitalism as companies seek success. The need for management systems to evolve over time is something that most organisations are well aware. The need for new skills is also a touchstone of current thinking. The problem is often with the issue of new values.

The Evolution of HRD in the KM Context

It seems straightforward enough to look at the KM and implications for HRD – to learn from and with employees rather than ignore or suppress their learning. If it was this simple, then KM and CoP would imply little more than a reinvention of the kinds of activity associated with old-style staff suggestion schemes. But, as this chapter has shown, there are various dimensions and aspects of management that are challenged by the concepts of KM and CoP. In practice, managers have been criticised for being too concerned with re-engineering processes to increase efficiency using past management principles, rather than embracing the principles of working with KM and CoP to improve HRD. This continuing concern with imposing structures for HRD and work stifles knowledge capture and the HRD that emerges from that. On the other hand, for organisations, there are problems with defining managers' roles in terms of the principles consistent with encouraging KM and CoP, and having to cope with HRD constantly bubbling up and leading to changes in working practices in an almost chaotic way. In organisations there is a tension between general management and the principles of KM and CoP. It manifests itself as the dilemma of balancing the freedom of KM and CoP to learn and change while maintaining the necessary elements of structure that can fix and stabilise such learning so that it can be more widely circulated and implemented.

These tensions in capturing and codifying learning from employees partly reflect the argument that knowledge is power. Knowledge capture and codification cannot be analysed in a vacuum; they are pursued in circumstances where different groups, with different interests, contest the same ground. In the context of HRD at work those circumstances are about the structuring of, control of and returns from work.

The KM and CoP context has implications for HRD, with its purpose to have processes and structures to help people create new knowledge, share their understanding, and continuously improve themselves and the results of the enterprise. CoP and KM are not just different ways of framing HRD programmes or projects, but a different kind of management philosophy.

Questioning Strategic HRD

An increasingly diverse range of themes, concepts and initiatives occupy the minds of theorists and practitioners in people management. At a superficial level this is reflected in the new language of people management. It is a world of excellence, competence, learning organisations, empowerment and strategic HRD itself.

While HRD deals with a range of problems, there are two major traditions or ways of classifying them – the radical and prescriptivist approaches. The radical tradition has emphasised the potential antagonisms between employer and employee in modern industrial economies, and has defined the problem of human resources as embedded in processes of exploitation and alienation. Value judgements about society and the development of modern economies were central, and, depending on a commentator's precise position, this concern might be translated into anything from radical blueprints for workers' control of work to systems for ensuring harmony within the existing order of industry and organisations. The increasing de-skilling of labour and the use of technologies in production and service systems were major focuses of concern. Much humanistic thinking from North America in the 1950s and 1960s also worked through the problem of alienation by seeking to map motivation as a positive framework for engaging with people.

The prescriptivist tradition, by contrast, has adopted a purportedly 'neutral' view. Indeed, it often characterised itself as scientific, and defined the problems of HRD in terms of efficiency and effectiveness. The classical and administration theorists, as well as much thinking in industrial psychology, are historical examples of this. Training managers or personnel specialists in this 'neutral' science were the keynote of this approach. The emergence of professional HRD can be seen as one aspect of it. Contemporary approaches such as competence-based theories and systems continue to embody this 'scientific' stream of thought. The continuing arguments that range around the issue of promoting professionalism in HRM and management reflect the persistent instability of the cultural claims to neutrality, a scientific foundation and ethical rigour as the means of solving human resource problems.

HRD as an area of interdisciplinary study offers to strategising two areas of knowledge: economics and behavioural science. Economics encompasses both the micro and macro levels of analysis. This means that it can provide an analysis both of individual firms and of the broader reality in which those firms operate. The evolution of economic thought has encompassed people at the core of both levels, as a factor of production and as the policy field of employment. The role of HRD has therefore been a major concern, in both the pursuit of profit and the realisation of broader goals such as full employment. Questions of efficiency (and productivity) go hand in hand with questions of equity (full employment, wage levels, etc.) – though which of these aims gets top billing depends on political factors, as the recent development of the social dimension of the European Union demonstrates.

Behavioural science includes psychology, social psychology and sociology. The roots of many developments in HRD lie in the development of fields such as industrial psychology, and experiments such as those at Hawthorn in the 1930s, through to the ideas of humanistic psychologists in the 1960s, and the insights of cognitive psychologists in the 2000s. The different frameworks of scientific or classical management and human relations management in some ways reflect the economic–social split. For classical management, people were a factor of production, motivated by money in organisations whose primary goal was profit – the pure microeconomic picture. For human relations research, people were social beings, motivated by needs for belonging and identity within organisations. Organisations were conceived of as communities with dynamics and processes of their own, beyond the entirely rational behaviour of economic man.

In the contemporary language of HRD, the economic and behavioural science disciplines are associated with the resource side (economics and efficiency, profit, the organisation as an economic system) and the human side (behavioural science and people interacting in communities/groups). At one level these may meet in a useful dialogue, providing complementary insights into an area of common focus, for example increasing productivity and group performance based on social psychology. For some, however, the future of HRD relies on behavioural science providing answers for business problems.

There is an insularity from which HRD thinking suffers is its lack of connection with key contemporary thinkers. There is not enough cross-fertilisation and interdisciplinary activity in HRD as a whole. Knowledge about people is therefore a central issue. This is not simply about the development of better models of HRD and employment systems. It is about dealing with substantially different views of people at work, and it is about being better connected with management in practice and broader developments in knowledge more generally. Only when the knowledge base is healthy, innovative and challenging can there be an effective link between theory and practice.

In any of its forms the concept of SHRD is subject to questioning. Identifying and analysing the links between strategy, HRD and effectiveness has proven to be conceptually and practically complicated. It is equally difficult to prove that HRD was not 'strategic' in the past but is 'strategic' now. Meanings, evidence and value judgements are unclear. In general there appears to have been a shift from the equilibrium model of HRD to a concern with change and activity to redress perceived weaknesses with HRD in order to compete or improve service standards. Rather than direct attention to proof for any definite link between strategy and HRD, it is more useful to analyse the status, functional tasks and power of HRD.

New approaches to people management have a substantially different set of emphases. First, the idea is that the foundation of effective HRD is culture rather than procedure. Having a culture in which human resources are valued, in which commitment is expected, and where all managers are highly skilled and trained can be seen to preclude the need for collective agreements and procedures. Second, the use of levers such as teamwork is much more important. Overall, there is a concern to restructure employment patterns, jobs and organisations. In this context, training and development assume a greater role, which involves more than the level of technical training being given and extends to initiatives such as empowerment. This is a difficult construct to pin down, but it refers, at a minimum, to a significant reconceptualisation of roles by both managers and employees.

In sum, the organisation as a unit of analysis has changed and the national context as a unit of analysis has changed. As a result of these changes, the roles and activities of management and personnel specialists appear to be changing. Stable structures and systems administered by specialist staff are perhaps necessary, but they are not sufficient.

Finally, perceptions of the challenges of SHRD are affected by how power in organisations is distributed and works. Power in organisations is commonly discussed in terms of unitarist, pluralist and radical perceptions (Perspective 13.5). SHRD may be perceived as either part of unitarist control in organisations, or part of democratic pluralism in organisations, or as a contributor to radical change in organisations. Equally barriers to SHRD can be associated with these theories of power; as unitarists desire control they inhibit the emergence of SHRD effective learning by regulating organisational life and alienating the workforce; as pluralists advocate involvement and participation there is a trade-off in HRD investments which compromises SHRD; the 'liberating' aspirations of the radical theory fuels scepticism about its advocates and the changes they propose in the name of 'learning organisations'.

Conclusion

In understanding SHRD as a context formal policies should be determined on a case by case basis, rather than representing a standard, single compendium of best practice. Here the contexts of strategising, of change and of business value propositions have been considered. What it means for learning about HRD is that the identification of relevant contexts and analysis of trends within those contexts is a key task. The continuation of strategising, change and value proposition analysis at the frontiers of work and organisation will all entail further thinking about SHRD. There is a whole new world to map and explore, beyond our previous certainties. SHRD is a field in which, for example, new models of competence are being developed. These can be used to profile the ideal workforce and employee and provide a framework for integrating human resource systems. A sense of reinventing people management, of discovery and opportunity with scope for progress is evident. The tone is optimistic, and the deconstruction of the old cannot happen fast enough. Creativity, innovation and progress are the main themes here.

A more critical analysis of the new rhetoric of SHRD can be given, revealing the abiding preoccupations. Despite superficial harmonisation and the rhetoric of commitment there are still the same old divisions between employer and employee. The issue of control in the workplace is still evident, whether that be in traditional sectors and industries or in new sectors and services. The problem of control at work and the consequences that has on HRD systems still applies. The gurus and consultants who market the new corporate fashions in HRD need to be exposed. The tone is more pessimistic, with a critique of the deconstruction of past strengths and scepticism about innovation.

Such critique does not begin or end with the concept of SHRD. We are in a period of uncertainty, which will not be resolved easily or quickly as new systems or simply duplicate old ones with new names. Prescribing strong and autonomous individuals and organisations who should be able to transform themselves almost at will to deal with a wide array of new situations. Our maps of HRD need to be capable of making sense of all this transformation and change; our images of ourselves, organisations and work have to alter.

Organising KM, codified knowledge has always been an issue in HRD. Yet performing well is rarely based on just having accumulated finite, codified pre-existing knowledge. The challenges are as follows:

– Organisational accessing new 'know what' and 'know why';
– Organisational accessing peoples' tacit knowledge;
– Sharing such knowledge freely and effectively.

  o People who will collaborate because they trust each other (across teams, projects, departments);
  o With win–win attitudes to knowledge-creation and sharing;
  o Able to manage emotions and challenges of sharing knowledge collaboratively – speaking up, being open and honest;
  o And there is a more general human challenge; to promote innovative solutions and thinking in constrained rationality.

No exemplar models of HRD shaped by KM or CoP are evident. There are prescriptions for changing the HRD process in the context of KM and CoP in general, but there are many unanswered questions. How to foster and further invention and innovation through supporting free practice and KM and CoP needs analysing. For some critics, instead of progress there has been a spiralling into greater and greater complexity, and obscurity. Perhaps more than any others in recent times the concepts of KM and CoP, based on developments in information systems, organisational learning and intellectual capital, have baffled and bemused. The glimpses have remained vague as a result of problems with defining, modelling and providing empirical evidence for these concepts, despite well over a decade of intensive interest.

One problem in accounting for developments in theory and practice is that there are different streams involved in the debate, which do not necessarily speak the same language. There is also a problem with the distinctiveness and separateness of regional interpretations of these concepts, particularly between European and US approaches. But none of this explains why developments in theory and practice have proved so problematic. These issues exist in many other areas of the human sciences. Why then should KM and CoP provide so many difficulties?

Case: PowerCo

As you read the following PowerCo case study and consider questions:

(1) In what ways could HRD help the organisation to realise its values?

(2) What HRD practices might this organisation adopt to help achieve progress on the highlighted four key workplace issues?

(3) Does this organisation appear to you to be which achieves what you might think of as 'strategic HRD', that is the integration of HRD with the development of the whole enterprise and its competitiveness, bear in mind the concerns raised by the HRD director when interviewed?

Organisation; Business and Background

PowerCo is an international energy company with annual sales of £5.2 billion, 13,800 employees and in excess of 5 million customers in the United Kingdom and western United States. They have a wide range of retail customers, including large industrial and commercial businesses and individual householders in the western United States and across the United Kingdom. Its business is electricity generation, transmission, distribution and supply services in both countries. PowerCo has a strategic aim of becoming a leading international energy company. In both the United States and the United Kingdom, their customers tell them that they are most interested in the same key issues: reliability, price and value, customer service and company reputation. In addition they are in a business that involves high profile and very sensitive technological and environmental issues as a result of their operations, including:

- Energy: how they reduce the carbon intensity of their generation emissions by investing in renewables; their customer energy efficiency programmes and how they link these to fuel poverty;

- Air quality and global climate change: how they minimise the effects of the use of fossil fuels, as well as emissions from the various forms of transport they use;

- Land and biodiversity: how they manage their impacts on land biodiversity as a result of our coal mining, hydro-electric and network activities;

- Resource management and waste: how they manage the resulting waste streams, including waste reduction programmes and recycling.

Altogether these pressures combined carry significant challenge and responsibility. PowerCo needs to strike a balance between competing imperatives, such as securing energy supply now and into the future, keeping that supply affordable and minimising their impact on the environment. They also need to maintain the trust of their key stakeholders in an age when levels of investor and public trust in corporations have declined and demand is growing for more transparency and accountability.

Company Basics

PowerCo as a large electricity and gas provider. It has all the usual HRD provisions you would expect of a large, multinational organisation. These include substantial management and professional development programmes, and in-house training centres for manual and clerical staff. These are all managed by a large HRD department with a large training staff, together with links with colleges and universities.

A special unit, PowerCo Learning, was founded in the late 1990s in partnership with trade unions in the company. It represents the company's commitment to lifelong learning for all its staff, and its belief in sharing its success and resources with the communities that support its operations. This entails a strategic framework with four areas of learning (see below).

The PowerCo learning unit have a mission statement; it is 'Whoever you are, you have the power to become what you want to be.' The staff believe that everyone can transform their lives, and that learning is the ultimate transformer. Whether the person is an employee or a relative, leaving school or unemployed, looking for a new challenge or career, they seek to put learners on track. They have learning centres and partner organisations, including schools and businesses, and others. They exist to provide access and choice. Whatever the learners want can be provided. Access may be in learning centres or via the Internet. The only question the staff in PowerCo learning department asks is: are you prepared to work for it?

> **Learning for life**: a broad range of personal development opportunities for employees and their families, for example a learning helpline, with common number, and a common e-mail account for internal and external learners to provide advice and brokerage about learning opportunities.

Learning for real: interesting and innovative approaches to encourage young people within communities to return to learning, for example support transition of young people from school, or FE or unemployment to work from socially deprived areas.

Learning for work: highly focused learning aligned to the specific job roles and career needs of employees, for example involving staff in work with young people participating in charitable trust based learning initiatives.

Learning for you: learning initiatives designed to help young people, in the communities the company serves, to take the first steps into employment, for example technology-driven learning link to schools with four school-based learning centres set up by them to deliver enterprise oriented learning.

Corporate Values

One reference point for managing this is to identify a set of values that they feel can help guide them into the future. These values, all, are as follows:

- Working at the highest levels of industrial safety and continuously improving health and safety performance;

- Well-earned customer loyalty: We shall deliver quality and value for money services which meet and influence our customers' needs;

- Enhanced shareholder value: we shall create shareholder value by building businesses and continuously seeking opportunities to gain advantage over competitors;

- Positive working environment: we shall seek to provide a positive working environment which inspires employees to fulfil their potential and maximise their contribution;

- Trust of communities: we shall maintain the respect and trust of communities through recognising and responding to the needs of both the local and the wider environment;

- Teamwork and leadership: we shall place continuing importance on the way we work together and increasing focus on developing our team-working skills.

Four key workplace issues to be expanded upon

1. Building a high-performance culture.
They aim to develop the leadership skills of their senior managers, to create a working environment that encourages this approach to optimising personal achievement and satisfaction.

What performance comes down is the security of energy supply; how to ensure a reliable supply of energy when and where it's needed to meet current and future demand.

(1) System availability: seeking to reduce the average length of time customers are without power due to supply interruptions;

(2) System reliability: seeking to reduce the average number of times customers experience supply interruptions to;

(3) Momentary interruptions: seeking to reduce the average number of momentary power interruptions customers experience;

(4) Worst-performing assessment: seeking to improve the five worst circuits performance;

(5) Restoring supply: seeking to ensure that at least 80 per cent of our customers who experience a power interruption have their power supply restored in less than three hours.

It also includes price and value of energy; how to deliver affordable energy. And, of course, customer service; how to ensure all contact with the company meets or beats customer expectations of service; for example they aim to answer 80 per cent of all telephone calls to their Customer Service Centres within 20 seconds. They have not reached industry-leading status on these measures yet.

Once they meet these basic customer needs, their stakeholders tell them they have other expectations. These include providing green energy options, educating the public about safety, improving energy efficiency, serving priority needs customers and ensuring accessibility to services for all customers.

2. Ensuring a consistent, positive working experience.
They seek to provide the kind of working experience that encourages and supports their employees in achieving their best personal performance. They have an annual staff survey which examines the following attitudes:

> I am proud of what the company is trying to achieve
> I feel valued as a member of a team
> My colleagues and I are able to produce high-quality work
> I feel a sense of personal accomplishment in my work
> I have developed my skills over the last six months
> I have recently spoken to my manager about my training/development
> I am able to act decisively on behalf of the company
> I am clear about where I add value.

3. Training and developing their people.
They seek to offer training and development programmes throughout their businesses to implement their policies, procedures and business plan and ensure that they comply with legislation and best practice standards

Their investment in work-based training over the year amounted to a cost of over £4.8 million and involved in excess of 460,000 employee hours. PowerCo Learning has helped train more than 6,500 young people and reached 1,200 in

2002/03 through joining a range of government funded programmes. The US division announced support for a new $1 million, 3-year early childhood literacy project that partners with agencies in cities in their region to deliver literacy programmes.

4. Providing equal opportunities to all individuals.

They aim to maintain and promote a foundation of fairness, mutual respect and understanding, recognising that all employees contribute to the success of the company and its reputation as an employer, service provider and member of the wider community

Across the PowerCo group, 72.8 per cent of employees are male and 27.2 per cent are female. In the United Kingdom, about 0.6 per cent of the workforce identify themselves as minorities compared to the general minority population of 2 per cent in Scotland and 9 per cent in England and Wales. In the United States, 9 per cent of the workforce identify themselves as minorities. This compares to 18 per cent of minorities in all other companies that report to the Equal Employment Opportunities Commission in their major areas of operation.

Finally, an interview with the HRD Director of PowerCo raised the following five training and development issues.

Issue 1

Specialist in-house HRD Staff had been mainly training needs assessors, but now the organisation expected line managers do that (with HR partners in the business). More in-house skills were needed in design and delivery and in Organisation Development.

Issue 2

PowerCo use many external training suppliers; they are seeking to reduce the number of these they work with, increase the volume of training they do and reduce costs by up to 20 per cent. They want to make them associate trainers, coming in to deliver SP material, not just pay for 'design and development' with costs that seem excessive and variable for no good reason. And they want innovations that add value; that for example may make use more e-learning material for technical training because that not only saves costs but also as it fits with strategy.

Issue 3

They want new programme for Engineers; emphasising skills in asset management, not so much 'people skills' as that is overdone and not critical to them. The engineers need to begin to have a knowledge transfer culture; where they must share what they learn. They can do new masterclasses in technical areas and support the professional accreditation of engineers. Leadership skills have been pushed until now, and professional neglected – but want people to see professionals as equally valued, and credible. There are gaps in engineering career management, with few apprentices and potential successors to current plant managers. This is compounded by workforce immobility in the United Kingdom; happy with their lot and reluctant to move even a little to a new post.

Issue 4

Talent potential is currently managed at three levels:

Level 1: on or potential for top tier board

Level 2: on or potential for MD, second tier

Level 3: in top 250, or potential to join at third tier

The development of that level 3 group, the 250 people involved in that, is owned by the CEO, individual reviews, coaching (via IoD) and plans. They want to develop partnerships with premier business schools for top-level management development and local business schools for others. They are using executive coaching extensively for level 1 and 2 talents.

Issue 5

PowerCo wants learning to be more learner driven. They have put in personal planning processes, but people are still dependent. They need to challenge what they see as a dependency culture.

3 Key Texts

(1) Argyris, C. and Schon, C. (1974) *Theory in Practice: Increasing Professional Effectiveness* (San Francisco: Jossey-Bass).

(2) Grieves, J. (2003) *Strategic HRD* (London: Sage).

(3) Senge, P. (1992) *The Fifth Discipline: The Art and Practice of the Learning Organisation* (London: Century).

3 Key Articles

(1) Garavan, T. (2007) 'A Strategic Perspective on Human Resource Development', *Advances in Developing Human Resources*, 9(1), pp. 11–30.

(2) Tseng, C. and McLean, N. (2008) 'Strategic HRD Practices as Key Factors in Organizational Learning', *Journal of European Industrial Training*, 32(6), pp. 418–432.

(3) Bartram, T. and Stanton, P. (2007) 'Developing the Professional Workforce: A Focus on Systems not Individuals', *International Journal of Human Resources Development and Management*, 7(2), pp. 161–176.

3 Key Web Links

(1) European Consortium on Organisational learning: http://www.eclo.org/.

(2) Society for Organisational learning: http://www.solonline.org/aboutsol/who/Senge/.

(3) The Tavistock Institute, which represents an example of activities reflecting a sociotechnical perspective: http://www.tavinstitute.org/.

14

National HRD

Learning Objectives

By the end of this chapter you will be able to:

- Describe the roles of states in public policy-making for National HRD;
- Discuss common factors in the historical context for National HRD policy in different national contexts;
- Critically evaluate the evolution and impact of National HRD policy and practice in a specific case study context.

Introduction

National HRD (NHRD) is the management of learning and change to support the development of people and organisations for economic, social and cultural purposes in countries. NHRD priorities and activities will reflect both local economic, social and cultural contexts and regional/global characteristics. The historical background to this in one context, the United Kingdom is outlined. Issues arising for transnational bodies, such as the European Union (EU), are identified.

Exercise 14.1: Themes from a NHRD Perspective: Prioritising Human Capital Development

Below are 15 possible public policy concerns that can have an impact on the quality of the workforce. Select a country you are familiar with, and rank them according to whether you believe they should be high, medium or low priorities for public policy in contributing to advancing workforce HRD. You can only use each ranking up to four times; so four priorities will be high, four medium and four low.

	Priority status for contributing to National HRD in the country you are considering?		
	High	Med	Low
Focus 'human capital' spending on investing in young adults, rather than spread across all the population			
Concentrate spending on the under 5-year-olds			
Intervene in dysfunctional families to protect the interests of vulnerable children			
Measure levels of IQ/talent among children and target HRD spending and systems accordingly on supporting the best			
Spend on giving higher education access to more people			
Increase subsidies for higher education participation among the least well off			
Promote spending on vocational skills, not academic knowledge and qualifications			
Reduce class sizes in schools and colleges			
Ensure access to good on-the-job training, and improve the quality of this			
Retrain older workers			
Transparency of qualifications and skills, including recognition of informal and non-formal learning			
Continuous training of learning professionals			
Working with under-represented groups			
Promote flexibility in labour markets			
Tax policies favouring individual and company spending on learning			
Heckman and Masterov 2004, and EU Lifelong learning thematic groups			

NHRD

NHRD is the management of learning and change to support the development of people and organisations for economic, social and cultural purposes. NHRD priorities and activities will reflect both local economic, social and cultural contexts and regional/global characteristics. NHRD policy is sometimes perceived to be a relatively recent concern, though Harbison and Myers (1964) recognised the enabling role of HRD in general development some time ago, and advocated policy and practice to meet key goals and needs in both economic development and industrial relations. In the contemporary HRD literature five models of NHRD (Perspective 14.1) have been identified (Cho and McLean 2004, Lynham and Cunningham 2006).

Perspective 14.1: Models of National HRD

NHRD System	Characteristics	Examples
Centralised	• Top-down, state driven approach to education • Critical role for government in HRD policy development • HRD addresses social and moral needs • HRD linked to multiyear national development plan	China, Poland, Kenya, Mexico, Morocco
Transitional	• Tripartite approach to HRD policy; government, employers, unions • Goals and initiatives to meet economic and social skill needs • Multiple government departments involved	India, Singapore, Philippines, Brazil
Government Initiated towards standardisation	• Standardisation of aspects of HRD a key theme • Stakeholder view of HRD needs • National needs framework, network of agencies • Private sector pressured to comply	United Kingdom, Australia, South Africa

Decentralised, free market	• Market forces push HRD • Education and training is for the private sector • State supports individual and private sector initiatives	USA, Canada
Small nations	• Need to cooperate regionally • 'Competition' – compete and collaborate • Regional intergovernmental bodies	Pacific islands, St Lucia South Africa/ Morocco, Brazil

Source: Cho and McLean (2004).

In developed countries, with generally high levels of income and productivity, well-developed educational infrastructures and constructive relationships between major stakeholders in employment including a concern with HRD the development of NHRD policy is an integral part of economic and social planning (see Debate 14.1). In developing countries, where there are low levels of income, patchy educational provision and a complex of relations among global agencies concerned with human development, the policy-making picture is different. A developing country is typified by a low average income, a relatively undeveloped infrastructure, and a poor human development index compared to the global norms. The following chapter on comparative HRD explores this in more detail.

Debate 14.1: Developing and Developed Country NHRD

Developing	Developed
Colonial pasts and legacies; a history of inequality	Legacies of past global influence, and current global status and power
Heterogeneous societies	Homogeneous societies
Young and unstable economies	Mature and stable economies
Political transformations, new democracies and civil societies – limiting the power of the state	Political transformations driven by democratic processes

Debate 14.1: (Continued)

High unemployment, marked differences in distribution of wealth; 'haves' and 'have-nots' (Gini index) and rural-urban	Lower unemployment, less marked differences in the distribution of wealth
Moving towards industrialisation, away from agrarian: developing human resources the key	Moving towards service economies from having been industrial: changing human resources part of that
Under pressure of debt, flight of skilled labour	Under pressures to sustain wealth and affluence, accommodating migrating labour
Redress education inequalities, and government partner with others (industry) to develop labour and skills	Reconfigure education and skills to meet changing employment demands

In doing and writing HRD research the National context needs to be understood and located as a context for any topic or group being studied, and as a context in which any findings will be disseminated and be enacted. NHRD incorporates:

- **Public HRD** programmes; large and oriented on disadvantage – social goals.
- **Private HRD** programmes; discrete and fragmented, evaluated in terms of learning and knowledge and ROI in organisations.
- **Partnership HRD** programmes; combinations of market and government action.

There is no single, clear structure or language for describing and analysing NHRD as a complex of public, private and partnership programmes. Evidence, very broadly, in the past comes in the form of:

- Impact studies of public programmes, and major company studies; America.
- Results measures for national programmes and national studies in HRD journals; Western Europe–EU based.
- Human development and modernising issues in transitioning economies; UN studies.

If we were to develop an index to capture and compare NHRD themes and issues which would enable action, what would that index include?

The issue is to find something between a crude single measure and a complex picture of a whole which can have many, many pieces. Crude quantitative measures would include data on HRD activity (lifelong learning in the last four weeks) and levels of public spending – these capture Public HRD. These figures tell us something, and can reveal significant differences which may be worth further action; but the implications are often associated with large-scale political change, and realistically not much can be done.

More complex quantitative and qualitative data are captured in Human Capital or more broadly PEST-type analyses. These can be rich in data, but paradoxically may miss important and significant details. The UN HDI index provides an example. It has three factors: (1) GDP, (2) longevity and (3) enrolments in education. These enable a classification of countries as very high, high, medium or low.

Possible factors for an index would include the following:

- Competence (themes and gaps, not just qualifications and frameworks of qualification);
- Maturity model of political support for HRD (not just a typology of different systems – is a single ministry or many HRD oriented units in several ministries the best way?);
- Modernising challenges (liberal/progressive agendas, not just cross-cultural differences between developed and transitioning countries. e.g. co-educational systems);
- Accreditation systems uptake and quality in HRD provisions (like IiP or ISO 9000 or other).

In driving change we are aware that:
Political systems make a difference as to which forms of communication will work.

- Centralised: influence policy authorities;
- Tripartite: consensus among stakeholders;
- Market systems: profile and spread of ideas through opinion formers.

Improving levels of maturity make a difference; how can this be operationalised?

- Basic NHRD;
- Intermediate NHRD;
- Advanced NHRD.

Short-term and long-term matters. Greenhousing real change begins with schools, if any significant change is going to take root. Influencing best practice meantime where that is possible in other parts of the system is also practicable. Generational differences rather than cross-cultural factors may be significant in understanding where the meeting points that matter are to be found; how the 'past' and the 'future' meet and find common interests.

The Role of Government

Government-led NHRD public policies and programmes are a major feature of the HRD landscape. These may address subjects ranging from early childhood development and engagement in education through to policy for retaining and retraining older people. They may address and include questions of taxation and benefit policy as well as outlining areas of subsidy and spending specifically in HRD. Policies in HRD are usually developed by government in partnership with other agencies and stakeholders, to support the development of a consensus approach to developing a knowledgeable, capable and committed workforce. Given this range of areas under the HRD banner, and the many agencies involved, the kinds of activity in NHRD can be bewildering to track in any specific national context. Equally, the levers of HRD are always being pulled, as they are seen to provide an easy option for quick change. For some critics this has become part of the problem, as there is a tendency to meddle with HRD policies before they have had a chance to settle in and make an impact. However, even if governments change the overall goals tend to stay the same or very similar: to ensure the existence of the necessary skills base for effective economic performance so that skills shortages are avoided and opportunities for economic development are taken, and that populations get the broader social benefits of learning and being skilled (Brynner et al. 2001):

- Improve their chances in the labour market;
- Suffer less from poor physical and mental health;
- Less likely to have children experiencing difficulty at school;
- More likely to be active citizens, for example in voting and expressing interest in politics;
- More liberal and less discriminatory in their attitudes.

Challenges in NHRD can be about finding a balance and compromise between proponents of government-led NHRD and those more sceptical of the wisdom and results of government-led NHRD. The former see a need to make better use of HRD to deal with the changing economic environment, responding to the effects of globalisation, technological innovation and a fast pace of change. They see a role for NHRD as changes occur in the composition of the workforce, in the types of work available and in career structures and patterns. HRD needs to enable and support these. And they see a role for NHRD in social change, with an apparent growing polarisation between those 'getting on' and those 'going nowhere'; the rich and the poor. These divisions can be manifest in polarised lifestyles, expectations and attitudes to education and development. Those who are more sceptical challenge the belief that public policy and government-led NHRD can be an effective response to any of these concerns; they would leave it to markets and employers to deal with and resolve the issues which emerge in workforce development (see Debate 14.2). An example of this is given with one relatively recent review of NHRD in the United Kingdom, the Leitch review (see below).

Debate 14.2: The Leitch Review of Skills in the UK

This review suggested there was still a long-term challenge in the UK, despite many previous reviews since the contemporary pro-HRD government was first elected in 1997. The UK had a strong economy and world-leading employment levels, but its productivity trailed many key comparator nations. Poor skills were a key contributor to this problem as well as having wider impacts on social welfare.

Over the last decade, the skills profile of the working-age population in the UK had improved. For example, the proportion of adults with a degree had increased from a fifth to over a quarter of the population. Despite these improvements, the UK still did not have a world-class skills base: over a third of adults in the UK did not have a basic school-leaving qualification and five million people had no qualifications at all. One in six adults did not have the literacy skills expected of an 11-year-old and half did not have these levels of functional numeracy.

Looking ahead to 2020, global, demographic and technological change would place an even greater premium on the UK's skills profile. New analysis conducted by the 2006 Review showed that, if the Government met its ambitious target for improving the UK's skills, by 2020 the proportion of working-age people without any qualifications would fall to 4 per cent; and the proportion of adults holding a degree would increase from 27 per cent to 38 per cent. This would have significant benefits for the economy; increasing annual productivity growth by 0.2 per cent with a net benefit to the economy of £3 billion a year, equivalent to 0.3 per cent of GDP.

However, even if the UK can meet these challenging targets, the nation's human capital would still fail to be world-class. Considerable problems would remain; at least 4 million adults would not have the literacy skills expected of an 11-year-old and 12 million would not have numeracy skills at this level. Ambitious scenarios were needed for tackling the stock of low-skilled adults without qualifications, basic literacy and numeracy; investing more in intermediate skills; and further increasing the proportion of adults holding a degree.

Significant economic and social benefits would result from higher productivity and employment gained through improving skills. The Leitch Review concluded that the UK must urgently raise its game and set itself a greater ambition to have a world-class skills base by 2020.

Source: Leitch (2006).

Themes and Issues in NHRD Public Policy

National HRD policy and decision-making ought to be grounded in rigorous, hard-headed analysis of the issues. Continuing reviews and change in many national contexts suggest this is not the case. Consequently, public policy in this area has not been successful, had the impact desired or engaged all the relevant government departments. Sorting out the basics is a recurring theme, with reports concluding that there is a need to do more to thoroughly analyse HRD problems and their causes, both the demand-side and supply-side factors that determine investment in workforce development. Fresh policy options ought to better include the aspirations and capabilities of stakeholders. The focus would then be on developing a coherent strategy that draws together all the key initiatives and actors involved in workforce development.

The goal is to ensure that government policy is genuinely strategic and not, as has so often been the case in the past, piecemeal, tactical, disjointed and low impact. If being piecemeal and disjointed means low impact, then being genuinely strategic means having a greater impact. Strategy is about plans and policy for major goals; however, it often seems that what happens here is institutional reform, not goal change.

To ensure that the analysis of the issues leads to real improvements in workforce development 'on the ground'. This contrasts with improvements in the abstract, which produce better-looking or better-sounding policy; improvements 'on the ground' are with real people, and real companies.

To engage fully with the different government departments with a stake in work-force development. In the United Kingdom, for example, this includes at least two different departments involved in skills and dealings with business, as well as the Treasury, which leads on fiscal and other matters.

The ambiguity here is that HRD at work is working across two major public policy agendas: improving productivity and employability on the one hand and achieving social inclusion or social justice on the other. A belief in a positive link between HRD and both private benefits for individuals and firms and social benefits for the economy and society at large.

Establishing indicators to evaluate policy in terms of HRD at work is a concern. These may include labour force participation rates, rates of participation in higher education and levels of expenditure on HRD at work. The volume of HRD (as opposed to numbers of people participating in it) has stagnated in recent years, and much HRD tends to be job-specific. In addition, institutional weaknesses have resulted in few businesses participating in training networks that promote workforce development, or accessing and using supportive government structures.

These problems relate to productivity issues. The quality of the labour force, as measured by the skill mix, can be compared with that in other countries. Problems may exist in both the current stock of people in the workforce and those entering the workforce. An underdeveloped workforce produces less, works harder and longer for the same pay, and attracts less capital investment. For government all these HRD concerns are not isolated and distinct; they need to be addressed in the wider context of government and business strategies towards innovation, information technology and other policy areas relevant to business.

There is evidence to show that HRD can contribute to enhanced productivity. Equally there is evidence of HRD's potential contribution to employability and social inclusion. More HRD means higher earnings. But, at present, the distribution of HRD tends to reinforce social exclusion. There is a link between skill levels and deprivation. Particular groups, for example disabled people and certain ethnic minorities, are disproportionately likely to have low skills. Such low skills are correlated with poor employment prospects in the labour market. The low-skilled are less likely to receive HRD opportunities that might help to overcome their disadvantage. The HRD-rich grow richer and the HRD-poor become poorer.

This problematic state of affairs has existed within HRD for some time. Why? There are three different explanations:

The economic development explanation. The premise is that NHRD provisions will match the demands of economic practices, and economic practices involve low skills. Therefore there is ineffective NHRD because employment as a whole, and skills and performance within that, are trapped in a 'low skills equilibrium'.

It does not make economic sense for people to invest in NHRD when organisational strategies and individual career success do not require it.

The flawed NHRD policy system explanation. The premise is that a coherent NHRD policy system could be constructed by government, but government has not done this yet. Therefore the assessment of needs, design and delivery of NHRD remain flawed. Although NHRD policy is a key part of the political agenda, the system that emerges – of agencies, initiatives and policies – is inconsistent, confusing, poor-quality and provider-driven NHRD policy.

The social factors explanation. The premise is that NHRD provisions can have an impact only if people are motivated, and are in a position to participate in NHRD, but many people are neither motivated nor able to participate. Therefore, any otherwise relevant and effective NHRD policy fails because it encounters the challenges of social exclusion, where the vulnerable and disadvantaged are alienated from and will not engage with, learning. Until NHRD policy deals as effectively with social inclusion issues as with economic development concerns it will always be hampered and obstructed. The provision of opportunity has to be an engine of policy.

The Background to NHRD

Skills 'revolutions' are perceived to be a necessary precondition of economic and social success, as each nation or region fears that it may stall and lag behind others in changing times. Changing times can mean producing a more skilled and better educated workforce, particularly with young people. Changing times can mean challenging perceptions and behaviours, for example the view that academic education has higher prestige than vocational training. Changing times can mean employers and the state arguing about who takes the lead, and who pays. Changing times can mean dealing with congestion within the field of local economic development where there is confusion, overlap, duplication and even active competition between the many agencies involved. These issues have long been debated, but they are now generally collated into one conclusion: that all these factors matter and that many countries are deficient in NHRD many respects.

To understand the current situation the historical background to NHRD policy and practice needs to be appreciated. The approach here is to review the distant, the recent and the immediate history of NHRD in one context, that of the United Kingdom. The themes and issues to explore can be applied in any national context. The distant past should be analysed because it puts more recent times and concerns in context. Recent concerns with change and unemployment have shaped the system substantially, and have influenced what happened in the 1990s when a complex web of programmes and agencies was created.

The Distant Past

There is an image, partly fact and partly myth, of a pre-industrial golden era when NHRD meant simply learning that was an organic part of the lives of working people in agricultural and home-based craft economy. Learning was something that happened within families or within guilds, or for the intelligentsia in institutions such as monasteries and a few medieval universities. Capabilities, knowledge and behaviour were shaped within these traditional, community-based environments. For most there was no contact with schools or colleges, no exams or qualifications, no government departments or agencies. Colleges, the few that there were, were institutes linked to the major medieval powers, either royal or religious, for the development of clerics through scholarship associated with the classical disciplines. People learned for work and employment as farmers, or clothmakers, or tanners, or smiths, or bakers, or masons or fishers, as a natural and integral part of their community.

With the rise of industrial capitalism, this 'golden era' of community-based learning ended and the whole approach to NHRD came to be radically transformed. The reasons why, and the effects of this, are many, but two are particularly relevant to understanding the subsequent history and current state of NHRD policy. The first relates to the requirements for efficiency in mechanised production in factory systems, and the large-scale bureaucracies and clerical factories required for business and government. This was a shift from a system based upon individuals being employed in whole jobs, with all the HRD that required and the skills it involved, to a system based upon a division of labour. That division of labour de-skilled many workers, as they were only responsible for part of a process, not a whole job. With little requirement for HRD the individual could be fit for work and employment quite easily.

This was a shift that curtailed the requirement for the complex development of independent and highly skilled work, and the identities that went with that. The realities of employment in unskilled 'production line' type environments were dominant. The accompanying social upheaval, involving the destruction of community, small town and country jobs and ways of life with the shift to urban and factory environments, had wider and well-documented social consequences. Unemployment, poverty, health and safety, and crime provided pressing issues for policy-makers and campaigners. As nations came to terms with the onset and evolution of industrialisation driven by capitalism, the question of NHRD was associated with and nested within greater social questions about welfare and the basic quality of life. On the one hand, development was less of a challenge, and on the other it was more significant.

The other major impact of industrialisation and the development of capitalism was the role of technologies and knowledge as forces driving economic growth. Together these formed a situation where the increase of wealth through the creation of profit-making firms required an increase in knowledge and skills, the development of new skills, and the establishment of new patterns of employment and work behaviour. This meant the social aspects of employment and the quality of the workforce would matter as much as technological innovation for economic growth and success. This required greater investment in HRD. This was the age when science, and scientific research into materials, production processes and engineering, was complemented by the growth of institutions and industry in areas such as banking and finance. These pillars of industrialisation and capitalism required many literate, numerate and knowledgeable professionals. They also required large workforces of literate, numerate and skilled clerical and administrative staff to push all the paper that had to be processed for the engineering innovations, the factories and the institutions to work. How were these people to be developed? The answer was to be investment in mass education; in the development and expansion of technical schools, colleges and universities, and the development of NHRD at work.

Since the onset of industrialisation and capitalism there has been a continuing interplay between factors dramatically increasing the requirement for such investment in NHRD and displacing investment in NHRD. Alongside the evolution of more highly skilled and knowledge-based work and employment there has been the evolution of de-skilled process work and employment. Governments, according to their ideological hue, made choices about what to do and where to invest. For example the craft, skills and knowledge involved in manufacturing cloth were made redundant, when all that was required was a 'hand' to mind the machine that did the work. But the skills and knowledge required to make the machines and manage the legal, financial and operational aspects of such manufacture were now in demand. What could governments do to help manage this?

Through industrialisation, the guild system for managing NHRD, where it was the responsibility of independent masters in trades and professions, was superseded by the growth of large employers. But apprenticeships in the major industries where crafts were practised, the factories and shipyards, publishing and mining, became industrial relations battlegrounds.Employers and trade unions shared certain interests and pursued their different interests. For trade unions, controlling the time serving of apprentices was one way of guarding their existing members' interests, pay and conditions of work. For employers, there was an interest in enforcing their control of work and changes to methods of work by challenging job demarcations and the kinds and levels of skill needed for jobs.

Such circumstances prevailed throughout much of the twentieth century in industrialised countries. These still form the background to ongoing debates in NHRD, economic and social policy, with major events tending to bring them into starker relief. The first such event, which created critical points for NHRD policy in the twentieth century, was the First World War in Europe. This brought an influx of unskilled people into the labour market and employment. The problems encountered in managing such an unskilled workforce, or in creating systems to develop more skills, were evident then – as was the trade unions' opposition to 'dilution', using unskilled, untrained people to do the work of skilled craftsmen.

The second event was the economic depression in the 1930s. The causes of this economic collapse were many, but mass unemployment was one of its greatest effects. Government policy in general, and NHRD policy in particular, were important in responding to this, and in providing some foundation for moving on to recovery. The depression, and unemployment, was implicated in the political instability that saw the growth of both political extremism, as well as in the acceptance of interventions by government in democracies elsewhere to cope with the effects of the recession. Some countries saw the development of government training centres, intervention designed (it seemed) more to get people off the streets than to fit any specific strategy for an NHRD-led economic recovery.

Finally, there was the period during and after the Second World War. In the United Kingdom this meant, among other things, once again the need to draw an influx of new people into work, which again exposed labour market deficiencies, as many of these were unskilled. This period is often best remembered for the influx of women into the workforce, proving their worth and value in a whole range of occupations for which they had never been considered suitable before. After the Second World War the demands of rebuilding after the destruction experienced in many regions and countries placed a premium on NHRD, and on the resourcefulness of people.

After each of these major and critical events there were changes, but there was also a return to the status quo. That is to say, lower priority was given to using NHRD to improve the quality and skills of the whole labour force, or to maintaining a central role for government, or to consolidating new entrants in the workforce. But each of these issues was to be encountered again during the 1960s, when concerns about the economic consequences of performance problems in industry as a result of skills shortages attained a greater strategic rather than situational significance. NHRD became a subject of real and sustained prominence. The conquered and vanquished regimes and destroyed economies of the Second World War were experiencing recovery, while those of the military victors were experiencing problems. The human capital factor was highlighted, and NHRD was to become a significant force.

Recent History

In more recent times the HRD problems were seen to lie with employers failing to invest in HRD. Schemes whose purpose was to promote investment in HRD by monitoring employers' spending on training and raising a levy for investment in NHRD became popular. Although this concern remained in the 1970s, the institutional context often changed; from a concern with employers' investments in training to government's role in dealing with the unemployment that accompanied economic change and the decline of traditional heavy industries. In some countries, such as the United Kingdom, this period saw the origins of schemes and agencies that, over the next three decades, would be set up, enlarged, reduced, re-named and re-launched almost constantly. By the 1980s, with the growth of new technologies and industries, the need to change the institutional context again was evident.

By the early 1990s, reviews deemed much NHRD policy activity to have been a failure. Investment had not changed the situation significantly: there were still skill gaps, concerns about productivity, and inequalities in access and opportunity. The United Kingdom's answer was a new strategy that gave more emphasis to the role of employer-led bodies, providing local leadership rather than a national Civil Service-led system. In addition, major initiatives, such as the Investors in People (IiP) standard, were developed as an advanced and substantial attempt to upgrade and improve HRD in the workplace.

Despite these attempts to ensure that NHRD was better focused as employers led the agencies that determined practices, barriers to attaining key goals still seemed to exist. In particular, the worlds of education and of training – of the academic and the vocational – seemed still disconnected, as far apart as ever, and even competing rather than collaborating to support NHRD. There were then further attempts at institutional reform to break down these barriers, with better 'joined-up' policy thinking and practice across NHRD as a whole. The 'schism' in thinking and policy about training and education can be embodied in separate government departments dealing with each issue, and the hope is that combining these in one body will remove the problem. There was also a challenge in establishing a culture where individuals and organisations who did not traditionally value their own HRD did recognise and take responsibility for their own HRD. Finally, there was also an investment of resources, and of hope, in the era of the Internet and the e-business boom – the hope that the use of these technologies could offer a new route to better NHRD policy and performance.

These kinds of issue confronted all governments, whether their political outlook was interventionist, voluntarist or abstentionist. As a rule versions of voluntarism predominated in the United Kingdom. This did not mean abstaining from NHRD; it meant a policy of encouragement by the state but a dependence on others to fulfil expectations. If this failed to produce results, the government would set about developing or changing policy; government was then quite active in NHRD as an actor and agent, not just a proponent. Voluntarism also does not mean that there is no state responsibility; a state role in education, and in responding to unemployment, has been constant. What it does mean is that the state will not take the primary leadership in a system where the state, employers and employee representatives will be partners. There is an uneasy dance about who should do what; who should take the lead. And there are issues where leadership rather than consensus is required. For example, the quality of higher education of professionals has always attracted much middle-class attention and seems, therefore, to receive more political attention, than deficiencies in intermediate-level development of skills. The outcome is the 'Cinderella' status of the further education sector, reflected in its low status and low levels of funding. Vocational education may be the better investment, but governments do not want to alienate the influential middle classes.

National HRD policy has been shaped by the rivalry between political philosophies, in essence between laissez-faire opponents of state intervention and liberal proponents of a social agenda for NHRD. This has been largely fought over interpretations of what voluntarism should involve, rather than taking issue with voluntarism itself. For the laissez-faire opponents of state intervention, NHRD policy should happen 'naturally' in the interests of all, as market forces drive investments and activities, and employers have a key role as they have the greatest knowledge of and interest in NHRD. Policy activity should be left free to track labour market supply and demand dynamics; wherever earnings and employment are growing there will be NHRD policy. Voluntarism is preferred to its alternatives. One is greater state intervention, involving greater taxing and spending. The other is a corporatist model, such as that found in some countries, which involves a degree of assumption of control and responsibility by employers for things that employers see that the state should rightly be concerned with. The conclusion is that there is no role for intervention through legislation on NHRD policy, nor the establishment of individual rights in matters of NHRD policy.

Liberal proponents of voluntarism argue that markets fail, for various reasons, to provide the necessary NHRD policy. Instead of a natural evolution of NHRD policy, and change in it being driven by change in labour markets, there are many failures; the skills required by employers are in shortage because the NHRD policy system is not developing them. Interventions by government are then needed to deal with these market failures, to shape and centrally allocate resources to the NHRD policy system. Laissez-faire voluntarism does not deliver sufficient NHRD policy quantity or quality. Some employers train; some do not. Some programmes are good; some are bad. There is value in the state and employers working together through institutional developments.

How far can we now see the development of a clear, coherent and comprehensive HRD policy system in most countries? This is open to debate. The muddle of different kinds of voluntarism may not be resolved, but new systems do seem to exist that are popular and well supported by employers, government and institutions in a range of areas. The 'cultural' blocks are being overcome, though there are still reservations; take-up is still low, and the performance of reformed institutions is still problematic.

More state investment and intervention in NHRD might mean, for example, legislation to make training compulsory, equivalent to the requirements on employers about health and safety, and employer responsibility. Or it might mean, for example, a new form of levy – in effect a tax – to be centrally controlled and redistributed to high-quality training facilities and centres (private or public sector) which employers can then use. Does your country need more state intervention like this or less?

The Contemporary Agenda: Lifelong Learning

Regions are developing an interest in NHRD policy. For example, in the past in the European area a major public policy focus was on standards in employment, together with associated matters of employee consultation and representation, but now the emphasis is firmly on learning. When the European Commission considered the direction of policy and action in the EU, it concluded that Europe had indisputably moved into the knowledge age, with all that this will imply for cultural, economic and social life. Patterns of learning, living and working are changing. This means that individuals must adapt to change, and long-established ways of doing things must change too.

The EU then highlighted a move towards lifelong learning as accompanying the successful transition to a knowledge-based economy and society (see Practice 14.1). The Commission defined lifelong learning, within an overall European employment strategy, as 'all purposeful learning activity, undertaken on an ongoing basis with the aim of improving knowledge, skills and competence'. Lifelong learning is no longer just one aspect of education and training; it must become the guiding principle for provision and participation across the full spectrum of learning. All those living in Europe, without exception, should have equal opportunity to adjust to the demands of social and economic change, and to participate actively in the shaping of Europe's future. The implication is that Europe's education and training systems are at the heart of the coming changes.

Practice 14.1: EU Programmes

With a budget of nearly €7 billion for 2007–2013, the EU funds a range of actions including exchanges, study visits and networking activities. Projects are intended not only for individual students and learners, but also for teachers, trainers and all others involved in education and training. There are four sub-programmes which fund projects at different levels of education and training:

- Comenius for schools
- Erasmus for higher education
- Leonardo da Vinci for vocational education and training
- Grundtvig for adult education

Targets have been set for the four sub-programmes:

- Comenius should involve at least 3 million pupils in joint educational activities, over the period of the programme;
- Erasmus should reach a total of 3 million individual participants in student mobility actions since the programme began;
- Leonardo da Vinci should increase placements in enterprises to 80,000 a year by the end of the programme;
- Grundtvig should support the mobility of 7000 individuals involved in adult education a year by 2013.

Source: EU (2011a) http://ec.europa.eu/education/lifelong-learning-programme/doc78_en.htm.

The Member States, the Council and the Commission within their respective areas of competence must identify coherent strategies and practical measures with a view to fostering lifelong learning for all.

A memorandum on lifelong learning was circulated to launch a Europe-wide debate on a comprehensive strategy for implementing it at individual and institutional levels, and in all spheres of public and private life. The implications of this basic change in perspectives and practices merit much debate. The Member States, which are responsible for their education and training systems, should lead this debate. The aim was to fix European guidelines and timetables for achieving specific agreed goals, establishing, where appropriate, indicators and benchmarks to compare best practice, and then regularly monitoring, evaluating and reviewing progress. This decentralised approach will be applied in line with the principle of subsidiarity, in which the Union, the Member States, the regional and local levels, and the social partners, will be actively involved using variable forms of partnership.

The EU argues that promoting active citizenship and promoting employability are equally important and interrelated aims for lifelong learning. Others may tend to emphasise competitiveness and organisational performance. Member States agree on the priority, but have been slow to take concerted action (see Practice 14.2). The argument is that the scale of current economic and social change in Europe demands a fundamentally new approach to education and training. Lifelong learning is the common umbrella under which all kinds of teaching and learning should be united. To put lifelong learning into practice, everyone must work together effectively, both as individuals and in organisations. This is analysed in terms of six key messages, which offer a structured framework for an open debate on putting lifelong learning into practice with priority areas for action.

Practice 14.2: Thematic Concerns in Lifelong Learning

Thematic Networking Groups (TNGs) in the EU provide opportunities for policy makers and experts in all parts of education to benefit from the lessons learned through the Lifelong Learning Programme.

They provide a forum to discuss policy developments, share information and exchange best practice around a common subject of expertise. TNGs bring together people who are passionate and knowledgeable about their subject areas, allowing them to work together to give recommendations for improvement. The TNGs are made up of four groups, each focusing on a specific theme:

Group 1: Transparency of qualifications and skills, including recognition of informal and non-formal learning

Group 2: Continuous training of learning professionals

Group 3: Meeting training and skills needs

Group 4: Working with under-represented groups

Source: EU(2011b)   http://www.lifelonglearningprogramme.org.uk/thematic-networking.

The EU has an interest in and influence on NHRD and HRD policy. The political foundations of EU-level government provide a means through which ends in both economic and social agendas can be attained. The union is not just about trade, but about managing a social dialogue between employers and employees to consider interests and resolve differences over issues such as HRD policy. The huge numbers of people involved in the elected bodies and associated institutions of the EU have considered many HRD issues and policies. The harmonisation of common systems and policies in HRD continues to be a central part of the EU project. The public policy aims are to:

- Guarantee universal and continuing access to learning for gaining and renewing the skills needed for sustained participation in the knowledge society;

- Raise visibly levels of investment in human resources in order to place priority on Europe's most important asset, its people;
- Develop effective teaching and learning methods and contexts for the continuum of lifelong and life-wide learning;
- Improve significantly the ways in which learning participation and outcomes are understood and appreciated, particularly non-formal and informal learning;
- Ensure that everyone can easily access good-quality information and advice about learning opportunities throughout Europe and throughout their lives;
- Provide lifelong learning opportunities as close to learners as possible, in their own communities and supported through ICT-based facilities wherever appropriate.

In the short term and long term these aims are central to sustaining an enlarged and competitive EU, and so require some form of agreed and joint policy and action.

A framework of partnership is needed to mobilise resources for lifelong learning at all levels. Working together to put lifelong learning into practice is required to build an inclusive society that offers equal opportunities for access to quality learning throughout life to all people, and in which education and training provision is based on the needs and demands of individuals. This in turn means a need to adjust the ways in which education and training are provided, and the way paid working life is organised, so that people can participate in learning throughout their lives and can plan for themselves how they combine learning, working and family life. This, it is argued, will help to achieve higher overall levels of education and qualification in all sectors, to ensure high-quality provision of education and training, and at the same time to ensure that people's knowledge and skills match the changing demands of jobs and occupations, workplace organisation and working methods. Ultimately it will encourage and equip people to participate more actively in all spheres of public life, especially in social and political life at all levels of the community, including the European level.

The key to success is argued to be the same at the European level: that is, to build on a sense of shared responsibility for lifelong learning among all the key actors. These include the Member States, the European institutions, the social partners (employers and trade unions) and enterprises, regional and local authorities, those who work in education and training, voluntary organisations, associations and groupings. The shared aim should be to build a Europe in which all citizens have the opportunity to develop their potential to the full and to feel that they belong. This European agenda clearly emphasises the broader social and political aspects of better HRD at work.

This can be compared with the approach of the Asia-Pacific Economic Cooperation (APEC) region (Practice 14.3). The EU was founded, as the European Economic Community, in 1957 with the Treaty of Rome. It is not just an economic and trade unit; it has an elected Parliament, a Council with policy-making power, and a Commission which acts as the executive body. This involves tens of thousands of staff in many institutions. In the EU the HRD concerns are to raise employment skill levels (not just deal with unemployment), to enable skills development and measures, to improve the quality of working life and to ensure social inclusion. Matters ranging from migration to qualifications are researched and discussed.

Practice 14.3: EU and APEC Compared

	EU	APEC
Model	Social model	Political economy of up-skilling
Integration	Deep and wide	Narrow and superficial
Dialogue	Social partners	Narrow financial approach
Spend	Partnerships and infrastructure	Very little

There are three key points to note regarding NHRD. The first is the integration of HRD into the policy- and decision-making of the EU – it is a central part of it. The second is the open method of coordination for compliance in HRD policy: this means that the major policies are to be reviewed each year, and progress determined and reviewed. The third point is the presence of social dialogue: the European social model is to involve employers and trade unions jointly in consultations. Together this provides a mechanism for dealing with difficult and complex issues and either avoiding or managing crises. The enlargement of the EU in 2004 was seen as a threat to strategy of the social model, because of weaknesses with unemployment and unions in some new accession states.

The APEC was set up in 1989, partly out of a concern to ensure that other supranational bodies such as the EU did not come to dominate the world scene. It includes 21 economies, including the USA, China, Japan and Australia, along with some much smaller countries. Together they represent around 50 per cent of world GDP. APEC works through a downward cascade mechanism: ministers from the countries meet and propose ideas, and set up working groups. These working groups arrive at decisions through the Kuching Consensus process of consensual decision-making. Any country can veto any decision, or simply not turn up to discuss a matter. There is no imperative to act following the decision-making. This is a 'thin' organisation, run from Singapore with around 40 staff.

There are many NHRD issues – improving the quality of teaching and the skills and labour force issues are central – but spanning the differences among the included economies is a huge challenge. This is not really a regional community with a political project like the EU. It has a trade and investment agenda. It is very conservative; refusing, for example, to research projects on labour migration. It adopts a technicist view that there are no politics in production. Alongside a unitarist philosophy this means that there are no discussions with social partners, and delegates are advised by business only. There may be myriad HRD projects, but there is no unifying political power which presents problems with the labour market response to economic crises. NHRD is on the agenda because its importance is accepted. APEC delegates are comfortable talking about that rather than other things. Yet a fear of human capital deficit does exist, and there is more than a trade agenda to consider.

Conclusion

To understand HRD from the perspective of NHRD public policy is to encounter a set of options, debates, historical legacies and public policy choices. These are managed through complex stakeholder relationships, and in any national setting, HRD public policy development and review will face common challenges. Tangibly there will be a mosaic of overlapping agencies and initiatives, varying from country to country and region to region, constituting NHRD. The underlying common issues are, from an economic and social policy perspective, that there are often gaps in NHRD provisions and contentious matters of 'who pays for what' to be resolved. These are long-standing concerns and, despite many studies, initiatives and policy reviews, there is still no settled agreement on what needs to be done. Continuing major reviews and country-based studies into workforce development are evident, such as the United Kingdom's Leitch review, along with initiatives from supranational bodies such as the European Commission's consultations on, and promotion of, lifelong learning.

Taking the long-term view, looking back and looking ahead, challenges with NHRD public policy are a symptom of the general problem of the complex interaction of the key partners and institutions in contemporary societies. Is the way to bring about change and improvement in HRD to influence either government policy or the practices of firms in free market capitalism? Neither alone can provide the NHRD at work required, but those seeking to influence either, or indeed both, find it difficult to get the right balance of partnerships and collaboration. This was true of the old global system, when certain nation-states in the developed world were pursuing national interests in conjunction with indigenous firms. It seems equally true of the contemporary world, with growing economies, new challenges for developed economies, and, with regional alliances such as the EU seeking to deal with the realities of governing a large region when international firms are operating in an open global economy.

On the one hand, there is a concern to provide a strategic, impartial and wide-ranging view of workforce development and its role, as exemplified by the more recent review in the United Kingdom. Yet for some countries' problems in HRD seem to reflect circumstances in which a commitment to a voluntarist philosophy has produced endless institutional reform in the hope of finally hitting the right approach to involve individuals, employers and government in an optimum way. On the other hand, the point is that, no matter how strong the argument for NHRD, a range of political, economic and social forces and factors exist and influence policy. Sustaining and directing policy support for NHRD remains a challenge for all countries in the future, developed and developing.

Exercise 14.1: Answer

If you were asked to justify adopting either a compulsory, non-legislative or 'do nothing' public policy' on NHRD in your national context, what would you choose and what factors would you say are in favour of your stance? Do this in the context of one specific national context.

The list was based on one proposed by Heckman and Masterov (2004) and incorporating thematic concerns in lifelong learning in the EU. There are no definitive rankings of priority here; it depends on the economic and political positions adopted. Your responses may show that government ought to intervene in all these areas, or stay out of all them, or pick and choose where to intervene. In terms of agreeing or disagreeing with the points listed there about the United Kingdom there is likely to be a range of responses. Some points are not controversial: for example, that the area of HRD is a complex one with many agents involved and with government playing some kind of facilitating role. Some points are open to more evidence-based analysis and should be judged on that: for example the costs and benefits of changing class sizes in primary schools. Others, however, are more controversial and political: that resources should be taken from elite higher education and invested in the general education of under 5-year-olds, or that those who 'benefit' from education should pay for it. Agreeing or disagreeing with these is a matter of values and world-view, not common sense or research evidence. Heckman and Masterov may be world experts on developing human capital, but their conclusions reflect as much a moral as an analytical approach to analysing human capital and behaviour. They take into account the following core beliefs and values:

- Learning begets learning as there are 'dynamic complementarities'; governments have to understand this and act accordingly. The challenge is not just about employers failing to train, but also about individuals and groups in various categories not engaging with learning at key stages early on, and therefore not engaging in later stages of life either.

- Families, schools and firms can all create 'human capital'. HRD policy can be related to all of these. In other words it can be a part of policy on the most fundamental social issues, including some of the most contentious arenas of policy: for example, the quality of parenting, and what parents want for their children. Paternalistic interventions by government may be seen to be strongly warranted in early life in dysfunctional families, or they may be fiercely resisted.

- There is a complex dynamic to the human capital creation and accumulation process because a multiplicity of actors and institutions are involved in determining investments. It is never possible for one central stakeholder to control all of this; a variety of powerful stakeholder interests need to be reconciled. Policy-making must recognise differences in abilities, and proceed with cost–benefit analyses on that basis. This realism rather than an ideology-based approach is important because, otherwise, policy-makers can skew the system badly. For example, rather than focus on higher education for the many – arguably because we are in the era of the knowledge economy but also because that appeals to key target voter groups – governments might do better to invest in improved care and education for the under-5-year-olds to produce a core productive labour force. But the latter option involves appealing to a group whose voting power is weak.

- People who benefit from HRD should pay for it.

Your beliefs and values will be different, so your priorities will be different. This illustrates how developing and implementing HRD public policy is embedded in wider policy debates and challenges. That may be helpful where these connections stimulate interest in workforce HRD and have a positive impact on it. Alternatively, it may be a challenge if these connections impede effective workforce HRD policy-making. In public policy there is no right and wrong answer. Of course those responsible for policy and its implementation seek to be 'evidence-based'; but often there is no definitive, or even very clear, evidence available. Social, political and moral factors inform and shape policy development.

3 Key Texts

(1) Cohen, S. (1994) *Human Resource Development and Utilization: Economic Analysis for Policy Making* (Aldershot: Avebury).

(2) Esland, G. (1991) *Education, Training and Employment*, Volumes 1 & 2 (London: Addison-Wesley).

(3) Harbison, F. H. and Myers, C. A. (1964) *Education, Manpower and Economic Growth: Strategies of Human Resource Development* (New York: McGraw Hill).

3 Key Articles

(1) Cho, E. and McLean, G. N. (2004) 'What We Discovered about NHRD and What It Means for HRD', *Advances in Developing Human Resources*, 6 (3), pp. 382–393.

(2) Lynham, S. A. and Cunningham, P. W. (2006) 'National Human Resource Development in Transitioning Societies in the Developing World: Concepts and Challenges', *Advances in Developing Human Resources*, 8 (1), pp. 116–135.

(3) Wang, G. and Swanson, R. (2008) 'The Idea of National HRD: An Analysis Based on Economics and Theory Development Methodology', *Human Resource Development Review*, 7(1), pp. 79–106.

3 Key Web Links

(1) APEC: http://www.apec.org/.

(2) India National HRD network: http://www.nationalhrd.org/.

(3) EU Lifelong Learning: http://ec.europa.eu/education/lifelong-learning-programme/doc78_en.htm.

15

Comparative HRD

Learning Objectives

By the end of this chapter you will be able to:

- Define the United Nations Human development Index;
- Examine and review three representative NHRD social, economic and cultural contexts;
- Describe how cultural differences can shape perceptions, understanding and practice in HRD;
- Reflect on the challenges of conceptual and functional equivalence in NHRD.

Introduction

Human Resource Development (HRD) broadly defined is of policy and practical concern in what the United Nations identifies as three kinds of national Human Development contexts: (1) affluent and developed nations, (2) developing nations facing critical challenges (3) and nations with basic, multiple problems in developing people. The United Nations has an index which classifies all nations in these terms, a Human Development Index (HDI). The cultural factors that are raised by studying Comparative HRD are discussed. On case is outlined in detail, that of Morocco. A further case in conclusion is given, Pakistan.

Comparative HRD

The desired outcome of HRD, within organisational contexts, ranges from learning or performance to learning and performance, whereas within larger community, national and international contexts, it ranges between the economic or humanitarian, to the economic and humanitarian (Paprock 2006). Mclean and Mclean (2011) have offered tentative definition of HRD after the analysis of HRD scholars and practitioners' definitions from various countries. HRD 'is any process or activity that, either initially or over the long term, has the potential to develop adults' work-based knowledge, expertise, productivity and satisfaction, whether for personal or group/team gain, or for the benefit of an organisation, community, nation or, ultimately, the whole of humanity'. The definition identified two dimensions which they perceived as more influential on the definition of HRD as considering the national contexts. These dimensions are scope of the activities, ranging from training and development to improving technical and productive skills, and the beneficiaries of these activities, for example individuals, organisations, nation and communities. HRD activities, when targeted at national level are termed as National HRD (NHRD). Wang and McLean (2007) used the term NHRD to replicate the concept of policy-oriented approach to HRD at the national level.

Cox et al. (2005) show that understanding how political, economic, socio-cultural and technological contexts drive and shape the necessary nature and role of national HRD in. Instead of developing countries having what makes for HRD imposed upon them externally; by multinational corporations or international organisations that are based in the developed, western world, comparative study is crucial for studying, understanding and legitimising the emergence of HRD from within national contexts. Each country has its own way of focusing and developing their human resources because of their varying political, economic and socio-cultural contexts. It is of essence importance to understand both past and present contexts as it helps understanding the emergence of HRD as a national priority.

The challenges and issues involved in understanding and applying HRD in these different contexts, given the different socio-cultural, economic and political backgrounds, can be appreciated by reviewing representative cases from each category. In each there are different challenges to be understood and engaged with; from the widespread and intensive human development required to sustain advanced economies, through the use of HRD as an engine of change in developing countries to the hope for basic progress in low HDI nations as a foundation for overall improvement in the quality of lives. In comparative HRD the challenge is to

> bridge the gap between the micro- and macro-level of national and international skills analyses...(can)...greatly improve networking and cooperation between all actors in the field. (Markowitsch and Plaimaur 2009, p. 833)

This is evident in the concerns of transnational organisations, such as the United Nations. HRD broadly defined is of policy and practical concern in what the United Nations identify as three kinds of national Human Development contexts; affluent and developed nations, developing nations facing critical challenges, and nations with basic, multiple problems in developing people. The United Nations has an index which classifies all nations in these terms, a Human Development Index (HDI) (Perspective 15.1).

Tome (2009) outlines the frameworks for evaluation that may be in use for evaluating HRD comparatively, across countries. Any of these might be further developed to provide a meeting point between the micro and the macro. What would this look like? What is possible? These can be considered ranging from the empirical and easy to measure through intermediate frameworks to more abstract and theoretical constructs.

Perspective 15.1: UN HDI

High HDI nations are affluent, developed nations. The top ten are Norway, Australia, Ireland, Canada, Ireland, the Netherlands, Sweden, France, Switzerland and Japan.

HDI medium status nation are developing nations with critical challenges. The top 10 in this category are Armenia, Ukraine, Azerbaijan, Thailand, Iran, Georgia, Dominican Republic, China, Belize, Samoa

Low HDI status nations are those facing multiple problems (the changing village). These include Afghanistan, Sierra Leone, central African republic, Mali, Burkina Faso, Congo, Chad, Burundi, Guinea-Bissau, Mozambique and Ethiopia.

Practice 15.1: United Nations Human Development Index (HDI) (ref UN)

One model for measuring levels of Human Development is the UN HDI. This uses data about three areas to produce an overall, single figure which places a country in one of three bands. The data is about;

Education; net enrolments in primary, secondary and tertiary education

Standard of living; GDP per capita

Health; longevity

The three bands are;

High HDI   0.8 to 1.000
Medium HDI   0.500 to 0.800
Low HDI   < 0.500

High HDI countries tend to be have high levels of enrolment in primary, secondary and tertiary education; high levels of GDP per capita, and populations with the greatest longevity. UN (2011)

Source: http://hdr.undp.org/en/, accessed 3rd March 2011.

Perspective 15.2:

	Issues	Quantitative
Measure activity (lifelong learning in last four weeks) and public spending: count investments and the number of people affected – what are the obvious priorities	Appeals to administrators, basic and easy	

Measure impact: what is the difference made? What works for public = social policy impact and public good. For private = productivity	Cover both public programmes and organisational activity	Combined
Skill classifications and qualifications frameworks	Demographic analysis of current and anticipated needs	
Index: UN HDI – educational only, not training – track financial investment – how to evaluate these as economic impacts		
Forcefield analysis; PEST – Political, Economic, Socio-Cultural, Technological	Human development, not resource oriented	
Political systems; Typology of NHRD (McLean 2004); compare different kinds of system (e.g. centralised vs. centralised, tripartite vs. tripartite	Plain and simple – shallow	Qualitative
Maturity levels; scope of HRD activities and beneficiaries (Mclean and Mclean 2011)	Institutional and stakeholder analysis- plans vs. markets	
Cross-Cultural Issues (e.g. Individualism vs. Collectivism, Confucian Values)	From basic to intermediate to advanced levels?	
Human development most broadly (Harbinson and Meyer 1964, UN HDI); in classical economics skills are a factor in development and growth. In neo-classical (1950s) HCT	Agreed framework to use	

In exploring comparative HRD an appreciation and mindfulness of the challenges of ethnocentrism is helpful. Ethnocentrism is like a filter with which people may view others level of development, projecting issues, problems and solutions, onto them. Ethnocentrism can result in superficial misunderstanding of situations, more significantly it can interfere with developing HRD, government skill policy, institutional development and the partnerships with international agencies needed to drive better HRD. Perceptions of human development, its purpose and its outcome, are embedded in some basic and deeply held cultural beliefs which show patterns of difference. There are many ways to map these, and Perspective 15.3 gives one fairly straightforward framework, from

Schwartz, of three dimensions of cultural influence. Studies in comparative HRD are lacking, as

> Studies have tended to focus on different training methods and methodologies rather than on cultural influences on the forms and relations of HRD processes in different countries (Metcalfe and Rees 2005, p. 457)

Perspective 15.3: Cultural Factors

Individuals	Conservatism	Autonomy
	Individuals are embedded in a web of social relationships and obligations, both intellectually and affectively	Individuals are primarily autonomous, free to be what they want to be.
Roles	Hierarchy	Egalitarianism
	Ascribing roles and legitimising unequal distributions of power, wealth, and influence	Citizens are all moral equals, with equal rights and responsibilities.
Goals	Mastery	Harmony
	Seek to influence and change the natural and social worlds	Accept the natural and social worlds as they are and emphasise fitting in harmoniously and adapting to them.

With globalisation, and the global re-shaping the local bringing greater inter-connectedness and interdependent economies there is a smaller world with greater scope for ethnocentrism to interfere (see Perspective 15.4). Cultures seen to be representative of the values of autonomy, egalitarianism and emphasising mastery, especially the global superpower of the USA, have been seen to be pre-eminent. In the twentieth century the rivalry was between superpowers divided along political lines, the collectivist socialist and communist countries and others. Now cultures perceived to have values that are more conservative, hierarchical and emphasising harmony, especially China economically and Islamic countries, are significant forces. The extent to which a new rivalry is taking shape, which in part is shaped by and around human development philosophies and practices, is a major political question. At a more personal level the continuing experience of migration of people from developing nations to advanced economies provides an everyday context in which the grand debates about ethnocentrism are real and present.

Another key issue is also one of generational change. The extent to which younger generations have different value profiles to older generations, whether or not these are lifestage differences only, presents an interesting set of issues when it comes to mapping and taking account of cultural differences.

One of the effects of ethnocentrism can be conflating cultural practice with good practice. For example, it can be assumed that individualism is reciprocal with affluence, cultural complexity and social mobility. If HRD both requires these and contributes to achieving these, then the conclusion is that encouraging more individualistic attitudes and behaviours is a positive policy. If, however, this is not assumed, and is rather seen as ethnocentric, then encouraging more individualistic attitudes and behaviours will be seen as part of the problem, not a solution.

Comparative studies can be of three kinds. One is 'Unicultural': with the intention being to examine HRD in one culture or country. Another is 'Polycentric': involving comparisons between multiple countries or cultures. Often these studies use 'Cross Cultural' Psychology models. Finally studies may be 'Synergistic': interested in specific phenomena in a multicultural organisation; for example, what team development issues are faced in different cultures or how processes like coaching might be taken up differently in different cultural contexts.

Perspective 15.4: Individualism and Collectivism

Reciprocal with individualism	Reciprocal with collectivism
Affluence	Under-development
Cultural complexity	Uniformity
Social mobility	Social Immobility

The search for universals, ways of making sense of the tremendous variety and complexity of national and individual behaviour and thought across the cultures of the world. The Schwartz framework above uses 'social values' to describe cultural difference, around three factors. More elaborate models have been proposed (see Perspective 15.5).

Perspective 15.5: Hofstede

Individualism (Caring)	Collective.......Individual self-centered
Power-Distance (Respected)	Large.............Small
Masculinity (Achievement)	Feminine. . ...Masculine Relationship Assertiveness
Uncertainty Avoidance	Avoid.............Tolerate No Ambiguity....Ambiguity OK
Long Term Orientation	Long term.......Short term Defer...........Gratify

Simplifying, the reductionist view emerges from noting that the largest number of empirical studies in cross-cultural psychology have been based on a single dimension of culture; individualism and collectivism (Kagitcibasi 1997). The conclusion is that

> it is probably safe to infer that this dimension is the most important yield of cross-cultural psychology to date. (Smith et al. 1996, p. 237)

By 'individualism' is meant the beliefs that the individual is an end in himself or herself; with an obligation to realise themselves; to cultivate one's own judgement; to resist social pressures towards conformity; to be 'oneself'. By collectivism is meant the beliefs that emphasise the views, needs and goals of the group; social norms and duty as defined by the group; shared beliefs and traditions; a readiness to cooperate and surrender personal goals to group interest.

Socialisation for self-reliance, independence and adeptness when entering new groups. It can be taken for granted, but this requires emotional detachment from the 'collective'; prioritising the self and the immediate family; having personal goals that take primacy over those of the larger group; behaviour being judged in terms of rationality and cost-benefit analyses.

Exercise 15.1: Scope your Own Culture

Consider the culture you are originally from. Rate the extent to which it tends to value one or other position in each of the three values below.

Conservatism   Autonomy
      5   4   3   2   1   2   3   4   5
Hierarchy   Egalitarianism
      5   4   3   2   1   2   3   4   5
Harmony   Mastery
      5   4   3   2   1   2   3   4   5

What form might ethnocentrism about HRD take for you?

What differences in perceptions about the purpose, role and style of HRD would you expect to find between cultures which were at opposite positions on all these factors?

It is important to keep in mind that the aims of HRD, developing skills, knowledge and attitudes for and in employment, cannot be taken apart from broader cultural development. However, the focus is on changing behaviour in work roles, not challenging or transforming an entire culture. Developing an appreciation of comparative issues, a sensitivity to them, is necessary to understand, notice and deal with both policy and day-to-day interactions in HRD. This can be achieved with some self-enquiry and awareness of one's own culture, and an appreciative enquiry outlook on HRD in others' culture.

Because most cross-cultural research situations involve encounters between researchers from one culture (Western/USA and individualist) and informants from another (generally more collectivist), self-enquiry is necessary. Even most fundamental concepts, the meaning of which is presumed to be obvious and universal, should be examined, for example performance, potential, learning, change, trust. Even when concepts have the same meaning across cultures, these concepts may perform different functions. The meaning of 'mentoring' may be similar, for example in the USA and China, the functional role of mentoring in the two cultures may be different. In China, mentoring is more focussed on the developmental. In the USA, mentoring is more focused on sponsorship. If studies and stories entail concepts, are these meaning the same? The concept of 'mentoring' then has different meanings in different national contexts. How it is to be defined and to whom it applies makes any comparative studies based on operationalising one universal concept difficult to uphold. People are not talking about the same thing (Ardichvli and Kuchinke 2002).

Cross-Cultural Issues

Cross-cultural psychological research is based on the assumption of a common value profile among citizens, representing shared acculturation and integration through a single or dominant language, institutions, political system, and shared mass media, products, services and national symbols. Understanding arises from the act of interpretation, an act in the comparative context of translating what is said in one language into the meanings and codes of another language. Comparative HRD raises to another level the need to understand and present accurately perspectives of different actors. Phenomena are studied by poorly informed outsiders who lack the background to understand the intricacies of local cultures and symbolic systems. Researchers in a peculiar position:

> All the talk about the ethnographer being 'accepted' by the natives is nonsense. He can, at best, hope to be regarded as a harmful village idiot. (Barley 1983, p. 46)

Accounts may control and distort the informant's voices by imposing their own interpretations, narrative styles and choices of the elements of the native's text to include in the research report. This is mitigated by appreciative enquiry, with mutual valuing being essential for understanding cross-culturally; promoting an open, uncritical approach to others' perspectives which attempts to understand others' points of view without criticising their knowledge claims. Bakhtin calls this 'Multivoicedness'; not centred on attempts to understand others' perspectives, as if these perspectives were rigid, once-and-for-all given (and one is better than another, one 'wins', the other 'loses') but through dialogue learning to understand, at the same time this very dialogue invariably also creates a space for new realities to be created. Western dominance has not only been economic, but also culturally, including the influence of social science, and in HRD the disciplines of psychology and OD. With their US and European traditions of individualism, newer and emerging economic powers can be contrasted with this, with their cultural profiles and differences on collectivism.

Morocco Case Study

Morocco is a country which is an example of a medium HDI society (see Cases 15.1 and 15.2). According to the UN HDI it has shown improvements in recent decades; from scoring an HDI of 0.429 in 1975 to a HDI of 0.620 in 1995. It is a transitioning society in the developing world, making significant progress. This is a relative success story, and over that period HRD has been a contributing factor:

> HRD related pressures include responding to an external environment that stresses global capitalism and international human rights and an internal environment that seeks economic growth and improvements in reducing social disparities. (Cox et al. 2006, p. 88)

Case 15.1: Morocco Socio-cultural Population	
1975–	17.3 Million
2003–	30.1 Million
Language	
Official language;	Modern Standard Arabic
Business and diplomacy;	French
Home language;	Moroccan dialect of Arabic or Berber dialects
Adult Illiteracy;	48.3 per cent
Disparities in human development	
Male-urban education enrolments;	98 per cent in 2002
Rural-female education enrolments;	78.6 per cent in 2002
Recent reform	
Legal age of marriage	Raised from 15 to 18
Divorce	Right of women to divorce

Understanding the lessons from the history and contemporary context of NHRD in a country like Morocco helps identify the policy and practice themes of NHRD in this context.

Case 15.2: Morocco Economic Facts

GDP; $45 Billion (2003)

Sectors	GDP	Employment (share of workforce)
Service sector	53 per cent	45 per cent
Industrial;	29.7 per cent	15 per cent
Agriculture;	18.3 per cent	40 per cent

Self sufficient in high level manpower needs, excepting scientific and technical fields; Surplus of graduates in humanities, shortage in engineering and business; Economic changes (free trade agreements) put a strain on education and training. Unemployment; 12.1 per cent

Economic Issues

Capital Intensive Agriculture

Irrigation and electricity projects

1970s/80s; rapid urbanisation

1990s; Privatizing state enterprises

Source: http://www.google.com/publicdata?ds=wb-wdi&met=ny_gdp_mktp_cd&idim=country:GBR&dl=en&hl=en&q=UK+GDP#met=ny_gdp

_mktp_cd&idim=country:GBR:MAR:AFG:CHN:USA:HTI

The political, economic and socio-cultural aspects can all be explored. Key reforms intended to promote HRD have been central, with National strategy for HRD is a priority. Cooperation among employers, unions and government exists, but there are still barriers to HRD. Under-developed Institutions. Corrupt business practices are an issue. There is disillusion among the disenfranchised, and a loss of strategic human capital to other countries, especially in Europe. Flight of young Moroccans to Europe legally and the flight of unskilled, lower class, illegally across the Straits of Gibraltar.

HRD Themes

There is a National Charter on Education and Training, with NHRD a top priority. Dealing with the interaction of values is a factor in this country; blending and balancing Islam, nationalism, culture, human rights, science and technology. There is a concern with lifelong learning, partnerships, universities and poverty, unemployment, illiteracy, educational deficiencies. A Ministry for Employment and Professional Training exists with 5,600 staff, managing 186 training centres, developing skills for 360 occupations. The country has democratic governance, trade liberalisation, protection of human rights, but also 'Palace centred' politics, business inefficiency, human rights restrictions.

Primary;	89.6 per cent enrolment – 67.5 per cent completion
Secondary;	37.5 per cent enrolment
Tertiary;	10.8 per cent enrolment
Workplace;	15 per cent receive formal training
Training levy of	1.6 per cent

The enabling factors seen here are:

- Reform-minded monarch
- Major reforms
- Desires of general population heightened

The impediments are:

- Centralised government direction
- Inefficient business practice
- Motivational deficits.

Morocco scores highest on the 'power distance' factor among 62 countries studied – suggesting a traditional 'command and control' attitudes among managers and staff). Other cultural issues and norms that impact on participating in HRD and its outcomes are:

- Flexible view of deadlines;
- Approximation rather than precision;
- Memorisation not critical thinking;
- Procedural not problem-solving approach to work.

Corruption is an issue (Transparency International monitor this at http://transparency.org/).

Morocco is placed 77th out of the 145 most corrupt. Corruption exists in politics, in public contracting, and in the private sector.

Overall there are more impeding than enabling factors to progress further. Much groundwork is done with political, socio-cultural and economic gains, though political, economic and socio-cultural challenges persist. Future needs to sustain and progress greater HRD include:

- Effective HRD professionals;
- Economic policies for skill development;
- Strategic sectors to grow;
- Improve literacy to encourage change in agribusiness;
- Support tourism;
- Retrain in the declining sectors.

Case: Pakistan

Below is a brief description of political, economic and socio-cultural historical-transitional contexts of Pakistan.

Politics

Pakistan was the part of Indian subcontinent which was ruled by Afghans and Mughals for centuries with various influences on the politics and culture of the area. Although they were unable to promote educational and human development initiates but they introduced various political and architectural systems. The British came to dominate the region in eighteenth century, and by the early twentieth century British India included all of modern Pakistan. During the British rule, education and railway system was introduced. Government College Lahore, University of Punjab and other well-known educational institutions were built during the British era in the present day Pakistan. Because of hostilities between Muslims and Hindus in the Indian subcontinent, the separate Muslim state of Pakistan was created when British India gained independence in 1947 (Country Watch 2009).

Pakistan was originally in two parts – the east wing and the west wing (present- day Pakistan). East Pakistanis felt that power was unfairly concentrated in the west, and in 1971 with the help of India, East Pakistan became a separate state of Bangladesh. This had huge influence on the human resources as East Pakistan had a population of almost 90 million at that time and literacy rate was also higher there. Pakistan and India fought four major wars mainly because of the disputed Kashmir territory. Although the dispute is ongoing, discussions and confidence-building measures have led to decreased tensions since 2002. This conflict has made government to focus on arm forces and nearly 70 per cent of the budget is allocated for army while only 2–3 per cent is allocated for education (Economic Survey of Pakistan, 2008–09). In this way and others the legacy of the period of the 'cold war' has influenced the political system. It has also brought about 4 million refugees to the country.

Politics in Pakistan in the past few decades has been marked by corruption, inefficiency and confrontations between various institutions. Alternating periods of civilian and military rule have not helped to establish stability. For about 32 years military has ruled with focus mainly on the improvement of arm forces. The most recent coup was in October 1999, when coup ousted the civilian government and the coup leader General Musharraf came to power. Mounting public dissatisfaction with President Musharraf, coupled with the assassination of the prominent and popular political leader Benazir Bhutto in late 2007, led to Musharraf's resignation in August 2008 and the election of Zardari, Bhutto's widower, as president (Country Watch 2009).

Pakistani government and military forces are challenged to maintain control over the tribal areas adjacent to the border with Afghanistan and other parts of the country, where Taliban-linked militants are firmly entrenched. In the meanwhile, through the support of international community, Pakistani government is focusing on new policies for human development and higher education. There have been many scholarships for higher education abroad and at home.

Economics

During the British reign, the present-day Pakistan included a railways infrastructure, irrigated land and some basic industry. The main focus was agriculture and mostly government policies were focusing this field. During 1960s, government introduced and implemented new policies which sustained an economic growth rate of 6.8 per cent for the whole decade. The political crisis of 1971 and nationalisation of mid-1970s led the country to a low economic growth. The economy recovered during the 1980s via a policy of deregulation, as well as an increased inflow of remittances from expatriate workers and foreign aid of the cold war.

The high-level corruption and governmental incompetence during 1990s has slow down the growth level (UNDP, 2002). The economic sanctions after the nuclear tests in 1999 also aid to economic slowdown. But the first few years of this century were economically better as the average GDP growth rate remain 5 per cent which include 9 per cent GDP growth rate of 2005 and 2 per cent of 2009. Over the last decade GDP has a growth pattern as from $ 75 billion in 1999; GDP has increased to $ 166.5 billions in 2009. Analysing the sectoral contribution to GDP, it is observed that agriculture contributes 23 per cent, industry 25 per cent while services contributes about 52 per cent. Pakistan is still an agrarian society with 44 per cent of workforce engaged with agriculture while industry engages 21 per cent and services 35 per cent (Economic Survey of Pakistan 2008–09; Labour Force Survey 2007–08; Budget Report 2009–10).

Socio-cultural

Pakistan comprises numerous diverse cultures and ethnic groups which have affected the socio-cultural system and ultimately influenced the HRD strategy. Pakistan's population is over 161 million which include 51 per cent of female population. Being a conservation society females are not let to get higher education and work which has huge influence on economy as well. Total workforce consists of 51 million which includes only 10 million females which means there is still 40 million more female workers which are not let to work in one way or the other. The overall Literacy rate in Pakistan is 56 per cent where literacy rate for male is 69 per cent while females' literacy rate is only 44 per cent. Life expectancy is 65.4 years which is less than average world life expectancy i.e.

67.2 years (Economic Survey of Pakistan, 2008–09; Labour Force Survey 2007–08; Country Watch 2009).

Human Development Index

Human Development index (HDI) is a composite index of three indices reflecting a country's achievements in health and longevity (as measured by life expectancy at birth), education (measured by adult literacy and combined primary, secondary and tertiary enrolments) and living standard (measured by GDP per capita in purchasing power parity terms) (UNDP, 2002). It was first introduced in 1990 by United Nations Development Programme (UNDP) to rank countries by the level of human development. UN HDI classify countries into three levels of human development based on their scores as high development countries score between 0.800 and 1.000, medium between 0.500 and 0.800 and low development countries are those who score below 0.500. UNDP in 2007 introduced a new category of very high development countries which are those countries which score above 0.900.

UNDP human development index issued on 5th October 2009 which used 2007 data ranked Pakistan as 141st country out of 180 countries analysed regarding the human development. Pakistan is still in the medium developed countries by scoring 0.572 in 2009. Observing the trend over the years, it may be depicted that Pakistan has improved in HDI. As in 1980, Pakistan score was as low as 0.400 which increased to 0.518 in 1995. The current priorities seem to improve the situation further. The recent 18th amendment in the constitution of Pakistan passed on 15th April 2010, government has shown its commitment to promote education and improve health which is a sign for further improvement in the HDI score.

National Human Resource Development in Pakistan

In case of Pakistan, it may be said that it fits in transitional model as its improvement in HDI and government priorities states that it is moving from a centralised system to a decentralised one. The recent government policies and international community pressure for the improvement of education is one of the reason for being in transitional period.

Transitional period in Pakistan even started during 1990s with introduction of Privatisation Commission for privatising public owned organisations. This process slow down later in 1990s but now it has almost ended. Presently, Pakistan is under pressure of international community for changing the current political, economic and socio-cultural situation as there are many stakeholders involved in it. There are many funds and grants announced for Pakistan recently which mainly include grants in the form of Kerry-Lugar Bill from United States. This bill includes a grant of $7.5 billion payable in five steps at $1.5 billion annually. The conditions attached for with this bill include focus on education and particularly higher education. This is a good sign for changing the NHRD priorities and improvement of human resources in the country (UNDP 2002).

Education System

The structure of education in Pakistan is divided into five levels: (1) primary school (grades one through five); (2) middle school (grades six through eight); (3) high school (grades nine and ten); (4) intermediate (grades 11 and 12, leading to a higher secondary school certificate); and (5) university programmes (leading to graduate and advanced degrees). The current government of Prime Minister Syed Yousuf Raza Gilani has introduced new educational policy where compulsory education will be until 10th class which was before until primary; grades 11 and 12 (intermediate education) is no more be part of college education but is merged into the school system. Primary school is upgraded to the middle level (CIA 2009).

The primary school finishing ratio in Pakistan is 63 per cent; furthermore, 72 per cent boys and 68 per cent girls reach to primary level. Higher education ratio was as low as 2.9 per cent in 2004 while it is reached to 4.0 per cent in 2008 and 4.7 per cent in 2009. The government of Pakistan plans to increase this figure to 10 per cent by 2015 and subsequently to 15 per cent by 2020. Education ratio varies in different age group in Pakistan. Between the years 2000–04, Pakistanis in the age group of 55–64 had a literacy rate of almost 30 per cent, those aged 45–54 had a literacy rate of nearly 40 per cent, those aged 25–34 had a literacy rate of 50 per cent, and those aged between 15–24 had a literacy rate more than 60 per cent. These data indicate that, with every passing generation, the literacy rate in Pakistan is rising by almost 10 per cent.

Labour Force

Pakistan has a total labour force of 51.78 million which includes 40.82 million males while 10.96 millions are females (Labour Force Survey 2007–08). The age intervals between 20 to 50 years rank as the most productive period of life. Although the male labour force of this age in Pakistan is involved in work at the rate of almost 80 to 85 per cent while female labour force of this age is only involved at the rate of 20 to 25 per cent. This shows that there is considerable space for female labour force to increase their involvement and participation in the economic development of the country.

Another important factor in the workforce is their competitiveness. It is an attribute important for the saviour of the country economic development after post quota regime. In the Global Competitive Index, World Employment Forum lists the profiles of South East Asian countries for the year 2007–08, where India dominates in competitiveness. It comes 55th in terms of Higher education and training and 96th in labour market efficiency while Pakistan is 116th and 113th in both respectively (Labour Force Survey Pakistan 2007–08). This explains why Pakistan is not doing so well in trade since it has very low offer in terms of efficiency and training of the labour force. Pakistan needs to step up its efforts in this regard if it wishes to compete in the global arena.

Implications for HRD Strategy in Pakistan

After describing the historical, transitional and current conditions of Pakistan, it is now easy to identify the elements influencing the emergence and development of a national approach to HRD in Pakistan. These elements help to notify factors important to an effective NHRD strategy which includes factors enabling and/or impeding the successful implementation of such a strategy.

Harbison and Myers (1964) explained four levels of countries in terms of human and economic development. Pakistan may best be fitted in level III as the conditions defined fits Pakistan current situations. They recommended elements for each of these levels for developing their human recourses. Their recommendation for level III countries includes improving higher education towards science and technology, making primary education universal, improving the quality of secondary education and focusing on non-academic professional training. Analysing the situation of Pakistan, the following factors may be placed as enabling and impeding for an effective HRD strategy.

Enabling Factors

It is imperative for Pakistan to focus on an effective NHRD strategy. The current conditions in Pakistan suggest that there are many factors which might be helpful for an effective NHRD strategy. Firstly, 161 million populations is itself a factor which can make the country to compete in the world markets. The cheap availability of labour can be a good attraction to investors. Female population, currently only participate in the development of the country at around 20 to 25 per cent, can be a good source of change if positive approach towards working of female is adopted. The current government approach towards education and economic development is also an enabling factor for implementing an effective NHRD strategy. This will help change the socio-cultural impediments towards human development. The recently passed 18th amendment has empowered provinces, protected human rights and pledged the improvement of education which will ultimately aid to an effective implementation of NHRD strategy. The announcement for compulsory primary education in the 18th amendment is one of the factors which help increase education ratio.

The current international pressure on Pakistan for social, educational and economic change is also one the enabling factor for an effective NHRD strategy. The Kerry Lugar bill from United States which pledge to give 7.5 billion dollar in 5 years is an effort to change the struggling situation of Pakistan. This bill includes the conditions to invest money in education and particularly in higher education. Similarly International Monetary Fund (IMF) World Bank and other institutions are also funding Pakistan for promoting different causes which includes the human development as priority. Another enabling factor is the Diaspora of Pakistan which currently is over a million. They are living in different developed countries including The United Kingdom, The United States of America, Canada, Australia, France, Germany, etc. They can have a good influence on the economic, social, and educational change of the country.

Impeding Factors

Pakistan imperative requirement is to overcome the impeding factors which are hurdle to the economic and human development of the country. These impeding factors include political instability, centralised governance, corruption, ethnic bias, terrorism, gender discrimination, energy crisis, ineffective budgetary distributions and globalisation. Pakistan basic problem is its political instable situation over the decades. Clashes between different institutions have made the country suffer. Incessant invasion of military into government and their rule for decades has aid to instable political environment. The undue power of military has made them more powerful and thus their budgetary share is as high as 70 per cent of GDP while education get only 2 to 3 per cent share. The lack of funds in the education sector has adverse affect on almost all the sectors and on the socio-cultural situation of the country.

The system of government is centralised with a complex procedure for decision making. Corruption is inhabited in almost every sector of the country. Transparency International report (2009) ranked Pakistan on 42nd number in corruption list of 180 countries. This has prevented institutions and talent to grow. The gender discrimination has also affected the country to a great extent which can be seen in the female work force participation ratio which is as low as 20 to 25 per cent as compare to 80 to 85 per cent of male. Some socio-cultural values at some points are a source of deprivation particularly for females. Pakistan is the country of five distinct nations; Punjabi, Pashtoon, Sindhi, Bolachi and Saraiki. The continuous deprivation of four of them by one nation has made the country to an unfavourable situation where a high level of ethnic bias can be seen. This has also caused the country to break in 1971 and now is prevented the talent to come forward.

One of the main problems currently faced by the country is the energy crisis. Pakistan currently requires additional 5,000 MW electricity for running the basic house hold and industry electric material. The shortage of power has caused millions to suffer and many industries are now shut down because of these crisis. Pakistan local industry is unable to compete in the international markets particularly because of low global competitive index and low technological and industrial development. This is also impeding the country to reach to a stable position and have a stable NHRD strategy.

Conclusion

The overall situation of Pakistan since independence has improved to a large extent. Pakistan is now in the medium human development category of UN HDI list. Education system is improving and literacy rate is growing almost 10 per cent for every generation, but it has contributed in another problem of generation gap and differences in their attitudes. The strategic location of Pakistan, it 161 million population, international funds and diaspora can help to built an effective NHRD strategy. Beside these factors, there are impeding factors like corruption, political instability, gender and ethnic discrimination and socio-cultural problems which are persistently making hurdles in the development of the country. Government has to take in consideration both enabling and impeding factors to shape and implement successful and sustainable policies which will help the country to develop it human resources.

3 Key Texts

(1) Hofstede, G. (1997) *Culture and Organizations, 2nd Edition.* (Thousand Oaks, CA: Sage).

(2) Usunier, J.-C. (1998) *International and Cross-Cultural Management Research* (London: Sage).

(3) Hansen, C. and Lee, Y. (2009) *The Cultural Contexts of Human Resource Development* (Basingstoke: Palgrave Macmillan).

3 Key Articles

(1) Ardichvli, A. and Kuchinke, P. (2002) 'The Concept of Culture in International and Comparative HRD Research: Methodological Problems and Possible Solutions', *Human Resource Development Review*, 1 (2), pp. 145–166.

(2) Metcalf, B. and Rees, C. (2005) 'Theorising Advances in International Human Resource Development', *Human Resource Development International*, 8 (4), pp. 449–465.

(3) Tome, E. (2009) 'The Evaluation of HRD: A Critical Study With Applications', *Journal of European Industrial Training*, 33 (6), pp. 513–538.

3 Key Web Links

(1) Transparency: http://transparency.org/.

(2) United Nations: http://hdr.undp.org/en/.

(3) World Factbook (CIA): https://www.cia.gov/library/publications/the-world- factbook/index.html.

16

Critical HRD

Learning Objectives

By the end of this chapter you will be able to:

- Describe what the concept of critical HRD means;
- Analyse constructivist thinking in HRD;
- Critically evaluate the place of HRD at work in the context of changes in management and organisation.

Introduction

Beyond links between theory and practice in organising learning, and applied analysis of that for organisations and countries, there is a growing concern with critical thinking and research in Human Resource Development (HRD). The realist and the constructivist framings of what critical HRD means, and why it matters, are discussed.

Critical HRD

Knowledge from several different academic disciplines is relevant in the study of HRD at work; including psychology, sociology, business policy, social policy and others. The boundaries of study of HRD at work can be set differently, according to the definitions employed; ranging from managing training to designing an entire organisation's strategy and purpose. Valuable contributions to the literature on HRD at work have been made in all of the last five decades, with the latest not necessarily superseding the earlier. This is particularly true in HRD where new journals have come onto the market. However critics of HRD as a discipline challenge the field's rationale as a force for promoting human capital development (Thody 1999, Elliott and Turnbull 2000, Stewart et al. 2006).

Discussions of critical HRD (Valentin 2006, Sambrook 2009) are emerging as the discipline of HRD matures, and aspects of that are considered here.

HRD Expectations

HRD carries a weight of expectation in modern societies: to develop learning, to create healthy individuals, to overcome deprivation, to test and guide individuals, to provide skills for a changing economy, to keep pupils happy and satisfied, to eradicate prejudice and so on. The list is endless. HRD exists to organise and transmit pre-existing knowledge, propositional knowledge, to create incentives and environments to encourage learning, to shape skills and techniques to facilitate autonomous learning, and to steer enquiry towards truth. The ideal standards of veritistic good practice should be at the heart of the system. Yet the realities can be quite different to this ideal. Bateson critique of schooling, applicable to HRD too, was that:

> It became monstrously evident that schooling...was so careful to avoid all crucial issues.. even grown-up persons with children of their own cannot give a reasonable account of concepts such as entropy, sacrament, syntax, number, quantity, pattern, linear relation, name, class, relevance, energy, redundancy, force, probability, parts, whole, information, tautology, homology, mass (either Newtonian or Christian), explanation, description, rule of dimensions, logical type, metaphor, topology, and so on. What are butterflies? What are starfish? What are beauty and ugliness? (Bateson 1979)

Expectations and activities in HRD are far wider than propositional knowledge, determining which truths to teach, where there is indeed 'true and false' involved; and further, when 'truth' is contested, what to actually teach. The issue and impact of multiculturalism and collaborative learning on the educational process, for example, have been contentious issues. The former gives all types of belief a level footing, raising up certain 'cultures' and pulling down others. Collaborative learning is, in practice, common as learning in groups with peers, in the extreme form suggesting students can only learn from and with their peers, not from any type of authority.

The critique is that there are truths, and there is a big role for telling, for learning based on evidence, and learners accepting supported assertions. The tried and true may be boring, while innovation in HRD attracts kudos but breeds faddishness.

The bigger problem, however, is the failure of HRD to achieve all the goals expected of it, and therefore of a disenchantment with its institutions and agents. Constraining the role of HRD, a return to learning, and the expectation of other agencies to meet broader social expectations is the conclusion.

It is also because, as a social practice, HRD is expected to incorporate elements of good practice from a veritistic point of view.

(1) The distribution of resources to investigate issues of interest in an optimal, truth seeking, way; to individuals and institutions which are truth seeking.

(2) That credit and reward exists in relation to truth seeking, helping to distribute efforts; through the honour as well as reward system.

(3) The dissemination and critical assessment of knowledge in publications centres on truthfulness.

(4) The use of domain specific expertise and authorities to control all these other aspects helps assure that truth seeking is maintained rather than error being compounded.

Is HRD a discipline based on veritism? In part the concern is that study of HRD at work contains evidence, examples and illustrations generated in a wide variety of organisations and from a diverse range of methodologies with varying degrees of rigour. Much material about HRD at work is not readily accessible to non-specialists (for example, internal company reviews or background economic policy review papers) and does not readily lend itself to cumulative review. The concepts included within the study of HRD at work range in scale from those debated between different academic schools of thought (constructivists and behaviourists), through to methodologies of practice (how to manage HRD) down to discrete single 'tools' (making mentoring work, for example).

Deeper and more critical concerns are that HRD is part of the commodification and subjugation of human development for organisational interests. It is part of maintaining control through surveillance, classification, normalisation, deficit assumptions and cultural engineering (Fenwick 2004). HRD is an integral part of employment and organisation. The general nature of that process is widely recognised, and detailed process analysis of the major phases provides the foundation for understanding HRD. But the many and varied practices that arise in the course of managing the HRD process are, in essence, about exploiting the workforce, not developing them.

The key propositions of HRD (Sloman 2006) can be read critically as putting a gloss on this:

- Effective individual learning is critical if employees are to acquire the knowledge and skill needed to support the organisation's business objectives and delivery targets.
- Review of training interventions must ensure that the learning achieved is aligned with business activity.
- Many HR roles are involved in the people development effort, and the boundaries between organisational development, management development and training are becoming increasingly blurred.
- The delivery of effective people development practices requires a considerable increase in commitment and enhanced skills from all managers, particularly first-line managers.
- A shift is taking place from training, an instructor-led content-based intervention, to learning, which is a self-directed work-based process leading to increased adaptive capacity.

- While off-the-job classroom-based training still has a place, it no longer occupies the central role in training provision as other forms of intervention are becoming more important

- Technology is becoming an important enabler in people development, but there are many conceptual and practical issues to be resolved in its implementation.

- It is important to demonstrate the value to be derived from people development activities, but traditional hierarchical training evaluation may not be the most appropriate method.

This is to stand back and think about 'Metaperspectives' (McGuire et al. 2007) and the language of HRD itself. Language is a metaperspective associate with constructivism. The central idea is that the kinds and structures of discourse determine what we 'see' and what is talked about; and these in turn reflect power relationships. What is seen and sanctioned as for debate in HRD reflects the interests of dominant powers. Being critical means showing this, and providing a channel for alternative, under-represented or repressed, voices.

HRD at work has been presented in terms of three related dimensions. First, workplace HRD is a process – a series of phases with associated tasks that need to be controlled and completed. There is a core process of observing, planning, acting and reviewing. This is, or should be, integrated with the performance management of the organisation and general HRM policy and practices. These tasks are about managing organisational intelligence and knowledge, capabilities and behaviours to achieve effective performance. Whatever else changes, this basic process remains constant. The theorising of process does evolve though; the major change has been being the change from theorising the process as being about the provision of training to the management of learning.

Second, HRD involves a range of concepts and methods for developing successful individuals, groups and organisations. HRD practice has been explored here in terms of HRD strategies, partnerships with providers, the increasing use of e-learning and working with groups. Concepts and methods of significance do change from time to time, and from era to era, to fit with changes in the worlds of business, organisations and technology.

Third, there are a range of contexts for making sense of and understanding HRD at work. These different contexts need to be appreciated, considered and combined to enable a complete picture of strengths, weaknesses, practicalities and potential of HRD at work as an area of problem-solving and decision-making of concern to various stakeholders. The perspectives reviewed in this book include the points of view of government and public policy development, the increasing concern with knowledge management, major themes like managing diversity, and new thinking on strategy and the place of HRD in that. Underlying all discussion of process, concepts and contexts there is the background of competing conceptions of HRD. These can be described as the realist and constructivist conceptions. The future of HRD will continue to be shaped and animated by the presence and rivalry of these different traditions in theory and in practice.

Realists versus Constructivists

Perspective 16.1: Realist and Constructivist Framings	
Realist conception of HRD	**Constructivist conception of HRD**
HRD is definable as 'one thing' that can be stated explicitly	HRD is many things, a synthesis of changing concerns, evolving socio-economic forces and adaptations to new circumstances
HRD is a means to win–win social ends; its nature is to ameliorate and improve, to drive and achieve progress	HRD is an arena in which shared and distinct interests exist; it is interconnected with the wider balance of power, and its exercise, in societies; some lose.
HRD theory should prescribe what is to be done	HRD theory should offer insights that open options
Good thinking about HRD shows premises and invites critique around empirical evidence	Good thinking about HRD helps to escape the limiting frames of mind inherited from past eras as change occurs
HRD should be based on 'strong' authorities; reputable scholars whose major theoretical and empirical works form a recognised, stable canon	HRD should be about encouraging and participating in 'languaging'; generating meaning anew, in a social context, original for its times, then obsolete

Realists and constructivist adopt different stances towards the psychological bases, which can interfere with developing knowledge and explain why, in general, people may fail to live the life of reason made possible by the possession of cognitive capacities (see Perspectives 16.1 and 16.3). Modern societies are based upon several systems of trial in specific contexts. These contexts arise with concerns in trials in education where debates are held, in justice systems with their trials before judges or juries, politics with the trials of elections and democratic institutions, mass communication and trial by media, and science with its trial by experiments.

There are a number of elements which are commonly identified as being involved in the normative social practices required for a fair trial in each domain, where there is a contest among the two sides to the story at issue. These normative social practices are used to attain the validation and verification of strong knowledge rather than depending upon unexamined dispositions to satisfactory truth in the context of concrete and contested issues (see Practice 16.1). Questions of what to teach, guilt and innocence, interpretations of current events, which party should govern, and which theory prevails involve contests among individuals and groups with various satisfactory truths; but truth can only be decided upon using a process of trial.

The outcomes are obvious in these special social domains. They are the strong knowledge to be able to accept into or reject from a curriculum, to judge specific questions of guilt and innocence, to report as true and accurate a version of events, the vote for a particular political party and the evaluation of the merits of specific hypotheses. In all these cases strong knowledge rather than false belief should be achieved through using normative procedures.

Normatively appropriate procedures to enable sound deductive inferences. The threat to these institutions of trial and their practices is not just from those who lose when subject to their trials, but it is also from an accumulating disenchantment with the institutions as they fail to live up to ideals and expectations. For Goldman this is because their procedures are flawed, not because their aims are wrong.

Practice 16.1: Elements of Collective Truth Seeking, based on Quinne and Ullian

φ	Observation	Information and analysis	Illusions & delusions
φ	Normal self	Emotions	Knowing oneself
φ	Memory	Learning and thinking	Fallibility
φ	Testimony	Fiduciary framework	Deceit and credulity

Observation is built into all the special domains of collective truth seeking and trial. Education based on observations now dominates the socialisation of children throughout the early stages of their lives up to adulthood. Justice is symbolically blind to the person and concerned only with weighing the actual evidence. Reporting is based on correspondents being on the scene, providing first-hand accounts of their own experience. Democratic government requires elections where the candidates and issues are presented transparently, subject to trial by professional and public questioning. Scientists manage experiments where trails involve verifiable and replicable observations.

But equally observation is problematic in all these domains. Education is most often about passing on accepted accounts rather than discovery under conditions of personal observation. Laws embody perceptions of right and wrong which can be argued to reflect particular powers and interests rather than transcendental principles. Reporter's access to scenes can be restricted, with the example of war coverage is a good example, or non-existent as they report second hand. Election campaigns are notoriously stage managed affairs, where spin matters more than substance. And, as many examples attest, scientific observations and experiments can be manipulated to reach amenable conclusions, at least for a period.

Finally, there are the normative procedures about testimony as a source of strong knowledge. Much of what people claim to 'know' is based on the testimony of others. In the social domains referred to here the examples are evident; the testimony of witnesses and defendants, of reporters and sources, of teachers and authorities, of politicians and experts, of scientists. Scepticism about the trustworthiness of people's testimony can be sparked by many things. There may be specific scepticism about an individual's testimony as a witness, a neutral reporter, a trustworthy politician or a reputable scientist. There may also be general scepticism about the trustworthiness of the systems dependent upon testimony as a whole; the justice system, the mass media, education and science.

Yet the norm is that people accept the testaments that are given, unless there are clear reason to doubt it. On the one hand, this can make people credulous, and prone to being deceived by those who would abuse the power of testimony to influence their beliefs, resulting in false beliefs. On the other hand, people have little scope for first hand verification of most matters affecting their lives and so credulity is a necessary human quality. The risks of being exposed to liars, romancers and hoaxers are offset by the benefits of learning from those with experience and truth to tell. Exchanges of testimony provide the environment for most knowledge formation and change, not experience of first-hand observation and evidence.

Realists versus Constructivist in HRD

Perhaps the greatest challenge in theory is the different structures favoured by two contrasting communities. Those with a realist 'path to truth' view of theory development; that of a scientific discipline which aims to supply knowledge to advance practice. And those with a constructivist language of theory is about accepting, enabling and encouraging the contest of competing views and options, competing theories.

Is useful knowledge based on theories established by experimental studies which show clear causality between well-defined variables regarding things as they are? Or is useful knowledge based on theories whose inherent purpose is to challenge and change things as they are, theories that can in themselves cause change? The former produce social sciences which, especially in psychology and economics, inform HRD with realism. The latter produce social science, especially in sociology and politics, which inform HRD with idealism.

Becher and Trowler (2001) outline how any area of knowledge can be considered as a kind of 'territory' occupied by a tribe, tribes they call 'realists' and 'constructivists'. The former presume that knowledge of a single, stable reality can be obtained; a search for truth is possible, and theory development is the path to that. The latter presume that no single, stable reality exists, and the search for truth is replaced with understanding which involves appreciating and accommodating several different theories.

For realists with a stable and continuing consensus on a core paradigm, a common theory is necessary for knowledge development; they share, work from, reinforce and extend the one clear, single paradigm. For constructivist's variation, disagreement and dissent is the norm, as there is no common and shared theory; knowledge development proceeds by accepting, enabling and encouraging the contest of competing views and options, competing theories.

Typically natural sciences are 'realist' and social sciences are 'constructivist'. Physicists, chemists and engineers share a common view of the world they investigate, and a belief that evidence for useful theories can be obtained. Economists, psychologists and sociologists do not share a common view of people as individuals, groups, organisations and societies, and factors other than evidence and usefulness are influential in what makes a theory successful.

Knowledge in HRD, founded as it is on social sciences, is generated and maintained in the constructivist tradition. That is, there is no single, common, theory shared by professionals, academics, policy-makers. What makes for a successful theory has to be that which helps in the constant contest of competing theories.

As Storberg-Walker outlined this, those factors are relevance, validity, evidence and impact as theorists and practitioners influence each other. This is the 'normal science' view, and aspiration, for theory in HRD. However the factors that determine what actually does succeed as theory in HRD can be thought of quite differently from this normal science view. The other factors can include stakeholder interests, power relationships, cultural influences and goal-driven thinking.

In HRD stakeholder interests are those of employers, employees and governments. In HRD a balance of power exists in relationships between the historically advantaged and disadvantaged, the young and the old, the teacher and the pupil, and others. Cultural influences, which were explored in more detail in Chapter 15, reflect values about individualism and collectivism.

A successful theory in HRD may then be one that is successful because it fits with what a powerful stakeholder in a particular culture is convinced ought to be true rather than the alternative proposed by a weak stakeholder from a different culture. The constructivist tradition in HRD has been manifest in the dominance of ideas, publications and theories from and around this reality. As HRD has become more prominent this has become more manifest. In HRD this perspective on theory in HRD has been centred on critiquing the dominance of pro-capitalist thinkers, partnering employers, adopting a generally Western (especially North American) set of values and outlook.

HRD is also subject to the advantages and disadvantages of being hyperconstructivist; because as an interdisciplinary area of study the multiplication of possible combinations of contested theories which might be relevant and involved in discussing any aspect of learning and change is significant. Contested ideas from psychology, economics and sociology combine in HRD, to make it a fascinating and perplexing area of study.

The extent to which the knowledge about HRD we have, the theory in use in HRD, is relevant, valid, evidence based and impactful are all issues that learners in HRD need to be concerned with. Each piece of research, past or present, and theory can be examined to test its relevance, validity, evidence and impact. Doing this can mean different things, depending on the approach taken to doing research, developing theory and producing useful knowledge. The two main frameworks for examining and testing knowledge are the real-ist and the constructivist frameworks. Appreciating the constructivist character of much of theory, theory development and the function of theory in HRD is helpful.

Beyond the Basic Critical Rivalry; More Voices, More Choices

Smith (1997) explores the nature of intellectual controversies. Intellectual con-troversies span many fields, but tend to reflect a universal debate; between those who hold to established ideas about wisdom and those who would challenge those. Wisdom is, in established terms, attained by the accumulation of truth, through knowledge, with certain meaning, requiring the use of reason, objec-tivity and justification in those terms. Those who challenge this will argue alternatively that there is no certain truth; knowledge is a socially constructed phenomena; and meanings are uncertain. Justifications for positions or stances do not have to be based on reason and objectivity; they can be based on a vari-ety of kinds of thinking and sources. The revisionists accuse the traditionalists of having confining, unreliable and ambiguous ideas about truth; they are trapped by them. The countercharge is that the revisionist opposition to truth is itself the trap; it only provides inadequate and fallacious wisdom. It is, ultimately, counterproductive, debilitating and irresponsible.

The merits of each approach to wisdom can be endlessly debated, but Smith's point is that a persistent, and indeed deepening, mutual misunderstanding and incomprehension accompanies these established ideas and the resistance to them. The pattern of adversarial embrace between sceptic and believer is played out, yet again, between traditionalists and revisionists.

This play of forces about belief and resistance in intellectual controversy is analysed by Smith in terms of cognition. The repeated eruption of regresses and quandaries accompanying these controversies, ending in deadlocks, are seen to mirror cognition. This is explored in a number of ways, in relation to question-begging, circularity in argument and cognitive conservatism. But the central concern is to consider the concept of cognitive dissonance. This involves dis-tress at being confronted with something at odds with an ingrained, taken for granted view; it gives rise to a sense of intolerable wrongness, and a consequent attempt to make it right. Beliefs provide the material of the ingrained, taken for granted, warranting the pursuit of normative rightness.

In order to maintain normative rightness, stable beliefs, 'The stability of every contested belief depends on a stable explanation for the resistance to that belief and, with it, a more or less coherent account of how beliefs generally are formed and validated, that is, an epistemology' (Smith 1997, p. xvi). The people who oppose the beliefs that underpin normative rightness are either devils, with character deficiencies, or fools with intellectual deficiencies. There is something wrong with them. There is symmetry that then emerges from this; with each side holding these views about the other.

What the revisionist theorists argue, against established ideas about 'truth', is that there is a; methodological symmetry for all beliefs. The credibility of beliefs whether framed as science or as other forms, is contingent. They are all equally the product of conditions, and need to be evaluated in that context; none can claim superiority as higher forms of 'truth'. Problems with 'middle way' or reformulations attempting to go 'beyond' the intellectual polarisations that occur tend to fail; the dynamics of belief cannot be so easily outflanked, as these don't satisfy the partisans, they are superficial or they fall towards the established anyway. There are no resolutions, just new alliances, alignments, mergings.

The conflict between two rival conceptions, and critical conceptions, emerges from this. Realist's assume that mistaken beliefs corrected by encounters with reality. Constructivists assume that there is no independence of prior beliefs and general assumptions. Smith is right to point out that such controversies are often seen to be between two distinct parties; opposed but in unsituated positions. This way of representing intellectual disagreement is common but inadequate. These controversies always involve others, and happen in concrete situations. It is not just a limited group of intellectuals arguing different positions.

The key conclusion, in terms of belief and resistance, is that 'intellectual polarisation will always occur. This is 'the tendency for an array of multiple, variously differing, more or less shifting, configurations of belief to move towards and become stabilised as contradistinctive and mutually antagonistic positions' (Smith 1997, p. xxv).

Smith is concerned to stay close to the field of intellectual controversies, and specifically the controversy between realists and constructivists. She does along the way raise important issues about the role and importance of cognition, the range of parties/groups concerned with questions of truth rather than just intellectuals and the broad context of what she terms 'institutional antagonisms' that energise and shape the course of contests.

A Broader Range of Groups and Critiques

The distinction being made in these kinds of terms can be more accurately classed as a contrast between 'superstrong knowledge' and 'unconsidered belief' Goldman (1999). Goldman uses the term 'superstrong knowledge' to suggest the top end of a hierarchical taxonomy with what he calls 'ignorance' or 'unconsidered belief' at the other end (see Perspective 16.2). This taxonomy differentiates among various types of knowledge and forms of belief. What he calls 'weak knowledge' provides the mid-point, straddled by strong knowledge and error on each side.

Perspective 16.2: Goldman's Hierarchy of Knowledge Related to Belief	
Knowledge	**Belief**
Superstrong knowledge	Definitively verified
Strong knowledge	Well verified
Weak knowledge	True belief
Error	False belief
Ignorance	Unconsidered belief.

Superstrong knowledge exists, in Goldman's definition, where there is a definitive and absolute explanation that excludes all other possible explanations. Goldman argues that the clearest attainment of this should be found in the work of truth-seeking institutions using normative procedures. Superstrong knowledge is, in theory, the goal for those involved in truth seeking in the pursuit of justice, in news reporting, in providing education, in seeking to govern in democracies, and in the practice of science. In practice, justice works with standards phrased in terms of being 'beyond reasonable doubt'. In practice, news is reported as purportedly 'objective' because it is impartial, checked or balanced. Schooling is a process which is ostensibly concerned with the practical transmission of agreed and neutral facts from teachers to pupils, but encompasses and achieves (or fails to achieve) much more than that. Voters make their decisions about what is in their best interests when judging those who aspire to govern on the basis of imperfect and flawed information. Science can use specific methods to approach strong and 'positive' knowledge about some natural phenomena, and possibly some aspects of the study of human phenomena, but has no claim on achieving superstrong knowledge (Mazlish 1998).

Claims to achieve superstrong knowledge in any domain of truth-seeking practice cannot be sustained; they appear to be about obtaining strong or weak knowledge at best. Indeed they may often not achieve even that. Innocent people can be convicted and guilty ones can be freed. Misleading stories, moral panics and propagandising may be found in even the most esteemed of mass media institutions, conforming to the norms of their host societies. Systems for teaching even the most basic skills, such as literacy and numeracy, are the subject of controversy because of the broader beliefs people have about learning and schooling in society. Voters are, it seems, often expected to find that their 'true' understanding of their own interests were mistaken, and feel that they were manipulated into a decision they regret. And the most secure and established of scientific views can be overturned by scientific revolutions.

A Typology of 'Critical' Life-Worlds

A typology of perspectives represent the range of 'critical' positions that exist (see Figure 16.1).

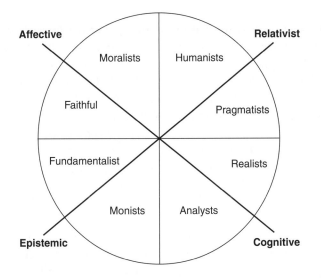

Figure 16.1   Groups and critical position

Perspective 16.3: A Typology of 'Critical' Life-Worlds	
Fundamentalist	Critique emerges from strong convictions associated with strong feelings and emotions.
Faithful	Critique emerges from a commitment to beliefs, but they are not all consuming.
Moralists	Critique emerges from values, but can and must be debated.
Humanists	Critique emerges from what is seen and judged in terms of what is good for people, not in relation to an overarching ideological systems and principles.
Pragmatists	Critique emerges from the context of actual experience and practice.
Realists	Critique emerges from fit with 'reality'. This is the 'realpolitik', hard-headed approach.

Perspective 16.3: (Continued)	
Analysts	Critique emerges from rigorous analysis of various kinds, and people should be open-minded and sceptical.
Monists	Critique emerges from truth being determined using methods appropriate to the context; justice, education, the media, science.

Modern culture is to be defined as involving a preference for secular rationality, the adoption of religious tolerance with tendencies to relativism and a culture of individualism. These are all sources of criticism in HRD, and criticised in their turn. Fundamentalists in particular see themselves as 'fighting back' against modernity, represented by pragmatism. Critiques are not frivolous, concerned with responding to peripheral differences; they respond to core perceived threats to personal and social identity that go straight to central issues which pragmatists would rather leave alone. They 'fight for'; for a definite world-view and a conception of what should happen in the family, in education, and in gender roles, based on beliefs. These are the features that are the key to reinforcing personal and social identity consistent with their beliefs; and shared belief is what defines and keeps the group together.

In this context critical HRD is not an academic sideshow, but it is about recognising and connecting with a range of voices and positions which can shape and influence how we perceive and approach human development.

Conclusion

HRD does not exist in isolation from the broader world of management and HRM, nor from debates and concerns in societies and cultures more generally. In fact HRD, as an area of human development, is at the heart of many key debates. By investing in HRD, there are better prospects for success; what that means is not only or all about resource management and skills, it is also about human development more broadly. Pragmatically the fear is that the failure to get HRD right will leave individuals, organisations, nations or regions disadvantaged, and struggling in the wake of others in the future. In other words, getting HRD right can be seen in win–lose terms, with those who gain doing so at the expense of others. Ethically the issue is different beliefs about the challenges entailed in managing human development in modern, complex societies and cultures.

Even where, as with many other aspects of HRM, HRD can be seen to create a win–win situation there is more at stake. Win–win situations through HRD exist for individuals where there are optimum outcomes for each, in the form of fulfilling and rewarding jobs, careers and employment across a wide range of types of capability and interest. They exist for organisations when HRD helps create and sustain employability and a capable workforce, often run in partnership with other stakeholders and meeting their interests rather than conflicting with them. And they exist for nations and regions where, through HRD, each can find a path to integration with world trade and industry by attaining reasonable standards that improve the quality of life above existing levels for the majority.

So HRD at work is critical because it is the means to give some individuals good career choices – the capacity to get on in life rather than 'going nowhere' – and it can ensure that the disadvantaged and disenchanted find a place and role rather than being left behind and neglected. HRD is critical because the world in which we live in general creates organisations with the capacity to develop their intellectual capital, capabilities and behaviours consistent with core values; organisations that will both compete and collaborate to provide products and services at the quality and cost that customers seek. And HRD is critical because the affects of globalisation further accelerate the speed at which people need to learn and develop in free-market economies. These circumstances present challenges for nations to compare themselves with the best and compete with each other for inward investment from the major multinationals. Economic imperatives among both developed and developing nations tend to highlight the roles of development and learning in creating and using knowledge, capabilities and behaviours consistent with employment in modern jobs and organisations.

These critical levels of development and learning interact, and can produce a virtuous or a vicious cycle. In the virtuous cycle the net effect is appropriate levels of investment in HRD that provides high levels of economic and social returns, thus creating a dependence upon development, learning and knowledge. In the vicious cycle a failure at any one level will feed into others. One example of this process is when individuals fail to learn, causing knowledge gaps, capability shortages or behavioural mismatches for organisations. Another is when organisations, already low on knowledge and skill requirements, fail to provide opportunities for educated and capable individuals, which, in turn, leads to frustrated expectations.

There are no value-free, transcendent prescriptions that can be found for HRD; no panacea policies and procedures that can be implemented, to invent or to copy others' success. Practices are embedded in antecedents of historical, political, social and educational contexts of particular business systems, and cannot be freed from these contexts and manipulated at will. And this is also true of perspectives; they too are embedded in antecedents of history and politics as much as evidence and argument.

The Future

It is helpful to look ahead, and reflect on the future for HRD. Having emphasised the need to take perspectives, cultural and institutional contexts into account, what are the prospects? Views on these questions are divided. One optimistic view, which has clearly been around for some time, is that there is now a consensus on a greater concern with effective HRD at work. Great economic and social advantages and benefits are to be gained from developing, effectively and efficiently, the kinds and levels of knowledge, capability and behaviour required in the jobs and organisations that are the foundations of a changed, and still changing, world of work. The levers of HRD, from access to greater learning opportunities through reforms within national education and training systems to persuading employers to spend more on training, offer areas for action where the most powerful stakeholders – employers, government, educationalists and employee organisations – can work together on common interests in developing and implementing schemes and initiatives. And in a context where commitments to improved HRM in the workplace are taken for granted, the rationale for investing in people as an integral part of a people-friendly business strategy creates circumstances in which support for HRD will be natural and strong.

What should not be overlooked, however, is the alternative and more sceptical and critical view; the systemic questioning and scepticism around firstly the value of HRD at work and secondly about the ability of HRD systems to deliver what is wanted. There are uncertainties and difficulties in responding to a changed and changing world of work by seeking, through supporting HRD, to achieve economic and social change of the scale and quality apparently required. Breaking free of an economic and social 'status quo', of low skills, low participation in learning and often inefficient systems, is no easy option that can provide overnight returns. Yet breaking free of the status quo where the 'rich' get richer, partly through access to HRD, with better facilities, support and returns being confined to those in the wealthier classes, nations and regions, is an integral part of the global HRD agenda on change. The debates about pulling the right levers to affect the policies of key institutions, the investments of thousands of organisations and the motivations of millions of people can then be come debates that divide stakeholders rather than unite them in consensus. Who pays, and where does the money go? Finally, there is the question of the extent to which commitments to HRD can be an integral part of HRM, when it seems that a 'new deal' in employee relations can lead to under-investment in staff because, in the long term, a commitment to mutually beneficial relations in employment are a thing of the past.

Such perceptions are neither right nor wrong. What is seen depends on where you looking from. One aim of this book has been to give several vantage points so that a 360-degree view of the area is available, not a limited and partial picture.

Developing and improving our understanding of these situations, from the smallest actions carried out in the name of learning to more significant actions, should help shape and influence what is and what is not done. There is then a great span and a great depth to the questions raised by thinking about doing and improving HRD at work, a one-day course in an organisation to the development of policy by government to achieve economic and social goals, and from the evolution of knowledge management in multinational organisations to the improvement of skills a medium-sized organisation increasing its productivity. Authoritative and final answers to these questions are not be found in any text. There are many voices which can help shape the many choices facing thoughtful practitioners wherever the power of learning is to be harnessed.

3 Key Texts

(1) Thody, P. (1999) *Researching Human Resource Development: Philosophy, Processes and Practices* (London: Routledge).

(2) Elliott, C. and Turnbull, S. (2005) *Critical Thinking in Human Resource Development* (London: Routledge).

(3) Stewart, J., Rigg, C. and Trehan, K. (2006) *Critical Human Resource Development: Beyond Orthodoxy* (London: Financial Times/ Prentice Hall).

3 Key Articles

(1) McGuire, D., Garavan, T., O'Donnell, D. and Watson, S. (2007) 'Metaperspectives and HRD: Lessons for Research and Practice', *Advances in Developing Human Resources*, 9 (1), pp. 120–139.

(2) Sambrook, S. (2009) 'Critical HRD: A Concept Analysis', *Personnel Review* Farnborough, 38 (1), p. 61.

(3) Valentin, C. (2006) 'Researching Human Resource Development: Emergence of a Critical Approach to HRD Enquiry', *International Journal of Training & Development*, 10 (1), p. 17.

3 Key Web Links

(1) A discussion of the ideas of the Frankfurt School, proponents of critical analysis: http://www.bbc.co.uk/programmes/b00pr54s.

(2) More conventional 'critical thinking' resources: http://www.learnhigher.ac.uk/Students/Critical-thinking-and-reflection.html.

(3) A resource for searching concepts and thinkers in philosophy generally: http://plato.stanford.edu/contents.html.

17

HRD Providers

Learning Objectives

By the end of this chapter you will be able to:

- Identify a range of HRD providers and partners;
- Describe the opportunities and threats of using different kinds of providers and partners in HRD;
- Analyse trends and changes in the use of providers and partners in HRD;
- Critically evaluate the issues involved in using external providers and partner consultants for HRD.

Introduction

In many instances, HRD is delivered by a specialist HRD Provider (HRDP). Such providers range from individuals to large organisations working in the training industry. HRDPs are an integral part of the practice of learning and change at work for many organisations. Because outsourcing and organisational partnership as ways of delivering HRD have increased, this institutional situation deserves a distinct examination. HRDP partnerships may be with a range of providers, from individual consultants through to major organisations such as large management consulting firms and universities. This market for HRD covers a large volume of HRD activity and is central to some of the most important HRD projects that organisations will pursue.

HRDP

One European study concluded that, of all the organisations which supply training, including employers in-house, colleges and universities, the highest proportion of training participation hours was accounted for by organisations which were private HRDPs (Eurostat 2002). Despite this it is often the other actors who are the centre of attention for research and policy analysis; employers, colleges and universities. Private HRDPs seem to be taken for granted, though their existence and performance is an integral part of both corporate and public spending on training.

HRDPs are organisations whose business is adult and workplace HRD. The learners are the post-16-year-old age group. The activities HRDPs can be involved in can be one or a mix of the following activities associated with learning for adults:

- Setting standards;
- Sourcing trainees;
- Delivering training;
- Monitoring progress;
- Assessing and/or certifying HRD.

HRDPs may be organisations whose rationale is to make a profit, or they may be functioning within the publicly funded and subsidised HRD economy. This means that, included in the HRDP category, will be actors in the institutional networks of public, community-based, FE and HE or Non Departmental Public Bodies (NDPB) that provide for and manage learning. These organisations may on occasion, or in some units, engage with commercial income generation activities. But they are not private companies which prosper or fail according to their ability to make a profit from learning. They may either prosper or fail according to their ability to obtain and manage public funds.

HRDPs will be defined here as:

> Organisations whose primary business is providing learning and development for employment for adults and involves one or a mix of the following activities: setting standards, sourcing trainees, delivering training, monitoring progress, assessing and certifying.

HRDPs may operate entirely in the free market for training, generating income from their activities, or be dependent on public funding, making them part of the public sector and voluntary sector. In these sectors there are HRDP providers with a history grounded in the provision of general learning in educational institutions, as well as colleges and universities. The structures of these may vary in some respects, but they are essentially alike: governed by boards of stakeholders and involved in all aspects of learning from setting standards to assessing and certifying. Their staff are subject specialists, often professionally qualified, though not all are accredited as teachers or trainers. These are organisations staffed by people who are, or who see themselves primarily as, providing public services. They have been primarily funded by state-directed spending on programmes which implement government policies on education, social policy and economic development. The public sector in this definition includes colleges, universities, local authority-funded units and much community learning.

The introduction and influence of commercial concerns is most visible, perhaps, in units in FE/HE institutions which are revenue- or profit-generating. On the other hand, there is also scope for a role for voluntary sector organisations and trusts. Others, such as companies whose core business is publishing but who provide learning materials, can also be included as HRDPs even though they are not directly involved in delivery, as they may partner learning providers in various ways.

HRDP details will vary with the national context, though patterns in their use can be very similar. For England, for example, information is available from the Skills Funding Agency (http://skillsfundingagency.bis.gov.uk/) and Young People's learning Agency (http://www.ypla.gov.uk/). The former aims to help employers better understand the help and support available to them from Government supported skills and employment and to provide information for adults looking for work or in employment who want to improve their skills and widen their horizons. The latter has a mission of championing education and training for young people in England, by providing financial support to young learners, by funding academies for all their provision and by supporting local authorities to commission suitable education and training opportunities for all 16- to 19-year-olds.

Audiences and Forms

The HRDPO sector deals with a set of audiences:

- Initial education for 16- to 19-year-olds;
- Continuing education for adults;
- Workforce development;
- Retraining;
- Community learning.

There is a need to deal with young people and others in schools, colleges and universities. HRDP organisations are funded and governed in various ways, and 'joined up' to an extent by shared visions and frameworks. As HRDPOs, they are major institutions dealing with large volumes of learners. The management and leadership development provision in these is often criticised as patchily developed. The second and third audiences are concerned with developing those in the work-force and employment, and are, again, to an extent 'joined up' in webs of policy and frameworks of support, such as, in the United Kindgom, Investors in People (IiP). Employers are to be motivated to engage with HRDPs and helped with initiatives and funding. Conventionally most large organisations are seen to invest fairly well and rationally in learning, while small- and medium-sized enterprises (SMEs) invest less but often need it more.

The HRDP provision in many countries is one where there have been two dominant organisational forms. In the initial education sector there have been specialist institutions of education, state-funded, planned and delivered as public services through bureaucracies directly owned and managed by the state. There may be examples of contracting the delivery of public services to private and voluntary organisations, blurring the public service nature of these. Continuing concerns to modernise public services, looking at patterns of provision and relationships, extends this. There have also always been private sector providers as well; organisations dedicated to providing training and learning for or along with government and employers, some involved in work-based training, others in distance learning or other methods.

Knowledge and understanding of these two sectors, the public and the private, including management and leadership development, is mixed. There is a gap in knowledge about private providers in the learning and skills sector. The interest is not in knowing more about HRDPOs for the sake of it, but to focus on how to create the conditions for positive learning outcomes to be achieved. This includes the following:

- Learners willing to identify with providers and engage with them, including brand and image;
- Productive learner–teacher and ancillaries relations;
- Adequate resourcing: capital investment strategy;
- Trusting relations with other agencies, inter-agency relations;
- Protecting the learner–teacher relationship from potentially damaging pressures but being open to clear signals about requirements, inspection regimes, targets, provider missions and ethos.

The growth of this private HRDP sector is not well documented. Some of it emerges from specific contexts, such as the development of a market for learning among young adults in periods of high unemployment. However HRDPs existed before such concern with youth unemployment in the 1970s. They were companies whose business was providing adult learners with learning which the state or enterprises did not provide, contracting with either individuals, organisations or the state to make a profit for their owners and investors. In these organisations either the sole business is learning, or the company has a significant interest in learning. Their activities may vary considerably, from small companies in niche markets to those operating as arms of major multinational companies like IBM or Accenture (Harris 2003).

Issues in HRDPs

HRDPs are central to improving access to and the quality of training for adults. Three common concerns often underlie publicly funded training policy and provisions for adults:

- It should be led by the needs of employers and learners;
- It should be shaped by the skill needs prioritised in each sector, region and locality;
- It should give the HRDP maximum discretion to decide how best to respond to needs.

To achieve this governments are interested in a range of actions on: providing wider choice for employers and learners of publicly funded providers of adult skills and training; reforming the funding system to give incentives for providers to be more responsive, while cutting bureaucracy; helping HRDPs to build their capacity to offer a wider range of support to local employers.

The public sector providers exist to fulfil government's policies through large-scale, 'big' education, both academic and vocational. Private providers exist to fill in the 'small' gaps these large institutions cannot manage. This has meant that they exist to meet both employer needs and small and local needs. The net effect is that they operate in areas where they encounter the greatest interaction of issues around economic development and social inclusion, often with people who have backgrounds of disadvantage and poverty. Another view is that the private sector exists to fulfil the demands enterprises have for learning services for their staff because, while some organisations may have their own training staff, most use external resources at some point for some needs. HRDPOs start to meet this market, and may then seek to interact with publicly funded programmes.

In contrast with the attention devoted to analysing employer behaviour and public sector partner behaviour less is known about the private sector in HRDPs. Even basic questions about where they come from, who they are, how they have evolved, what their business models are, and many more are unanswered. There may, however, be niche providers, for particular occupational skills or types of client, who deliver a significant share of particular provisions. Yet it would seem few HRDPs dominate any market. While staffing information about the public sector, the FE and HE institutions, is publicly available, the private sector HRDP sector is less visible. The number of colleges and universities is known, their spending is known, their staffing is known and their quality is known. This is not true of the private sector HRDPs. The quality of what is provided by colleges and universities is well reviewed. Some private sector provision, where it involves publicly funded programmes or links with public institutions, may be assessed using formal quality management systems (QMS) or other frameworks, but not others.

Clearly organisations in the public sector, colleges and universities, identify and seek to meet demands that arise from enterprises; often to generate income streams of their own, additional to those provided by government. Equally, many government programmes are implemented by private provider organisations, and some of these providers are entirely dependent on government programmes for their revenues. Rather than there being a split between the public and the private, then, there is some overlap, and therefore some scope for both partnership and competition.

This is often seen to require a strategy that is more joined up than in the past. To that end reviews of new policy are undertaken, and new institutional arrangements created. The question has always been about the development of a system which ensures each sector is contributing to best effect (Gospel and Foreman 2002) and that their combined efforts and activities produce the desired outcomes: effective learning for the benefit of individuals, organisations and society.

It is expected, or hoped, that the number of providers will increase where existing providers are unable to meet any additional demand as a result of new strategies. However, it has been noted that dependency on government-funded programmes presents substantial problems and risks to HRDPs. Many HRDPs seek to diversify into other aspects of learning, non-state-funded, or into other areas of business. The danger is that effective and efficient HRDP organisations fail to engage with government initiatives and funding as they are not sufficiently attractive to them. This leaves less effective HRDPs serving the state-funded sector. Broadly speaking, the corporate direct sector is more lucrative, less bureaucratic and provides more motivated learners and more interesting projects. As many organisations may seek to outsource their learning (Harris 2003), the HRDP sector may grow but not engage with government policy areas and priorities.

HRDP Functions and Activities

HRDPs may be involved in a variety of different kinds of activity:

- Setting standards;
- Sourcing learners;
- Delivering learning;
- Monitoring progress;
- Assessing;
- Certifying.

Here there is potential for three different kinds of HRDP: single-purpose agencies, multiple-purpose agencies, total process agencies (see Practice 17.1).

Practice 17.1: HRDP Roles

	Activities					
HRD provision contexts	Setting standards	Sourcing learners	Delivering learning	Monitoring	Assessment	Certifying power
Single employer	Own performance issues	Employees	Training dept	Internal	Internal	Not certified
Formal education contexts	Subject benchmarks	From schools or community	Classroom-based and other facilities	Retention and progress of learners	Methods for continuous assessment	Internal power and quality assurance
Private sector learning providers	Government-funded or commercial scheme standards	Government-funded or commercial opportunities	Own premises or employer premises	May monitor only during own training	May assess or rely on others	Arrange to certify or do own certification
Multi-employer organisations	As above	As above	As above	Employers' needs	External standards	Arrange to certify
Issues	Balance of technical and other skills and knowledge	Attractiveness of provider to targets	Quality of trainers and training	Completing, changing, succeeding	Validity and accuracy of assessments	Paperwork and esteem involved in certification

The Market Context for HRD

The market for HRD at work is part of two bigger markets: the market for management consultancy and the market for HRM provision and services. The market for management consultancy is made up of buyers and sellers of independent advice and assistance about management issues. This typically includes identifying and investigating problems and/or opportunities, recommending appropriate action, and helping to implement those recommendations.

Consultants are experts playing the role of external adviser to organisations, based on their experience and their expertise, though they may be hired for many reasons. These reasons may be broad and high level, connected with the organisation's plans and policy for achieving major goals. For example, a client company might want help in putting in a new financial system, or it might want advice on redesigning the organisation. The reasons may also be more specific and low level. For example, a client company might require an external review of its pay structures or recruitment policies, or it might need help in product design and marketing. One common perception is that buying in consultants means that a company has inadequate internal management resources. In principle, consultants are valued because they are external resources, who can bring in knowledge of best practice.

As traditional consultancy firms have prospered and grown, other kinds of business have also started to offer consultancy services. Advertising agencies and design firms offer consultancy, as do IT companies and law firms. Many specialist management consultancies start up when redundant executives set up on their own as consultants. Today the consultancy industry is both huge and amorphous. All kinds of companies can become partners in providing HRD at work in the course of their work with organisations.

Management consultancy can also be analysed by looking at its market sectors and those who provide consultancy. The second market for HRD at work is the HRM consultancy market. This includes services and provisions in HR planning, recruitment, reward, training, development, appraisal, career development, leadership and communication. It interfaces and overlaps with two other segments of the consultancy market – corporate communications and organisation development. This market expands with the outsourcing of HR activities.

The HRD market can also be analysed by identifying the kinds of sector and organisation that use consultants. For example, in the United Kingdom the importance of the financial services sector has been rising each year, and consultancy earnings from the energy and water industries increased dramatically in the 1990s as these industries were subject to much public interest both as takeover targets and as public service providers. Public sector work as a proportion of total consultancy revenues declined during the 1990s. In part, this was because the public sector was much smaller than it had been and, in part, because the major privatisations had been completed.

So the market for consultancy involves various kinds of provider, offering a range of different kinds of service including HR-related and HRD services, working with diverse kinds of organisation.

Partners in Training

Organisations have always involved consultants in their HRD activities, as they can support the improvement of performance systems. Partners may be able to identify needs, to plan and design HRD, or to deliver a programme of HRD. But more recently, although many companies have retained and developed their in-house training function, an increasing number of organisations have cut back their internally managed provisions, and therefore have to choose a specialist HRDPO to meet their HRD requirements.

- Technical independence: not tied to one kind of solution;
- Financial independence: not dependent on 'getting results' to earn fees;
- Administratively independent: not part of the organisation;
- Politically independent: not tied to any power grouping in the organisation;
- Emotionally independent: not emotionally involved with the organisation or its people.

Organisations select an outside provider in order to obtain the best training available, and because the required training cannot be supplied in-house. Factors of quality and capacity combine to lead organisations into partnerships. Factors that influence the choice of partner include the training facilities available and the quality of the HRD design. A dedicated HRDP is likely to have broad experience in designing different courses for the needs of various clients. An in-house training department is unlikely to have this breadth of knowledge and experience.

Training managers play a significant role in the selection of trainers. Although external partnerships may be required for design and delivery, companies still need internal HRD departments and HRD professionals with a knowledge of training suppliers.

Despite this apparent shift towards the use of external HRD resources, various factors still make in-house HRD both attractive and economic. The Industrial Society suggests three factors that play a crucial role in persuading companies to carry out their own training rather than use partners:

- Price, as external providers can be very expensive;
- For many organisations, the need to tailor the training to their own needs – they do not want 'off-the-shelf' training from an external provider;
- The number of people being trained: the larger the number, the more likely the company is to opt for internal training to control costs.

In the HRD Market

Marketplaces in the form of trade fairs exist for selling HRD products and services, and the activity there is an indication of who is in the market. Independent training organisations are probably the most important type of HRDP. They can be public companies, private limited companies or, occasionally, charities. Most are small businesses, with under 100 employees. Most of the trainers they employ are full-time, although some training companies rely heavily on contract staff.

Colleges of further education and business schools are also important. Colleges of further education provide vocational training, whereas business schools offer general management training with an academic input, which is mainly for managers and executives. Information technology (IT) companies are expanding rapidly in the HRD market: it has become a natural additional service to their traditional products. The provision of HRD can also help to increase their customer base.

The HRD market is served by many sole practitioners. These have often developed their skills at a larger management consultancy, training organisation or business school, and then gone independent. They may have worked as training managers with specific companies, designing and managing training courses in-house. Some may have started up on their own when their former employer decided to outsource all the company's training needs. Some will work for their former employers as HRD consultants.

Partnerships with these kinds of organisation and people will involve either bringing consultants into the organisation, or sending staff out to events or courses – or a combination of both. The issues and tensions of managing this effectively are about ensuring the quality of the person coming in or the external provider. Good consultants give value for money and care about the working relationships they have with clients. Partnership is a way of working not an opportunity to 'dump' things on consultants or abdicate responsibility because a consultant has been paid to manage an aspect of HRD. If that approach is taken, disappointment is almost inevitable. Before any organisation uses a partner it should be clear about why it is using consultants, what it wants the consultant to do, and how that will be managed, and it should then be effective in choosing the right person or company.

Good HRDPs work in a high-risk environment, and have to be commercially focused. They seek a good relationship as a partner with the client to earn their fees or their living. An effective partnership begins with a clear written brief from the client, detailing the outcomes wanted, and the scale and scope of the project, and making clear what is needed in a submission. To select an HRDP from a written submission to a brief, the HRDP must tell clients what they need to know about them. Clients must feel confident that they can work with the partner, and that other key stakeholders feel the same.

What is required for organisations to work with the HRDP? This varies according to the project. If they are to be used to provide one-off courses then, once the format is agreed, they can be left to get on with it. If they are to be involved in a larger scale project then regular meetings, and perhaps some kind of project steering group, will be appropriate. It will be more difficult to maintain a good partnership over a longer term project, as challenges and issues may arise in the course of the project. The conclusion to any partnership should be an evaluation that mirrors the usual evaluation of HRD. What were people's reactions? What learning has occurred? What improvements in performance are there? What have the costs and benefits been? Questions to ask when using HRDPs:

Perspective 17.1: Why HRDP?		
Why?	Partners are needed because of:	
	The scale of a project;	
	A lack of resources;	
	A need for objectivity;	
	A need for credibility;	
	A lack of confidence among internal staff.	

Perspective 17.1: (Continued)		
What?	What outcomes are being sought? How you will these be identified and measured? Agree outcomes with all the key stakeholders, including the consultants.	
How?	Consider in detail what the project is likely to involve. Be prepared to consider ideas and options the consultants have. Keep in mind the implications of any options for budgets and other resources. Be realistic about expectations.	
Who?	Know the HRD consultancy market, and test it by asking for tenders. Be clear about what you want from a consultant. Consider the stakeholder relationships. Be clear about the skills a consultant can offer; they are not all things to all people.	

HRDPs and HRD Strategy

The overall objective of HRD strategy is to contribute towards raising productivity and competitiveness by creating a more highly skilled, more productive workforce. In this context external partners are organisations seeking to operate independently and privately, alongside the state sector and work organisations, to fulfil government policy aims. Government can direct funding into these high-priority areas. The priorities in this respect are currently:

- Skills needed for employment for social reasons, for example basic skills;
- Areas of skill shortage, for example, vocational technician/craft skills;
- Identified areas of deficiency such as management and leadership, maths and science.

HRDPs will respond to these priorities and adjust the balance of current learning provision and learners. Colleges and providers will also have to develop effective marketing strategies to encourage much greater numbers of low-skilled individuals to engage in learning. This group is typically among the most difficult to engage in learning, and are least likely to be offered training by their employers. Effective engagement of both low-skilled individuals and their employers will be an important aspect of successfully delivering the strategy. There are issues involved in recruiting new tutors to deliver different provisions and in structuring the teaching workforce to ensure that skills are appropriate for the new, more relevant, provision.

A skills strategy needs to open the door to the funded training market to new providers. This may mean some existing providers being replaced by ones of higher quality. From a quality point of view the best option is training provided by a single employer. However there are two major problems with seeking to rely on this or expand it further. The first problem is the recognition that there are islands of high skill in a low-skill sea; not all employers invest in training equally. The second problem is that the expense of effective training cannot be met by SMEs. Conventionally FE colleges are meant to help overcome these problems by providing for equal access and national coverage, offering cost-effective development of knowledge and skills. However there are also problems with this option. The FE colleges may be considered too remote from employers' needs, unable to provide development on their own, be somewhat out of date, and unattractive to young people.

One study (Gospel and Foreman 2002) that analysed the relative size and activity of various kinds of training provider in the United Kingdom, based on data concerning the review of government-funded programmes, particularly Modern Apprenticeships (MAs), showed that what are termed here 'private sector HRDPs' constituted 29 per cent of all learning providers and dealt with 38.5 per cent of all trainees. This is substantially ahead of other specialist NDPB providers (18.2 per cent of all trainees) and all the other three public sector types of learning provider, namely FE colleges (19.1 per cent of trainees), local authorities (5.8 per cent of trainees) and charities/not for profit sector (6.2 per cent of all trainees).

Organisational Form Issues

The issue of organisational form in the HRDP sector is increasingly important. Should there be more private sector providers, more public sector providers or more original forms of HRDP from new social enterprises? The issue is partly about whether private is better than public, or voluntary better than either of those. Some locate the issue as part of a bigger understanding matters of organisational form in analysing the effectiveness of the learning and skills sector (Cameron and Marashi 2003). In other areas of activity debates about organisational form are prominent, including debates about developing Public Interest Companies (PICs) or foundation hospitals, or transferring social care from the public to the voluntary sector. Questions about legal form and legitimacy, and who owns, coordinates and manages resources and performance, are widely discussed in other sectors. The same is arising in HRD. Questions about organisational form that arise in general can be applied to the learning and skills sector (see Debate 17.1).

Debate 17.1: HRDP Organisational Form Questions

- What model of governance in an organisation is to be adopted to enable effective accountability, authority and decision-making?

Debate 17.1: (Continued)

- How does organisational form, whether hierarchical, professional, collegial or consultative, affect the way that the work of learning is managed?
- How is the organisation legitimised for its users: through membership, choice, image?
- How does the organisation secure resources: fees, contracts, grants, donations, loans, equity, reserves?
- How does the organisation allocate resources: rationing, vouchers, price?
- How does the organisation protect and manage its resources: safeguard, secure borrowing, actively managed?
- How are inter-provider relationships affected by organisational form: the capacity for collaboration – joint planning, referral, joint provision, sharing resources, joint delivery?

Consequently the HRDP sector is a complex sector, with public, private and voluntary organisational forms all represented to some degree. For some, at heart, the voluntary sector exists to deliver vocational education and second chances to those who have not gained from initial schooling. The primary partnerships are, then, between FE colleges, HRDPs and employers.

One concern is that some contexts lack a healthy HRDP sector. A problem may be then that there are too many 'small gaps' in learning needs. These are not met by either employers or large institutions, nor are there HRDPs around to deal with these, or if they exist they deal with them ineffectively. Another concern may be that the sector is not operating effectively. There are not enough HRDPs and there is an imbalance between private and public forms, with too many social justice-oriented HRDPs embedded in public or voluntary sector models and not enough strong private HRDPs concerned with economic returns. Alternatively, some companies may perceive that HRDPs charge too much for what they do, while other HRDPs struggle to remain viable going concerns. The uncertainty of short-term contracts for government work and similar problems with stability in work for employers is a factor. HRDPs may also struggle with too many targets, an underdeveloped cadre of management and staff with limited qualifications. Solutions then are focused on long-term contracts, fewer, clearer targets based on outcomes and strengthening managerial competence.

Cameron and Marashi identify a number of interconnected policy contexts in which the question of organisational form arises. With a view to improving learning outcomes these include the following:

- Wanting to expand the sector but there is a high cost of entry for new providers, as regulation, inspection and targets regimes are prohibitive.

- The inertia encountered given the sunk costs in certain forms of provision and existing loyalties; it can be hard to rationalise provisions.

- The problem of transaction costs; collaborative working creates transaction costs that are easier for large organisations to bear than small organisations. This drives small providers out.

- The use of inspection as a proxy for the voice of the user; consumers cannot have a comprehensive understanding.

- Maintaining efforts at reaching the most excluded; the hard-to-serve are difficult, the easy-to-serve are demanding. Embed the interests of non-participants.

The concept and application of the principal–agent relationship in the sector is critical A principal–agent relationship occurs when one person or an organisation acts on behalf of another. If the relationship is too loose, then the principal's intentions are not realised. If it is too tight, then the agent has no discretion to innovate.

Issues

More public and private HRDPs activity mean more targets, and more inspectors, so as investment goes up bureaucracy increases. Leaders in these organisations may lose motivation and become more cautious. They may begin to focus on back-watching not delivery. To influence and change government policy and practice in those circumstances, the points of leverage need to be identified:

- Treasury interests: they aim to set simple targets agreed with departments and seek to control public expenditure on education, training;

- Departments and Ministers: they like initiatives which show they are active. Targets and rules are needed to ensure expectations are clear;

- Departmentalism: with several departments involved, there is scope for inter-departmental 'turf wars'.

HRDPs have played a part in learning and training in the past, but are now of greater interest in the context of Lifelong Learning (LLL) and skills strategy goals. They are of some significance, but it is conceivable that they may play a bigger role in the future. In the past they have existed to fill 'gaps' in either government provision or the corporate sector, but their quality has been questioned. Now the best HRDPs are seen to provide better quality learning in either state-funded programmes or internal company provisions. In the future, if the increasing outsourcing of training in the corporate sector continues, then external partners may become players whose voice and interests become even stronger; to equal or indeed rival those of the state or employer organisations. Three key themes underpin this.

First, improving the quality of providers is an issue, along with innovation and creativity. The learning provider sector includes many and varied kinds of provider; ranging from the single, self-employed consultant specialising in one subject to the complex, multi-faceted modern university. The quality of learning found in these different areas is seen to be patchy. While all kinds of learning providers have their share of failures the perception is that those motivated by profit are most at risk of failure, or of exploiting learners. Why this is so, and what can be done to change that, requires research.

Second, while the level of employers' commitment to training in general is hard to gauge, it is a constant theme among many commentators that it is low and weak. For the particular group of most current concern – low-waged, low-skilled, adults in work – employer neglect of HRD remains an issue and, unless employers engage with the HRDPs who can aid these people, this group will remain neglected.

Finally, there is the issue of work-based training. In its formal guise in the United Kingdom, for example, this is represented by initiatives like Modern Apprenticeships (MAs). In its 'informal' guises work-based learning has also come to be recognised as a major, if often hidden, contributor to skills and knowledge development. Work-based learning in both of these senses presents a continuing challenge for the role of external partners. In formal schemes the issues are those of providing effective instruction and experience rather than simply using trainees as a source of cheap unskilled labour, combining basic skills with vocational development and ensuring that standards are maintained while trainees actually complete their training. These are not new, but are all abiding challenges. Some of the attractions of work-based training are firmly founded in sound principles of adult education; but some of the realities of work-based learning are deeply rooted in a system in which there is no parity of esteem, and academic learning is still seen to be, and funded as if it were, the best path to career development and success. This is true for both formal and informal work-based learning. One hope is that subsidised job-specific training, subsidised management training and wage compensation for the time employees spend training would help SMEs to give more attention to training.

Conclusions

Much HRD at work is supplied by HRDPs working with an organisation, or by staff going outside the organisation into an HRDP. This approach to HRD has always been used, but seems to be increasing for various reasons, including the greater use of outsourcing of HR services by many organisations. Effective management of HRD therefore means effective management of partnerships with HRDPOs. The nature of the market for HRD services and products is evolving, but the main sectors and providers are fairly well-established. Being able to research and access them as needed is an integral part of modern HRD at work. In developing relationships the building of positive partnerships should be the key. This requires clarity about what is wanted, and skills to ensure that the right partners are selected.

Organisations are partly dependent on what the market offers. The effectiveness of market forces as a driver of improvements in the provision and quality of HRD remains a concern for many stakeholders – for work organisations as buyers, for providers as sellers and for the government – as they seek to evolve better HRD at work provisions over the years ahead. Changes in government policy, trends in outsourcing HRM work, and the merging of organisations in the consulting and HRM sectors will all provide impetus for change in the market for HRD at work. New forms of, or areas for, partnership may emerge and evolve.

HRDPs represent a sector which faces challenges across all five key policy areas:

(1) High quality – people should demand, and providers should deliver, high-quality learning: Where are the best practices among HRDPs?

(2) Participation – giving people the confidence, enterprise, knowledge, creativity and skills to take part: How can HRDPs help to achieve this? Do we need more HRDPs, bigger HRDPs?

(3) Recognition – knowledge and skill should be recognised, used and developed in the workplace: How do HRDPs respond to an environment where this is desired?

(4) Information, guidance and counselling (IGC) – giving people the information, guidance and support to make decisions and transitions: What issues for HRDPs arise from seeking to improve IGC via private sector HRDP?

(5) Chances – giving people chances to learn irrespective of background or circumstances: How well do HRDPs meet this expectation?

HRDPs operate in the context of, and often in partnership with, the other sectors as well. Thus there are also research issues about these relations and partnerships.

Taken together, there is a set of issues relating to questions about the structure, strategies and challenges facing HRDPs. Making these more visible in the first instance is a prerequisite of considering the extent to which the existing HRDP sector is providing an effective contribution to achieving lifelong learning; and the extent to which support for a better understanding of structure, strategies and challenges might be of benefit to the sector itself, and those who interact with them.

Case: Impact Arts

Impact Arts was established in 1994 by Susan Aktemel as a small business. She identified the need for the development of excellent projects that make a difference to individuals and community groups, and the opportunity to create work for freelance artists who are committed to operating within the community environment.

Impact Arts is a charity with both social and enterprising aims. They work within a network of other Social Enterprises, sharing their knowledge with them and supporting each other where they can. They believe this is the right way of working.

Fifteen years later, they are the leading community arts company in Scotland. They want to make a real difference in communities at a local, city-wide and national level through developing excellent work with partners. They see the arts and creativity as catalysts for positive, lasting change in people's lives, and through their work they want to enable people to flourish. They want to be a successful, profitable social business, recognised for excellence, innovation and creativity. They have stayed true to their aims and values. They are now a creative social enterprise with charitable status, and they successfully balance our commitment to social change with being a dynamic and responsive business. Social enterprises are 'dynamic businesses with a social purpose working to deliver lasting social and environmental change'.

- They are the leading community arts company in Scotland, specialising in youth arts, employability and regeneration;
- They create positive futures for young people;
- They tackle social isolation amongst the elderly;
- They make ideas happen.

They offer training and development in many forms, including programmes in Art, Fashion, Drama, Music and Interior design. Impact Arts are well known for some key flagship programmes. These include;

Creative Pathways

Creative Pathways is a 24-week creative engagement project working with young people aged 16–19 who were previously not in education, employment or training. Participants are engaged full-time with Impact Arts' dedicated and inspiring art tutors. Young People can choose between Fashion, Furniture Design or Community Challenges to develop artistic and social skills that are transferable into a work setting. They also take part in drama, cultural trips, outward-bound days, team building and retail challenges. Their journey culminates in a high-profile final show in a city-centre venue.

Fab Pad

Fab Pad is an Interior Design programme. OIt is their longest-running project operates throughout Scotland. The programme is for 16- to 34-year-olds and provides a chance for young people in their first tenancy or at risk of homelessness to personalise their home and make it their own.

The programme runs for 6–12 months during which time participants attend local weekly workshops with professional interior designers to develop their ideas, plan design and create their space. Activities include personal design consultation, shopping and inspiration trips, whilst meeting other young people in the same situation as themselves.

Participants are also provided with help to improve their employability and encouraged to take positive steps to secure training, education or employment and to become more active citizens.

Over 90 per cent of participants sustain their tenancy for 12 months or more. Many of those who take part in Fab Pad progress onto other opportunities. Participants receive travel expenses and a budget of £100 to spend on their home. Referrals are taken at any time.

Clients

Children and Schools

Children and Schools are some of their biggest clients! They deliver bespoke packages ranging from Big Bag shows for primary-aged children, to community consultations in regeneration areas, making artwork for competition or with a message for a whole school or community. In this highly rewarding area they get children to use their imaginations in all kinds of creative ways.

They are often asked for creative educational approaches to tackle various issues, and this has been the catalyst for many fantastic projects. They create programmes of activity across a range of themes: environment; bullying; water and fire safety; racism; territorialism; health and even in just learning to be creative!

Young People

Young people are their priority target group and they engage with them on a number of levels. Our creative employability programmes are for 16- to 19-year-olds. However they have also successfully delivered projects for other agencies and organisations such as the Restorative Justice team and a wide range of other youth groups and youth services. They engage young people in positive activities, with outcomes that can, for instance, leave a legacy for a community and that engender a sense of pride. They also ensure that the work of the young people is celebrated and showcased to the groups they are working for.

Older People

Older people can find themselves isolated and with little stimulus. Impact Arts believes how beneficial arts activities can be for them in many ways, particularly health-wise. Sometimes just the company and conversation of contemporaries is enough to help but in their Craft Café projects, aimed at the over 50s, they often see a re-awakening or an unexpected discovery of creative abilities which are truly rewarding.

They think you have to go the extra mile to provide such opportunities, as problems faced by the elderly stem from lack of mobility, lack of confidence and a lack of communication, information and support. They will work locally and in partnership with other relevant organisations, such as local housing authorities, to ensure we find ways of engaging older people. Getting information out and making sure they can get to the café are two fundamental and practical issues that we tackle.

They also work with older people extensively in our public art and regeneration projects, including reminiscence and intergenerational workshops.

Events and Festivals

Everyone loves an event and none more than Impact Arts! They can provide services from comprehensive event management and staffing to event programming, contributions such as face-painters, visual arts workshops, event spectaculars or stage acts.

Our Values and Principles

As a team of people Impact Arts share the following values:

Integrity: in all their dealings with clients, funders, participants and colleagues they are honest, and act with integrity and transparency.

Positivity: they treat everyone we work with well, forming positive and supportive relationships. They are committed to overcoming barriers and problem-solving – there is no room for negative thinking!

Ambition: in their own work we are ambitious in what they want to achieve, and they encourage our partners and the people who take part in our projects to raise their own aspirations.

Openness: they are open to new ideas; we create opportunity and are happy to be challenged in our thinking. They communicate in an open, approachable way with everyone they work with.

Potential and equality: they think that everyone has the ability to achieve great things. Whatever the starting point or circumstances of staff or participants, they encourage personal and professional development as fundamental to being able to flourish and maximise their own potential.

Creativity: creativity is at the centre of what they do. They are creative in all aspects of their work – be it project based or simply in the ideas they generate and the way they work.

Work ethic: they expect to work hard to achieve our company aims, the needs of their clients and their own personal and professional goals.

Our Principles

The following principles underpin and direct their work:

Quality: doing the very best job they can within available resources.

Profile: continuously raising awareness of the role the arts have in a social and regeneration context with all partners.

Growth: continuous improvement of company practices, operational and project, and change to structures to meet increasing demand in a planned way.

Innovation: trying new ways of doing things – developing solutions for emerging external agendas.

Teamwork: recognise the role each person has to play in Impact Arts' and our partners' success, and be committed both to fulfilling our own roles and helping our colleagues to achieve that success.

Flexibility: maintaining a balance between planning for future work levels and priorities, and being able to respond to opportunities and requests as they arise.

Source: http://www.impactarts.co.uk/

3 Key Texts

(1) Whitfield, K. and McNabb, R. (1991) *The Market for Training: International Perspectives on Theory, Methodology, and Policy* (Aldershot, Brookfield, VT: Avebury).

(2) Booth, A. and Snower, D. (1996) *Acquiring Skills: Market Failures, Their Symptoms and Policy Responses* (New York: Cambridge University Press).

(3) Crouch, C., Finegold, D. and Sako, M. (1999) *Are Skills the Answer?: The Political Economy of Skill Creation in Advanced Industrial Countries* (New York: Oxford University Press).

3 Key Articles

(1) Cameron, H. and Marashi, M. (2003) 'Form or Substance in the Learning and Skills Sector: Does Organisational Form Affect Learning Outcomes?', *Report to Learning and Skills Research Centre*.

(2) Ganey, T. and Klass, B. S. (2005) 'Outsourcing Relationships between Firms and Their Training Providers: The Role of Trust', *Human Resource Development Quarterly*, 16 (1), pp. 7–26.

(3) Harris, P. (2003) 'Outsourced Learning: A New Market Emerges', *Training and Development*, 57 (9), pp. 30–38.

3 Key Web Links

(1) Skills Funding Agency: http://skillsfundingagency.bis.gov.uk/.

(2) Young People's learning Agency: http://www.ypla.gov.uk/.

(3) In Training; A Private training Company: http://www.intraining.co.uk/.

Bibliography

Accountability Publication Pakistan (2005–06) available at: http://www.accountancy. com.pk/docs/economic-social-indicators-pakistan-2005-06.pdf. Budget Report (2009–10) available at: http://www.fbr.gov.pk/budget2009-2010/fb/FinanceAct.pdf.

Adler, N. J. (1997) *International Dimensions of Organizational Behavior* (Belmont, CA: Wadsworth).

Albarracin, D., Johnson, B. T. and Zanna, M. P. (2005) *The Handbook of Attitudes* (Mahwah, N.J: Lawrence Erlbaum Associates Publishers).

Allen, J. and Allen, B. (2005) *Therapeutic Journey, Practice and Life* (Oakland California: TA Press).

Allen, M. (2007) *Designing Successful E-Learning: Forget What You Know About Instructional Design and Do Something Interesting* (San Francisco, CA: Pfeiffer).

Allen, R. (1994) 'The Need for Diversity in Corporate Training: One Size Doesn't Really Fit', *Industrial and Commercial Training*, 26(10), pp. 15–17.

Andresen, M. (2003) 'Corporate Universities als Instrument des Strategischen Managements von Person, Gruppe und Organisation', *Zeitschrift für Personalforschung*, 17(4), pp. 391–394.

Antonacopoulou, E. (2000) 'Employee Development through Self-development in Three Retail Banks', *Personnel Review*, 29(3), pp. 491–508.

Argyris, C. (1994) *On Organizational Learning* (Cambridge, MA: Blackwell).

Arnold, J., Randall, R., Patterson, F., Silvester, J., Robertson, I., Cooper, C. and Burnes, B. (2010) *Work Psychology*, 5th edn. (London: Pearson).

Artizeta, A., Swailes, S. and Senior, B. (2007) 'Belbin's Team Role Model: Development, Validity and Applications for Team Building', *Journal of Management Studies*, 44(1), pp. 96–118.

Attwell, G. (2007) 'The Personal Learning Environments – The Future of E-learning?', *E-learning Papers*, 2(1).

Axtell, C. (1997), 'Predicting Immediate and Longer Term Transfer of Training', *Personnel Review*, 26(3), pp. 201–213.

Bacharach, S. B. (1989) 'Organizational Theories; Some Criteria for Evaluation', *Academy of Management*, 14(4), pp. 496–515.

Bakhtin, M. M. (1981) *The Dialogic Imagination: Four Essays* (Austin: University of Texas Press).

Barrell, J. and Ryback, D. (2008) *Psychology of Champions: How to Win at Sports and Life with the Focus Edge of Super-Athletes* (Westport, CO: Praeger Publishers).

Bartlett-Bragg, A. (2006) *Reflections on Pedagogy: Reframing Practice to Foster Informal Learning with Social Software.* Available from: http://www.dream.dk/uploads/files/ Anne%20Bartlett-Brag.pdf, accessed 3rd October 2010.

Bartram, S. and Gibson, B. (1994) *Training Needs Analysis: A Resource for Identifying Training Needs, Selecting Training Strategies, and Developing Training Plans* (Aldersho: Gower).

Baumard, P. and Starbuck, W. (2006) *Is Organisational Learning a Myth?* Advanced Institute of Mananagement, Executive Briefing.

Becher, T. and Trowler, P. (2001) *Academic Tribes and Territories: Intellectual Enquiry and the Cultures of Disciplines*, 2nd edn. (Buckingham: Open University Press/SRHE).

Beech, N. et al. (2000) 'Transient Transfusion: Or the Wearing Off of the Governance of the Soul?', *Personnel Review*, 19(4), pp. 460–473.

Belbin, R. M. (1996) *Management Teams: Why They Succeed or Fail* (Oxford: Buterrworth).

Bentley, T. (1994) *Facilitation* (Maidenhead: McGraw-Hill).

Berry, M. (1993) 'Changing Perspectives on Facilitation Skills Development', *Journal of European Industrial Training*, 17(3), pp. 22–32.

Bion, W. R. (1977) *Experiences in Groups* (London: Tavistock).

Blass, E. (2007) *Talent Management: Maximising Talenttfor Business Performance* (Chartered Management Institute and Ashridge Consulting Limited).

Bloom, B. S. (1965) *A Taxonomy of Educational Objectives: Handbook 1; Cognitive Domain* (New York: McKay).

Bonebright, D. A. (2010) '40 Years of Storming: A Historical Review of Tuckman's Model of Small Group Development', *Human Resource Development International*, 13(1), pp. 111–120.

Boud, D. and Garrick, J. (1999) *Understanding Learning at Work* (London: Routledge).

Boydell, T. and Leary, M. (1996) *Identifying Training Needs* (London: CIPD).

Boyle, D. (2001) *The Tyranny of Numbers: Why Counting Can't Make Us Happy* (London: Harper Collins).

Bramley, P. (1991) *Evaluating Training Effectiveness* (London: McGraw-Hill).

Brewster-Smith, M. (1974) Humanising Social Psychology (San Francisco: Josey-Bass).

Briggs, L. J., Gustafson, D. L. and Tillman, M. H. (1990) *Instructional Design: Principles and Applications* (New York: Springer-Verlag).

Briley, S. (ed.) (1996) *Women in the Workforce: Human Resource Development Strategies into the Next Century* (Edinburgh: HMSO).

Brockbank, A. and McGill, I. (2006) *Facilitating Reflective Learning Through Mentoring & Coaching* (London: Kogan Page).

Brown, J. and Duguid, P. (1991) 'Organizational Learning and Communities-of-Practice: Towards a Unified View of Working, Learning, and Innovation', *Organization Science*, 2(1), pp. 40–57.

Brown, J. S., Collins, A. and Duguid, P. (1989) 'Situated Cognition and the Culture of Learning', *Education Researcher*, 18(1), pp. 32–42.

Brynner, J., McIntosh, S., Vignoles, A., Dearden, L., Reed, H. and Van Reenan, J. (2001) *Improving Adult Basic Skills: Benefits to the Individual and to Society*, DfEE research report RR2S1 (London: HMSO).

Bunge, M. A. (1983) *Exploring the World: Epistemology and Methodology* (Reidel: Dordrecht).

Butler-Bowden, T. (2008) *50 Success Classics* (London: Nicholas Brealey Publishing).

Cameron, K. S., Quinn, R. E., Degraff, J. and Thakor, A (2006) *Competing Values Leadership: Creating Value in Organizations* (Cheltenham, UK: Edward Elgar).

Canell, M. and Harrison, R. (1997) 'What Makes Training Pay?', *Management Development Review*, 10(6), pp. 225–227.

Carroll, M. and Gilbert, M. (2008) *Becoming an Executive Coachee: Creating Learning Partnerships* (London: Vukani Publications).

Case, P. and Gosling, J. (2010) 'Where Is the Wisdom We Have Lost in Knowledge? A Stoical Perspective on Personal Knowledge Management', in Pauleen, D. and Goran, G. (eds) *Personal Knowledge Management* (Oxford: Gower).

Cennamo, L and Gardner, D (2008) 'Generational Differences in Work Values, Outcomes and Person-Organisation Values Fit', *Journal of Managerial Psychology*, 23(8), pp. 891–906.

Central Intelligence Agency (CIA) (2009) The world factbook: Pakistan. Available at: https://www.cia.gov/library/publications/the-world-factbook/geos/pk.html.

CETIS (2007) Personal learning Environments, Report Available from: http://wiki.cetis.ac.uk/Ple/Report.

Chalofsky, N. (2007) 'The Seminal Foundation of the Discipline of HRD: People, Learning and Organizations', *Human Resource Development Quarterly*, 18(3), pp. 431–442.

Chambers, E. G., Foulon, M., Handfield-Jones, H., Hankin, S. M. and Michaels, E. G. (1998) 'The War for Talent', *The McKinsey Quarterly*, 3, pp. 44–57.

Chapman, P. (1993) *The Economics of Training* (London: Harvester Wheatsheaf).

CIPD (2010) 'Annual Survey Report 2010: Learning and Talent Development', Chartered Institute of Personnel and Development, viewed 24 July 2010, retrieved from http://www.cipd.co.uk/NR/rdonlyres/BC060DD1-EEA7-4929-9142-1AD7333F95E7/0/5215_Learning_talent_development_survey_report.pdf.

Cheese, P., Thomas, R. and Craig, C. (2008) *The Talent Powered Organization: Strategies for Globalization, Talent Management and High Performance* (London: Kogan Page).

Chiu, W. et al. (1999) 'Re-thinking Training Needs Analysis: A Proposed Framework for Literature Review', *Personnel Review*, 28(1/2).

Clawson, J. G. (1985) 'Is Mentoring Necessary?' *Training and Development Journal*, April, pp. 36–39.

Clutterbuck, D. and Megginson, D. (2000) *Mentoring Executives and Directors* (Oxford: Butterworth-Heinemann).

Cluttterbuck, D. (2004) *Everyone Needs a Mentor* (London: IPM).

Coffield, F., Moseley, D., Hall, E. and Ecclestone, K. (2004) *Should We Be Using Learning Styles? What Research Has to Say to Practice* (London: Learning and Skills Research Centre).

Cosier, R. A. and Schrenk, C. R. (1990) 'Agreement and Thinking Alike: Ingredients for Poor Decisions', *Academy of Management Executive*, 4(1), pp. 69–74.

Cottrell, S. (2003) *Skills for Success: The Personal Development Planning Handbook* (Basingstoke: Palgrave Macmillan).

Country Watch (2009) Country Profile Pakistan, available at: http://www.countrywatch.com/country_profile.aspx?vcountry=131.

Covey, S. (1989) *The Seven Habits of Highly Effective People: Restoring the Character Ethic* (New York: Simon & Schuster).

Cox, J., Al Arkoubi, K. and Estrada, S. (2006) 'National Human Resource Development in Transitioning Societies in the Developing World: Morocco', *Advances in Developing Human Resources*, 8(1), pp. 84–98.

Cross, R., Abrams, L. and Parker, A. (2004) 'A Relational View of Learning: How Who You Know Affects What You Know', in Connor, M. L. and Clawson, J. G. (eds) *Creating a learning Culture* (Cambridge: CUP).

D'Abate. P., Eddy, E. and Tannenbaum, S. (2003) 'What's in a Name? A Literature-Based Approach to Understanding Mentoring, Coaching, and Other Constructs that Describe Developmental Interactions', *Human Resource Development Review*, 2(4), pp. 360–384.

Davenport, T. and Prusak, L. (1998) *Working Knowledge: How Organizations Manage What They Know* (Boston, Mass: Harvard Business School Press).

Davidson, P. (1972) 'Value Theory: Toward Conceptual Clarification', *British Journal of Sociology*, 23, pp. 172–187.

Davis, B. and Sumara, D. J. (2006) *Complexity and Education: Inquiries into Learning, Teaching and Research* (Mahwah, NJ: Erlbaum).

Dealtry, R. (2009) 'The Design and Management of an Organisation's Lifelong Learning Curriculum', *Journal of Workplace Learning*, 21(2), pp. 156–165.

De Bono, E. (1985) *Tactics: The Art and Science of Success* (London: Collins).

de Geus, A (1999) *The Living Company: Growth, Learning and Longevity in Business* (London: Nicholas Brealey).

De Haan, E. (2005) 'A New Vintage: Old Wine Maturing in New Bottles', *Training Journal*, November, pp. 20–24.

De Haan, E. (2008) *Relational Coaching* (Chichester: John Wiley & Sons).

Denny, R. (1997) *Succeed for Yourself: Unlock Your Potential for Success and Happiness* (London: Kogan Page).

DfEE (1996) *Equal Opportunities Ten Point Plan* (London: DfEE).

DfES (2003) *Success for All* (London: Df ES).

DfES (2003) *21st Century Skills – Realigning Our Potential* (London: HMSO).

DiMaggio, P. and Powell, W. (1983) 'The Iron Cage Re-Visited: Institutional Isomorphism and Collective Rationality in Organizational Fields', *American Sociological Review*, 48(2), pp. 147–160.

Downes, S. (2005) E-Learning 2.0. Available from: <http://www.elearnmag.org/subpage.cfm?section=articles&article=29-1>.

Dubois, D. and Rothwell, W. (2004). *Competency-Based Human Resource Management* (Paol Alto, CA: Davies-Black Publishing).

Dweck, S. (2008) *Mindset: The New Psychology of Success* (New York: Ballantine Books).

Earl, A. (1987) *The Art and Craft of Course Design* (London: Kogan Page).

Easterby-Smith, M. et al. (1992) *Management Research* (London: Sage).

Easterby-Smith, M. et al. (1999) *Organizational Learning and the Learning Organization* (London: Sage).

Economic Survey of Pakistan (2008–09), available at: http://www.finance.gov.pk/finance_ survery_chapter.aspx?id=21.

Edinger, E. (2010) 'An Outline of Analytical Psychology', Edward R. Edinger, M. D. http://www.capt.org/using-type/c-g-jung.htm, accessed 5th August 2010.

Ehrenreich, B. (2009) *Bright-Sided* (New York: Metropolitan Books).

ELLD (2003) 'Life Through Learning, Learning Through Life: The Lifelong Learning Strategy for Scotland', Enterprise and Lifelong Learning Department.

English, F. (2005) 'How Did You Become a Transactional Analyst?', *Transactional Analysis Journal*, 35(1), pp. 294–303.

Entwistle, N., Thompson, S. and Tait, H. (1992) *Guidelines for Promoting Effective Learning in Higher Education* (Edinburgh: Centre for Research on Learning and Instruction).

European Commission (2003) Choosing to Grow: Knowledge, Innovation and Jobs in a Cohesive Society (European Commission).

Eurostat (2002) 'Continuing Vocational Training Survey (CVTS2)', European Social Statistics, Eurostat Working Paper, Luxembourg, Eurostat.

Evans, C. and Dion, K. (1991) 'Group Cohesion and Performance: A Meta-Analysis', *Small Group Research*, 22, pp. 175–186.

Fenwick, T. (2010) 'Re-thinking the "thing": Sociomaterial Approaches to Understanding and Researching Learning in Work', *Journal of Workplace Learning*, 22(1/2), pp. 104–116.

Fenwick, T. A. (2004) 'Toward a Critical HRD in Theory and Practice', *Adult Education Quarterly*, 54(3), pp. 193–209.

Fiedler, S. (2006) 'Landscapes of Tools and Services Reconsidered: New Directions for Informal Learning Support in Higher Education?' Available from: http://www.dream.sdu.dk/uploads/files/Sebastian%20Fiedler.pdf>.

Fineman, S. (ed.) (1993) *Emotions in Organizations* (London: Sage).

Finkelstein, S., Harvey, C. and Lawton, T. (2006) *Breakout Strategy: Meeting the Challenge of Double digit Growth* (New York: McGraw-Hill).

Flynn, G. (1998) 'The Nuts and Bolts of Valuing Training', *Workforce*, 77(11), pp. 80–85.

Foley, M. (2010) *The Age of Absurdity* (London: Simon & Schuster).

Foote, E. and Ruona, W. (2008) 'Institutionalizing Ethics: A Synthesis of Frameworks and the Implications for HRD', *Human Resource Development Review*, 7(3), pp. 292–308.

Foray, D. (2004) *The Economics of Knowledge* (Cambridge: MIT press).

Ford, D. (1999) *Bottom Line Training* (Houston, TX: Gulf Publishing Co).

Ford, V. (1996) 'Partnership is the Secret of Progress', *People Management*, 2(3), pp. 34–36.

Forsyth, P. (1992) *Running an Effective Training Session* (London: Gower).

Gagne, R. (1985) *The Conditions of Learning*, 4th edn. (New York: Holt, Rinehart & Winston).

Garavan, T. (1991) 'Strategic Human Resource Development', *Journal of European Industrial Training*, 15(1), pp. 17–31.

Garavan, T. and Morley, M. (2006) 'Re-dimensionalising Boundaries in the Theory and Practice of HRD, *International Journal of Learning and Intellectual Capital*, 3(1), pp. 3–13.

Garger, E. (1999) 'Goodbye Training, Hello Learning', *Workforce*, 78(11), pp. 35–42.

Garvey, B. and Williamson, B. (eds) (2002) *Beyond Knowledge Management: Dialogue, Creativity and the Corporate Curriculum* (Harlow, UK: Pearson Education).

Garvey.B. and Garrett-Harris, R. (2005) 'The Benefits of Mentoring: A Literature Review', The Mentoring and Coaching Research Unit, Sheffield Hallam University.

Gebauer, A. (2006) 'Viele kleine Schritte, kein großer Wurf. Kritische Rekonstruktion der Entwicklungsverläufe von Corporate Universities', *Personalführung*. Fachbeiträge, 12, pp. 60–71.

Gibb, S. (1999) 'The Usefulness of Theory: A Case Study in Evaluating Formal Mentoring Schemes', *Human Relations*, 52(8), pp. 1055–1075.

Gill, J. and Johnson, P. (1991) *Research Methods for Managers* (London: Paul Chapman Publishing).

Gladwell, M. (2002) 'The Talent Myth', New Yorker, retrieved on 3rd March 2010 from http://www.gladwell.com/2002/2002_07_22_a_talent.htm.

Gladwell, M. (2008) *Outliers: The Story of Success* (London: Allen Lane).

Glotz, P. and Seufert, S. (eds) (2002) Corporate University. Wie Unternehmen ihre Mitarbeiter mit E-Learning erfolgreich weiterbilden (Wien: Huber).

Goffee, R. and Jones, G. (2006) *Why Should Anyone Be Led by You? What it Takes to Be an Authentic Leader* (Boston, Massachusetts: Harvard Business School Press).

Goffee, R. and Jones, G. (2009) *Clever: Leading Your Smartest Most Creative People* (Boston, MA: Harvard Business Press).

Goldman, A. (1999) *Knowledge in a Social World* (Oxford: Clarendon Press).

Goldsmith, M. (2007) *What Got You Here Won't Get You There* (New York: Hyperion).

Goleman, D. (1995) *Emotional Intelligence: Why it can Matter More than IQ* (New York: Bantam).

Gosling (2010) retreived from http://homepage.psy.utexas.edu/HomePage/Faculty/Gosling/scales_we.htm, 5th August 2010.

Gospel, H. and Foreman, J. (2002) 'The Provision of Training in Britain; Case Studies of Inter-Firm Coordination', The Centre for Economic Performance, London School of Economics and Political Science.

Green, F., Felstead, A., Mayhew, K. and Pack, A (2000) 'The Impact of Training on Labour Mobility: Individual and Firm Level Evidence from Britain', *British Journal of Industrial Relations*, 38(2), pp. 261–275.

Hager, P. (1999) 'Finding a Good Theory of Workplace Learning', in Boud, D. and Garrick, J. (eds) *Understanding Learning at Work* (London: Routledge).

Hamblin, A. (1974) *Evaluation and Control of Training* (London: McGraw-Hill).

Hammersley, M. and Atkinson, P. (1992) *Ethnography: Principles in Practice* (London: Routledge).

Handfeld-Jones, H. and Axelrod, B. (2001) *The War for Talent* (McKinsey Report: Mackinsey & Company Inc).

Hanft, A. and Knust, M. (2007) 'Internationale Vergleichsstudie zur Struktur und Organisation der Weiterbildung an Hochschulen', *Bundesministerium für Bildung und Forschung*. Available from: http://www.bmbf.de/pub/internat_vergleichsstudie_struktur_und_organisation_hochschulweiterbildung.pdf, Accessed 11 October 2010.

Hansen, C. and Lee, Y. (2009) *The Cultural Contexts of Human Resource Development* (Basingstoke: Palgrave Macmillan).

Harbinson, F. and Myers, C. (1964) Education, Manpower, and Economic Growth: Strategies of Human Resource Development (New York: McGraw-Hill).

Hardingham, A. (2000) *Psychology for Trainers* (London: CIPD).

Harrison, R. (2009) *Learning and Development*, 5th edn. (London: CIPD).

Harrison, R. and Kessels, J. (2003) *Human Resource Development in a Knowledge Economy* (Basingstoke: Palgrave Macmillan).

Harvey, R. J. (1999) 'Job Analysis', in Dunnette, M. D. and Hough, L. (eds) *Handbook of Industrial and Organization Psychology*, 2nd edn. (Palo Alto, CA: Consulting Psychologists Press).

Hawkins, P. and Smith, N. (2006) Coaching, Mentoring and Organizational Consultancy: Supervision and Development (Maidenhead: Open University).

Hay, J. (2009) *Working it Out at Work* (Hertfordshire: Sherwood Publishing).

Hay, J. (1996) *Transactional Analysis for Trainers*, 2nd Rev edn. (Hertfordshire: Sherwood Publishing).

Hay, M. (2002) 'Strategies for Survival in the War for Talent', *Career Development International*, 7(1), pp. 52–56.

Heckman, J. J. and Masterov, D. V. (2004) 'Skill Policies for Scotland', Institute for the Study of Labour, Discussion paper No. 1444.

Heuser, M. (2001) 'Corporate Universities als strategiegetriebene "Schulen des Geschäfts" – Das Beispiel Lufthansa School of Business', in Friederichs, P. and Althauser, U. (eds)

Personalentwicklung in der Globalisierung. Strategien der Insider (pp. 343–359), Neuwied: Hermann Luchterhand Verlag.

Hills, H. and Francis, P. (1999) 'Interaction Learning', *People Management*, 5(14), pp. 731–737.

Hochschild, A. R. (1983) *The Managed Heart: Commercialisation of Human Feeling* (Berkeley and Los Angeles: University of California Press).

Hodell, C. (2000) *ISD From the Ground Up: A No-Nonsense Approach to Instructional Design* (Alexandria, VA: American Society for Training & Development).

Holton, E. F. and Naquin, S. (2005) 'A Critical Analysis of HRD Evaluation Models from a Decision-Making Perspective', *Human Resource Development Quarterly*, 16(2), pp. 257–280.

Homer (trans. E. V. Rieu) (1946) *The Odyssey* (Harmondsworth: Penguin).

Honey, P. and Mumford, A. (1982) *Manual of Learning Styles* (London: P. Honey).

Hunt, M. and Clarke, A. (1997) *A Guide to the Cost Effectiveness of Technology-based Training* (London: DfEE).

Huselid, M., Beatty, R. and Becker, B. (2005) 'A Players' or A Positions'? The Strategic Logic of Workforce Management', *Harvard Business Review*, December, pp. 110–117.

Iles, P. (1995) 'Learning to Work with Difference', *Personnel Review*, 24(6), pp. 44–60.

Iles, V. and Sutherland, K. (2001) Organisational Change: A Review for Health Care Managers and Professionals (NCCDSO).

Ipe, M. (2003) 'Knowledge Sharing in Organizations: A Conceptual Framework', *Human Resource Development Review*, 2(4), pp. 337–359.

James, O. (2007) Affluenza: How to Be Successful and Stay Sane (London: Vermillion).

James, O. (2008) The Selfish Capitalist: The Origins of Affluenza (London: Vermillion.)

Janis, I. (1982) *Groupthink*, 2nd edn. (Boston, MA: Houghton-Mifflin).

Jarvis, P. (1987) *Adult Learning in the Social Context* (London: Croom Helm).

Jun Jo. S., Jeung, C-W., Park, S. and Jun Yoon, H. (2009) 'Who is Citing Whom: Citation Network Analysis Among HRD Publications from 1990–2007', *Human Resource Development Quarterly*, 20(4), pp. 503–538.

Kagitcibasi, C. (1997) 'Individualism and Collectivism', in Berry, J. W., Segall, M. H. and Kagitcibasi, C. (eds) *Handbook of Cross-cultural Psychology*, Vol. 3, 2nd edn. (Boston: Allyn & Bacon).

Kahnwald, Nina (2008) 'Social Software als Werkzeuge informellen Lernens', in Hug, Theo (ed.) *Media, Knowledge & Education. Exploring New Spaces, Relations and Dynamics in Digital Media Ecologies* (pp. 282–295), Innsbruck: Innsbruck University Press.

Kaplan, R. and Norton, D. (1996) 'The Balanced Scorecard', *Harvard Business Review*, January–February.

Kasl, E., Marsick, V. J. and Dechant, K. (1997) 'Teams as Learners: A Research-Based Model of Team Learning', *Journal of Applied Behavioral Science*, 33, pp. 227–246.

Katzenbach, J. R. and Smith, D. K. (1993) 'The Discipline of Teams', *Harvard Business Review*, 71, pp. 111–146.

Keely, B. (2007) *Human Capital: How What You Know Shapes Your Life* (Paris: OECD).

Kerres, M. (2006a) Web 2.0 und seine Implikationen für E-Learning, deutsche Fassung von: Web 2.0 and its implications to E-Learning, presented at Microlearning Conference, Innsbruck, Available from <http://mediendidaktik.de>.

Kirkpatrick, D. (ed.) (1975) *Evaluating Training Programs: The Four Levels* (New York: Berett-Koehler).

Kline, N. (1998) *Time to Think* (London: Cassell Illustrated).

Knoll, L., Owsen, D. M. and Karmon, D. J. (2003) 'Universitätsdiplom vom Arbeitgeber? Anmerkungen zum wachsenden Anspruch von "Corporate Universities"', *Personal*, 8, pp. 50–52.

Knowles, M. (1984) *Andragogy in Action* (San Francisco: Jossey-Bass).

Knowles, M. (1995) *Designs for Adult Learning: Practical Resources, Exercises, and Course Outlines from the Father of Adult Learning* (Alexandria, VA: American Society for Training & Development).

Kolb, D. (1984) *Experiential Learning* (New Jersey: Prentice Hall).

Kraiger, K., Ford, J. K. and Salas, E. (1993) 'Application of Cognitive, Skill-Based and Affective Theories of Learning Outcomes to New Methods of Training Evaluation', *Journal of Applied Psychology*, 78, pp. 311–328.

Kram, K. (1985) 'Improving the Mentoring Process', *Training and Development Journal*, April, pp. 40–43.

Kuchinke, P. (2010) 'Human Development as a Central Goal for Human Resource Development', *Human Resource Development International*, 13–15, pp. 575–585.

Labour Force Survey of Pakistan (2007–08), available at: http://www.statpak.gov.pk/depts/fbs/publications/lfs2007_08/lfs2007_08.html.

Lally, P., van Jaarsveld, C., Potts, H. and Wardle, J. (2009) How Are Habits Formed: Modelling Habit Formation in the Real World, *European Journal of Social Psychology*, Published Online: July 16, 4:54AM, DOI: 10.1002/ejsp.674.

Lanchester, J. (2010) *Whoops; Why Everyone Owes and No One Can Pay* (London: Penguin).

Lange, T. et al. (2000) 'SMEs and Barriers to Skills Development: A Scottish Perspective', *Journal of European Industrial Training*, 24, pp. 5–11.

Laurillard, D. (2002) *Rethinking University Teaching A Conversational Framework for the Effective Use of Learning Technologies* (London: Routledge).

Lave, J. and Wenger, E. (1991) *Situated Learning: Legitimate Peripheral Participation* (Cambridge: Cambridge University Press).

Leatherman, D. (1996) *Designing Training Programmes* (Aldershot, England: Gower).

Legge, K. (1997) 'Morality Bound', *People Management*, 2, p. 25.

Leigh, D. (1991) *A Practical Approach to Group Training* (London: Kogan Page).

Leitch, S. (200 retrieved from http://www.hm-treasury.gov.uk./independent_reviews/leitch_review/review_leitch_index.cfm, accessed 25 July 2006.

Leonard-Barton, D. (1995) *Wellsprings of Knowledge* (Boston, MA: Harvard Business School Press).

Levinson, D. et al. (1978) *The Seasons of a Man's Life* (New York: Alfred Knopf).

Li, C. and Bernoff, J. (2008) *Groundswell* (Boston, MA: Harvard Business School press).

Likierman, A. (2009) 'Measuring the Success of Custom Programmes', EFMD Global Focus, March.

LLUK (2010) 'National Occupational Standards for Learning and Development Final version', Lifelong Learning, UK.

London, M. and Sessa, V. (2007) 'The Development of Group Interaction Patterns: How Groups Become Adaptive, Generative and Transformative Learners', *Human Resource Development Review*, 6(4), pp. 353–376.

Longstaff, S. (2011) 'Ethical Issues and Human Resource Development', http://www.ethics.org.au/ethics-articles/ethical-issues-and-human-resource-development, accessed February 3, 2011.

LSC (2003) 'Success for All – Implementation of the Framework for Quality and Success', Learning and Skills Council *Circular 03/09*.

Lynton, R. and Pareek, U. (2000) *Training for Organisational Transformation: Part I for Policy Makers and Change Managers* (London: Sage).

Machin, S. and Vignoles, A. (2001) *The Economic Benefits of Training to the Individual, the Firm and the Economy: The Key Issues* (Centre for the Economics of Education, London School of Economics).

Mager, R. (2000) *What Every Manager Should Know About Training* (Chalford: Management Books).

Manning, S. (2002) *Resource Base of a Research Project Cluster Related to Human Resource Development in Europe* (WIFO:Berlin)

Marlow, H. (1984) *Success: Individual Corporate and National: Profile for the Eighties and Beyond* (London: Institute of Personnel Management).

Markowitsch, J. and Plaimauer, C. (2009) 'Descriptors for Competence: Towards an International Standard Classification for Skills and Competences', *Journal of European Industrial Training*, 33(8/9), pp. 817–837.

Mayo, A. (2000) 'The Role of Employee Development in the Growth of Intellectual Capital', *Personnel Review*, 29(4), pp. 521–533.

Mazlish, B. (1998) *The Uncertain Sciences* (New Haven, CT: Yale University Press).

McCracken, M. and Wallace, M. (2000) 'Towards a Redefinition of Strategic HRD', *Journal of European Industrial Training*, 24–25, 281–290.

McEnrue, M. P. and Groves, K. (2006) 'Choosing Among Tests of Emotional Intelligence; What is the Evidence?', *Human Resource Development Quarterly*, 17(1), pp. 9–42.

McGoldrick, J., Stewart, J. and Watson, S. (2002) *Understanding Human Resource Development: A Research Based Approach* (London: Routledge).

McLean, G. N., & McLean, L. D., (2010). 'If We Can't Define HRD in One Country, How Can We Define It in an International Context?' *Human Resource Development International*, 4(3) 313–326.

McLean, G. (2006) 'National Human Resource Development: A Focussed Study in Tranisitioning Societies in the Developing World', *Advances in Developing Human Resources*, 8(1), pp. 3–11.

McLean, G. N. (2004). 'National Human Resource Development: What in the World Is It?' *Advances in Developing Human Resources* 6 (3), 269–275.

Megginson, D. and Pedler, M. (1992) *Self-Development: A Facilitator's Guide* (London: McGraw-Hill).

Metcalfe & Rees (2005) 'Theorising Advances in International HRD', *Human Resource Development International*, 8(4): 572–592.

Michaels, E., Handfield-Jones, H. and Axelrod, B. (2001) *The War for Talent* (Boston, Massachusetts: Harvard Business School Press).

Milano, M. and Ullius, D. (1998) *Designing Powerful Training: The Sequential Iterative Model (SIM)* (San Francisco: Jossey-Bass).

Miller, L., Rankin, N. and Neathey, F. (2001) *Competency Frameworks in Organisations* (London: Chartered Institute of Personnel and Development).

Mithen, S. (1996) *The Prehistory of Mind* (London: Thames & Hudson).

Mohrman, S. A., Cohen, S. A. and Mohrman, A. (1995) *Designing Team-Based Organizations* (San Francisco, CA: Jossey Bass).

Morris, C. (1965) *Varieties of Human Value* (Chicago: University of Chicago Press).

Mumford, A. (1989) *Management Development1*, (London, IPD).

Nadler, L. and Nalder. Z. (1970) *Developing Human Resources: Concepts and a Model*, 1st edn. (San Francisco: Josey-Bass).

Natrins. N. and Smith, V. (2004) 'Rethinking the Process: Strategies for Integrating On- and Off-the-job Training', *Learning and Skills Development Agency*.

Newby, T. (1992) *Training Evaluation Handbook* (London: Gower).

Ng, T., Eby, L., Sorensen, K. and Feldman, D. (2005) 'Predictors of Objective and Subjective Career Success: A meta Analysis', *Personnel Psychology*, 58, pp. 367–408.

Nonaka, I. (1991) 'The Knowledge-Creating Company', *Harvard Business Review*, 69(6), pp. 96–105.

Norman, D. (1982) *Learning and Memory* (San Francisco: WH Freeman and Co).

OECD (2003) *Adult Learning* (Paris: OECD).

Palmer, S. and Whybrow, A. (2007) *Handbook of Coaching Psychology* (London: Routledge).

Paprock, K. E. (2006) 'National Human Resource Development in Transitioning Societies in the Developing World: Introductory Overview', *Advances in Developing Human Resources*, 8(1), pp. 12–27.

Parry, E. and Urwin, P. (2009) Tapping into Talent: The Age Factor and Generation Issues (London: CIPD).

Parsons, D. (1997) 'A Qualitative Approach to Local Skills Audits', *Skills and Enterprise Briefing*, Issue 6.

Paul, R. (2010), 'Engaging the Multi-Generational Workforce', *HR Management*, 6, 17 August 2010, Available at <http://www.hrmreport.com/article/Engaging-the-Multi-generational-Workforce/>.

Pawson, R. (2004) 'Mentoring Relationships: An Exploratory Review', ESRC UK Centre for Evidence Based Policy and Practice; Working Paper 21.

Pawson, R., Greenhalgh, T., Harvey, G. and Walshe, K. (2004) 'Realist Synthesis: An Introduction, ESRC Research Methods Programme', RMP Methods Paper.

Pedler, M. et al. (1991) *The Learning Company: A Strategy for Sustainable Development* (London: McGraw-Hill).

Peters, T. and Waterman, R. (1990) *In Search of Excellence* (London: Harper & Row).

Pfeffer, J. and Sutton, R. (2000) *The Knowing-Doing Gap: How Smart Companies Turn Knowledge into Action* (Boston: Harvard Business School Press).

Pfeffer, J. and Sutton, R. (2008) Hard Facts, Dangerous Half Truths and Total Nonsense: Profiting from Evidence-Based Management (Boston: Harvard Business School Press).

Phillips, J. (1991) *Handbook of Training Evaluation and Measurement Methods* (Houston, TX: Gulf Publishing).

Pinker, S. (1997) *How the Mind Works* (London: Penguin).

Piskurich, G. M. et al. (eds) (2000) *The ASTD Handbook of Training Design and Delivery* (New York: McGraw-Hill).

PIU (2001) 'In Demand: Adult Skills in the 21st Century', Performance Innovation Unit 1.

Plutchik, R. (1980) 'A General Psychoevolutionary Theory of Emotion', in Plutchik, R. and Kellerman, H. (eds) *Emotion: Theory, Research, and Experience: Vol. 1 Theories of Emotion* (New York: Academic Press).

Polanyi, M. (1958) *Personal Knowledge: Towards a Post Critical Philosophy* (London: Routledge & Kegan Paul).

Prensky, M. (2000) *Digital Games Based Learning* (New York: McGraw-Hill).

Prochaska, J. et al. (1992) 'In Search of How People Change; Applications to Addictive Behaviors', *American Psychologist*, 47(9), pp. 1102–1114.

Puybaraud, M., Russell, S., McEwan, A. M., Leussink, E. and Beck, L. (2010) *Generation Y and the Workplace Annual Report 2010* (London: Johnson Controls).

Rademakers, M. (2005)' Corporate Universities: Driving Force of Knowledge Innovation', *The Journal of Workplace Learning*, 17(1/2), pp. 130–136.

Reich, B. et al. (1976) *Values, Attitudes and Behaviour Change* (London: Methuen & Co).

Reid, M. A., Barrington, H. and Brown, M. (2009) *Human Resource Development; Beyond Training Interventions*, 7th edn. (London: CIPD).

Reilly, R. and Kort, B. (2003) *The Science Behind the Art of Teaching Science: Emotional States and Learning*, (Boston MA: MIT) (Working Paper).

Reynolds, A., Sambrook, S. and Stewart, J. (1997) Dictionary of HRD, Gower.

Robbins, A. (1994) *Giant Steps: Small Changes to Make a Big Difference: Daily Lessons in Self-mastery* (London: Pocket Books).

Robbins, P. (1993) *Organizational Behaviour* (London: Prentice Hall).

Robinson, I., and Swap, W. (2005) *Deep Smarts: How to Cultivate and Transfer Enduring Business Wisdom* (Boston, MA: Harvard Business School).

Roche, G. (1979) 'Much Ado About Mentors', *Harvard Business Review*, January–February.

Rogers, C. (1969) *Freedom to Learn* (Columbus: Charles E Merrill).

Rokeach, M. (1960) *The Open and Closed Mind: Investigations into the Nature of Belief Systems and Personality Systems* (New York: Basic Books).

Rokeach, M. (1973). *The Nature of Human Values*. New York: Free Press.

Rokeach, M. (1970) *Beliefs, Attitudes and Values: A Theory of Organisation and Change* (San Francisco: Jossey-Bass).

Rosenberg, M. J. (ed.) (2001) *E-learning: Strategies for Delivering Knowledge in the Digital Age* (New York: McGraw-Hill).

Rossett, A. (2002) *The ASTD E-learning Handbook* (New York: McGraw-Hill).

Rothwell, W. J. and Kazanas, H. C. (1992) *Mastering the Instructional Design Process* (New York: Jossey-Bass).

Rothwell, W. J. and Kazanas, H. C. (2003) *The Strategic Development of Talent* (Amherst: HRD Press).

Sadler-Smith, E. Down, S., Lean. J. (2000) 'Modern Learning Methods: Rhetoric and Reality', *Personnel Review*, 9(4), pp. 474–490.

Salas, E. and Kosarzycki, M. P. (2003) 'Why Don't Organizations Pay Attention to (and Use) Findings from the Science of Training?' *Human Resource Development Quarterly*, 14(4), pp. 487–492.

Sambrook, S. and Stewart, J. (2007) 'Teaching, Learning and Assessing HRD; FINAL REPORT', Higher Education Academy: Business, Management, Accounting & Finance (BMAF) & University Forum for Human Resource Development (UFHRD).

Schamari, U. W. (2001) 'Firmenuniversitäten als Alternative'. *Management & Training*, 9, pp. 34–35.

Schank, R. C. (2002) *Designing World Class E-learning* (New York: McGraw-Hill).

Schiemann, W. (2009) *Reinventing Talent Management: How to Maximize Performance in the New Marketplace* (Hoboken, New Jersey: John Wiley & Sons Inc).

Schon, D. A. (1987) *Educating the Reflective Practitioner* (San Francisco: Jossey-Bass).

Schuller, T., Baron, S. and Field, J. (2000) 'Social Capital: A Review and Critic, in Baron, S., Field, J. and T. Schuller (eds) *Social Capital* (Oxford: Oxford University Press).

Schwartz, S. H. and Bilsky, W. (1990) 'Toward a Theory of the Universal Content and Structure of Values: Extensions and Cross-Cultural Replications', *Journal of Personality and Social Psychology*, 58, pp. 878–891.

Scott, A. (1997) *Learning Centres: A Step-by-step Guide to Planning, Managing and Evaluating an Organizational Resource Centre* (London: Kogan Page).

Scottish Executive (2003) 'The Lifelong Learning Strategy for Scotland', *Scottish Executive*.

Seely Brown, J. and Duguid, P. (2000) 'Balancing Act: How to Catch Knowledge without Killing It', *Harvard Business Review*, May–June.

Seligman, M. (2002) *Authentic Happiness* (New York: Free Press).

Senge, M. (1990) *The Fifth Discipline* (London: Doubleday).

Shank, P. (2007) *The Online Learning Idea Book* (San Francisco: Pfieffer).

Shapiro, E. C. et al. (1978) 'Moving Up: Role Models, Mentors, and the 'Patron System', *Sloan Management Review*, Spring.

Sieger, R. (2004) *Natural Born Winners* (London: Arrow).

Simon, W. (2002) 'Sinn oder Unsinn von Firmenuniversitäten', *Personal*, 8(8), pp. 22–32.

Skiffington,S. and Zeus, P. (2005) *Behavioral Coaching; How to Build Sustainable Personal and Organizational Strength* (Sydney: McGraw Hill).

Sloman, M. (2006) 'A New Context for the Trainer', *Impact, CIPD Policy and Research*.

Smith, B. (1997) *Belief and Resistance: Dynamics of Contemporary Intellectual Controversy* (Cambridge, Massachusetts: Harvard University Press)

Smith, P. B., Dugan, S. and Trompenaars, F. (1996) 'National Culture and the Values of Organizational Employees: A Dimensional Analysis across 43 Nations', *Journal of Cross-Cultural Psychology*, 27, pp. 231–264.

Smith, P. M. and Aufenast, J. (2001) 'Emotional Competence at Work; Implicit Theories, a New Model and Supporting Data', *British Academy of Management*, Cardiff.

Steedman, H. (1993) 'Do Work Force Skills Matter?', *British Journal of Industrial Relations*, 31, pp. 285–292.

Stern, E. and Sommerlad, E. (1999) *Workplace Learning, Culture and Performance* (London: Institute of Personnel and Development).

Stewart, J. (1999) *Employee Development* (London: Financial Times/Pitman).

Storberg-Walker, J. (2003) 'Comparison of the Dubin, Lynham, and Van de Ven Theory-Building Research Methods and Implications for HRD', *Human Resource Development Review*, 2, pp. 211–222.

Storey, J. (1989) 'Management Development: A Literature Review and Implications for Research; Part 1, Conceptualisations and Practices', *Personnel Review*, 18(6), pp. 3–19.

Strongman, K. (1996) *The Psychology of Emotion: Theories of Emotion in Perspective*, 4th edn. (New York: John Wiley).

Swanson, R. A. and Holton, E. F. (2001) *Foundations of Human Resource Development* (San Francisco: Berret-Koehler).

Swinney, M. (2007) 'One More Time – What Training Is and Isn't', *Performance Improvement*, 46(5), pp. 6–9.

Tabbron, A. et al. (1997) 'Making Mentoring Work', *Training for Quality*, 5(1), pp. 6–9.

Talbot, C. (1995) 'Evaluation and Validation: A Mixed Approach', *Journal of European Industrial Training*, 16(5), pp. 26–32.

Tamkin, P., Pearson, G., Hirsh, W. and Constable, S. (2010) *Exceeding Expectations: The Principles of Outstanding Leadership* (London: Work Foundation.

Tannenbaum, S. I. (1997) 'Enhancing Continuous Learning: Diagnostic Findings from Multiple Companies', *Human Resource Management*, 36(4), pp. 437–452.

Tapscott, D. (2008) *Grown Digital* (New York: McGraw Hill).

Tarique, I. and Schuler, R. S. (2010) 'Global Talent Management: Literature Review, Integrative Framework, and Suggestions for Further Research', *Journal of World Business*, 45(2), pp. 122–133.

Thagrad, P. (1996) *Mind: Introduction to Cognitive Science* (Cambridge, MA: MIT Press).

Thomas, D. (1993) 'Racial Dynamics in Cross Race Developmental Relationships', *Administrative Science Quarterly*, 38, pp. 169–194.

Thompson, M. and Walsham, G. (2004) 'Placing knowledge Management in Context', *Journal of Management Studies*, 41(5), pp. 725–747.

Tuckman, B. W. and Jensen, M. A. C. (1977) 'Stages of Small Group Development Revisited', *Group and Organizational Studies*, 2, pp. 419–427.

Tulgan, B. (2001) *Winning the Talent Wars* (New York: W.W. Norton & Co.).

UNDP (2009) Human Development Report; Morocco, Available at http://hdr.undp.org/en/media/HDR_2009_EN_Summary.pdf, accessed 25 November 2009.

United Nations Development Programme (UNDP) (2002) *'Pakistan National Human Development Report'* (New York, UN Publications).

VA (2009) http://www.trainingreference.co.uk/news/gn090916.htm, Video Arts.

Van de Ven, A. H. (1989) 'Nothing is Quite So Practical as a Good Theory', *Academy of Management*, 14(4), pp. 486–489.

Wenger, E. (1998) *Communities of Practice: Learning, Meaning and Identity* (Cambridge: Cambridge University Press).

Wenger, E., McDermott, R. and Snyder, W. (2002) *Cultivating Communities of Practice* (Boston: Harvard Business School Press).

West, M. (2002) 'A Matter of Life and Death', *People Management*, 21, February, pp. 30–35.

Whitmore, J. (2005) *Coaching for Performance* (London: Nicolas Brealey).

Wilson, E. (1996)'Managing Diversity and HRD', in Stewart, J. and McGoldrick, J. (eds) *HRD Perspectives, Strategies and Practice* (London: Pitman).

Wilson, J. (2001) *Human Resource Development* (London: Kogan Page).

Wimmer, R., Emmerich, A. and Nicolai, A. T. (2002) Corporate Universities in Deutschland. Eine empirische Untersuchung zu ihrer Verbreitung und strategischen Bedeutung. [online]. *Bundesministerium für Bildung und Fortbildung*. Available from: http://www.bmbf.de/pub/corporate_universities _in_deutschland.pdf, Accessed 11 October 2010.

Wolfe, P. et al. (1991) *Job Task Analysis: Guide to Good Practice* (Englewood Cliffs, NJ: Educational Technology Publications).

Wolpert, L. (2008) *Six Impossible Things Before Breakfast* (New York: W.W Norton & Company).

Yang, B. (2004) 'Can Adult Learning Theory Provide a Foundation for Human Resource Development', *Advances in Developing Human Resources*, 6(2), pp. 129–145.

Yi, X., Ribbens, B. and Morgan, C. (2010) 'Generational Differences in China; Career Implications', *Career Development International*, 15(6), pp. 601–620.

Yorks, L. and Saquet, A. (2003) 'Team Learning and National Culture: Framing the Issues', *Advances in Developing Human Resources*, 5(1), pp. 7–25.

Zemke, R. (1985) 'The Honeywell Studies: How Managers Learn to Manage', *Training*, 22(8), pp. 46–51.

Zey, M. (1991) *The Mentor Connection* (New Brunswick: Transaction).

Zimmermann, V. (2008) 'Corporate Universities', in Adelsberger, H. H., Kinshuk. Pawlowski, J. M. and Sampson, D. (eds) *Handbook on Information Technologies for Education and Training* 2nd edn.

Index